Wissenschaftliche Untersuchungen
zum Neuen Testament · 2. Reihe

Herausgeber / Editor
Jörg Frey (München)

Mitherausgeber / Associate Editors
Friedrich Avemarie (Marburg)
Judith Gundry-Volf (New Haven, CT)
Hans-Josef Klauck (Chicago, IL)

235

Desta Heliso

Pistis and the Righteous One

A Study of Romans 1:17
against the Background of Scripture and
Second Temple Jewish Literature

Mohr Siebeck

DESTA HELISO, born 1964; studied at London School of Theology and King's College London, UK; currently lecturer at the Ethiopian Graduate School of Theology in Addis Ababa, Ethiopia.

BS
2665.6
.F3
H45
2007

ISBN 978-3-16-149253-2
ISSN 0340-9570 (Wissenschaftliche Untersuchungen zum Neuen Testament, 2. Reihe)

Die Deutsche Nationalbibliothek lists this publication in the Deutsche Nationalbibliographie; detailed bibliographic data is available in the Internet at *http://dnb.d-nb.de*.

The book was printed by Laupp & Göbel in Nehren on non-aging paper and bound by Buchbinderei Nädele in Nehren.

Printed in Germany.

To my sister Aregash Heliso (1980 – 2003)

Preface

This monograph is a revision of my doctoral dissertation. I am very grateful to Prof Dr Jörg Frey, Prof Dr Friedrich Avemarie and Dr Henning Ziebritzki for their initial interest in the work, subsequent approval of it for publication in the WUNT II series, and their valuable editorial comments and suggestions on the manuscript. Mr Matthias Spitzner of Mohr Siebeck guided me efficiently and patiently with regard to the formatting and other technical aspects of the manuscript, for which I am thankful. I should make a special mention of Prof Dr Jörg Frey who made it possible for me and my wife to stay in Munich during the preparation of the manuscript by securing a scholarship from Evangelische Kirche in Deutschland, arranging accommodation at Collegium-Öcumenicum München, and by providing excellent working space at his Evangelisch-Theologische Fakultät, in Universität München. I am eternally grateful for his kindness. I also express my thanks to Evangelische Kirche in Deutschland for providing funding for my transport and living expenses.

The doctoral dissertation, from its inception through to the final stage, owes a great deal to many as well. Although the dissertation was eventually submitted to Brunel University and the London School of Theology, much of the work had been done at King's College London. I would like to thank Dr Douglas Campbell, Prof Judith Lieu and Prof Michael Knibb for their contributions to the work during my time at King's College London. I would also like to thank Prof Max Turner of the London School of Theology for taking me on after a difficult and discouraging academic experience and for giving me skillful guidance and wonderful support, which enabled me to finish the project successfully.

I have benefited financially from various organisations and individuals during my doctoral studies. The Overseas Scholarship Trust at King's College London, Golden Stable Trust in UK, Overseas Council International and Miss Barbara Smith are some of them. I thank them all.

During my studies in London, Fairfield Church in Northwood Hills provided very warm Christian fellowship for me as well as giving financial support when needed, all of which is much appreciated. In connection with Fairfield, I must mention Roger and Frances Pearce whose love and support I will never forget.

My friend (and brother-in-spirit) Jim Bradford, in whose flat I lived for many years while working on my PhD, stuck by me through thick and thin, and all the highs and lows. No words can express my gratitude to him.

The leadership, staff and students of the Ethiopian Graduate School of Theology (EGST), the institution I work for, have been very supportive in every way, for which I am thankful. I also express my deep appreciation to Dr Peter Cotterell, who was the first director of EGST, for all his support over the years.

I remember fondly my conversations with Annette Glaw, Cor Bennema, Volker Rabens and André Munzinger. I am grateful for their dialogical partnership, friendship and critical input to my interpretations of some Jewish texts and the text of Romans.

There are also so many without whose love, friendship, encouragement and practical support my academic journey would not have been possible. To mention but only a few: Fecadu Abraha and his family, Dr Jean Orr, Mr David Mackinder, Mrs Sylvia Colley, Mr and Mrs Allcock, Mr and Mrs A. Absalom, Fasil Belete and his family, Andy and Haimie Walter, Mr and Prof J. Fox-Rushby, Mr and Mrs A. Abernethie, Mr and Mrs P. Carey, Miss Christina Muir, Mr and Mrs N. Pearson, the late Mrs Maggie Taylor, the leadership of the Ethiopian Kale Heywet Church, my house group in Northwood, and my family and friends back in Ethiopia.

Joanna Jeffery, as my girlfriend towards the end of my doctoral studies and as my wife during the preparation of the manuscript for publication, was a great source of support in every way. Without her companionship and handling of much of the technical work, I would not have been able to meet Mohr Siebeck's deadline for submission of the manuscript. I am immensely grateful to her.

Finally, I thank God for his love, through which he has continued to sustain me, challenge me and change me. As Apostle Paul says in Rom 11:36: ὅτι ἐξ αὐτοῦ καὶ δι' αὐτοῦ καὶ εἰς αὐτὸν τὰ πάντα· αὐτῷ ἡ δόξα εἰς τοὺς αἰῶνας, ἀμήν.

Addis Ababa 2007 Desta Heliso

Table of Contents

Abbreviations

ABD	*The Anchor Bible Dictionary*, 6 vols
BDB	Brown, Driver and Briggs, *Hebrew and English Lexicon of the Old Testament*
BDF	Blass and Debrunner, *A Greek Grammar of the New Testament and Other Early Christian Literature* (trans. and rev. R. W. Funk)
BNTC	Black's New Testament Commentary
BZ	*Biblische Zeitschrift*
CBQ	*Catholic Biblical Quarterly*
DSD	*Dead Sea Discoveries*
EvQ	*Evangelical Quarterly*
ExpT	*Expository Times*
FRLANT	Forschungen zur Religion und Literatur des Alten und Neuen Testaments
HeyJ	*The Heythrop Journal*
HNT	Handbuch zum Neuen Testament
HTR	*Harvard Theological Review*
ICC	The International Critical Commentary
IDB	*Interpreter's Dictionary of the Bible*, 4 vols
IJST	*International Journal of Systematic Theology*
IVP	Inter-Varsity Press
JBL	*Journal of Biblical Literature*
JJS	*Journal of Jewish Studies*
JPS	*The Jewish Publication Society*
JSJS	Supplements to the Journal for the Study of Judaism in the Persian, Hellenistic and Roman Period
JSNT	*Journal for the Study of the New Testament*
JSNTS	Journal for the Study of the New Testament Supplement Series
JSOT	Journal for the Study of the Old Testament
JSP	*Journal for the Study of Pseudepigrapha*
JSPS	Journal for the Study of the Pseudepigrapha Supplement Series
JTC	*Journal for Theology and Church*
JTS	*Journal of Theological Studies*
KEK	Kritisch-exegetischer Kommentar über das Neue Testament
LXX	Septuagint (Greek Bible)
MT	Masoretic Text (Hebrew Bible)
NIGTC	New International Greek Testament Commentary
NIV	New International Version
NRSV	New Revised Standard Version
NovT	*Novum Testamentum*
NT	New Testament
NTF	Neutestamentliche Forschungen
NTS	*New Testament Studies*

OT   Old Testament
OTL   Old Testament Library
RB   *Revue biblique*
RevQ   *Revue de Qumrân*
RSV   Revised Standard Version
SBL   Society of Biblical Literature
SJT   *Scottish Journal of Theology*
ScEspr   *Science et Esprit*
SCM   Student Christian Movement
SPCK   Society for the Promotion of Christian Knowledge
SP   Sacra Pagina
SPB   Studia Postbiblica
ST   *Studia Theologica*
SUNT   Studien zur Umwelt des Neuen Testaments
TDNT   *Theological Dictionary of the New Testament*
TDOT   *Theological Dictionary of the Old Testament*
ThHK   Theologischer Handkommentar zum Neuen Testament
ThLZ   *Theologische Literaturzeitung*
TSK   *Theologische Studien und Kritiken*
TynB   *Tyndale Bulletin*
VT   *Vetus Testamentum*
WBC   Word Biblical Commentary
WUNT   Wissenshaftliche Untersuchungen zum Neuen Testament
ZAW   *Zeitschrift für die alttestamentliche Wissenschaft*
ZNW   *Zeitschrift für die neutestamentliche Wissensch*

Introduction

Rom 1:17 is one of Paul's climactic statements in the introductory section of the letter (1:1-17), which is traditionally broken up into two sections, i.e. 1:1-15 and 1:16-17,[1] and is followed by one of the distinct parts that is

---

[1] Since the statement must be explained along with its immediate context, particularly 1:16, it may be helpful to set out the textual variants of Rom 1:16-17 with brief comments and translations from the NRSV, the NIV and the Jerusalem Bible.

Rom 1:16-17 reads: οὐ γὰρ ἐπαισχύνομαι τὸ εὐαγγέλιον, δύναμις γὰρ θεοῦ ἐστιν εἰς σωτηρίαν παντὶ τῷ πιστεύοντι, Ἰουδαίῳ τε πρῶτον καὶ Ἕλληνι. δικαιοσύνη γὰρ θεοῦ ἐν αὐτῷ ἀποκαλύπτεται ἐκ πίστεως εἰς πίστιν, καθὼς γέγραπται· ὁ δὲ δίκαιος ἐκ πίστεως ζήσεται.

Textual Notes: 1) The Majority Text, the Athos (044 or Ψ) and the Leningrad (D^c [9th century CE], copy of 06 or D located in Paris [6th century CE]) manuscripts have τὸ εὐαγγέλιον τοῦ Χριστοῦ, instead of the reading τὸ εὐαγγέλιον, which is maintained in the majority of the textual witnesses: Papyrus 26 (P^26vid), Codex Sinaiticus (ℵ), Codex Vaticanus (B), Codex Ephraemi (C), Codex Claromontanus (D), Codex Boernerianus (G), some minuscules (33 81 1506 1739 1881 2495), a few other Greek manuscripts, parts of Old Latin and Vulgate versions, all Syriac witnesses and Coptic versions. The minority reading probably stemmed from a later scribal attempt to bring the expression in line with 1:9, εὐαγγέλιον τοῦ υἱοῦ, and also probably with Paul's occasional association of εὐαγγέλιον with Christ elsewhere in his Seven Letter Corpus (so 1 Cor 9:12, 18; 2 Cor 2:12; 9:13; 10:14; Gal 1:7; Phil 1:27; 1 Thess 3:2) – it is to be noted here that in Romans Paul also associates εὐαγγέλιον with God (Rom 1:1; 15:16; cf. 1 Thess 2:8) and himself (Rom 2:16; 16:25). From a text-critical standpoint, the insertion with notably slender and late witnesses is not decisive.

2) In 1:16b, MS G omits εἰς σωτηρίαν. The motivation is not very clear, but it could be attributed to either a later scribal corruption or a conscious attempt to make the text read more smoothly.

3) In 1:16b again, MSS B, G, the Sahidic version and, predictably, Marcion omit πρῶτον. The question as to whether Marcion preserves an early variation or some of the early manuscripts are influenced by Marcion's text is an interesting one. Metzger (*A Textual Commentary on the Greek New Testament* [2nd edn], 447) suggests that the omission 'is perhaps due to Marcion, to whom the privilege of the Jews was unacceptable' (For a discussion of this and other textual issues, see Sanday and Headlam, *Epistle*, lxiii-lxxxv). Whatever the answer, the majority of Greek manuscripts read πρῶτον, which appears to be original in the light of the recurrence of the formula Ἰουδαίῳ τε πρῶτον καὶ Ἕλληνι in 2:9-10 and the fact that the priority or privilege of the Jews is evident in 3:1; 9:1-5; 11:16ff and 15:9. This view appears to be in tension with Paul's assertion that there is no διαστολή between Jews and Greeks (3:22; 10:12).

4) From among the fifth-century manuscripts, only MS C adds the possessive pronoun μου after ὁ δὲ δίκαιος. The influence may have come from either one of the LXX texts

itself broken up into two major sections: 1:18-3:20 and 3:21-5:21[2] or 1:18-3:20 and 3:21-4:25.[3] What follows in this study is an attempt to critically evaluate existing interpretations of the passage in the light of exegetical considerations of relevant texts from the OT and Second Temple Judaism

---

(e.g. A) that read ὁ δὲ δίκαιός μου ἐκ πίστεως ζήσεται or the reading in Heb 10:38. It is secondary.

Selected Translations: 1) 'For I am not ashamed of the gospel; it is the power of God for salvation to everyone who has faith, to the Jew first and also to the Greek. For in it the righteousness of God is revealed through faith for faith; as it is written, "The one who is righteous will live by faith"' (NRSV).2) 'I am not ashamed of the gospel, because it is the power of God for the salvation of everyone who believes: first for the Jew, then for the Gentile. For in the gospel a righteousness from God is revealed, a righteousness that is by faith from first to last, just as it is written: "The righteous will live by faith"' (NIV). 3) 'For I am not ashamed of the Good News: it is the power of God saving all who have faith – Jews first, but Greeks as well – since this is what reveals the justice of God to us: it shows how faith leads to faith, as scripture says: *"The upright man finds life through faith"'* (The Jerusalem Bible).

[2] See, for example, Dunn, *Romans 1-8* (WBC Series), vii-viii, 38; Stuhlmacher, *Paul's Letter to the Romans*, 14-15; Keck, 'What Makes Romans Tick?', in Hay and Johnson (eds), *Pauline Theology III: Romans* (SBL Symposium Series), 3-29, 24.

[3] See Cranfield, *Romans 1-8* (ICC), xi; Fitzmyer, *Romans: A New Translation with Introduction and Commentary*, ix. See also R. Longenecker, 'A Realised Hope, a New Commitment, a Developed Proclamation: Paul and Jesus', in R. Longenecker (ed.), *The Road from Damascus: The Impact of Paul's Conversion on His Life, Thought and Ministry*, 18-42, 37f. There is a question as to whether the structural division 1:16-4:25 (or 1:18-4:25) and 5:1-8:39 is to be preferred against 1:16-5:21 (or 1:18-5:21) and 6:1-8:39 or *vice versa*. Scholars such as Nygren (*Commentary on Romans*, 26-35) and Cranfield (*Romans 1-8*, 102) have followed the former and argued that the Habakkuk citation is expounded in 1:18-4:25 and 5:1-8:39. Along this line, R. Longenecker ('Realised', 38) argues that 1:16-4:25 is the type of proclamation commonly held by all Jewish 'believers in Jesus' and 5:1-8:39 'the distinctive features of the gospel' proclaimed to the Gentiles. This may mean that Rom 1-4 (as Rom 9-11) was a homily intended for a Jewish audience and 5-8 for a Gentile audience (Scroggs, 'Paul as Rhetorician: Two Homilies in Romans 1-11', in R. Hamerton-Kelly and R. Scroggs (eds), *Jews, Greeks, and Christians: Religious Cultures in Late Antiquity: Essays in Honor of William David Davies*, 271-298). In any case, 1-5 (or 1:16-5:21) and 6:1-8:39 probably is a better division, because, as Cranfield (*Romans 1-8*, 253) has rightly recognised, there are some significant connections, particularly linguistic, between chapter 5 and chs 1-4. We wish to outline the occurrence in respective chapters of some relevant terms and phrases as follows:

Chapters 1-4	Chapter 5
δίκαιος = 4x (1:17; 2:13; 3:10, 26)	= 2x (5:7,19;cf.7:12)
δικαιόω = 9x (2:4; 3:4, 20, 24, 26, 28, 30; 4:2, 5)	= 2x (5:1, 9)
δικαιοσύνη = 14x (1:17; 3:5, 21, 22, 25, 26; 4:3, 5, 6, 9, 11, 13, 22)	= 2x (5:17, 21)
δικαίωμα = 2x (1:32; 2:26)	= 2x (5:16, 18)
δικαίωσις = 1x (4:25)	= 1x (5:18)
ὀργή = 6x (1:18; 2:5, 8; 3:5; 4:15)	= 1x (5:9)
ἐκ πίστεως = 6x (1:17a, 17b; 3:26, 30; 4:16a, 16b)	= 1x (5:1)
ἐν τῷ αὐτοῦ αἵματι = 1x (3:25)	= 1x (5:9)

as well as from Paul's Seven Letter Corpus and the rest of the NT. The importance of Rom 1:17 is undisputed, because since Luther the declarations it contains have shaped not only the ways in which Paul's expressions in the letter of Romans are understood but also the living, thinking and praxis of many in ecclesiastical, socio-political and cultural landscapes. Rom 1:17, along with its immediate and wider contexts, has also played a very significant role in the centuries-long diverse scholarly explications of the Law-Gospel or Judaism-Christ[ianity] antithesis. The reason behind such importance is that many regard the passage, which contains Paul's own declarative statement and its scriptural proof from Hab 2:4, as the thesis of the letter. How the passage is read therefore determines how the whole letter should be interpreted.

So, that Rom 1:17 is an important passage probably goes without saying. But why is our task in this study important? We will indicate a specific reason below, but here it is worth mentioning three general and, perhaps, obvious reasons why our task is important. First, many in the post-Sanders era may no longer view Judaism as a legalistic religion that has no place for grace, but over twenty years down the line since Sanders fundamentally challenged such a view and its interpretative basis, a focussed and extensive endeavour to deal with the passage and its context in the light of Jewish literature has not yet been made. Second, although a common understanding developed over the years between the Catholic and Protestant churches has resulted in the signing of a joint declaration that (at least, in theory) renders the longstanding doctrinal condemnations ineffectual,[4] the underlying exegetical problems in Rom 1:17 remain and the dialogue between the two ecclesiastical traditions continues. Third, the issues embedded in the passage continue to have far-reaching social, religious and existential implications, necessitating continued effort for fresh study.

As is well known, the majority of scholars go along with the traditional understanding of 'justification by faith' that depends, by and large, on Luther's initial interpretation of the passage. A few scholars have, however, offered a reading where the person of the Habakkuk citation is understood as Christ. If this christological reading is shown to be cogent, it poses a serious problem to the traditional view that Rom 1:17 introduces and provides a framework for the doctrine of justification by faith. However, no extensive study that evaluates both readings in the light of external-contextual and internal-textual evidence has so far been done. As this study seeks to remedy that and offer a fresh and coherent reading of the passage, it will adopt several strategic steps in order to achieve its central

---

[4] See also Lane, *Justification by Faith in Catholic – Protestant Dialogue: An Evangelical Assessment*, 100-107, 239-259 (Appendix II: *Joint Declaration on the Doctrine of Justification*).

objective. The rationale of each step will be discussed at the end of the following chapter, but it might be helpful to outline those steps briefly here.

The study will start by analysing existing interpretations and isolating issues. Then the second chapter will examine the sort of interpretations given to Hab 2:3-4 by the Septuagintal translator, the producer of the Qumran commentary (1QpHab), the translator or reviser of the Nahal Hever text (8HevXIIgr) and the author of the letter of Hebrews (Heb 10:37-38). In the third, fourth and fifth chapters, we will make exegetical attempts to answer three questions from the text. The questions respectively are, first, do Paul's linguistic images in the immediate context of the Habakkuk citation, 1:16-17a in particular, in any way reflect his christological perspective? Second, is ὁ δίκαιος in the Habakkuk citation a reference to a generic individual or messianic figure? Third, is the implied subject of ἐκ πίστεως in both halves of Rom 1:17 human faith or Christ's faithfulness? In the process of answering these questions, our discussions will be informed by the results of our exegetical analyses of the interpretations of Hab 2:3-4 in the traditions of the LXX, *Pesher* Habakkuk, the Nahal Hever text and the letter of Hebrews. The process will also involve combining a comparative analysis of external evidence from Second Temple Judaism in general and the Enochic Book of Parables (*1 En* 37-71) in particular with an exegetical treatment of Rom 1:17 and internal evidence.

Chapter 1

Analyses of Existing Interpretations

1. Introduction

This chapter will focus on analysing theories and exegetical considerations relating to Rom 1:17. The result will provide us with a clearer picture of the scholarly perspectives on the passage and the interpretative problems surrounding πίστις and ὁ δίκαιος. It is probably natural to start such a task with Luther because of the relative novelty of his interpretation of Rom 1:16-17. Following a brief discussion of Luther's reading of this passage, we shall summarise scholarly views on δικαιοσύνη θεοῦ, because the meaning assigned to this phrase to an extent influences the ways in which the Habakkuk citation is interpreted.

We will then organise issues raised and arguments proposed in relation to ἐκ πίστεως and ὁ δίκαιος under two interpretative categories, namely anthropological (the faith by which a justified person lives or the faith by which a person is justified) and christological (the faithfulness of Christ, by which he gains eschatological life). We do this not because we believe that these categories should be universally applicable to all texts of Romans or Galatians, but simply because such a categorisation is expedient for our discussion in this chapter. We shall analyse both categories in turn.

Subsequently, we shall overview the effect of the so-called Old and New Perspectives on Rom 1:17. In the course of this, we pay attention to the recent defences of the Lutheran view of justification by faith. Finally, we shall conclude our largely descriptive analysis by clarifying what the major problems are with the two competing readings and how the study will attempt to adjudicate between them.

2. Luther's Reading of Romans 1:17

As is well known, Luther's new interpretation was driven by his concern over the concept of the Latin *iustitia* by means of which the term δικαιοσύνη θεοῦ ('righteousness of God') in his day was customarily understood as God's retributive justice. It was that concern that led Luther to

revive the Augustinian tradition where δικαιοσύνη θεοῦ was thought to be
a gift that comes from God.[1] What he says in his preface to the Latin
edition of his works encapsulates the extent to which Rom 1:17 influenced
his thinking:

I had confidence in the fact that I was more skilful, after I had lectured in the university
on St Paul's epistles to the Romans, to the Galatians, and the one to the Hebrews. I had
indeed been captivated with an extraordinary ardor for understanding Paul in the Epistle
to the Romans. But up till then it was not the cold blood about the heart, but a single
word in Chapter 1 [:17], 'In it the righteousness of God is revealed,' that had stood in my
way. For I hated that word 'righteousness of God,' which, according to the use and custom of all the teachers, I had been taught to understand philosophically regarding the
formal or active righteousness, as they called it, with which God is righteous and punishes the unrighteous sinner.

   Though I lived as a monk without reproach, I felt that I was a sinner before God with
an extremely disturbed conscience. I could not believe that he was placated by my satisfaction. I did not love, yes, I hated the righteous God who punishes sinners, and secretly,
if not blasphemously, certainly murmuring *greatly*, I was angry with God, and said, 'As
if, indeed, it is not enough, that miserable sinners, eternally lost through original sin, are
crushed by every kind of calamity by the law of the Decalogue, without having God add
pain to pain by the gospel and also by the gospel threatening us with his righteousness
and wrath!' Thus I raged with a fierce and troubled conscience. Nevertheless, I beat

---

[1] For analytical discussions of both Augustine's perspective and Luther's appropriation of it, see McGrath, *Iustitia Dei: A History of Christian Doctrine of Justification I
(Beginnings to 1500)*, 23-36; *II (From 1500 to the Present Day)*, 10-19. As space does
not permit us to study the use of the δικ- terms in Hellenistic Greek, it may be helpful to
note a few things here. In Hellenism the meaning of δίκαιος and δικαιοσύνη developed
out of the concepts surrounding the figure of δίκη. A δίκαιος is someone who conforms
to δίκη ('custom', 'the divine law of universal and civic life', 'justice' [cf. Acts 28:4]).
In literature and art, the figure of δίκη served to inform Zeus of evils done by humans
and to punish injustice. On the whole, the idea of δίκη's cosmic rule took the shape of
laws for family, natural and social orders, and norms for justice (δικαιοσύνη) developed
in the political and ethical realms. In Plato's *Republic* (1-4), we notice that δικαιοσύνη
became the basic virtue for Plato's ideal state, the key for ordering society and educating
citizens, the foundation of the *polis*. For Aristotle, justice, in contrast with injustice (*Nic
Ethics* 5.1.1, 1129a), refers to conformity to the law and fairness. In Stoicism,
Chrysippus in the 3rd century BCE took up the old notion of δικαιοσύνη as (a virgin)
goddess watching in heaven. As the virtue concerned with distributing things,
δικαιοσύνη, which, already in Aristotle, had been brought into connection with friendship
(*Nic Ethics* 8:9-12, 1159b 25-1162a 33), was divided into goodness, good fellowship and
an accommodating disposition, explained as being disposed towards kindness, fairness in
sharing and blamelessly dealing with one's neighbour. In subsequent thinking,
δικαιοσύνη often came to be united closely with piety and also with philanthropy. For
detailed discussions, see Schrenk, 'δίκη, δίκαιος, δικαιοσύνη, δικαιόω, δικαίωμα,
δικαίωσις, δικαιοκρισία', *TDNT II*, 174-225; Reumann, 'Righteousness (Greco-Roman
World)', *ABD V*, 742-745; Ziesler, *The Meaning of Righteousness*, 48-51, 255-258;
Cranfield, *Romans 1-8*, 93; Blumenfeld, *The Political Paul: Justice, Democracy and
Kingship in a Hellenistic Framework*, 36-44, 55-63, 415-450.

importunately upon Paul at that place, most ardently desiring to know what St. Paul wanted.

At last, by the mercy of God, meditating day and night, I gave heed to the context of the words, namely, 'In it the righteousness of God is revealed, as it is written, "He who through faith is righteous shall live."' There I began to understand that the righteousness of God is that by which the righteous lives by a gift of God, namely by faith. And this is the meaning: the righteousness of God is revealed by the gospel, namely, the passive righteousness with which a merciful God justifies us by faith, as it is written, 'He who through faith is righteous shall live.' Here I felt that I was altogether born again and had entered paradise itself through open gates. There a totally other face of the entire Scripture showed itself to me. Thereupon I ran through the Scriptures from memory. I also found in other terms an analogy, as, the work of God, that is, what God does in us, the power of God, with which he makes us strong, the wisdom of God, with which he makes us wise, the strength of God, the salvation of God, the glory of God. And I extolled my sweetest word with a love as great as the hatred with which I had before hated the word 'righteousness of God.' Thus that place in Paul was for me truly the gate to paradise.[2]

Luther's perspectives above were set against the Scholastics who, according to him, based their philosophical and theological frameworks on Aristotelian ethics, where one becomes righteous by performing righteous actions (*Nic Ethics* 2:1; 3:7, 9, 10), and, in doing so, attributed to human beings the potentialities of moral and religious attainment (i.e. the love of neighbour and of God, by natural powers or will).[3] Central to his perspectives was his distinction between the 'righteousness of human beings', which is revealed through human teachings and in terms of which human beings can *be* and *become* righteous in themselves and before fellow human beings, and the 'righteousness of God', which is revealed through the gospel and in terms of which human beings can *be* and *become* righteous before God – the former comes from works, while the latter from 'faith alone'.[4] That is, the 'righteousness of God' as that righteousness by which we are made righteous (justified) by faith.[5] Faith, in Luther's view, is not only a divine gift but also an ongoing belief that 'the righteous person' is 'justified', as in the Habakkuk citation.[6] Luther maintains that human beings are always in need of being made 'righteous', for in themselves they are always unrighteous even if they think they are

---

[2] *Luther's Works* 34:336-337.

[3] See Luther's *Lectures on Romans*, 18, 105-118; see also the general introduction to this work, esp. xxxiv-lxvi.

[4] Luther, *Lectures*, 17-18.

[5] Luther, *Lectures*, 18. Or as Luther puts in his Romans translation, δικαιοσύνη θεοῦ is 'the justice [of God] that counts before God' (*die Gerechtigkeit, die vor Gott gilt*) and by which the just (ὁ δίκαιος) lives (ζήσεται) by a gift of God, namely by faith (ἐκ πίστεως). See also *Luther's Works* 25:9, 30-31, 89, 151-152, 241-250, 440f.

[6] Luther, *Lectures*, 19.

righteous. Thus his famous formula *simul justus et peccator* ('at the same time righteous and sinner').

Luther's new interpretation of Rom 1:17 and related texts was increasingly important during the Reformation period, as attempts were made to answer questions such as what is 'righteousness', who is 'righteous' and what is the role of 'faith' in one's existence in relation to God, Christ and the Church.[7] These questions have also dominated much Pauline scholarship in Europe and North America throughout the modern period. Before analysing a reading of Rom 1:17 that is influenced by Luther's perspective, we summarise meanings afforded concerning the righteousness of God.

3. Meanings of Δικαιοσύνη Θεοῦ

Although δικαιοσύνη θεοῦ is not a widespread phrase in NT writings outside the Pauline Seven Letter Corpus,[8] where the genitival construction occurs eight times (Rom 1:17; 3:5, 21, 22, 25; 10:3 [2x]; 2 Cor 5:21) out of fifty uses of δικαιοσύνη terminology (thirty-four or 68% of those being in Romans), it has been a focus of long-standing scholarly debate, because the meaning it is given, as we noticed above, is decisive not only for our reading of Rom 1:17 and related texts such as 3:21-26 but also for our understanding of Paul's theology as a whole. Four main perspectives on the phrase probably are predominant: a righteous status that counts in God's court (θεοῦ as objective genitive), God's gift of 'righteousness' (θεοῦ as genitive of origin), God's salvation-creating power (θεοῦ as subjective), or God's own activity and status (θεοῦ as subjective) expressed within a covenant that establishes mutual relationship and obligation (the covenantal reading).[9] The difficulty of explaining the term and even translating it

---

[7] Calvin (*The Epistles of Paul the Apostle to the Romans and to the Thessalonians*, 5), for instance, argued that '[m]an's only righteousness is the mercy of God in Christ, when it is offered by the Gospel and received by faith'. Melanchthon also answered the questions within the forensic framework where emphasis was laid on the notion of *iustitia aliena* ('an alien righteousness') imputed to 'the believer' so that she may be 'declared righteous' or 'accepted as righteous'. See McGrath, *Iustitia II*, 20ff.

[8] Indeed, it appears only in Jas 1:20 (δικαιοσύνην θεοῦ), 2 Pet 1:1 (ἐν δικαιοσύνῃ τοῦ θεοῦ) and Matt 6:33 (τὴν δικαιοσύνην αὐτοῦ [θεοῦ]).

[9] On these interpretations, see, for example, H. Cremer, *Die paulinische Rechtfertigungslehre im Zusammenhang ihrer geschichtlichen Voraussetzungen*, 33f; Sanday and Headlam, *The Epistle to the Romans: A Critical and Exegetical Commentary*, 24-25; Dodd, *The Epistle of Paul to the Romans*, 9-13; Schlatter, *Romans: The Righteousness of God*, 20-21; Barth, *The Epistle to the Romans*, 40-41; *A Shorter Commentary on Romans*, 22; Nygren, *Commentary on Romans*, 74-78; Käsemann, *Commentary on Romans*, 23-30; *New Testament Questions of Today*, 168-182; Wilckens, *Der Brief an die Römer I*, 88; Stuhlmacher, *Paul's Letter to the Romans*, 28-32; Cranfield, *Romans 1-8*,

into modern European languages is compounded by an ongoing controversy that has chiefly concentrated on the grammar.[10] As the objective
genitive argument is often combined or aligned with the genitive of origin
argument, the grammatical question focuses on whether the genitive in
δικαιοσύνη θεοῦ should be read with a genitive of origin or a subjective
sense, which we wish to summarise briefly here.[11]

The gift sense of the righteousness of God is based on the genitive of
origin interpretation, which is firmly founded on Luther's understanding of
Rom 1:17. Although some scholars argue that the righteousness of God
denotes a quality that is to be acquired by humanity and approved by God
as something that is able to stand before God during his juridical adjudication,[12] it is this gift sense as explained particularly by Bultmann that remains predominant. For Bultmann, Paul's use of the righteousness of God
stands against the idea of *iustitia* with a punitive sense.[13] So the phrase has
a 'forensic-eschatological' meaning, where it expresses one's relation to
God in a court context.[14] While the pious Jew would understand the phrase
in terms of God's 'rightwising' verdict (i.e. giving a favourable standing
before him) through keeping the law, Paul understood it in terms of God's
eschatological adjudication of the person of 'faith' by pronouncing her

---

95-100; Fitzmyer, *Romans*, 254-262; Byrne, *Romans*, 51-60; Leenhardt, *The Epistle to the Romans*, 49-58; Dunn, *Romans 1-8*, 40-48; Moo, *The Epistle to the Romans*, 69-89; Wright, 'The Letter to the Romans: Introduction, Commentary and Reflections', in *The New Interpreters Bible*, 398-405.

[10] There is difficulty with regard to rendering δικαιοσύνη θεοῦ into English. In this study, we have followed the more conventional rendering of δικαιοσύνη θεοῦ in the Eng-
lish speaking world, namely the 'righteousness of God'. But it should be borne in mind that translations such as 'the uprightness of God', 'the justice of God', 'God's rectifying act' and 'God's act of covenant faithfulness' can also be used. To be sure, it is difficult to find a rendering that is directly compatible with what we think the phrase denotes (i.e. God's power of salvation), but we have chosen the conventional translation because it is perhaps more flexible than others. On the translation problem, see Sanders, *Paul*, 44-49; Fitzmyer, *Romans*, 257-263; Reumann, *'Righteousness' in the New Testament: 'Justification' in the United States Lutheran-Roman Catholic Dialogue*, 11; Dunn, *The Theology of Paul the Apostle*, 334ff.

[11] Käsemann (*Commentary*, 28), perhaps rightly, complains that focussing on grammatical rules may have contributed to the difficulty by wrapping 'material problems in a thick fog'. But grammar cannot and should not be neglected. For good summaries of the grammatical discussions relating to the genitival phrase in question, see Sanday and Headlam, *Epistle*, 24-25; Cranfield, *Romans 1-8*, 97-99; Wright, *What Saint Paul Really Said: Was Paul of Tarsus the Real Founder of Christianity?*, 100-107.

[12] See, for example, O'Neill, *Paul's Letter to the Romans*, 38, 70-72, 168; Ridderbos, *Paul: An Outline of His Theology*, 159-181.

[13] Bultmann, *Theology of the New Testament I* (*TNT I*), 270-285; see also Reumann, *'Righteousness'*, 3-11.

[14] Bultmann, *TNT I*, 272.

'sinless' not in the sense that she is ethically perfect but in the sense that on her is conferred the divine free gift as a result of which she is placed in a new relation to God and no sins are counted against her.[15]

Several grammatical and exegetical arguments have been put forward in favour of this interpretation: first, in 10:3 τὴν τοῦ θεοῦ δικαιοσύνην means the status of 'righteousness' given by God as opposed to a status achieved by one's efforts (cf. Rom 5:17; 1 Cor 1:30; 2 Cor 5:21; Phil 3:9).[16] Second, the words ἐκ πίστεως εἰς πίστιν cannot be shown to be a natural expression for Paul unless the righteousness of God is understood as the status conferred on humanity. In other words, 'faith' has to be both the beginning and culmination in terms of sharing the 'righteousness of God' through it.[17] In connection with this, third, in 3:22, the reading δικαιοσύνη θεοῦ ... εἰς πάντας τοὺς πιστεύοντας makes it clear that the righteousness of God is received by those who believe. Fourth, the Habakkuk citation is in favour of this argument because of its focus on the 'justified' person rather than God's act of 'justifying' a person.[18] Fifth, the fact that '1:18-4:25 expounds the words ὁ δίκαιος ἐκ πίστεως and 5:1-8:39 the promise that the man who is righteous by faith ζήσεται'[19] agrees with the interpretation that takes δικαιοσύνη θεοῦ in 1:17 as the righteous status bestowed by God.

Notwithstanding these arguments, some scholars have resisted the interpretation that takes θεοῦ as a genitive of origin and δικαιοσύνη as the status graciously conferred on humanity. Schlatter at the turn of the 20th century pointed out the interpretation's tendency to exclude the denotation of the phrase as God's activity in divine-human relations.[20] Schlatter's concern was revived by Käsemann, who, without rejecting the gift sense, defined δικαιοσύνη θεοῦ as God's power that creates salvation (*heilsetzende Macht*).[21] Müller,[22] Stuhlmacher,[23] Kertelge,[24] and Fitzmyer[25] (to

---

[15] Bultmann, *TNT I*, 276f, 281-285; see also 'ΔΙΚΑΙΟΣΥΝΗ ΘΕΟΥ', *JBL* 83 (1964) 12-16. Conzelmann (*An Outline of the Theology of the New Testament*, 218-220) basically agrees with this Lutheran-Bultmannian explanation, although he concedes that in Rom 3:5 the phrase denotes a 'property' of God.

[16] See also Nygren, *Commentary*, 74-76.

[17] So Nygren (*Commentary*, 78-81).

[18] See also Nygren, *Commentary*, 81-92.

[19] Cranfield, *Romans 1-8*, 98.

[20] Schlatter, *Romans*, 20. Dodd (*Epistle*, 10-13) too argued that, for Paul, δικαιοσύνη along with the genitive θεοῦ denotes the divine action in redressing the wrongful oppression and delivering his people from the powers of evil. See also Barrett (*The Epistle to the Romans*, 29-31), who, like Dodd and others, argues that δικαιοσύνη θεοῦ is not merely God's property or attribute of being righteous, but also his activity of doing right as the righteous judge.

[21] With extreme caution, Käsemann (*Commentary*, 30) also thought it probable that

mention only a few) have followed Käsemann's interpretation in various ways. Fitzmyer gives a forensic-ethical definition to the phrase: God's uprightness manifested in judicial activity. For Kertelge, the phrase denotes God's redemptive activity on the basis of 'faith in Christ'.[26] Kertelge more or less agrees with Stuhlmacher, who interprets the phrase in terms of the cosmic power of God as Creator (*Schöpfermacht*).[27] God's creative or salvific activity, for Stuhlmacher, takes place 'in and through Christ' and is strictly related to 'faith/believing'.[28] He differs slightly from Müller, whose work focuses on Rom 9-11 but who takes the block as an integral part of the theme announced in 1:17 and, in so doing, interprets the phrase within the lawsuit framework, where God is victorious against Israel (and the world).[29]

Amongst post-Sanders scholars, Wright is happy to adopt the subjective genitive interpretation of δικαιοσύνη θεοῦ but unhappy to go along with Käsemann and his followers completely.[30] He understands the term with a sense of 'covenant faithfulness'.[31] This is similar to the views held by Moo

---

'Paul did take over this characteristic catchword as a fixed formula from Jewish apocalyptic'.

[22] Müller, *Gottes Gerechtigkeit und Gottes Volk: Eine Untersuchung zu Römer 9-11*.

[23] Stuhlmacher, *Reconciliation, Law, and Righteousness: Essays in Biblical Theology*, 68-109.

[24] Kertelge, *'Rechtfertigung' bei Paulus: Studien zur Struktur und zum Bedeutungsgehalt des paulinischen Rechtfertigungsbegriffs*.

[25] Fitzmyer, *Romans*, 254-262. In his recent commentary, Schreiner (*Romans*, 66) too appears to accept this perspective as valid.

[26] Kertelge, *'Rechtfertigung'*, 67, 85.

[27] Stuhlmacher, *Gerechtigkeit Gottes bei Paulus*, 78-83; *Letter*, 30. See also Michel (*Der Brief an die Römer*, 88-92), who understands δικαιοσύνη θεοῦ in terms of divine judgement and eschatological gift of salvation.

[28] Stuhlmacher, *Letter*, 31.

[29] Müller, *Gottes*, 57ff, 104f.

[30] Wright (*Saint*, 103) regards an understanding of δικαιοσύνη θεοῦ on the basis of the technical usage of the phrase in Judaism as 'an ingenious impossibility'. Others have also argued against the phrase being a fixed formula on the grounds that a genuine technical term does not vary in its formulaic use, as happens in Judaism and Paul where the phrase or its equivalent is used. See, for example, Ziesler, *Meaning*, 170; Way, *The Lordship of Christ: Ernst Käsemann's Interpretations of Paul's Theology*, 190-193; Sanders, *Paul and Palestinian Judaism (PPJ)*, 494f; see also Manfred Brauch's Appendix in Sanders *PPJ*, 523-542. But see Campbell (*The Rhetoric of Righteousness in Romans 3.21–26*, 163; Romans 1:17 – A *Crux Interpretum* for the Πίστις Χριστοῦ Debate', *JBL* 113 [1994] 265-285, 270), who does not speak of the technical usage of the phrase in the Second Temple period but goes along with Käsemann.

[31] Wright, *Saint*, 101, 103, 107; see also his Unpublished DPhil Dissertation (1980), *The Messiah and the People of God: A Study in Pauline Theology with Particular Reference to the Argument of the Epistle to the Romans*, 57, 64; and 'A New Tübingen School? Ernst Käsemann and His Commentary on Romans', *Themelios* 7:3 (1982) 6-16.

and Dunn.[32] Wright has recently adopted a political reading of the term within the framework that in Romans Paul is setting Κύριος 'Ιησοῦς Χριστός over against Κύριος Καῖσαρ and, in doing so, countering the imperial ideology.[33]

In any case, several grammatical and exegetical arguments have been put forward in favour of the subjective genitive reading of δικαιοσύνη θεοῦ:[34] first, in view of the connection between 1:16b and 1:17, δικαιοσύνη θεοῦ can be understood in the light of δύναμις θεοῦ. That is, as θεοῦ is subjective and δύναμις is God's power in action, so also are θεοῦ and δικαιοσύνη. Second, in ὀργή θεοῦ in 1:18, θεοῦ is a subjective genitive and ὀργή an activity of God. So on the basis of the parallelism between 1:17a and 1:18, δικαιοσύνη θεοῦ should again be understood similarly. Third, in Rom 3:5, 25 and 26 the genitives θεοῦ and αὐτοῦ must be subjective, hence Paul must have understood δικαιοσύνη as a power rather than a status. Fourth, in some of the relevant OT texts (e.g. 1 Sam 12:7; Ps 98:2),

---

[32] Moo, *Epistle*, 70ff. Differing from Wright, Dunn (*Romans 1-8*, 41; *Theology*, 340-346) explains δικαιοσύνη θεοῦ with a notion of discharging sociological responsibilities or meeting relational obligations generally. Martin (*The Righteousness of God in Romans: A Study in Paul's Use of Jewish Tradition* [Unpublished PhD Dissertation, Marquette University, 1991] has argued that Paul was interested in none of the interpretations given so far. For Martin, Paul's main concern was to address through the use of scripture the social/cultural issues of 'soteric domain' (whom God saves rather than how God saves humanity), so δικαιοσύνη θεοῦ is viewed as God's salvation of the faithful person *qua* faithful, the paradigm of whom is Jesus, whose resurrection stood for the 'vindication' of the faithful.

[33] See Wright, *Saint*, 88; 'Letter', 404-405; Blumenfeld, *Paul*, 302-414. Other scholars, in an essay collection entitled *Paul and Empire: Religion and Power in Roman Imperial Society*, have also contended that Romans is part of Paul's gospel which stands against Roman imperial ideology. Georgi, in an article ('God Turned Upside Down', 148-157) that condenses the thesis of his earlier work *Theocracy in Paul's Praxis and Theology*, which was first published in German in 1987 and translated into English in 1991 (see esp. 81-104), for example, argues that the *Acts of Augustus* (ch 34) has δικαιοσύνη as one of the four attributes demonstrated by Augustus, whose birthday (September 23) is considered as the day that gave a new aspect and beginning to the whole universe. Elsewhere, the *princeps* was identified with *Iustitia*. So for Georgi, Paul's use of δικαιοσύνη (and other terms mentioned above) betrays his intention to counter the imperial political ideology that has the new cult of *Iustitia* in its centre (see also Neil Elliott's article 'The Anti-Imperial Message of the Cross', 167-183). Georgi admits that Paul's use of δικαιοσύνη θεοῦ is derived from the Jewish Bible, but he still argues that the evidence stated above suggests that δικαιοσύνη θεοῦ is to be understood against the Roman ideological and judicial framework (p. 149). According to Hays (*The Faith of Jesus Christ: The Narrative Substructure of Galatians 3:1-4:11* [2nd ed], xlii), although the parallels that Georgi adduces between the imperial ideology and the situation Paul addresses in Galatia are 'few and imprecise', Georgi's suggestions 'may actually make better sense in relation to Romans'.

[34] See also Cranfield, *Romans 1-8*, 96.

when צְדָקָה or δικαιοσύνη is attributed to God, it is referred to as the activity of his saving and judging power. Fifth, δικαιοσύνη θεοῦ or an equivalent phrase was a fixed formula in some Jewish apocalyptic traditions of the Second Temple period, and if Paul took over the formula from those traditions he would have understood it with the sense of God's activity/power within a cosmic setting.[35]

4. Two Competing Readings

The idea of justification by faith is based as much on the meaning of Paul's declarations in Rom 1:17 as on the way in which the verb δικαιόω (or the passive δικαιοῦσθαι) is understood in relation to πίστις/πιστεύω.[36] Indeed, the first half of Rom 1:17 is thought to be about 'righteousness by faith' while the second half (namely the Habakkuk citation) is about 'the person who by faith is justified'.[37] Thus the righteousness in the first half is the righteousness that is acquired by the person of the citation (the Christian) through 'faith'. We have termed this reading anthropological, as against christological – in the latter the person of the Habakkuk citation is Christ. We wish to analyse both readings in turn.

4.1. Anthropological Reading

There are perhaps three things that characterise what we call the anthropological reading of Rom 1:17. First, the syntax of the passage suggests that the righteousness of God is to be understood as righteousness given to believers and ἐκ πίστεως as the faith exercised by any individual person. Second, ὁ δίκαιος in the Habakkuk citation represents a person who was ungodly but is now justified or declared righteous. Third, the means through which one's justification takes place is 'faith'. It may be helpful to elucidate these factors briefly.

---

[35] Stuhlmacher, *Gerechtigkeit*, 74-91, 174-175. Stuhlmacher (*Letter*, 31-32) warns us against establishing a false alternative between God's activity/power and God's gift, but for this to be true δικαιοσύνη θεοῦ has to be understood as something embodied in Jesus rather than a mere status one receives at the judgement forum. Otherwise, in Rom 1:17 in particular, it has got to be one or the other.

[36] The English word 'justification' is based on Paul's use of the substantive δικαίωσις in Rom 4:25 and 5:18, which is probably based both on the Hebrew מִשְׁפָּט (cf. Lev 24:22) and the Greek δικαιόω (Exod 23:7; Deut 25:1; 1 Kgs 8:32; Ps 50 [MT 51]:6 [cf. Rom 3:4]; Isa 5:23; 50:8; 53:10-11; Mic 7:9 [cf. Job 4:17; Ps 7:9-12; 119:1-8; 143:2; Ezra 9:15]). All 18 occurrences of the verb in Romans (cf. 1 Cor 4:4; 6:11; Gal 2:16, 17; 3:8, 11, 24; 5:4) are: 2:13; 3:4, 20, 24, 26b, 28, 30; 4:2, 5, 25; 5:1, 9, 18; 6:7; 8:30, 33.

[37] Fitzmyer, *Romans*, 254.

14 *Chapter 1*

First, *Justification by Faith and the Syntax of Rom 1:17*. The argument
that 'justification by faith' is the theme of Rom 1:17 is based on the syntactical link between ἐκ πίστεως and δικαιοσύνη θεοῦ (as opposed to ἐκ
πίστεως and ἀποκαλύπτεται) in the first part of Rom 1:17 and ἐκ πίστεως
and ὁ δίκαιος (as opposed to ἐκ πίστεως and ζήσεται) in the second part.[38]
So Rom 1:17a is understood as saying that 'the righteousness of God from
(through) faith to (for) faith is revealed' rather than 'the righteousness of
God is revealed from (through) faith to (for) faith'. Similarly, Rom 1:17b
is understood as saying that 'the righteous one by faith shall live' rather
than 'the righteous one shall live by faith'. Nygren admits that such a syntactical link is not self-evident, but he and Cranfield still espouse it on the
grounds that the accent is 'definitely' on δικαιοσύνη θεοῦ; δικαιοσύνη ἐκ
πίστεως becomes a technical term for Paul (cf. 9:30; 10:6); 'Paul almost
certainly meant ἐκ πίστεως to be connected with δίκαιος'; and the central
thought in 1:17 is 'about faith, and only about faith'.[39]

The significance of accentuating δικαιοσύνη θεοῦ and linking it with the
prepositional phrase, it is said, is that the resulting meaning decisively
marks a distinction between the righteousness (in the sense of ethical perfection that merits forgiveness from and acceptance by God) earned by the
'law' and the righteous status proffered altogether by 'faith'.[40] So on the
basis that δικαιοσύνη θεοῦ is synonymous with δικαιοσύνη ἐκ πίστεως (as
opposed to δικαιοσύνη ἐκ νόμου), the former is (also) 'human righteousness' because 'it is proffered to him and accepted by faith'.[41] This argument is corroborated by the following things. First, in Rom 3:21-22 where

---

[38] See also Oepke, 'εἰς', *TDNT II* (420-434), 430; Leenhardt, *Epistle*, 56; Wilckens,
Brief I, 88-89.

[39] See, for example, Nygren, *Commentary*, 78-81; Cranfield, *Romans 1-8*, 100. But
other anthropological readers such as Michel (*Der Brief*, 90-91) and Lohse (*Der Brief an
die Römer*, 82) take ἐκ πίστεως with ζήσεται.

[40] Cranfield (*Romans 1-8*, 100) sets out the sense of 1:17a: 'For in it (i.e. in the gospel
as it is being preached) a righteous status which is God's gift is being revealed (and so
offered to men) – a righteous status which is altogether by faith.' Williams ('The
"Righteousness of God" in Romans', *JBL* 99 (1980) 241-290, 257), also, ventures this
paraphrase: 'when the word is proclaimed that he who is righteous (that is, reckoned
righteous, justified) on the basis of faith shall live in God's presence and when this word
is effective in creating its own proper response, which is also faith, the righteousness of
God is being revealed by God and experienced by man'.

[41] Nygren, *Commentary*, 77-79. Barrett (*Epistle*, 29-31) also equates the manifestation
of 'the righteousness of God' with God's act of doing his righteous judgement in his
court. His verdict is either Guilty or Righteous. The articular ὁ δίκαιος in the Habakkuk
citation, therefore, refers to the person who by faith is declared 'righteous' and who will
live, i.e. experience salvation at the last judgement. For Barrett, ἐκ πίστεως εἰς πίστιν is
rhetorical ('faith from start to finish') and ἐκ πίστεως in the Habakkuk citation modifies
the adjective.

δικαιοσύνη θεοῦ is taken with πίστις Ἰησοῦ Χριστοῦ ('faith in Jesus Christ'), that appears to be contrasted with the law. Second, Romans 1-4 as a whole is about who through/from faith is righteous. Third, when he makes the transition from the first part of the letter to the next, Paul sums it up thus: δικαιωθέντες οὖν ἐκ πίστεως (5:1). The phrase ἐκ πίστεως in relation to δίκαιος, δικαιοσύνη and δικαιόω in various references in Romans (e.g. 3:30; 5:1; 9:30, 32; cf. Gal 3:8; 5:5) denotes 'the believer's faith'.[42] In short, since the titular adjective ὁ δίκαιος in Rom 1:17b refers to the justified person and such an interpretation does not involve taking ἐκ πίστεως in 1:17a in a sense other than the believer's faith, δικαιοσύνη θεοῦ in connection with ἐκ πίστεως means justification through faith rather than through the law.

Second, *Justification in Rom 1:17 as the Justification of the Ungodly.* The idea of justification, as indicated above, partly depends on the meaning of the verb δικαιόω, which is given diverse senses: 'declarative' ('declared righteous' in a forensic sense, i.e. 'acquitted by God from charges'),[43] 'effective' ('made righteous' in an ethical sense, i.e. made virtuous or morally regenerated)[44] and 'creative' ('made righteous' not in the sense of 'made virtuous' but 'forgiven' or 'cleared' by grace within a relational context)[45] – many subscribe to both declarative and effective senses.[46] More to the point, Paul's expressions in Rom 1:17 are informed by the notion of the justification of the ungodly, as in Rom 4:5. As this is clearly and representatively explained by Wilckens, a brief summary of his discussion will suffice. Wilckens argues that Paul's declarations in Rom 1:17 explain his statement in 1:16. That is, in the first half of Rom 1:17 Paul explains why the gospel is the power of God for salvation: because it reveals righteousness that is by faith. Then in the second half Paul asserts that salvation or life is given to those who believe (παντὶ τῷ πιστεύοντι). The goal of εὐαγγέλιον is actualised in 'faith' (*Glaube*) and the goal of 'faith', which can be exercised by both Jews and Greeks, is the justifica-

---

[42] Cranfield, *On Romans and Other New Testament Essays*, 91.

[43] Fitzmyer, *Romans*, 116-118; Moo, *Epistle*, 227-228; Morris, *The Epistle to the Romans*, 177-179.

[44] So Käsemann (*Commentary*, 96), though he admits that this sense does not exclude the forensic sense of 'declaring righteous'. But see Campbell (*Rhetoric*, 171) who prefers the effective sense of δικαιόω ('set right') and equates this sense with 'to save', hence 3:26c is understood as expressing God's active involvement in 'saving (or "setting right") the one who lives out of the faithfulness of Jesus'.

[45] Barrett, *The Epistle to the Romans*, 76. For Barrett, 'justification' means an act of forgiveness on God's part, so '[f]ar from being a legal fiction, this [act] is a creative act in the field of divine-human relations' (p 76).

[46] See, for example, Dunn, *Romans 1-8*, 40-41; Cranfield, *Romans 1-8*, 95; Fitzmyer, *Romans*, 116-119, 347; Stuhlmacher, *Letter*, 63-64.

tion of the ungodly without the law (Rom 3:21f); a perspective that is radi-
cally opposed to the Jewish idea of the justification of the righteous by the
law.[47] This means that ἐκ πίστεως εἰς πίστιν is an abbreviation of a more
complex notion, as can be found in Rom 1:5 (cf. Gal 3:2) and 3:21f.
Within that notion, εἰς πίστιν may be understood as the universal mark of
the effect of the proclamation of 'the righteousness of God' that creates
salvation and is received ἐκ πίστεως. Only 'faith in the crucified Christ',
hence faith in the God who justifies the ungodly, can be the foundation of
this universal salvific effect of 'God's righteousness'. Paul uses Hab 2:4 to
reinforce this inclusive claim.[48] In contradistinction to the notion of πίστις
in Judaism, where it denotes trusting-faithfulness (Glaubenstreue) that
shows itself in keeping the law, Paul understands ἐκ πίστεως in close connection with ὁ δίκαιος in the sense that the foundation for Christian righteousness or justification is Glauben an Christus. In doing so, Paul understands Hab 2:4 differently from not only the Jewish understanding represented in the OT and Second Temple Judaism, but also from those that ad-
here to the Jewish-Christian tradition.[49]

    Third, *Faith as a Means of Justification*. As indicated above, anthropo-
logical readers take δικαιοσύνη θεοῦ ἐκ πίστεως as synonymous with
δικαιοσύνη ἐκ πίστεως. Both phrases are made consistent with the reading
that ὁ δίκαιος in Rom 1:17b is someone who by faith is 'justified' (hence
ὁ δίκαιος = 'the justified one').[50] The language of πίστις (and πιστεύω) is

---

[47] Wilckens, *Brief I*, 84-86.

[48] Wilckens, *Brief I*, 89.

[49] Wilckens, *Brief I*, 90. Stuhlmacher (*Letter*, 32, 61-65), like Wilckens, sees in Rom
1:16-17 the cosmic dimension of the Pauline view of justification, namely God's act of
acquitting Jews and Gentiles of all guilt by 'faith', together with his creation theology,
namely God's act of creating and ordering a new world. This interpretative perspective,
for Stuhlmacher, includes Luther's understanding of the passage in question, although he
insists that Paul does not develop the theme of the letter from the standpoint of Luther's
concern, which centred on finding a mechanism by which comfort is afforded to the as-
sailed conscience of the sinner.

[50] We will be dealing with the meaning of ἐκ πίστεως εἰς πίστιν later in the book.
But it may be helpful to indicate three main readings of the double preposition. First,
Barth (*Epistle*, 41) and Dunn (*Romans 1-8*, 49) have read it as God's faithfulness and
human faith respectively. This reading was first proposed by Ambrosiaster: 'from God's
faithfulness to man's faith' (ex fide Dei promittentis in fidem hominis credentis) – cited
in Cranfield, *Romans 1-8*, 99 and n. 7. Second, Dodd (*Epistle*, 13-14) and Morris (*Epistle*, 70; cf. NIV: 'faith from first to last') have read the double preposition rhetorically:
the revelation of God's righteousness is a matter of faith 'from start to finish'. Cranfield's reading (*Romans 1-8*, 100) is not that different from this in that, for him, εἰς
πίστιν is 'an emphatic equivalent of ἐκ πίστεως' and has much the same effect as the
sola of *sola fide*. Third, there are some who read the double preposition progressionally.
E.g. Sanday and Headlam (*Epistle*, 26-28: 'starting from a smaller quantity of faith to
produce a larger quantity'), Fitzmyer (*Romans*, 263: 'from a beginning faith to a more

generally understood as integral to the mode through which God 'justifies' the ungodly.[51] But there are diverse interpretative categories as to what senses πίστις carries.

For some, the term carries the sense of a subjective quality in a person where she plays a co-operative role with God by responding to the 'gospel' message. This response can be explained in terms of faith in Jesus that necessarily involves an intellectual assent.[52] From this, one might allege, πίστις is itself in the last resort a human meritorious work whereby a person establishes her own claim on God by virtue of something in or achieved by herself. Differently from this, however, others insist that πίστις has nothing to do with a person's contribution to her 'salvation', but rather, as Nygren argues, it is another way of speaking about belonging to Christ and through him participating in the new aeon.[53] Speaking of πίστις as one's participation in God's eschatological saving act rather than a condition does not diminish its decisive importance for salvation, because πίστις as divine gift is associated with God's promise as found in Hab 2:4b.[54] Cranfield provides a similar but even more nuanced argument. For

---

perfect or culminating faith' in the process of 'justification') and Robinson (*Romans*, 15: 'a way that starts from faith and ends in faith'). Stuhlmacher (*Letter*, 77) defines πίστις as *fides ex auditu* (Rom 10:17). It is something that grows from the obedient hearing of the gospel. Such faith is the gift of God which leads to justification (Eph 2:8). The term also refers to one's humble and liberating resignation to the hidden epiphany of the Lord who comes in the 'word'. Stuhlmacher, *Gerechtigkeit*, 81f.

[51] Cranfield (*On Romans*, 96) distinguishes those denotations: (a) faithfulness, trustworthiness of God (e.g. Rom 3:5) or of believers (e.g. Gal 5:22); (b) a special charisma given only to some (e.g. 1 Cor 12:8-11); (c) faith in the sense of *fides qua creditur*; (d) one's confidence that one's *fides qua creditur* allows one to do or not to do certain things (e.g. Rom 14:1, 2, 22, 23); (e) faith in the sense of *fides quae creditur*, the body of doctrine believed. See also Seifried, *Christ*, 37.

[52] Or in the words of Sanday and Headlam (*Epistle*, 11), πίστις is 'the lively act or impulse of adhesion to Christ' or 'the act of assent by which the Gospel is appropriated'. Schreiner (*Romans*, 61, 64f, 72-73, 181-189) also argues that πίστις is a condition that one must meet in order to experience salvation or be right with God. According to Hay ('*Pistis*', 471), Paul thought of πίστις in both cognitive and non-cognitive ways: 'Subjective *pistis* for the apostle is, to a considerable degree, intellectual assent to what God has accomplished through Jesus. It is not, however, so much assent to particular propositions as it is affirmation that the Christian kerygma is valid and determinative for the experience, outlook, and decisions of the individual believer.'

[53] Nygren (*Commentary*, 71-72) denies that faith is the condition necessary for salvation. But by equating πιστεύω/πίστις with one's removal from the realm of darkness and being received into the new aeon, Nygren comes close to equating 'salvation' with πιστεύω/πίστις, which is rather absurd.

[54] Kertelge, *Paul's Epistle to the Romans*, 15. In understanding 'faith in Jesus' as a way of participating in δικαιοσύνη θεοῦ, Kertelge does not seem to construe πιστεύω/πίστις in Rom 1:16-17 in terms of a person's mental acquiescence to the gospel message or certain ideas within a belief system, although it is not clear whether he

him, πίστις, according to Rom 1:16-17, is 'faith in the message, and so faith in Jesus Christ who is its content and in God who has acted in Him and whose power the message is'.[55] This response should not be understood as a person's contribution in fulfilling a condition so that the gospel is εἰς σωτηρίαν for her. If that were the case, πιστεύοντι in Rom 1:16 denotes a meritorious work through which a person establishes her own claim on God to reward her action. This view cannot be claimed to be Pauline.

So, in Cranfield's perspective, 'faith' should be understood in terms of 'the openness to the gospel which God Himself creates', although he goes on to say: '[a]nd yet this faith, as God's work in a man, is in a real sense more truly and fully the man's own personal decision than anything which he himself does of himself; for it is the expression of the freedom which God has restored to him – the freedom to obey God.'[56] One may wonder how 'faith' as one's personal decision to surrender to God would square with 'faith' as divine gift or divinely occasioned openness to the gospel, but in Cranfield's view, it seems, the distinction between one's act of decision and God's act is artificial, because the former is based on God's liberative act.[57] Fitzmyer, on the other hand, holds both categories equally so that πίστις is a gift of God (just as is the whole salvific process) as well as a reaction to Paul's εὐαγγέλιον, which leads to an assent of the mind that acknowledges that 'Jesus is Lord' and to obedient submission of the whole person in her relation to God, other human beings and the world.[58]

---

equates πίστις as a way of participating in δικαιοσύνη θεοῦ with πίστις as a person's faith-decision within an existential framework.

[55] Cranfield, *Romans 1-8*, 89.

[56] Cranfield, *Romans 1-8*, 90; *On Romans*, 96-97. Cranfield's position reflects – to an extent – Bultmann's ('πιστεύω κτλ,' *TDNT VI*, 217, 225) view on faith-decision as God's free gift. The positions of Bultmann, Nygren and Canfield are, by and large, rooted in Luther's understanding of Rom 1:17a (*Luther's Works* 25, 151-153). For Luther, the righteousness that is freely given and counts before God's judgement forum is based on 'faith', which is also God's free gift and taught in the Gospel in accordance with divine revelation. In Schlatter's view (*Romans*, 25), Luther equates what is taught in the gospel with doctrine.

[57] Cranfield (*On Romans*, 92) protests that those who take πιστεύω/πίστις and also πίστις Χριστοῦ as the believer's faith do not 'share that horrible distortion of evangelical teaching which makes faith into a human meritorious work, a distortion which admittedly is to be found in some circles, but which it is quite unfair to attribute to all those who accept the objective genitive explanation of the πίστις Χριστοῦ passages'.

[58] So Fitzmyer (*Romans*, 137-138; *According to Paul*, 109; *Paul and His Theology: A Brief Sketch*, 84-85). Slightly differently, Kertelge (*Paul's Epistle to the Romans*, 15) comments that Paul regards πίστις 'not as a condition to be fulfilled by men before they reach salvation, but as the way by which they participate now in God's eschatological saving act ... Only God can give faith in Jesus Christ such decisive importance for salvation, and therefore Paul refers back to God's promise as found in Hab. 2:4b'. In understanding 'faith in Jesus' as a way of participating in δικαιοσύνη θεοῦ, Kertelge does not

4.2. Christological Reading

All major commentaries on Romans (Sanday and Headlam, Dodd, Barth, Schlatter, Nygren, Käsemann, Barrett, Stuhlmacher, Wilckens, Michel, Lohse, Haacker, Cranfield, Dunn, Fitzmyer, Byrne, Moo, Morris, Schreiner) take the likely referent of ὁ δίκαιος in the Habakkuk citation of Rom 1:17 to be any individual Jew or Gentile who receives the gospel and goes on believing.[59] But some scholars such as Anthony Hanson,[60] Richard Hays,[61] Douglas Campbell[62] and Ian Wallis[63] have challenged this traditional interpretation by taking both ὁ δίκαιος and ἐκ πίστεως in the citation christologically. We shall analyse each of them in turn.

4.2.1. Anthony Hanson

Hanson's main premise for understanding ὁ δίκαιος as an individual messianic figure is that in various passages of Paul's letters the faith of the Messiah is implied. Hanson takes πίστις Χριστοῦ as meaning 'both Christ's personal faith during his historical existence and our faith in him – and that the latter is based on the former.'[64] In his analysis of the Habakkuk citation in Rom 1:17, Hanson rejects the syntax that connects ἐκ πίστεως with ὁ δίκαιος, because had Paul intended the citation to be read with such a syntax he would have said ὁ δὲ ἐκ πίστεως δίκαιος ζήσεται. Even more important, in the context of Gal 3:11, where he cites the same text, Paul contrasts living by νόμος with living by πίστις, hence suggesting that πίστις is a way of life for ὁ δίκαιος.[65] By adopting the syntax that takes ἐκ πίστεως with ζήσεται, Hanson contends that 'the Righteous One [who] shall live by faith' is one particular individual, the Messiah.

Hanson does not explain how this syntax would enable one to read ὁ δίκαιος messianically, but he defends his reading by appealing to the LXX reading of Hab 2:3-4, which he takes as eschatological. And, following T. W. Manson, he understands ἐρχόμενος as having a messianic tone.[66] But he

---

seem to construe πιστεύω/πίστις in Rom 1:16-17 in terms of a person's mental acquiescence to the gospel message or certain ideas within a belief system.

[59] See also Sanders, *PPJ*, 484 and n. 38; Wright, *The Climax of the Covenant, Christ and the Law in Pauline Theology*, 148, 149 and n. 41; Dunn, *Romans 1-8*, 48-49; *Theology*, 374.

[60] Hanson, *Studies in Paul's Technique and Theology*, 39-51.

[61] Hays, '"The Righteous One" as Eschatological Deliverer', in Marcus and Soards, *Apocalyptic and the New Testament: Essays in Honor of J. Louis Martyn*, 191-215.

[62] Campbell, *Rhetoric* (Appendix 1), 204-213.

[63] Wallis, *The Faith of Jesus Christ in Early Christian Traditions*, 78-82.

[64] Hanson, *Studies*, 40.

[65] Hanson, *Studies*, 41-42.

[66] Manson, 'The Argument from Prophecy', *JTS* 46 (1945) 129-136.

argues against Manson's view that in Romans and Galatians the messianic prophecy is applied to Christians rather than Christ. For Hanson, in order for Paul to interpret the passage of Christians he should first have understood it of Christ, 'the Messiah who was to be justified by faith'.[67] That would be possible if the LXX's ἐρχόμενος and ὁ δίκαιος were understood to be the same being. In the course of arguing this case, Hanson partly depends on C. H. Dodd, who argued that '[i]t is much more likely that he [Paul] drew upon a tradition which already recognised the passage from Habakkuk as a *testimonium* to the coming of Christ' and which may well have been formed even before Paul began to write his letters.[68] But Dodd clearly distinguishes between the LXX's ἐρχόμενος and ὁ δίκαιος,[69] whereas Hanson understands both as referring to the same being, the Messiah.

Despite the scantiness of internal textual evidence, Hanson presses his messianic reading of Rom 1:17b and Gal 3:11. He appeals to OT (Jer 23:5-6; 33:15), NT (Acts 7:52; 22:14; Matt 10:41; 1 Pet 3:18 [Isa 53:11]; 1 Jn 2:1) and Enochic (*1 En* 38:2) texts as evidence, because, in his view, these texts use ὁ δίκαιος as a messianic description and/or title. Hanson further argues that ὁ δίκαιός μου in Hebrews 10:38 is messianic where the 'shrinking back' could refer to his Gethsemane experience.[70] He goes on to support this view by providing a sort of commentary on Gal 3:1-20, where he argues that Paul's scripturally based contrast between two ways of life, the way of the law (Deut 27:26; Lev 18:5) and the way of faith (Hab 2:4), in verses 10-12 shows that Paul regards Torah as a whole as a way of life and that the Messiah must have lived either by faith or by the law.[71] Hanson interprets the difficult citation of Deut 21:23 in Gal 3:13 (ἐπικατάρατος πᾶς ὁ κρεμάμενος ἐπὶ ξύλον) in terms of Christ dying to the law through the verdict of the law but without incurring the curse because he did not make the law his way of life.[72] The Messiah was 'put to death but in the resurrection he was vindicated or justified by God ... This justification was a justification by faith, because the Messiah was always destined to live by faith and actually did so ... if Christ was justified by faith, not only are Christians justified by faith in Christ, but they are also justified in Christ by Christ's faith'.[73] Hanson concedes that it 'cannot be taken

---

[67] Hanson, *Studies*, 43.

[68] Dodd, *According to the Scriptures: The Substructure of NT Theology*, 51.

[69] Because he (*Scriptures*, 41) says Paul's 'argument would be much more effective with his Jewish Christian antagonists if it was already common ground between them that when the Coming One should come ὁ δίκαιος ἐκ πίστεως ζήσεται'.

[70] Hanson, *Studies*, 43-45.

[71] Hanson, *Studies*, 45-47.

[72] Hanson, *Studies*, 48-51.

[73] Hanson, *Studies*, 51.

as proved that Hab 2.4 is regarded by Paul as a prophecy of the Messiah', but he still argues that 'it is at least a reasonable suggestion and one that fits in with what else we know of Paul's approach'.[74]

4.2.2. Richard Hays

Hays builds on Hanson's arguments and attempts to strengthen the chris-tological reading of the Habakkuk citation. Two of his works will be the focus of our attention here. In his *The Faith of Jesus Christ*, Hays argues that the key to a proper understanding of the citation in Gal 3:11 'lies in the recognition that the word ζήσεται has eschatological connotations and that it is used in 3:11b as a virtual synonym of δικαιοῦται in 3:11a'.[75] That is, 'the righteous one shall live by faith' is equivalent to 'the righteous shall be justified by faith', the *meaning* of which is 'substantially identical to the affirmation that "the one who is righteous [= justified] by faith shall live"'. Unlike Hanson, Hays does not see any material distinction between taking ἐκ πίστεως as modifying ὁ δίκαιος and taking it as modifying ζήσεται, because in either case the focus is the manner in which ὁ δίκαιος finds life (= is justified).[76] But who is ὁ δίκαιος?

Like Manson, Dodd and Hanson, Hays too notices messianic elements in Hab 2:3-4 and argues that Hanson's identification of ὁ δίκαιος with [ὁ] ἐρχόμενος is not unreasonable as Gal 3:16 with its messianic exegesis of Gen 17:8 shows. In this passage, the seed (σπέρμα) of Abraham, which can be exegetically linked with the 'seed of David', refers to a single individ-ual who is destined to be the heir of the promise to Abraham. This individ-ual obviously is the Messiah, Χριστός.[77] Hays attempts to strengthen the 'messianic σπέρμα' through considering Isa 53:10b-12a, where in verse 12 in particular the Righteous One is said to 'inherit many'.[78] So according to Paul's understanding of Hab 2:4, 'the Messiah's faith becomes the key to his inheritance of life and the promises'. In the light of this interpretation, οἱ ἐκ πίστεως in Gal 3:7, 9 must be understood as those who live 'on the basis of the faith of the Messiah'.[79] But Hays also suggests that Paul's fail-ure to make explicit choice between the MT and the LXX readings leaves room for πίστις to have 'multivalent significance'. That is, the referent of ἐκ πίστεως can be God, the Messiah and the righteous individual. The first possibility cannot be sustained due to the absence of explicit discussion of

---

[74] Hanson, *Studies*, 45.
[75] Hays, *Faith*, 133.
[76] Hays, *Faith*, 134.
[77] Hays, *Faith*, 136.
[78] Hays, *Faith*, 137.
[79] Hays, *Faith*, 138.

God's faithfulness in Galatians coupled with the omission of μου. But the remaining two interpretations serve Paul's purpose very well.[80]

In a separate article, Hays further advances the argument by proposing two interrelated hypotheses: first, ὁ δίκαιος 'was a standard epithet for the Messiah in early Jewish Christian circles', and, second, Paul's citation in Rom 1:17 (and indeed Gal 3:11) of Hab 2:4 'presupposes an apocalyptic/messianic interpretation of that text'.[81] To substantiate these hypotheses, Hays, like Hanson, appeals to Enochic texts (the Parables in particular: 38:2; 53:6; cf. 39:6; 46:3; 48:2; 62:5ff), Acts (3:14, 7:52; 22:14), the so-called Catholic Epistles (e.g. 1 Pet 3:18 [echoing Isa 53:11]; 1 Jn 2:1) and Hebrews (10:38), all of which, except Hebrews, present 'the Righteous One' as a distinctive designation of Jesus, whose role as the eschatological deliverer is executing divine justice.[82] For Hays, the author of Hebrews presents ὁ δίκαιός μου as 'the faithful Christian believer during the present eschatological interval before the coming of the Coming One'.[83] But Hays also says that the author in the context does 'project a vision of faithfulness for which Jesus is the prototype'.[84]

As far as Rom 1:17 is concerned, Hays admits that the 'compressed formulaic character' of the passage prevents one from definitively saying whether Paul in Rom 1:17 understood ὁ δίκαιος as a messianic designation or read the passage as a whole messianically without construing the articular as direct reference to Jesus (like the author of Hebrews).[85] But Hays suggests three factors that might favour a messianic interpretation: the reading that takes Jesus the Righteous One as the subject of ἐκ πίστεως in Rom 1:17a so that God's saving righteousness is revealed through the πίστις of Jesus (rather than the human disposition of faith towards God, which Jews also had), the description of Jesus as the δίκαιος whose righteousness is efficacious for 'many' in Rom 5:19 and the fact that ὁ δίκαιος was a common designation for Jesus in other NT and Jewish texts.[86] Hays accepts that none of these arguments is entirely compelling but still argues that 'the strongly apocalyptic theological context of Romans 1 creates at least a presumption in favor of the messianic exegesis of Hab 2 that would have been most readily at hand for Paul and that makes the best sense out of the letter.'[87]

---

[80] Hays, *Faith*, 140.
[81] Hays, '"Righteous"', 192.
[82] Hays, '"Righteous"', 194, 198, 205-206.
[83] Hays, '"Righteous"', 203.
[84] Hays, '"Righteous"', 204.
[85] Hays, '"Righteous"', 208.
[86] Hays, '"Righteous"', 208-209.
[87] Hays, '"Righteous"', 209.

4.2.3. Douglas Campbell

In his book *The Rhetoric of Righteousness in Romans 3:21-26*, Campbell treats issues in Rom 1:17 mainly in the appendices, although before that he understands πίστις in 3:22-26 in relation to Christ, which, in his view, is 'probably determined by, among other considerations, [Paul's] messianic reading of Hab 2:4'.[88] Campbell's purpose in discussing Rom 1:17 in an appendix is to show the significance of Hab 2:4 for τὸν ἐκ πίστεως 'Ιησοῦ in Rom 3:26, but in his discussion on the whole he does not seem to go beyond arguments proposed by Hanson and Hays. What he mainly does is that taking ἐκ πίστεως in Rom 1:17a with reference to the faithfulness of Christ on the grounds of the reading's agreement with Paul's statements in 1:2-4, 9, he argues that the Habakkuk quotation in 1:17b in general and ὁ δίκαιος in particular can be understood with christological reference.[89]

In his article 'The Meaning of ΠΙΣΤΙΣ and ΝΟΜΟΣ in Paul: A Linguistic and Structural Perspective',[90] Campbell starts by attempting to clarify the prepositional confusion incurred in Paul's use of ἐκ πίστεως and διὰ τῆς πίστεως, for example, in Rom 3:30. He argues that both prepositions stand for the same thing rather than the faithfulness of Jews and the faithfulness of Gentiles respectively, as argued by Stowers. For Campbell, the unified soteriology suggested by the unity of God on which Paul bases πίστις, the interchangeable use of the phrases in question in Gal 3:22, 24, and 26, and Paul's use of διὰ [τῆς] πίστεως and ἐκ πίστεως 'Ιησοῦ in Rom 3:25 and 3:26 respectively indicate that these phrases, despite their stylistic variation, function paradigmatically and express the same basic idea in Paul.[91] Campbell argues that the same is true in the use of νόμος whereby ἐκ νόμου and διὰ νόμου are semantically interchangeable.[92] In all this, Campbell's concern is not only to show that driving a wedge between the ἐκ and δία phrases in Romans and Galatians is wrong, but also to argue that the meaning of the latter must be informed and determined by that of the more numerous and dominant ἐκ πίστεως.[93] Since Paul cites Hab 2:4 only in Romans and Galatians, the motivation to use ἐκ πίστεως and related linguistic structure in both letters must have originated from the prophetic text and therefore it must be the interpretation of the Habakkuk citation that must determine the meaning of the troublesome πίστις Χριστοῦ construction.[94]

---

[88] Campbell, *Rhetoric*, 186.
[89] Campbell, *Rhetoric* (Appendix 1), 207-210.
[90] Campbell, *JBL* 111 (1992) 91-103.
[91] Campbell, 'ΠΙΣΤΙΣ', 93-96.
[92] Campbell, 'ΠΙΣΤΙΣ', 98-99.
[93] Campbell, 'ΠΙΣΤΙΣ', 100.
[94] Campbell, 'ΠΙΣΤΙΣ', 101-103.

A couple of years later, Campbell argued that Rom 1:17 is the programmatic text for the πίστις Χριστοῦ debate, as 'this text clearly deploys
the critical phrase ἐκ πίστεως as an intertextually motivated allusion to the
faithful death of Christ – a deployment that includes, perhaps surprisingly,
Hab 2:4.'[95] The basis for this thesis again is the dominance of ἐκ πίστεως
in the interlocked paradigms where the ἐκ and διά phrases are used in Romans and the correlation of ἐκ πίστεως with Paul's citation of Hab 2:4.[96]
Then in a Käsemannian fashion, he understands δικαιοσύνη θεοῦ as 'an
eschatological saving power, both of and from God',[97] but he characterises
the syntax that takes ἐν αὐτῷ adjectivally and with δικαιοσύνη θεοῦ as
anthropocentric or even Cartesian because it assumes the righteousness of
God to be already within the gospel and so the gospel's offer of salvation
to individuals is mediated by faith. Campbell wishes to emphasise what he
calls a 'cosmic eschatological reading' where ἐν αὐτῷ functions as an instrument to ἀποκαλύπτεται so that the focus is on the revelation of the
righteousness of God as God's eschatological salvation *in [the gospel]*.[98]
Campbell prefers the latter reading because it avoids making the accomplishment of the revelation dependent on the individual's faith as opposed
to God's grace and sovereignty.[99] He then argues that ἐκ πίστεως must refer to either the faithfulness of God or of Christ rather than human faith.
Although Campbell sees considerable strength in the theocentric reading of
ἐκ πίστεως, he notices some disadvantages that undermine its cogency.
The main disadvantage is that the theocentric interpretation fails to recognise the close relationship between the phrase in the first part of Rom 1:17
and in the Habakkuk citation. On the basis of Paul's failure to follow the
majority LXX textual tradition that has ἐκ πίστεώς μου and the reading in
Rom 3:26 *vis-à-vis* 4:16, Campbell, predictably, argues for a christological
construal of ἐκ πίστεως in both halves of Rom 1:17.[100] Along this line,
Campbell again attempts to defend ὁ δίκαιος as a titular reference to Christ
through arguments proposed by Hanson and Hays.[101]

---

[95] Campbell, 'Romans 1:17 – A Crux Interpretum for the Πίστις Χριστοῦ Debate',
JBL 113 (1994) 265-285, 267.

[96] Campbell, 'Romans 1:17', 268.

[97] Campbell, 'Romans 1:17', 270.

[98] Campbell, 'Romans 1:17', 272.

[99] Campbell, 'Romans 1:17', 273.

[100] Campbell, 'Romans 1:17', 277-281.

[101] Campbell, *Rhetoric* (Appendix), 204-213; 'Romans 1:17', 282. See Stowers, 'ΕΚ
ΠΙΣΤΕΩΣ and ΔΙΑ ΤΗΣ ΠΙΣΤΕΩΣ in Romans 3:30', *JBL* 108 (1989) 665-674, 672 and
n. 37. Stowers supports Hays by suggesting that it is likely that Paul's citation of Hab 2:4
is messianic and has influenced Paul's language, while conceding that Hays' thesis is
difficult to prove and that the reference to 'the Righteous One' could be used for Abraham as well. See also Lee, *A Developing Messianic Understanding of Hab 2:3-5 in the*

4.2.4. Ian Wallis

Wallis, in his brief treatment of Rom 1:17, argues that the construal of ὁ δίκαιος as an individual believer in our passage is based on a questionable assumption; questionable because it 'permits – if not encourages – a meritorious understanding of faith'[102] and diminishes the idea that Christ is 'the only one person, who in addition to God, is truly righteous'.[103] Wallis distinguishes between the πίστις of the Jew or Greek and the πίστις of the Righteous One (i.e. Jesus), but without linking ἐκ πίστεως with ὁ δίκαιος.[104] In any case, Wallis' objection is based on his interpretation of δικαιοσύνη θεοῦ as both 'righteousness from God' and 'covenant faithfulness' channelled to believers through Christ's πίστις.[105] So against the framework that advocates 'the law' versus 'faith in Christ'[106] or 'response to God mediated by Jewish "works of the law"' versus 'response to God mediated by the law fulfilled through faith',[107] he offers a framework that contrasts 'justification on the basis of human response' with 'justification on the basis of God's universal grace in Christ (or 'God's righteousness or covenantal faithfulness').[108] In Wallis' view, believers are not considered righteous but they receive righteousness from God, as can be noticed in Romans 4. Christ alone is righteous because he is the only one who knew no sin and to whom righteousness was not reckoned.[109] Depending on Hanson, Hays and Campbell, and without any fresh argument, Wallis

---

New Testament in the Context of Early Jewish Writings (Unpublished PhD Dissertation, Southern Baptist Theological Seminary, 1998). He has also argued that Paul and other NT writers developed a messianic understanding of ὁ δίκαιος from a non-messianic text with great emphasis on the importance of 'faith', i.e. 'justification by faith' and 'living by faith'.

[102] For Wallis (*Faith*, 80), 'as long as ὁ δίκαιος in Rom 1:17 is identified with each believer, this verse, which is considered by many commentators to set out the theme for at least the first half of the epistle, places the emphasis upon humanity's response to God and not on God's initiative in Christ'.

[103] Wallis, *Faith*, 81.

[104] Wallis, *Faith*, 79, 82. Cranfield (*On Romans*, 88) criticises Wallis on this and goes on to say: 'And I think that Wallis' claim (in arguing against connecting ἐκ πίστεως with ὁ δίκαιος) that appropriation of justification by believing in Christ and appropriation of justification by responding to God's revelation of his law by a life of covenantal faithfulness are in fact much the same sort of thing, and that it would be more in keeping with Paul's thought to see the significant contrast being between justification on the basis of human response and justification on the basis of God's universal grace in Christ than between "works" and "faith", must surely be rejected.'

[105] Wallis, *Faith*, 76-78, 80-81.

[106] E.g. Cranfield, *Romans 1-8*, 218-220.

[107] E.g. Dunn, *Romans 1-8*, 46, 187.

[108] Wallis, *Faith*, 80, 89, 99.

[109] Wallis, *Faith*, 81.

claims that the Habakkuk citation refers to Christ who lived by faith.[110] He says: 'Paul demonstrates that the reason why reliance must not be placed upon works of the law is because the Righteous lives by faith (Hab 2:4), not because those with faith are righteous.'[111]

5. The Effect of Old and New Perspectives on Romans 1:17

As mentioned above, the majority of Pauline scholars would argue that ὁ δίκαιος in the Habakkuk citation is an individual believer and ἐκ πίστεως refers to her faith or believing. As this argument is based on the Lutheran or, what we would call, Old Perspective, it may be helpful to overview this over against the so-called New Perspective. The result will not only set a stage for our later discussions but also show how one's interpretation of Rom 1:17 can be influenced by the Old or New Perspective, depending which line of interpretation she follows.

Within the Old Perspective, Luther's reading of Rom 1:17 has been adapted in various ways since the Reformation. Most influentially, Bultmann made Luther's understanding fit into his existentialist thought, which was explained within a broader Law-Faith antithetical framework where 'justification by faith' was related to Paul's self-understanding as someone who was utterly convicted in his conscience by the law about the impossibility of attaining righteousness (ethical perfection) by meritorious works. In the Bultmannian understanding of the passage, πίστις is one's relation to Jesus and the mode by which one responds to the 'gospel' through a 'faith-decision' on the basis of which a righteous status is bestowed so that one becomes ὁ δίκαιος. Like πίστις, δικαιοσύνη θεοῦ is God's gift in the sense that it is God's own decision to pronounce a person 'righteous' and graciously lavish such a status in the judgement forum.[112] Numerous scholars, directly or indirectly, have followed this Lutheran-Bultmannian reading in their endeavour to explicate Rom 1:17 and the letter as a whole.[113]

---

[110] Wallis, *Faith*, 81 and n. 77.

[111] Wallis, *Faith*, 111.

[112] See Bultmann, *Theology of the New Testament I* (*TNT I*), 270-285.

[113] It should be noted here that the understanding of the doctrine of 'justification by faith' is not entirely homogeneous, but it seems to have largely similar emphases in different circles of Protestantism. For a Wesleyan, it ('justifying faith') is a divine gift instantaneously given and a personal decision followed by an unfolding development. For a Lutheran-Bultmannian, it means one's resolve by 'faith' to accept Jesus' event as God's saving event, which, in return, leads her to 'justification' and gaining a new self-understanding (on this, see Thomas, *John Wesley's and Rudolf Bultmann's Understanding of Justification by Faith, Compared and Contrasted* [Unpublished PhD Dissertation, Bristol

Before Bultmann, however, Schweitzer had branded the doctrine of 'justification by faith' as incomplete and individualistic and declared it 'a subsidiary crater' to Paul's central idea and the psychological considerations adopted to explain it as simply inadequate, particularly compared with his Christ-mysticism theory.[114] But his theory ceased to be a popular option after the application of existentialism to NT studies, although it paved the way for the 'participation in Christ' approach that has been advocated to a degree by Käsemann, Sanders and Dunn.[115] In a different way, Stendahl regarded the Lutheran-Bultmannian view of 'justification by faith in Christ without the works of the Law' as a product of Western mental and emotional self-examination that resulted originally from medieval piety and theology. Stendahl rejected the negative assessment of the Law where it is considered as a force armed with moral imperatives and convicts one's conscience about its insatiable requirements for righteousness, leading to faith in Christ. Relating this idea to Paul's subjective struggle with his conscience, as in Rom 7, in Stendahl's view, would reduce Paul's positive solution embedded in his ἐφάπαξ (Rom 6:10) and available by the Spirit through faith in the Messiah (Rom 8) to something repeated by an individual whose introspective conscience is plagued by an awareness of sin and guilt.[116]

Sanders went further by treating 'justification by faith' versus 'works righteousness' as a mistaken understanding of Second Temple Judaism, where the latter is regarded as a religion of legalism (i.e. a system that teaches the earning of salvation by good works) rather than 'covenantal nomism' (i.e. a system where a covenant relationship regulated by the law is the way of living within the covenant).[117] Sanders' so-called 'New Perspective' thus revolutionised Pauline and NT scholarship. Pertinent to our purpose, Sanders set out to resolve the problems surrounding the doctrine of justification by analysing the ways in which the 'righteous' word-group

---

University, 1990]). For those who understand 'justification by faith' from a covenantal perspective, it has to do with God's covenant faithfulness to Israel that can have a saving effect in one's life followed by becoming part of the covenant community upon a believing response to the gospel. The complexity of the issue in Paul is considered by Dunn, 'Paul and Justification by Faith', in R. Longenecker, *Road*, 85-101.

[114] Schweitzer, *The Mysticism of Paul the Apostle*, 225-226; see also his *Paul and His Interpreters: A Critical History*, 245.

[115] Käsemann, *Commentary on Romans*, 165; Sanders, *Paul and Palestinian Judaism, A Comparison of Patterns of Religion (PPJ)*, 467-468; Dunn, *Theology*, 390-412.

[116] Stendahl, *Paul among Jews and Gentiles, and Other Essays*, 78-96. His seminal article 'The Apostle Paul and the Introspective Conscience of the West' (*HTR* 56 [1963], 199-215) is incorporated in this book.

[117] Sanders, *PPJ*, 1ff; *Paul, the Law, and the Jewish People (PLJP)*, 1ff.

is understood in Judaism and Paul.[118] Despite his helpful contribution, however, Sanders did not make any attempt to explicate the expressions in Rom 1:17 and offer a fresh understanding of such a crucial passage. All we can deduce on the basis of his overarching thesis is that ὁ δίκαιος in Rom 1:17, for Sanders, would be an individual who has been transferred to the body of the saved.[119]

Dunn criticises Sanders not for failing to offer a covenantal nomistic reading of Rom 1:17 over against the Lutheran interpretation of the passage but for accusing Paul of arbitrarily jumping from covenantal nomism to Christianity and leaving his idea of the law incoherent and contradictory.[120] Even more puzzling, for Dunn, is Sanders' failure to make a clear distinction between Jewish covenantal nomism and the religion of Paul – for in both, in Sanders' view, God's prior acceptance by grace results in good works.[121] This means that Sanders did not sufficiently explain what Paul was actually standing against. Dunn, therefore, wishes to remedy that by focusing on Paul's reference to 'the works of the law', which in his view does not mean 'good works' in general or one's attempt to establish merit by complying with a code of commandments, but 'that pattern of obedience by which "the righteous" maintain their status within the people of the covenant, as evidenced not least by their dedication on such sensitive "test" issues as Sabbath and food laws'.[122] So Paul's motivation in penning the letter of Romans is to resolve the situation where some thought that the coming of the Messiah Jesus was the fulfilment of God's promises to Abraham and insisted on having 'faith in Messiah Jesus' while some argued that since the claims of the new movement were legitimate expressions of Jewish belief and praxis its adherents must observe 'the works of the law'.[123] Dunn's explanation is basically socio-religious, where Paul is understood to be standing against a system that sees rituals

---

[118] What Sanders (*PPJ*, 544) says here seems to encapsulate his overarching view: 'To be righteous in Jewish literature means to obey the Torah and to repent of transgression, but in Paul it means to be saved by Christ. Most succinctly, righteousness in Judaism is a term which implies the *maintenance of status* among the group of the elect; in Paul it is a *transfer term* ... Thus when Paul says one cannot be made righteous by works of law, he means that one cannot, by works of law, "transfer to the body of the saved". When Judaism said that one is righteous who obeys the law, the meaning is that one thereby stays in the covenant. The debate about righteousness by faith or by works of law thus turns out to result from different usage of the "righteous" word group'.

[119] See Sanders, *PPJ*, 484 and n. 38; *PLJP*, 196f.

[120] According to Deidun ('James Dunn and John Ziesler on Romans in New Perspective', *HeyJ* [1992] 79-84, 79), Dunn wrongly represents Sanders as saying that 'Paul's repudiation of Judaism is arbitrary'.

[121] Dunn, *Romans 1-8*, lxvii.

[122] Dunn, *Romans 1-8*, lxxii.

[123] Dunn, *Romans 1-8*, lxiv-lxxii; *Theology*, 366f.

such as circumcision, Sabbath and food-laws as national identity markers and test cases of covenant loyalty for ethnic Jews. Paul frees the law from such a narrow nationalistic understanding and redefines it in such a way that it becomes a social guideline for the eschatological people of God.[124]

This framework affects Dunn's interpretation of Rom 1:17. He understands ὁ δίκαιος in relation to the generic Jew or Greek who receives the gospel as an initial act (πίστις), is able to see (ἀποκαλύπτεται) that she is being brought into relationship with God (δικαιοσύνη θεοῦ), and goes on believing (πιστεύω/πίστις) within a continuous progress towards salvation (1:16). Dunn, following Barth,[125] not only takes ἐκ πίστεως in 1:17a as God's faithfulness and εἰς πίστιν as human faith, he also takes ἐκ πίστεως in the Habakkuk citation as referring to both God's faithfulness and 'faith'. The latter, in Dunn's view, cannot be the counterpart of the former if it is interpreted in keeping with the Hebrew אמונה (= 'faithfulness'), which signified the same thing as observance of the law and which Paul would regard as a serious misunderstanding of 'faith' in relation to the person who accepts the gospel.[126]

Some scholars have pointed out the difficulties or shortcomings they think the New Perspective involves.[127] Some have even regarded the New Perspective as a serious misunderstanding of Paul and Luther. But others have criticised the New Perspective for not going far enough in terms of removing the anti-Semitic exegesis that has long been part of Pauline studies.[128] For example, Stowers alleges that Dunn's readings, as are Sanders',[129] are controlled by *a priori* assumptions like the idea of 'faith in Christ' and that Judaism is an inadequate religion for salvation on a universal level.[130] For Stowers, as the first four chapters of the letter show, the problem amongst Paul's readers in Rome stems from some Gentiles' great concern for 'moral self-mastery' (an alternative to the imperial cult) and acceptance by God. Some Jews (represented by the 'Jewish teacher' in 2:17-4:22) were advocating following Jesus and embracing the 'works of the law' as a means to achieve self-mastery and be accepted by God. This was a welcome view for some Gentiles (represented by the 'imaginary Gentile' in 2:1-16). Their commitment to the teachings of the Jewish

---

[124] Dunn, *Romans 1-8*, lxxi-lxxii; see also his 'Paul', 90ff.

[125] Barth, *The Epistle to the Romans*, 41.

[126] Dunn, *Romans 1-8*, 49.

[127] E.g. Deidun, 'Dunn', 79-84; Byrne, 'Interpreting Romans Theologically in a Post – "New Perspective" Perspective', *HTR* (2001) 227-241; Kim, *Paul and the New Perspective: Second Thoughts on the Origins of Paul's Gospel*.

[128] See, for example, Elliott, *Liberating Paul: The Justice of God and the Politics of the Apostle*, 69-72.

[129] See also Sanders, *PLJP*, 172.

[130] Stowers, *A Rereading of Romans: Justice, Jews, and Gentiles*, 22-29.

teacher led them to consider the followers of mainstream Judaism as those who had been rejected by God for rejecting Jesus.[131] Paul seeks to correct both the Gentile and Jewish followers of Jesus by arguing that God has not based his relations on moral betterment of Gentiles and Jews but on the faithfulness of Jesus (Rom 1:16-17; 3:22-26) and that of Abraham (4:1ff).[132] Stowers interprets ἐκ πίστεως in Rom 1:17 as the 'faithfulness of Jesus' as against 'the faithfulness of God' and identifies ὁ δίκαιος as Christ, albeit with some reservations.[133] Although Stowers wishes to go further than Dunn and others, he too sees the Lutheran view of justification by faith *vis-à-vis* Judaism as a mistake.

Recently, however, a number of scholars have published a two-volume work entitled *Justification and Variegated Nomism* and all contributors to the second volume, which is subtitled *The Paradoxes of Paul*, appear to agree that Luther has been badly misunderstood by the advocates of the New Perspective, as developed and defended by Sanders, Dunn and others. For the contributors, Paul's doctrine of justification by faith resulted from neither Luther's plagued conscience nor his view of Judaism as legalistic religion. Towards the end of the volume, for example, Timothy George argues that Luther did not proclaim the gospel of sheer inwardness where Christ's purpose in coming to the world was to calm anxious consciences. This was what Kierkegaard proclaimed.[134] George accepts that Luther's theology was intensely personal, experiential and relational, but he denies that it was as theologically egocentric as Stendahl presupposed. Indeed, Luther is regarded as a religious subjectivist mainly because of the interpretative categories applied to Scripture nowadays rather than because of his departure from Paul's thinking.[135] Luther and Paul had similar concerns. While Luther confronted the 'covenantal nominalism' of late medieval piety, Paul confronted the 'synergistic nomism' in Galatia.[136] Luther's insistence that we receive God's grace and hence are declared righteous by faith alone (not works that establish merit) originates from his under-

---

[131] Stowers, *Rereading*, 36-38, 104-109.

[132] Stowers, *Rereading*, 38.

[133] Stowers, *Rereading*, 198-202.

[134] George, 'Modernizing Luther, Domesticating Paul: Another Perspective', in Carson *et al* (eds), *Justification and Variegated Nomism: The Paradoxes of Paul*, 437-463, 444. For George, after his breakthrough insight into the freely given 'passive' righteousness of God, which is revealed by the gospel and with which the merciful God justifies us by faith, Luther's focus was on listening to the 'alien word' of God's promise in Scripture. It is that word that delivers us 'from the burden of introspection and self-justification. This is why there is no room for boasting or self-assertion in the Christian life.'

[135] George, 'Luther', 445.

[136] George, 'Luther', 451.

standing of such contextual parallelism and theological correspondence between the medieval piety and Galatian controversy. George admits that a Lutheran reading can lead to 'a dehistoricizing of the New Testament and, as in the case of Bultmann, to the evisceration of the very kerygmatic content it sets out to promote'.[137] He contends, however, that the New Perspective, in its claim to be objectively reading the Second Temple Judaism or the original *Sitz im Leben* of the Pauline communities, tends to do two things: to bypass 'a retrospective vision of the past'[138] and domesticate Paul by reading contemporary issues into his texts.[139]

This too seems to be the opinion of Westerholm, who opens the volume by summarising 33 scholars from the whole spectrum of perspectives.[140] More pertinent to our purpose, the last scholar in his treatment is Seyoon Kim who argued against Dunn's explanation of Paul's doctrine from a developmental viewpoint. For Kim, Paul's conversion did not entail a devaluation of the law as the means of justification. Also, Paul's gradually evolved doctrine should be understood as a defence of his mission that is about Gentiles' inclusion in the people of God without merging their ethnic identity into that of the Jewish people. In short, the apostle's doctrine must be understood from the angle of the Damascus Christophany where Paul was provided with a 'new soteriology', namely 'justification through faith in Christ without works of the law'.[141] Kim, like Seifrid,[142] for example, emphasises the forensic dimension of 'justification' and understands Paul as being opposed to 'works of the law' practised within Judaism, because in his conviction they were inadequate attempts of sinful human beings to be acquitted from God's wrath. For Paul, it is *only by God's grace through faith in Christ* that sinners can be delivered from God's wrath at the last judgement. The traditional interpretation of the doctrine of 'justification by faith' is legitimate.[143]

While accepting the fundamental role that grace played in Jewish theology, which is also the case in the soteriology of Pelagius and the 16th century church, it is this *exclusive* reliance on God's grace of Paul and Luther that Westerholm himself also wishes to underline.[144] Westerholm argues that the pre-Damascus Paul believed that one could enjoy the life and blessing that the law promises when it is properly observed, but the post-

---

[137] George, 'Luther', 447.

[138] George, 'Luther', 447.

[139] George, 'Luther', 460.

[140] Westerholm, 'The "New Perspective" at Twenty Five', in Carson *et al*, *Justification: Paradoxes*, 1-38.

[141] Westerholm, '"Perspective"', 36.

[142] Westerholm, '"Perspective"', 27-30.

[143] Westerholm, '"Perspective"', 36.

[144] Westerholm, '"Perspective"', 37.

Damascus Paul believed human beings, who are at enmity with God and in slavery to sin, have no ability or inclination to God's law and that 'a new divine act of creation is needed before people can be "put right" with God'.[145] This 'new divine act of creation' leads to 'justification' that 'must be received (by faith) as a gift of God's grace'.[146] Seifrid also contends that Rom 1:18-3:20 shows that what makes Paul different from his contemporaries is his understanding of divine grace as something through which *righteousness is given* to the guilty and condemned.[147] His conclusion is reinforced by Gathercole who discusses the idea of 'justification by faith and blood' in Rom 3:21-4:5.[148]

Gathercole, largely based on his earlier work,[149] argues that against his Jewish compatriots Paul thought that obedience to the Torah could not be a condition of divine deliverance or the way to eschatological vindication because of the impossibility of obedience in the flesh and God's new way of acting in Jesus.[150] Rom 3:27-28 shows that even Israel's justification or final vindication (like that of the Gentiles) is dependent on 'faith' as opposed to obedience to the Torah. This means that Israel does not have irreversible and exclusive assurance of final vindication, because there is strong evidence in Jewish writings (e.g. *Test Moses* 9:3-6; 1QS 5:21; 6:18; 4QMMT) that Israel's justification or vindication is based on the comprehensive obedience to the Torah rather than national boundary markers that set Israel apart. In Paul's view, the Torah failed to deliver vindication (Rom 3:20).[151] This is evidenced by the fact that Paul regards Abraham, who was in the 'ungodly' category (Rom 4:5),[152] and David, who was the example of a wicked man because of his guilt of adultery and murder (Rom 4:6-8),[153] as people who were reckoned as righteous without works. So in 4:1-8, 'Paul is establishing first and foremost that the Jewish understanding of obedience and justification is seriously mistaken ... Paul wants to announce through Abraham and David the justification of Israel

---

[145] Westerholm, "'Perspective'", 37.
[146] Westerholm, "'Perspective'", 37.
[147] Seifrid, 'Unrighteous by Faith: Apostolic Proclamation in Romans 1:18-3:20', in Carson *et al* (eds), *Justification: Paradoxes*, 105-145, 143-145.
[148] Gathercole, 'Justified by Faith, Justified by his Blood: The Evidence of Romans 3:21-4:5', in Carson *et al* (eds), *Justification: Paradoxes,* 147-184.
[149] Gathercole, *Where is Boasting?: Early Jewish Soteriology and Paul's Response in Romans 1-5.*
[150] Gathercole, 'Faith', 152.
[151] Gathercole, 'Faith', 154-156.
[152] Gathercole, 'Faith', 157.
[153] Gathercole, 'Faith', 159.

as the justification of the ungodly (4:5) and as the reckoning of righteousness without works (4:6).'[154]

So, in Gathercole's view, Paul must be understood within the framework of the distinction between justification on the basis of obedience to the Torah (Jewish) and justification on the basis of faith (Christian), which is 'a divine gift evoked by the action of the Spirit in conjunction with the preaching of the gospel'[155] but which genuinely becomes 'a human act, as God graciously permits the human person to share in the divine gift'.[156] But Gathercole also seeks to show from Rom 3:21-4:25 Jesus' centrality to justification through the connection between wrath and justification and Jesus' role in dealing with the latter in order to bring about the former. Here Jesus' death obviously is significant, so Gathercole argues that in his discussion of atonement in Rom 3:21-26 that follows 'God's infallible punishment of sin' delineated in Rom 1-2, Paul sees judgement on sin as punishment brought about by God's own action rather than as the effects of sin that are bound up with the nature of sin itself with no demand of divine active punishment, as argued by C. H. Dodd and Ulrich Wilckens.[157] As God's forbearance was not open-ended and sin ought to have been punished, Jesus was handed over by God and human beings (4:25) to death so that he would bear human sin as well as God's response to it.[158]

Neither Gathercole nor other contributors treat Rom 1:17 in any detail. But paying some attention, as we have done, to their defences of the Lutheran understanding of 'justification by faith' will inform our detailed analysis of Rom 1:17 and its context in the ensuing sections of the book. The central argument of the contributors is that Paul in Romans and Galatians is neither opposing Jewish exclusivism nor attempting to legitimate Gentile inclusion into the people of God. Paul is doing something different: he is showing the failing of the Torah in its promise to deliver justification if obeyed and, in so doing, presenting Jesus' death along with the punishment of sin in it as the ground of the justification of the ungodly Jew and Gentile through her faith.

To conclude this section: while the majority of scholars in the camps of both Old and New Perspectives seem to accept (albeit tacitly in some cases) that Paul introduces and provides a framework for the doctrine of justification by faith, the scholars in one camp clearly differ from those in the other on *what Paul set justification by faith against*. According to those who have recently provided new defences for the Lutheran view of the

---

[154] Gathercole, 'Faith', 160.
[155] Gathercole, 'Faith', 161.
[156] Gathercole, 'Faith', 162.
[157] Gathercole, 'Faith', 169-175.
[158] Gathercole, 'Faith', 179-183.

doctrine of justification by faith, Paul set this doctrine against the Torah that failed to deliver the righteousness it promised.[159]

6. Conclusions, Problems and Prospect

As we said above, the main difference between the Old and New Perspectives is to do with what Paul used the doctrine of justification by faith against. For those who wish to defend and advance the Old Perspective, the question is to be answered against the backdrop of a legalistic conception of Judaism where righteousness is earned by works that establish merit. Justification by faith, therefore, means God's gracious declaration of the ungodly person as righteous in the divine court on the grounds that sin is reckoned to Jesus and is punished in him on the cross. The revelation of this reality brings about peace and comfort for a troubled conscience in this life and assurance of eternal existence in the afterlife. The means for this process is 'faith' (God's gift mediated by the word and evoked by the Spirit or one's intellectual assent to the gospel message or religious truths based on the gospel) rather than the 'law'. In short, Paul set justification by faith against justification by law. On the other hand, the advocates of the New Perspective would generally argue that Paul set the doctrine against not the law as a means to earn salvation but rather against Jewish identity markers whose observance alone would ensure the legitimacy of one's membership of the people of the covenant. Scholars in both camps would, however, agree that justification or righteousness is attained by faith. Furthermore, although Paul does not use ἐκ πίστεως in Rom 1:17 with a subject or object and Christ is not mentioned in the passage, scholars in both camps seem to assume that the prepositional phrase stands for 'faith or believing [in Christ]', an idea that Paul develops and extensively argues in Rom 3:21-5:11.

Our analysis also shows that in order to sustain the argument that Rom 1:17 introduces the doctrine of justification by faith, one must interpret the righteousness of God in Rom 1:17a as the righteousness that is given by God to a person who believes [in Christ]. Along this line, the revelation in the gospel is the revelation of this new idea: *righteousness by faith in Christ* as opposed to *righteousness by observing the law or works of the law*. This is claimed to be a scripturally based understanding, because ac-

---

[159] Moises Silva ('Faith versus Works of the Law in Galatians', in Carson *et al* (eds), *Justification*, 217-248) sums it up as follows: 'the Protestant doctrine of justification by faith alone – and not by works of obedience to the law – reflects fundamentally important and exegetically valid understanding of Paul's teaching ...' (p. 248). We shall engage with some of Silva's arguments later in the study.

cording to Hab 2:4 a person is said to acquire her righteousness (and the resulting life) by faith. This means that Rom 1:17a and 1:17b speak about one and the same thing: while the former is about the righteousness that is divinely given to a believer, the latter is about an individual person who by faith has become righteous and gains life (or a person who has become righteous and lives by faith). We, therefore, categorised this reading as *anthropological*. One notable exception in this interpretation is Dunn's construal of ἐκ πίστεως in Rom 1:17a as God's faithfulness and in 1:17b as both God's faithfulness to his covenant and human faith. But since Dunn argues that the 'righteous one' in the Habakkuk citation is an individual person who is in relationship with God and lives through her faith (that is, her faith in Christ) as well as God's faithfulness, his reading too is more or less consistent with the conventional view. In short, the core issue that characterises the anthropological argument of Rom 1:17 is that the passage as a whole is about Paul's declaration that justification is attained by faith.

On the other hand, the core issue that characterises the christological reading of Rom 1:17 introduced by scholars such as Hanson, Hays, D. Campbell and Wallis is that human justification is achieved through the faithfulness of Christ. This is argued on the basis that the subject of ἐκ πίστεως is Christ. None of the christological interpreters has offered a coherent and comprehensive reading of Rom 1:17 and shown whether or how their reading fits into relevant passages in the rest of Romans and indeed Galatians. Nor is their interpretation completely homogenous. For example, while Hanson takes the Habakkuk citation in Rom 1:17 as a basis for his claim that our justification by faith is founded on the justification or vindication of the Messiah through his own faith, Hays and Campbell would not go that far. Also, while Hays and Campbell follow the Käsemannian interpretation of the righteousness of God with a power sense, Hanson and Wallis do not adopt such an interpretation. Furthermore, while Hays, in agreement with Dunn, construes ἐκ πίστεως in Rom 1:17a as God's faithfulness, Campbell (along with others) reads the prepositional phrase as Christ's faithfulness. But all four scholars argue that the Habakkuk citation should be understood in terms of the Messiah gaining eschatological life through his own faithfulness. Thus, to organise their readings under the christological interpretative category is appropriate. It is this interpretation that led us to the central question of this study. That is: can the christological reading of Rom 1:17 be shown to be sufficiently strong so as to threaten the viability of the widely accepted anthropological reading of the passage?

Both readings, of course, have problems, whether those problems are shared or specific to each reading. In our view, the main problem with the christological reading is twofold. First, Christ is not mentioned in the pas-

sage in question and there are not sufficiently clear immediate contextual
signals that unambiguously suggest that ὁ δίκαιος in the Habakkuk citation
can be construed messianically. So on what basis can we argue that ὁ
δίκαιος refers to Christ? There are other observations that relate to this
question. For example, in his Seven Letter Corpus Paul does not (directly)
use ὁ δίκαιος with reference to Christ. Neither can we find any such use in
letters attributed to Paul but deemed to be secondary. Furthermore, none of
the christological interpreters has been able to point out any pre-Pauline or
contemporary tradition within both Judaism and Christianity where Hab
2:4 was used messianically. Second, as the text does not indicate that the
subject of ἐκ πίστεως is Christ, how can one claim that the preposition
stands for Christ's faithfulness? This problem is exacerbated by the fact
that Christ is not mentioned in Rom 1:16-18. There are references to Christ
in earlier verses of chapter 1 (vv 2-4, 9), but nowhere in the immediate
context is Christ used as the subject of πίστις. Some attempts have been
made to explain ἐκ πίστεως in Rom 1:17 in the light of the πίστις Χριστοῦ
formulation in Rom 3:21-26. These attempts are legitimate, because the
πίστις Χριστοῦ formulation almost certainly is a development of the abbreviated form ἐκ πίστεως. However, that the formulation in question has
itself been debated for over a century further complicates the problem.
Given all this, one might wish to settle for the anthropological reading.

But the anthropological reading is not problem-free either. The problem
with this reading, in our view, is threefold. First, it equates the 'righteousness of God' with 'righteousness', which is taken to mean any believer's
righteous status. But it is not evident that Paul employs the term
righteousness of God with the same meaning as righteousness (or any
person's righteous status). Nor does any Second Temple Jewish writing
use the righteousness of God as any person's righteous status. In
connection with this, second, if the righteousness of God is not understood
as a righteous status, it cannot be understood as the righteousness of the
person of the Habakkuk citation (ὁ δίκαιος) either. If ὁ δίκαιος is not the
person to whom the righteousness of God is given, it should then be asked
who the referent of the epithet is. Third, anthropological interpreters take
ἐκ πίστεως as human faith. This meaning is entirely dependent on the
conventional meaning of the righteousness of God in the sense that an
individual acquires this righteousess by means of faith. But if the
Käsemannian interpretation of the righteousness of God ('God's saving
power') is shown to be more probable than the traditional meaning, the
anthropological interpretation of ἐκ πίστεως becomes unviable. For it
would be absurd to talk about human faith serving as instrumental for the
appearance of God's saving power, which, according to Rom 3:21-26,
seems to have first taken place in the Christ event. In brief, the

conventional view that Rom 1:17 is Paul's compact declaration of the Protestant doctrine of justification by faith cannot be regarded as conclusive.

Despite all this, no extensive work that critically evaluates both christological and anthropological readings in the light of external-contextual and internal-textual evidence has so far been done. In our attempt to remedy this and offer a fresh perspective on Rom 1:17 and related texts, we will first examine whether Hab 2:3-4 was understood messianically by the Septuagintal translator/s, the Qumran commentator, the translator or reviser of the Nahal Hever text (8HevXIIgr) and the author of the letter of Hebrews. That will set a stage or background for our own understanding of Paul's use of Hab 2:4 in both Gal 3:11 and Rom 1:17 and enable us to see not only where Paul adopts or departs from the ways in which his predecessors and contemporaries interpreted and appropriated Hab 2:4 but also how he develops his thoughts based on Hab 2:4.[160]

Before attempting to determine the meaning Paul affords concerning the citation, however, in chapter 3 we will ask whether or how far Paul's linguistic images in Rom 1:16 and 1:17a are christologically orientated. In order to answer this question, we will adopt several exegetical steps. We will first provide a fresh syntactical and structural observation regarding Rom 1:16-18. That will be followed by an attempt to understand whether δύναμις θεοῦ in Rom 1:16b is a linguistic image for Christ. Then we come to our exegesis of δικαιοσύνη γὰρ θεοῦ κτλ in Rom 1:17a that focuses on the question whether Paul's declaration about the revelation of the right-

---

[160] Paul's scriptural quotations present us with matters of great complexity, not least due to his rabbinic formation, his interest in the Gentile world, his possible knowledge of textual variants, and so on. Furthermore, there are hermeneutical questions as to whether Paul's use of scripture in Rom 1:16-17 is unintentional or intentional, the former implying that Pauline scriptural quotations carry meanings which were hidden from even Paul himself. All these questions are important, although given the limited scope of this study, the broader phenomenon of intertextuality and methodological questions will not be the focus of our discussions. But see, for example, Davies, *Paul and Rabbinic Judaism: Some Rabbinic Elements in Pauline Theology*, 1-16. Wright, *Saint*, 25ff; Légasse, 'Paul's Pre-Christian Career According to Acts,' in Bauckham (ed.), *The Book of Acts in Palestinian Setting*, 365-390; esp. 373-379; Lim, *Holy Scriptures in the Qumran Commentaries and Pauline Letters*, 123-175; Bruce, 'Paul in Acts and Letters,' in Hawthorne *et al*, *Dictionary of Paul and His Letters*, 679-692; Trebolle Barrera, 'The Bible and Biblical Interpretation in Qumran,' in García Martínez and Trebolle Barrera, *The People of the Dead Sea Scrolls: Their Writings, Beliefs and Practices*, 117f; Stanley, *Paul and the Language of Scripture: Citation Technique in the Pauline Epistles and Contemporary Literature*, 1ff; R. Longenecker, *Biblical Exegesis in the Apostolic Period*, 1ff; Hays, *Echoes of Scripture in the Letters of Paul*, 1-33; Moyise, 'Intertextuality and the Study of the Old Testament in the New Testament', in S. Moyise (ed.), *The Old Testament in the New Testament: Essays in Honour of J. L. North*, 14-41.

eousness of God had any christological significance. This question will be
answered through considering syntactical issues in Rom 1:17a and related
textual evidence from Rom 3:21-22 and 16:25-26 and through exploring
OT background texts from Pss 98 and 143 and other Jewish texts, *1 Enoch*
in particular, which contains an equivalent form of δικαιοσύνη θεοῦ
(71:14; 99:10; 101:3).[161]

After examining the traditions in which Hab 2:3-4 is interpreted and
dealing with the immediate context of Rom 1:17a in conjunction with relevant background texts, we will then be ready to treat the question as to
whether ὁ δίκαιος in the Habakkuk citation of Rom 1:17 is a generic individual or messianic reference. This task will be undertaken in chapter 4.
Our focus in this chapter will concentrate on testing christological and anthropological readings through considering the ways in which the epithet
in question is used in some non-Pauline NT texts and in the so-called Book
of Parables in *1 Enoch*.[162] We will then engage in a detailed adjudication
of various scholarly arguments for and against the christological construal
of ὁ δίκαιος. We will finally examine the origin of the antithetical pattern
between Rom 1:17 and 1:18-3:20. Our main question here will be whether
Paul's new understanding of Adam in relation to Christ influenced his
ideas in Rom 1:18-3:20. It is important to note here, however, that our discussions in this section and the chapter as a whole will not amount to a
study of the origins of Pauline christology in Romans.[163] For our task will

---

[161] *1 Enoch* is also known as *Ethiopic Enoch*, because it, along with *Jubilees* and
other Jewish-Christian literature, has existed in Ethiopia probably since the 4th century
CE. See also Isaac, '1 (Ethiopic Apocalypse of) Enoch', in Charlesworth, *The Old Tes-
tament Pseudepigrapha I*, 10; Yefru, 'An Inquiry into the Ethiopic Book of Henok: The
European and Ethiopian Views', in W. Yefru (ed.), *Henok* (1994) 56-72; VanderKam, '1
Enoch, Enochic Motifs, and Enoch in Early Christian Literature', in VanderKam and
Adler (eds), *The Jewish Apocalyptic Heritage in the Early Christianity*, 33-101.

[162] *1 Enoch* contains ideas and beliefs about a figure designated as the Righteous
One/Son of Man/Chosen One/Messiah and portrayed as an eschatological judge. So it can
provide us with important background material for our exploration of Paul's christology
in general and Rom 1:17 in particular. See also Charlesworth, *The Old Testament Pseudepigrapha & the New Testament* (*OTP & NT*), 87-90.

[163] For this, we refer to other existing studies, where Paul's christology is understood
from the point of view of (1) a development of existing messianic conceptions (Moule,
The Origin of Christology), (2) an evolution or expansion of categories as a result of
Christian attempts to express the significance of Jesus (Dunn, *Christology in the Making:
An Inquiry into the Origins of the Doctrine of the Incarnation*), (3) a mutation of categories within Jewish monotheism where a second figure alongside God becomes an object
of religious devotion (Hurtado, *One God, One Lord: Early Christian Devotion and Ancient Jewish Monotheism*), (4) the transference to Jesus of ideas already developed in
Second Temple Judaism (Charlesworth, *OTP & NT*, 81), or (5) an identification of Jesus
with God through worship (Bauckham, *God Crucified: Monotheism and Christology in
the New Testament*; 'The Throne of God and the Worship of Jesus', in Newman *et al* (eds),

be tightly limited to exegetically and contextually determining if ὁ δίκαιος in Rom 1:17 can be shown to be a reference to Christ. The result will hopefully enable us to answer our subsequent question.

In chapter 5, we will ask whether the implied subject of ἐκ πίστεως in both halves of Rom 1:17 is human faith or Christ's faithfulness. After considering text-critical and translational issues in relation to the Habakkuk citation in Rom 1:17, we will examine the viability of reading ἐκ πίστεως as God's faithfulness to his covenant. Then focussing on the christological and anthropological interpretative options, we will first discuss the citation in Gal 3:11 and then in Rom 1:17. As ἐκ πίστεως most probably is a short form for ἐκ/διὰ πίστεως 'Ιησοῦ Χριστοῦ in 2:16 and 3:22, any decision regarding the prepositional phrase in the Galatians and Romans citations must depend on a meaning we afford concerning πίστις Χριστοῦ. We will, therefore, examine Gal 2:16 and Rom 3:22 (and their contexts) in turn. As Romans 4 and 9:30-10:13 play an important role in the process of determining whether πίστις Χριστοῦ means Christ's faithfulness or human faith in Christ, we will discuss those passages as well.

So our answer to the central question, namely whether the traditional interpretation of Rom 1:17 in terms of justification by faith [in Christ] can be maintained if the subject of ἐκ πίστεως and ὁ δίκαιος are shown to be Christ, will depend on the cumulative findings of the investigations we shall undertake in the ensuing chapters. We start that task with an exegetical analysis of Hab 2:3-4 as interpreted in translational, revisional and interpretative contexts.

The Jewish Roots of Christological Monotheism, 43-69; see also Kreitzer, *Jesus and God in Paul's Eschatology*).

Chapter 2

Background: Interpretations of Hab 2:3-4

1. Introduction

That Hab 2:4 (along with its immediate context) was significant within biblical tradition and for subsequent theological reflection is demonstrated by citations of it in Rom 1:17, Gal 3:11 and Heb 10:38, and the references in the Rabbinic texts.[1] Our reason for investigating Hab 2:3-4 in this section, however, is not so much to appreciate the text's significance for NT, Rabbinic and Christian traditions in general as to set up a backdrop that might inform and illumine our attempt to understand whether Paul cited Hab 2:4b in Rom 1:17 (and Gal 3:11) with a messianic or generic meaning. As Hab 2:4 cannot be understood apart from Hab 2:3 and the writer of Hebrews cites Hab 2:3-4, our study will focus on both verses. Hab 2:3-4 has suffered modification in the process of Jewish and Christian interpretation. That will become apparent in our subsequent examination of the ways in which the passage is read in the Septuagint (LXX), as represented in its preserved variations, in Qumran *Pesher* (1QpHab), in the text from Nahal Hever (where the Minor Prophets Scroll [8HevXIIgr] was found) and Hebrews.

But as we embark on that task, we need to remind ourselves of an important textual issue that needs to be borne in mind in the course of our discussion. The finding in the Dead Sea Caves of a few Greek and Hebrew biblical manuscripts that represent to a degree the probable *Vorlage* of the so-called Old Greek (i.e. the 'autographs' from which the uncial manuscripts [or their predecessors] of the fourth and fifth century were copied)

---

[1] See *Exod Rab* 23:5; *Mid Ps* 17a:25; *bMakk* 23[b] [24[a]]. In *bMakk* in particular Rabbi Simlai (250 CE) is said to have asserted that the 613 Mosaic commandments had been summed up by David in eleven commandments (Ps 15), by Isaiah in six (Is 33:15f), by Micah in three (Mic 6:8), by Isaiah again in two (Is 56:1), and by Amos in one (Amos 5:4). The tractate then continues to say that Rabbi Nachman ben Isaac (350 CE) had substituted Hab 2:4b for Amos 5:4 as the summary in one commandment. For an overview of the most important problems and themes in the Habakkuk research conducted in the 1990s, see Dangl, 'Habakkuk in Recent Research', *Currents in Research: Biblical Studies* (CR: BS), vol 9, 2001, 131-168.

suggests that in the case of certain books the Hebrew text with which the LXX translators worked was not necessarily the same as the MT.[2] It has been shown that 40% of the Qumran writings reflect the medieval MT in their consonantal framework etc, in which case the predecessors of the MT or texts that resembled them to a large degree were extant in Qumran, but there are sufficient orthographical and morphological variations between some texts of the MT and some Qumran texts (e.g. 1QIsa[b] and MS L 48-51) to suggest that there existed biblical texts which differed from the predecessors of the MT.[3] This, coupled with the noticeably large amount of differences between the MT and our earliest witnesses to the Greek OT (as will also be noticed from subsequent discussions), prevents us from readily regarding the MT (or its predecessor) as the parent text of the Septuagintal translation of Habakkuk available to us. It should be added here that the Greek fragments of Habakkuk from the Nahal Hever text (8HevXIIgr) appear to show that there was Jewish Septuagintal revision taking place before the turn of the Christian Era.[4]

With this in mind, we now turn to our exegesis of Hab 2:3-4 focussing especially on the question as to whether the passage was interpreted messianically by the LXX translators, the Qumran commentator and the reviser of the Nahal Hever text. Consequently, we will consider the ways in which the author of the letter of Hebrews appropriates the passage for his Jewish-Christian audience. All this will not only arm us with knowledge of textual modifications, adaptations and interpretations exercised by Jewish and Jewish-Christian writers, but also it will hopefully provide us with interpretative guidance when we examine Paul's use of Hab 2:4 in subsequent chapters.

---

[2] For extensive discussions of this and the general intersection between the LXX and the Scrolls, see Tov, *Textual Criticism of the Hebrew Bible*, 101-117; *The Text-Critical Use of the Septuagint in Biblical Research*, 1ff; 'Groups of Biblical Texts Found at Qumran', in Dimant & Schiffman [eds], *Time to Prepare the Way in Wilderness*, 85-102; Greenspoon, 'The Dead Sea Scrolls and the Greek Bible', in Flint & VanderKam (eds), *Scrolls*, 101-127. For full analyses of the notion of text types and related issues, see Lim, *Scriptures*, 16-27. See also Ulrich ('The Dead Sea Scrolls and the Biblical Text', in Flint & VanderKam [eds], *Scrolls*, 79-100) who argues that MT, LXX and SP (Samaritan Pentateuch) are not text types, but rather 'collections of texts'.

[3] See Tov, 'Groups', 90-94.

[4] See Tov, 'The Greek Minor Prophets Scroll from Nahal Hever (8HevXIIgr): The "Seiyal" Collection' (with the collaboration of R. A. Kraft and a contribution of P. J. Parsons), in *Discoveries in the Judean Desert VIII*.

2. Septuagintal Interpretation of Habakkuk 2:3-4

Hab 2:3-4 in the LXX reads: Διότι ἔτι ὅρασις εἰς καιρόν, καὶ ἀνατελεῖ εἰς πέρας, καὶ οὐκ εἰς κενόν· ἐὰν ὑστερήσῃ, ὑπόμεινον αὐτόν, ὅτι ἐρχόμενος ἥξει, καὶ οὐ μὴ χρονίσῃ. Ἐὰν ὑποστείληται, οὐκ εὐδοκεῖ ἡ ψυχή μου ἐν αὐτῷ· ὁ δὲ δίκαιος ἐκ πίστεώς [μου] ζήσεται.[5] Our investigation into this text will centre on a threefold question. First, are there messianic elements in Hab 2:3? Second, is ὁ δίκαιος in Hab 2:4 messianic? Third, how can we understand the addition of μου after ὁ δίκαιος (minority texts) and its addition after ἐκ πίστεως (majority texts) in relation to our overall exegetical results?

2.1. Messianic Elements in Habakkuk 2:3?

Are there messianic elements in Hab 2:3? Hanson assumes that the occurrence of ἀνατελεῖ in the LXX of Hab 2:3[6] is influenced by Jeremiah's ἀνατολή in Jer 23:5. In so doing, he suggests that Habakkuk is probably informed by Jeremiah's messianic conception.[7] But Hanson does not pay any attention to Hab 2:3 as a whole. Nor does he point out the discrepancy between the LXX and the MT: while the MT's ויפח לקץ means 'and it will testify to the end',[8] its LXX rendering καὶ ἀνατελεῖ εἰς πέρας can

---

[5] The MT reads:

כי עוד חזון למועד ויפח לקץ ולא יכזב
אם־יתמהמה חכה־לו כי־בא יבא לא יאחר
הנה עפלה לא־ישרה נפשו בו
וצדיק באמונתו יחיה

'For the vision is yet for an appointed time, but it will testify to the end; it will not lie. If it/he tarries, wait for it/him; for it/he will surely come, it/he will not delay. Behold, his throat in him is swollen, not smooth. But the righteous one shall live through his faithfulness.'

[6] It is interesting that LXX א[2] reads ἀπαγγέλει ('will proclaim') instead of the majority reading ἀνατελεῖ ('will rise up' or 'will appear'), but this probably is a redactor's attempt to correct the previous reading. In any case, it is subsequently erased.

[7] Hanson, *Studies*, 43.

[8] That is, when עוד, which is translated as ἔτι in the LXX, is emended as עד ('witness', 'testifier') and יפח is understood in the light of that. The root and etymology of יפח is uncertain. For a long time, the term was given the sense of 'panting' (with haste) in the light of the verbal form of the root פוח (BDB, *Hebrew and English Lexicon of the Old Testament*, 806). However, on the basis that יפח is used in our text as the synonym and counterpart of עד ('witness'), as also elsewhere in the OT (e.g. Ps 27:12; Prov 6:19; 12:17; 14:5, 25; 19:5, 9), scholars have reasonably emended עוד to עד and, consequently, given יפח the same meaning as עד ('witness', 'testifier'). See, for example, Pardee, 'YPH "Witness" in Hebrew and Ugaritic', *VT* 28 (1978) 204-213; Janzen, 'Hab 2:2-4 in the Light of Recent Philological Advances', *HTR* 73 (1980) 53-78; Haak, *Habakkuk*, 56; Roberts, *Nahum, Habakkuk, and Zephaniah*, 106; Fitzmyer, 'Habakkuk

mean 'and it/he shall rise up [=appear] in the end'. The LXX translator basically replaces the act of 'testifying' with the act of 'rising up' or 'appearing'. This makes the subject of the second part of 2:3a (i.e. καὶ ἀνατελεῖ κτλ) more ambiguous in the LXX than in the MT. That is to say, while חָזוֹן ('vision') in the MT is clearly the subject ('the vision' is a 'witness' 'to the appointed time' [לְמוֹעֵד] or 'to the end' [לַקֵּץ]), it is difficult to say the same about ὅρασις in the LXX. For one thing, to speak about the 'rising' of 'vision'/'revelation' is absurd. For another, as will be discussed below, if the pronoun αὐτόν in 2:3b is taken as referring back to some subject, ὅρασις cannot be it, because it is feminine. So the LXX translators have left us wondering what or who the subject of καὶ ἀνατελεῖ εἰς πέρας κτλ is.

As Hanson suggests, however, the terminological relation between ἀνατολή ('a rising' [of the sun?] or 'the east' [e.g. Gen 2:8; Ex 27:13]) and ἀνατελεῖ is evident, as in between the Hebrew noun צֶמַח (*tsemach*) ('growth', 'sprout' or 'branch'), which is rendered by ἀνατολή in Jeremiah, and the qal צָמַח (*tsamach*), which is rendered by ἀνατέλλω ('to cause to rise' or 'to rise') elsewhere in the LXX (e.g. Gen 2:5; Ex 22:3). Jer 23:5 is obviously messianic. If Habakkuk shares the same view the referent of καὶ ἀνατελεῖ εἰς πέρας may not be difficult to assume. Although no certainty is possible as to how or whether Habakkuk could have shared Jeremiah's messianic viewpoint *vis-à-vis* the term in question, one can construe ἀνατελεῖ εἰς πέρας in 2:3a messianically. But such a construal would not be plausible unless it is shown to be consistent with the reading in 2:3b.

In 2:3b, the intensifying infinitive absolute בֹּא יָבֹא (prefixed by the loosely causal כִּי) is translated as ὅτι ἐρχόμενος ἥξει ('for he will surely come').[9] Here the causal ὅτι connects ἐὰν ὑστερήσῃ, ὑπόμεινον αὐτόν ('if he should tarry, wait for him') with ἐρχόμενος ἥξει. So for the LXX translator, the one who tarries is not ὅρασις but ἐρχόμενος as the grammatical dissonance between the masculine αὐτόν and the feminine ὅρασις and the harmony between αὐτόν and ἐρχόμενος – further supported by the αὐτῷ that appears to refer back to ὑστερήσῃ in 2:3b – clearly show. To be sure, the LXX translator could only have translated the masculine חָזוֹן with the feminine ὅρασις, but such a translation seems to limit the role of ὅρασις to the first part of 2:3a where what is seen or revealed seems to be the prophetic message given by YHWH regarding the appointed 'time' (καιρόν).[10] On the other hand, καὶ ἀνατελεῖ εἰς πέρας functions in

---

2:3-4 and the New Testament', in Fitzmyer, *To Advance the Gospel*, 236-246, 237-238.

[9] On the renderings of combinations of the infinitive absolute and finite verbs in the Septuagint, see Tov, *The Greek and Hebrew Bible: Collected Essays on the Septuagint*, 247-256.

[10] See also Andersen, *Habakkuk*, 207.

connection with ὅτι ἐρχόμενος ἥξει with the result that the one who rises (ἀνατελεῖ) is ἐρχόμενος.[11] The idea of the coming vision is not conveyed in ἐρχόμενος.[12] But there is a problem: what is the difference between the Lord who speaks in 2:2f and ἐρχόμενος?

In order to answer this question adequately, we need to appreciate the contribution of the MT's text. In the MT of Hab 2:1, YHWH is the one who is awaited to speak, reply or even to act as a court official (cf. 1:1-4). If the same is judged to be the case in 2:3, then the referent of בא יבא and, as a result, the subject of 2:3b can be חזון or מועד/קץ.[13] Either option is difficult to sustain.[14] The difficulty cannot be resolved fully by taking YHWH as the subject of 2:3, but such an option may work for 2:3b in general and כי־בא יבא in particular.[15] The notion of YHWH being the one who 'will surely come' is consistent with the perspective that is expressed in chapter 3[16] in the sense that the Lord who comes as a divine warrior to save the people of his משיח and shatter the 'head' of the house

---

[11] See also Hays, *Faith*, 135.

[12] As Gheorghita (*The Role of the Septuagint in Hebrews*, 214) says: 'For a Greek text to have conveyed the idea of the coming vision, (ὅρασις), the translator should have supplied a construction involving the feminine participle ἐρχόμενη ἥξει.'

[13] See Janzen ('Hab 2:2-4', 53-78), who argues for חזון being the antecedent of 2:3b. See also Roberts, *Nahum*, 105, 110 ('If it seems slow, wait for it. For it will surely come; it will not delay'); NRSV ('If it seems to tarry, wait for it... .').

[14] For one thing, the vision itself is not something to be waited for but rather something that refers to the subject that is to be waited for (2:2-3). Dan 8:15ff shows that חזון refers to 'the appointed time'/'the end' (למועד קץ, vv 17, 19, cf. v 27) that culminates in the arising of 'a king of bold countenance' (vv 23-25) and so confirms this. See also Strobel, *Untersuchungen zum eschatologischen Verzögerungsproblem: Auf Grund der spätjüdisch-urchristlichen Geschichte von Habakuk 2,2ff*, 49-50.

[15] See also Haak, *Habakkuk*, 55-57 ('He tarries!? Wait for him! For surely he comes. He will not delay'); Andersen, *Habakkuk*, 207-208; and Janzen, 'Hab 2:2-4', 73; 'Eschatological Symbol and Existence in Habakkuk', *CBQ* 44 (1982) 394-414, 404. Haak (*Habakkuk*, 57) takes אם in Hab 2:3b as a hypothetical particle that could function as an 'emphatic negative' and, then, paraphrases 2:3b: 'He tarries? You have got to be kidding!! He surely comes.' For the use of אם as an 'emphatic negative' in the Hebrew Bible, see BDB, 50a.

[16] There is an ongoing debate with regard to the question as to whether Habakkuk 3 was composed by the same person who composed Hab 1 and 2. Hiebert (*God of My Victory: The Ancient Hymn in Hab 3*, 129-136), for example, argues that Hab 3 existed independently of its present canonical context. To support this argument, the difference between the literary genre of ch 3 and the previous chapters and the absence of Hab 3 in 1QpHab are pointed out. However, although why 1QpHab ends in Hab 2:20 is difficult to explain (see Lim, *Scripture*, 93 and n. 33), no Qumran *pesher* has a complete Hebrew text (see also Haak, *Habakkuk*, 7-8). Another argument that supports the unity of the book is that 3:1 has 'Habakkuk the prophet' as the title of the poem and Hab 3 seems to provide a logical resolution to the problems raised in chs 1 and 2. See also Holladay, 'Plausible Circumstances for the Prophecy of Habakkuk', *JBL* 120 (2001) 123-130.

of 'the wicked one' here (vv 3, 8, 12-13; cf. 2:20)[17] is the same Lord who speaks and is expected to come at the appointed time/the end in 2:2-4.[18] If this appears awkward because YHWH is understood to refer to himself in the third person singular in 2:3, it can be argued that בא יבא depicts the eschatological coming of another figure, but that is not clear in the Hebrew reading.

The LXX translator, however, puts a different complexion on the issue not only by translating כי־בא יבא as ὅτι ἐρχόμενος ἥξει, but also by making this translation consistent with καὶ ἀνατελεῖ εἰς πέρας in 2:3a. Issues regarding our translators' lexical choices, translation techniques and exegetical traditions cannot be discussed here for reasons of space,[19] but the LXX's ἐρχόμενος ἥξει, as the masculine active participle that represents the infinitive absolute of the Hebrew original (בא יבא), could imply personal subject and be understood in terms of a messiah's coming. The translator either understood the Hebrew words in 2:3b with a messianic significance without necessarily realising that the referent of בא יבא could be YHWH, the vision or the appointed time/the end, or transposed the idea of the coming God to the idea of messianic coming by employing ἐρχόμενος ἥξει as the representation of בא יבא. Textual witnesses to the arthrous reading (ὁ ἐρχόμενος ἥξει) can be found, but they are significantly few and inferior.[20] The presence or absence of the definite article is not important as to whether ἐρχόμενος ἥξει is messianic anyway. For example, while in Ps 117:26 ὁ ἐρχόμενος is used in relation to a messiah, in Theodotionic Daniel (7:13) ἐρχόμενος is used in relation to the 'son of man', who appears to be messianic as well. Later, of course, the author of

---

[17] Hiebert (*God*, 8-9, 36-40) renders מחצת במת רשע 'You struck the back of the wicked one'. He translates במת on the basis of the Ugaritic cognate *bmt* ('back') rather than its customary use in Hebrew for heights. But as במת is followed by רוש ('head'), the rendering 'back' hardly makes sense.

[18] This is a prevalent Jewish royal military ideology, which is also shared by other Second Temple Jewish writings. Hiebert (*God*, 92-134) argues that the hymn in Hab 3 is in tension with the motifs of 'apocalyptic' literature. But this should be corrected by citing the striking verbal similarities between some texts of Hab 3 and *1 En* 1:3-9:
Hab: 'God came from Teman, the Holy One from Mount Paran' (3:3; cf. 2:20)
1 En: 'The Holy and Great One will come out from his dwelling' (1:3)
Hab: 'In fury you trod the earth, in anger you trampled nations' (3:12)
1 En: 'and the eternal God will tread from there upon mount Sinai, and he will appear in the strength of his power from heaven' (1:4-5)
Hab: 'You came forth to save your people, to save your anointed' (3:13)
1 En: 'But for the righteous he will make peace, and he will keep safe the chosen...'(1:8)

[19] But see Tov, *Greek*, 85ff; Lim, *Holy Scriptures in the Qumran Commentaries and Pauline Letters*, 16-27, 140ff.

[20] As Gheorghita (*Role*, 171) notices, outside the Church Fathers the arthrous reading is found only in minuscules 46 of the Lucianic group and 130, 311 of the Catena group.

Hebrews titularises Habakkuk's ἐρχόμενος in order to make it unambiguously messianic (Heb 10:37) and Matthew refers to Christ as ὁ ἐρχόμενος (Matt 11:3).

In conclusion, the evidence so far may not be absolutely conclusive that ἀνατελεῖ εἰς πέρας and ἐρχόμενος ἥξει are messianic, but our exegesis on the whole shows that Manson[21] and, after him, Hanson and Hays[22] cannot be seen as exaggerating in reading Hab 2:3 in general and ἐρχόμενος in particular messianically.

2.2. Is the Righteous One in Hab 2:4 Messianic?

A messianic reading of much of 2:3 in the LXX, however, does not smoothly fit into 2:4a, whose reading ('Εὰν ὑποστείληται, οὐκ εὐδοκεῖ ἡ ψυχή μου ἐν αὐτῷ ['if he should shrink back, my soul has no pleasure in him']) shows a startling divergence from the Hebrew reading in the MT: בו נפשו לא־ישרה עפלה הנה. To understand the Hebrew text could inform our reading of the LXX text. But the Hebrew text itself is problematic. For example, in עפלה, the qal עפל is understood to mean 'to swell', 'to be heedless', 'to be fainthearted', or 'to perish'.[23] The renderings 'to perish'[24] and 'to be fainthearted'[25] are based on textual emendation, and 'to be heedless' is based on the root which is found only in Num 14:44 but whose precise meaning is unclear.[26] The rendering 'to swell' can perhaps be shown to fit in with the sense given to the key terms in the construction, particularly ישר and נפש. The NRSV,[27] Emerton[28] and Roberts[29] contrast

---

[21] Manson, 'Argument', 129-136. See also Strobel, *Untersuchungen*, 47-55.

[22] Hanson, *Studies*, 45f; Hays, *Faith*, 134ff.

[23] See BDB (779) for different meanings. The LXX's rendering ἐαν ὑποστείληται ('if he should shrink or draw back') does not help to explain it.

[24] Emerton, 'The Textual and Linguistic Problems of Habakkuk II.4-5', *JTS* 28 (1977) 1-18, 16-17. Emerton emends עפלה to עף לה ('to fly away', i.e. 'pass away' or 'perish') in the light of Ps 90:10, in which case the word is proverbial in character and is intended to describe the downfall of 'the wicked one'. This is possible, but for it to work נפש is to be rendered as 'personality', which, as will be shown below, may not fit the context.

[25] See Roberts, *Nahum*, 105-107. Roberts sees textual corruption in the MT and gives an emended nominal sense to עפלה, namely 'the fainthearted' (Jer 4:31). This emendation takes 'the vision' as the antecedent of 2:3b. In this case, the vision urges one to wait patiently for its fulfilment, hence 'the righteous person will live by its (that is, the vision's) faithfulness' (Roberts, *Nahum*, 106-107; see also Halladay, 'Circumstances', 123-130). But 'the vision' does not appear to be the antecedent of 2:3b, so a negative meaning that suggests failure to wait may not suit עפלה.

[26] So Haak (*Habakkuk*, 59).

[27] The RSV translates 2:4a: 'Behold, he whose soul is not upright in him shall fail'. The NRSV is even more elaborate: 'Look at the proud! Their spirit is not right in them.' The term 'upright' or 'right' is, in a sense, made up. As there is no other case than Hab 2:4

the attitude of 'the proud' (Emerton and NRSV) or 'the fainthearted' (Roberts) with that of 'the righteous one'. If the contrast between two figures exists, יָשַׁר can be understood as meaning 'even, level, smooth',[30] in which case a literal meaning 'throat, gullet' is appropriate for נֶפֶשׁ and a better rendering for עֻפְּלָ would be 'to swell'. The result of this is that 2:4a has the sense of someone having a swollen rather than smooth gullet or throat, hence it is rendered: 'Behold, his throat in him is swollen, not smooth'.[31] In the light of 1:13 and 2:5, the referent in the third person singular suffix (נפשׁו בו) contrasted with צַדִּיק in 2:4b can only be 'the wicked one', and therefore it is the throat of 'the wicked one' that is swollen so that he cannot swallow 'the righteous one'.[32] Such an interpretation seems to be consistent with the prophet's portrayal of 'the wicked one' (1:4, 13; 2:5).[33]

That contrast is not conspicuous in the LXX and the meanings of עֻפְלָה and יָשְׁרָה obviously do not fit with that of ὑποστείληται and εὐδοκεῖ respectively. These Septuagintal renderings may have resulted from the translator's guesswork based on some existing assumption[34] or his igno-

---

in the OT, where נֶפֶשׁ is used in conjunction with יָשַׁר, the accuracy of RSV's and NRSV's translations should be doubted.

[28] Emerton ('Textual', 11) renders the verb יָשַׁר 'to be [morally] upright' on the grounds that the cognate adjective is often used in the same sense elsewhere and is found with לֵב ('heart') (e.g. Ps 7:11; 11:2), which is perhaps comparable with נפשׁו in our text. He ('Textual', 17) also translates נֶפֶשׁ 'personality'. So Emerton's translation of 2:4 is as follows: 'Behold, he whose personality within him is not upright will fly away (i.e. pass away, perish), but the righteous man will live because of his faithfulness' (p. 17).

[29] Roberts (*Nahum*, 111) gives יָשַׁר the sense 'to be right in the eyes of', 'to be pleasing', and argues that it is used negatively to express one's wavering walk in the light of the vision or one's faintheartedness or inability to expect the fulfilment of 'the vision' and walk in a manner of life consistent with the message of 'the vision'.

[30] See also Emerton, 'Textual', 11f.

[31] So Haak's (*Habakkuk*, 25) translation: 'Behold, swollen, not smooth, will be his gullet within him'. By way of contrasting 'the wicked one' with 'the righteous one' in 2:4, Haak (*Habakkuk*, 138) paraphrases, 'The "righteous one" will live and the wicked who gorges his gullet (cf. 1:13) will be choked.' See also Is 45:2: 'I will go before you and level the mountains'. Here the 'levelling' (אֲיַשֵּׁר) is combined with a word for hills or mountains (וְהֲדוּרִים). Whether הֲדוּרִים with the meaning of 'mountainous land' denotes 'swelling', we cannot be certain. But note Is 40:3-4 where יָשַׁר is used and the prophetic tones are similar to that of 45:2.

[32] S. Schreiner ('Erwägungen zum Text von Hab 2.4-5', *ZAW* 86 [1974] 538-542) also understands the suffixes in 2:4a as רָשָׁע in the light of 1:4.

[33] Emerton ('Textual', 5-10) takes the subject of 2:4a and 2:5 as 'the proud man'. While this may be right, it should be remembered that the motif of swallowing in 1:13 with reference to 'the wicked one' could explain the expression in 2:5 where a figure is depicted as having a gullet that is as wide as Sheol.

[34] Koch, 'Der Text von Hab 2:4b in der Septuaginta und im Neuen Testament', *ZNW* (1985) 68-85.

rance of the meanings of the words in their *Vorlage*.[35] But it is equally possible that they resulted from a deliberate attempt to minimise equivocation. Syntactically, the subject of [ἐ]ὰν ὑποστείληται probably is ἐρχόμενος because the conditional particle ἐάν followed by ὑποστείληται (masculine third person singular) points to what precedes, namely the masculine adjective ἐρχόμενος. It follows then that while the one who should not shrink back must be ἐρχόμενος, the one whose soul will not be pleased is the God who speaks in 2:2f. This explanation does not work if the LXX translation is understood to follow the MT's contrast between the one whose gullet is swollen (= 'the wicked one') in 2:4a and 'the righteous one' in 2:4b. Andersen does not see this, because he suggests that the 'LXX is on the right track to find in the two parts of the verse [i.e. 2:4a and 2:4b] a contrast between two kinds of person' [i.e. 'the wicked one' and 'the righteous one'].[36] Andersen's view implies that the referent of the one who might shrink back is 'the wicked one'. However, grammatically, the αὐτῷ in the first half of 2:4 refers back to the one who ὑποστείληται in the same half as well as, as argued above, to the one who ὑστερήσῃ in 2:3b, who, in both cases, must be ἐρχόμενος.

Pace Andersen, the Greek reading does not imply that God expects 'the wicked one' not to shrink back. Were that the case, the logical extension of such a reading would be that what displeases God is the wicked one's recoil rather than his identity. That obviously is absurd, not least because it divorces who the wicked one is from his actions.[37] But Gheorghita points out another logical problem. That is that the one who shrinks back cannot logically be the same person as the one who will surely come. To deal with this logical difficulty, Gheorghita interprets ἐρχόμενος as the Lord in chapter 3.[38] But, as argued above, the LXX reading of Hab 2:2-4 does not display the same sort of grammatical consistency as the Hebrew reading. For example, in the latter the Lord who speaks to the prophet can be understood as the same Lord who will certainly come at the appointed time. That is not the case in the former. Moreover, in the logic of the Greek reading, the identity of the one who shrinks back can be found in the subsequent as well as the preceding line. When he says οὐκ εὐδοκεῖ ἡ ψυχή μου ἐν αὐτῷ, the LXX translator refers to ἐρχόμενος in the same way, albeit negatively, as Deutero-Isaiah refers to the Servant in Isa 42:1 (Ιακωβ ὁ παῖς μου ἀντιλήμψομαι αὐτοῦ· Ἰσραηλ ὁ ἐκλεκτός μου προσεδέξατο αὐτὸν ἡ ψυχή μου). In brief, in the LXX reading of Hab 2:3-4, the one who will

---

[35] See Tov, *Greek*, 217.

[36] Andersen, *Habakkuk*, 210.

[37] Koch ('Text', 73) fails to see the point in insisting that the one who shrinks back is any individual, who, upon such action, faces divine rejection.

[38] Gheorghita, *Role*, 214-216.

come and would not displease YHWH by shrinking back and about whom Habakkuk is told by the Lord in 2:2 is ἐρχόμενος.

The result of this reading is that 'the righteous one' in 2:4b is to be set against the arrogant man or the scoffer (καταφρονητὴς ἀνὴρ ἀλαζών) in 2:5 rather than the one who shrinks back. Consequently, ἐρχόμενος can be understood as the same figure as ὁ δίκαιος, in which case δέ introduces a result clause rather than a contrastive clause. He who will come is 'the righteous one' whose survival depends on πίστις. Manson noticed such an interpretative possibility 60 years ago. He preferred the minority LXX reading as represented in MSS A and C and argued that ἐρχόμενος is a divinely chosen human leader who was awaited and whose hanging back would be a sign that he is not God's chosen. Manson writes: '[t]he leader who plays the coward *eo ipso* shows that he is not God's chosen. The genuine choice of God, God's righteous one, will be faithful to his God, his people, his task, and so he will win life... and the LXX interpretation of Hab ii.3ᵇ-4 is through and through Messianic'.[39]

Is Manson right in preferring the minority text and reading ὁ δίκαιός μου messianically? It can certainly be argued that ὁ δίκαιός μου is messianic. The epithet seems to have the same tenor as 'my son' in Ps 2:7 or 'my righteous servant' in Isa 53:11. That 'my righteous servant' in Isa 53:11 is a messianic reference can be defended – at least on the basis of terminological parallelism – from Ps 89 where a Davidic messiah is referred to as 'my servant' (vv 3, 20; cf. v 39). But does ὁ δίκαιός μου carry a messianic conception within the context of Habakkuk? As far as the MT is concerned, the protagonist(s) and antagonist(s) behind רשׁע and צדיק (1:4, 13; 2:4) cannot be identified with certainty. That has engendered diverse, in the main, speculative suggestions.[40] Some scholars have suggested that 'the wicked one' refers to an internal force within the institution of the monarchy,[41] while others have understood it as external forces such as the Chaldeans (cf. 1:6),[42] the Greeks (Kittim)[43] or the Seleucids.[44] With regard to 'the righteous one', it has been proposed that the title refers to Judah,[45] Habakkuk himself,[46] or, as Nielsen[47] and Haak[48] have sug-

---

[39] Manson, 'Argument', 134.

[40] For a brief introduction in relation to these questions, see Mason, *Zephaniah, Habakkuk, Joel*, 60-64.

[41] Ringgren, *Israelite Religion*, 82-84; Haak, *Habakkuk*, 35, 112f.

[42] Otto, 'Die Stellung der Wehe-Worte in der Verkündigung des Propheten Habakuk', *ZAW* 89 (1977) 73-107. Johnson, 'The Paralysis of Torah in Habakkuk I 4', *VT* 35 (1985) 257-266, 257-258; Roberts, *Nahum*, 83ff.

[43] Siegfried, *A History of Israel in Old Testament Times*, 334 and n. 2.

[44] Fohrer, *Introduction to the Old Testament*, 454.

[45] Fitzmyer, 'Hab 2:3-4', 237. See also Wright, *Climax*, 148.

[46] The suggestion that 'the righteous one' refers to Habakkuk could be based on the

gested, a royal figure opposed by another of the same kind.[49] The LXX translator may not have been troubled by the question as to who the king of Judah was at the time of Habakkuk. But from a historical perspective, it could be argued that the translator may have understood the looming conflict between the Chaldeans and the Judahites in terms of the wicked Greeks or Selucids and the righteous Judahites. But no certainty is possible again.

From a textual-exegetical perspective, however, despite limited information within Habakkuk, the contrast between the expression ἐὰν ὑποστείληται κτλ in 2:3b and 2:4b suggests that ὁ δίκαιός μου could have been understood specifically. That is, the figure who is not expected to shrink back in 2:3b, the referent of ἐρχόμενος, might be the same figure as the one who will live through πίστις. This is probably consistent with what we find in 3:12-13 in that while YHWH is expected to prevent 'the wicked one' from swallowing 'the righteous one' in 2:3-4, in 3:12-13 YHWH's coming results in the salvation of the anointed one of the Lord (τοῦ σῶσαι τὸν χριστόν σου). This means that 'the righteous one' contrasted with the one whose gullet is as wide as Sheol in 2:4b-5 ('the wicked one' [cf. 1:4, 13]) is the same figure as the 'messiah' of the Lord contrasted with 'the lawless' (ἀνόμων) in 3:12-13.[50] Is ὁ χριστός here generic or specific? The

---

first person singular style that dominates the book (cf. 1:2-4; 2:1; 3:1, 7, 9, 16, 18-19). See Haak (*Habakkuk*, 112) for the discussion on this.

[47] Nielsen, 'The Righteous and the Wicked in Habaqquq', *ST* 6 (1952) 54-78; cf. Malchow, 'A Manual for Future Monarchs', *CBQ* 47 (1985) 238-245.

[48] Haak, *Habakkuk*, 114-149.

[49] The reference to 'the Chaldeans' in Hab 1:6 indicates that Habakkuk is addressing a specific historical and socio-political situation in Judah during the Neo-Babylonian Empire, perhaps after the time when the Egyptian king Pharaoh Neco replaced Jehoahaz by his brother Jehoiakim (2 Kgs 23:31-24:7). Then, the context of the book, whenever it was composed – dates from late 7th century (605) to early 6th century BCE (597), to early 4th century BCE (the period of Alexander the Great) have been suggested (see Haak, *Habakkuk*, 112ff; Andersen *Habakkuk*, 25-27) – can be understood in terms of Habakkuk's disillusionment by immaterialised expectations (following Josianic reforms) compounded by the removal of, in Habakkuk's view, the rightful king, Jehoahaz. Hiebert (*God*, 134) argues that the referent of משיח would have been the reigning king Jehoiakim or Zedekiah. Does that mean that Habakkuk favoured Babylon and opposed Jehoiakim and his anti-Babylonian policy (cf. Jer 7:1-15; 26:1-19)? If the answer is yes, it means that Habakkuk shares with some Jewish prophets, historians and sectarian groups an apparent neutrality or even positive attitude towards foreign powers. Jeremiah's Babylon (Jer 28 and 29), Deutero-Isaiah's Cyrus (Isa 44:28-45:13), Habakkuk's Chaldeans (Hab 1:6), the Habakkuk *Pesher*'s Kittim (1QpHab 2:12; 4:11; 6:1), Josephus' Vespasian (*Ant* 12:128; *War* 3:6) and Paul's Roman powers (Rom 13:1f) are good examples. See also Ringgren, *Israelite*, 82f; Haak, *Habakkuk*, 108f and n. 5; Johnson, 'Paralysis', 262-264.

[50] See also Otto, 'Stellung', 101f; Haak, *Habakkuk*, 112f. The use of 'the wicked one' and 'the righteous one' is used with reference to royal figures in Prov 28 and 29 and the

use of εἰς σωτηρίαν λαοῦ σου as a parallel to τοῦ σῶσαι τὸν χριστόν σου suggests that the articular is a collective reference. But there are numerous references in the LXX where משׁיח is stereotypically translated as χριστός, and in almost all of the references, the term unambiguously denotes a priestly figure (e.g. Lev 4:5, 16; 6:15; 21:10), a king (1 Sam 12:5; 16:6; 2 Sam 2:14; Isa 45:1), prophets (1 Chr 16:22) or a Davidic messiah (e.g. Ps 2:2; 17:51; 131:10). This, coupled with the apparent conceptual similarity between Hab 2:3-4 and 3:13, seems to tip the balance towards a conclusion that 'the righteous one' and 'messiah' probably refer to the same figure and that the LXX translator may have understood both in terms of an individual with a messianic role.[51]

2.3. Issues Relating to the Personal Pronoun Μου

The meaning of Hab 2:4 is further complicated by the renderings of יחיה וצדיק באמונתו in the variations of the LXX. None of the LXX variations is consistent with the MT text. MSS א, B, Q, V, W* and numerous minuscules, which are followed by the Göttingen edition published in 1931, read ὁ δὲ δίκαιος ἐκ πίστεώς μου ζήσεται ('The righteous one shall live through my faithfulness'), hence the grammatical difference between the Hebrew באמונתו (third person) and the Greek ἐκ πίστεώς μου (first person). On the other hand, MSS A, C and minuscules such as 26, 49 and 407 have ὁ δὲ δίκαιός μου ἐκ πίστεως ζήσεται ('My righteous one shall live on the basis of/through faithfulness'), thus rendering וצדיק as though it has the first person singular pronoun suffix (וצדיקי [ὁ δὲ δίκαιός μου]).[52] MSS W^{c78}, 763*, 130 and 311 differ from both sets of MSS: ὁ δὲ δίκαιος ἐκ πίστεως ζήσεται ('The righteous one shall live through faithfulness'). Aquila and Symmachus depart from both the MT and other LXX MSS, as the former reads καὶ δίκαιος ἐν πίστει αὐτοῦ ζήσεται while the latter ὁ [δὲ] δίκαιος τῇ ἑαυτοῦ πίστει ζήσει. As will be discussed below, the translation in the scroll from Nahal Hever (8HevXIIgr) has the third person pronoun αὐτοῦ. It seems to conform to the MT of Hab 2:4, particularly with respect to the personal pronoun αὐτοῦ as opposed to μου.

---

whole idea could reflect what is said elsewhere in the OT about Judean kings, namely 'X did what was wicked in the sight of the Lord' (e.g. 2 Kgs 21:2, 11) and 'Y did what was right in the sight of Lord' (e.g. 2 Kgs 22:2) respectively. See also Holladay ('Circumstances', 23-30) who argues that the arrogant man (גבר יהיר) or the scoffer (καταφρονητὴς ἀνὴρ ἀλαζών) is associated with Jehoiakim, hence the context Jehoiakim versus Babylon (Nebuchadnezzar).

[51] 'The righteous one' and 'messiah' are epithets for a continuing royal-messianic and forensic-eschatological ideology within Judaism. Cf. Prov 28 & 29; Jer 23:5; Isa 11:1-5; 53:11f; *Ps Sol* 17:32; 4Q161; 4Q252; 4Q285; *Wis* 4:10-16; *1 En* 38:2-3; 52:4; 53:6.

[52] As Koch ('Text', 80-81) points out, the copier of W^c deletes μου after ἐκ πίστεως, which betrays a clear influence of Pauline citations in later periods.

The omission of the personal pronoun μου is easier to explain than its addition, for the reason for the omission can be attributed to scribal error. If the error was unintentional, it could be regarded as a case of haplography.[53] But if it was intentional, it could be seen as an attempt to harmonise the LXX's reading with that in Paul (Rom 1:17; Gal 3:11).[54] The problem, however, is: why did the majority of LXX manuscripts translate the clause with μου rather than αὐτοῦ? It could be said that the LXX translator had access to a Hebrew text that differed from the MT and read not only נפשי (2:4a) but also באמונתי (2:4b). This is purely hypothetical and the fact that Hab 2:4b in the Qumran *Pesher* is missing altogether does not help this case.[55] Also, the Hebrew third person singular possessive pronoun suffix ו is translated by the Greek αὐτοῦ almost consistently throughout Habakkuk. The deployment of ἐκ πίστεώς μου for באמונתו in 2:4b is one of the three exceptions in Habakkuk. The other two are in 1:11 and 2:4a. In 1:11, לאלהו is translated as τῷ θεῷ μου. In 2:4a, נפשו is rendered by ἡ ψυχή μου (נפשי). These exceptions could simply have been accidental; or they could have resulted from a mechanical error caused by orthographic similarity between the Hebrew suffixes י and ו. The latter option is more plausible, because as both letters are difficult to distinguish in the Qumran MSS and since the text used by the LXX translators probably resembled the Qumran text, the translators may mistakenly have read באמונתו (ἐκ πίστεως αὐτοῦ) as באמונתי (ἐκ πίστεώς μου).[56]

But the addition of μου could equally have been deliberate. If the Hebrew text of Hab 2:4 is the same as the parent text of the LXX, the rendering of באמונתו by ἐκ πίστεώς μου could have been intentional. Theological reasons could lie behind this deliberate alteration. So, for example, the LXX translation of Hab 2:4b in the majority text can be understood to reflect a well-known interpretation that makes the 'life'[57] of 'the righteous

---

[53] Gheorghita, *Role*, 173.

[54] Fitzmyer, *Romans*, 265; 'Paul and the Dead Sea Scrolls', in Flint & VanderKam (eds), *The Dead Sea Scrolls After Fifty Years*, 599-621, 606 and n. 15.

[55] This problem is complicated further by the possibility of the existence of multiple texts of the Bible in both Hebrew and Greek, but this is an issue that falls well beyond the scope of our study. For the 'multiple texts theory, see Tov (*Criticism*, 114-116; 'Groups', 85-102) who divides the Qumran text families into five categories: (1) the family of the proto-Masoretic texts, (2) texts written in the 'Qumran Practice' of orthography and morphology, (3) texts that are closely related to the LXX, (4) pre-Samaritan texts and (5) non-aligned or independent texts. See also Lim, *Scripture*, 14-27, 140-142.

[56] So Jepsen ('אמן', *TDOT I*, 292-323, 318-319). See also Fitzmyer, 'Habakkuk', 240; Lim, *Scriptures*, 118.

[57] חיה in our text seems to denote an idea that goes beyond lifespan (e.g. Gen 9:28; 47:28), survival (life as opposed to death – e.g. Gen 42:2; Ps 118:17), some restored functionality (e.g. Neh 4:2 [MT: 3:34]; 1 Chr 11:18) or even well-being (when combined with שלום [e.g. Prov 3:17f]). When the referent of צדיק is understood as an individual

one' dependent not on the quality produced by 'the righteous one' but on God. Only the addition of μου after ἐκ πίστεως could be consistent with this perspective. Furthermore, if the translator was aware of the uniqueness of the link between the 'living' of 'the righteous one' (an Israelite) and אמונה[58] in the Hebrew Bible, he could have decided to modify the reading in such a way that πίστις is God's.[59] This makes ἐκ πίστεώς μου in the majority texts a product of scribal and revisional activity. If true, the position of μου in the minority texts, where the pronoun comes after ὁ δὲ δίκαιος, probably owes to the same sort of activity. That means that while πίστις is God's in the majority texts, it is that of the 'righteous one' in the minority texts (despite the absence of αὐτοῦ after ἐκ πίστεως). But which of the two readings fits the context best?

Koch does not see both readings equally, because, for him, the wording of the majority texts is original, while that of the minority texts is the product of later adaptation based on Hebrews.[60] This seems to render our question above irrelevant. But Koch's argument is not plausible. It is conceivable that the Christian copyists of the latter knew and had access to Hebrews and that the reading δίκαιός μου ἐκ πίστεως could well have been a product of a scribal attempt to align the minority reading to this Jewish-Christian tradition.[61] However, an argument that considers either of the readings as original is overconfident, not least because none of the LXX uncial manuscripts antedates the fourth/fifth century CE and therefore none of them could have been immune from some Christian influence. Furthermore, that the copyists of the minority reading failed to add the

---

royal figure, may חיה for Habakkuk have to do with the living/life of a true king with power and success (cf. 2 Sam 16:16; 2 Kgs 11:12; 2 Chr 23:11)? See also Ringgren, 'חיה', *TDOT IV*, 324-344, esp. 332-336.

[58] אמונה is to do with a conduct that is in accordance with אמח ('stability', 'reliability', 'durability', 'permanence', 'faithfulness') and therefore includes 'sincerity', 'faithfulness', 'stability' and 'reliability'. See also Jensen, 'אמן', 318; cf. also 309-316. For some linguistic considerations of אמונה, ἀλήθεια, πίστις and δικαιοσύνη, see Barr, *Semantics*, 161-205.

[59] Numerous texts speak about 'life' through keeping the commandments (e.g. Lev 18:5; Deut 4:1; 5:33; 8:1; 30:16, 19; Neh 9:29; Ezek 18:5-9; 20:11, 13, 21), but not through אמונה. Gen 15:6 that connects אמן, attributed to Abraham, with צדקה, and Isa 26:2-3 that connects אמן/אמונה, kept/exercised by 'the righteous', with שלום, are the closest passages we can find. While discussing Paul's use of Hab 2:4, Davies (*Faith and Obedience in Romans, A Study in Romans 1-4*, 41) suggests that Hab 2:4b echoes Gen 15:6. But despite important verbal similarities between the two texts the verb יחיה (ζάω) is not used in Gen 15.

[60] Koch ('Text', 75, 85). For a comparative study of the use of Hab 2:4 in Rom 1:17 and Heb 10:37-38, see Strobel, *Untersuchungen*, 173-179. See also Gheorghita, *The Role of the Septuagint in Hebrews*, 173-174.

[61] See also Fitzmyer, 'Habakkuk', 244.

definite article to the participle ἐρχόμενος, in keeping with the author of
Hebrews (ὁ ἐρχόμενος ἥξει [10:37]), makes us doubt that the addition of
μου after ὁ δίκαιος could have come from the author of Hebrews. If the
reading in the minority texts of Hab 2:4b was the outcome of an attempt to
align the Septuagintal reading with the reading of Hebrews, ἐρχόμενος
should have been articular, at least for two reasons. First, the copyists of
the minority texts were Christians who would have been as concerned with
christological issues as the author of the Hebrews was. Second, the copyists would have known that adding the article to ἐρχόμενος would have
made the Septuagintal reading more explicit and hence easily exploit-
able.[62] That the minority texts fail to articularise ἐρχόμενος is an argument
against ὁ δίκαιός μου resulting from Christian influence.

In any case, the use of ὁ δίκαιός μου originated from the Christian era,
as did ἐκ πίστεώς μου. So no certainty is possible as to which reading is
original and which is not. Nor is it possible to determine with a reasonable
degree of certainty which manuscripts bear more or less Christian influence than others. Given all these uncertainties, one is forced to make an
inevitably subjective judgement as to which reading suits the context best.
If that judgement were to depend on one criterion, it should be the cumulative exegetical outcome of Hab 2:3-4. In our view, the minority reading
appears to make sense of the overall expressions of the passage, because
ἐρχόμενος, the one who, even if he delays (ὑπόμεινον αὐτὸν), will rise or
appear in the end (ἀνατελεῖ εἰς πέρας) and is not expected to
ὑποστείλασθαι, can be understood as ὁ δίκαιός μου, a titular phrase that
might also carry a messianic tenor (cf. Ps 2:7; 89:3, 20; Isa 53:11).[63]

3. Pesher Habakkuk (1QpHab)

Over the years, many attempts have been made to set *Pesher* Habakkuk
(1QpHab) within the framework of the historical situation of the Macca-
bean/Hasmonean era. Since various scholars have comprehensively summarised those attempts, no detailed discussion is necessary here.[64] Our

---

[62] This is evident in manuscripts from the Lucianic and Catena groups, which are regarded as bearers of NT influence and responsible for the variant reading δίκαιός μου ἐκ
πίστεως. See also Gheorghita, *Role*, 174.

[63] My translation of Hab 2:3-4 in the LXX: 'Therefore, the vision (revelation) is still
for the time, and he shall rise up in the end, and it is not without purpose; if he should be
(come) late, wait for him, for he will surely come, and he will not delay. If he should
shrink back, my soul will not be pleased in him; but the [my] righteous one shall live
through [my] faithfulness.'

[64] See Davies, 'The Teacher of Righteousness and the "End of Days"', *RevQ* (1988)
313-317; Knibb, *The Qumran Community*, 1-12; 'The Teacher of Righteousness – A

present concern is to examine whether the ways in which the author of *Pesher Habakkuk* interprets Hab 2:3-4 involve messianic elements. Before that, it may be helpful to reproduce 1QpHab 7:5-8:3 where Hab 2:3-4 is quoted and interpreted by the pesherist.

כיא עוד חזון ⁶למועד יפיח לקץ ולא יכזב *vacat*	Hab 2:3a
⁷פשרו אשר יארוך הקץ האחרון ויתר על כול	Interpretation
⁸אשר דברו הנביאים כיא רזי אל להפל	
⁹אם־יתמהמה חכה לו כיא בוא יבוא ולוא¹⁰יאחר *vacat*	Hab 2:3b
פשרו על אנשי האמת ¹¹עושי התורה	Interpretation
אשר לוא ירפו ידיהם מעבודת ¹²האמת	
בהמשך עליהם הקץ האחרון כיא	
¹³כול קיצי אל יבואו לתכונם כאשר חקק ¹⁴להם ברזי ערמת	
הנה עופלה לוא יושרה ¹⁵נפשו בו[*vacat*	Hab 2:4a
פשרו אשר יכפלו עליהם ¹⁶[...] ו]ל[וא]ירצו במשפטם [...]	Interpretation
[...]¹⁷[...]וצדיק באמונתו יחיה]	Hab 2:4b
¹פשרו על כול עושי התורה בבית יהודה אשר	*Col viii* Interpretation
יצילם אל מבית המשפט בעבור עמלם ואמנתם ³במורה הצדק	

Hab 2:3: For the vision has an appointed time⁶, it will have an end and not fail. *Blank* ⁷Its interpretation: the final age will be extended and go beyond all that ⁸the prophets say, because the mysteries of God are wonderful. ⁹*Hab 2:3b*: Though it might tarry, wait for it; it definitely has to come and will not¹⁰ delay. *Blank* Its interpretation concerns the men of truth, ¹¹those who observe the Law, whose hands will not desert the service ¹²of truth when the final age is extended beyond them, because ¹³all the ages of God will come at the right time, as he established ¹⁴for them in the mysteries of his prudence. *Hab 2:4a:* See, it is conceited and does not give way ¹⁵[his soul within him.] Its interpretation: they will double upon them ¹⁶[... and] find [no] mercy at being judged. [...] ¹⁷[... *Hab 2:4b*: But the righteous man will live because of their loyalty to him.] *Blank* Its interpretation concerns all observing the Law in the House of Judah, whom God will free from the house of judgement on account of their toil and of their loyalty to the Teacher of Righteousness.⁶⁵

While Hab 2:3 is quoted in full in 1QpHab 7:5-10, much of Hab 2:4 does not appear in the composition, most probably owing to textual mutilation.

Messianic Title?', in W. D. Davies *et al* (eds), *A Tribute to Geza Vermes, Essays on Jewish and Christian Literature and History*, 50-65; 'Eschatology and Messianism', in Flint & VanderKam (eds), *Scrolls*, 379-402; VanderKam, 'Identity and History of the Community', in Flint and VanderKam (eds), *Scrolls*, 487-533. See also Murphy-O'Connor, 'The Essenes and their History', *RB* 81 (1971) 215-244; 'The Damascus Document Revisited', *RB* 92 (1985) 239-244; Vermes, *The Dead Sea Scrolls: Qumran in Perspective* (*TDSS*), 119-141; *The Complete Dead Sea Scrolls in English* (*CDSSE*), 49-66; García Martínez and Trebolle Barrera, *People*, 86-96; Bernstein, 'Pesher Habakkuk', in Schifmann & VanderKam (eds), *Encyclopedia of the Dead Sea Scrolls* I, 647-650.

⁶⁵ The quotation is from García Martínez's and Tigchelaar's *The Dead Sea Scrolls: Study Edition*.

However, it is possible to assume that since the pesherist quoted Hab 2:3 in full he would have quoted Hab 2:4 in full as well. Such an assumption should take into account our complete ignorance about the orthographical and morphological alterations that might have taken place in the missing text. As far as the quotation of Hab 2:3-4 is concerned, there are some orthographical and morphological differences between the *Pesher* and MT, but the quotations of the Qumran *Pesher* betray very minimal and perhaps insignificant divergence from the MT, hence shedding very little or no light on the meanings of the difficult terms such as the MT's ויפח and עפלה and their Septuagintal translations.[66] The orthographical and morphological differences here and elsewhere in 1QpHab (cf., for example, Hab 2:5 and 1QpHab 8:3) and other Qumran *Pesharim*, however, are sufficient to prompt the question as to whether the pesherist used a different underlying *Vorlage*, but this issue goes beyond the purpose of the present study.[67] It is worth asking, though, what the pesherist's interpretative equivalents for the expressions in Hab 2:3-4 are.

The interpretation of 2:3 (in 7:5-14) in general and the emphasis on הקץ האחרון ('the final age') in particular suggest that the pesherist took למועד ('appointed time') to be the subject of both 2:3a (חזון in the MT) and 2:3b, hence the antecedent of כי בא יבא for him being 'the final age' rather than God, as is the case in the MT. In 8:1-3, 'the final age' is not repeated but the notion is embedded in the interpretation of the MT's יחיה, i.e. יצילם אל, God's eschatological deliverance of those who observe the Torah. צדיק, which in Hab 1:8, 13 is interpreted as the Teacher of Righteousness, is interpreted here in terms of the those who observe the Torah, who are also referred to as אנשי האמת ('the men of truth', 7:13-14).[68] So while the contrast in the MT's text is between צדיק and the 'arrogant man' (גבר יהיר) (Hab 2:5), for the pesherist it is between those

---

[66] It may be helpful to categorise these differences, including the variants of the LXX.

MT		LXX	1QpHab	
ויפח	2:3a	καὶ ἀνατελεῖ	יפיח	7:5
א			בוא	7:9
יבא	2:3b	ἐρχόμενος ἥξει	יבוא	7:9
לא	2:3b	---	לוא	7:9
עפלה	2:4a	ἐὰν ὑποστείληται	[עופלן]ה	7:14

See also Lim, *Scripture*, 83-86.

[67] For an extensive and expert treatment of this issue, see Ulrich, 'Dead Sea', in Flint & VanderKam (eds), *Scrolls*, 79-100; Lim, *Scripture*, 70ff; Tov, 'The Significance of the Texts from the Judean Desert for the History of the Text of the Hebrew Bible: A New Synthesis', in Cryer & Thompson (eds), *Qumran Between the Old and New Testaments*, 277-309, esp 282-283.

[68] Brownlee (*The Midrash Pesher of Habakkuk*, 126) suggests that the singular צדיק in the MT is generic and that the *Pesher* correctly interprets it by plurals, i.e. all who observe the Torah.

who are faithful to the Torah and loyal to the Teacher of Righteousness (7:10-12; 8:1-3) and the 'traitors' who side with the Man of Lies, the Wicked Priest (2:1-5; 5:8-11). The Teacher of Righteousness is seen as a divinely appointed interpreter of the words of the prophets (2:1-3), for all the mysteries are disclosed to him (7:1-8). Those 'mysteries' chiefly concern what will happen in the 'last days', the 'final age' (2:5-6; 7:7-14). In the 'last days', God will mobilise the Kittim (Greek Selucids or Romans) (2:12-3:14; 6:1-12), who will deal with 'the last priests of Jerusalem', portrayed as corrupt and oppressive (9:5-7).[69] Specifically, the Wicked Priest would be dealt with for his acts against God's elect, his religious failure and his economic plundering of the poor (9:9-12; 11:12-15; 12:1-15). So, for the Qumran commentator, מורה הצדק, as opposed to הכוהן הרשע (probably a word play on the biblical הכהן הראש[70]), is the central figure. This is also reflected in his interpretation of במורה הצדק אמנתם,[71] which could mean 'and their reliance upon, faithfulness to or trust in the Teacher of Righteousness'.[72]

From our observations above, three things can be said. First, it seems clear that צדיק is not interpreted as the Teacher of Righteousness, who is set against the Wicked Priest. Second, the Wicked Priest and the Teacher

---

[69] In Vermes' view (*TDSS*, 127, 131-132), 'the last priests of Jerusalem' in 1QpHab (9:1-14) are those who succeeded Simon the Maccabee.

[70] On this basis, VanderKam ('Identity', 528-529) argues that the latter is Jonathan who assumed the high priesthood and, as a result, probably came to violent conflict with the Teacher. VanderKam swiftly admits that הכוהן alone does not designate the high priest, but he nonetheless maintains that the proposal fits the religious, political and military power of Jonathan, and that disputes over the interpretation of the Torah, which centre in calendrical issues, played a role in causing the split between the Teacher and Jonathan. See also VanderKam's *Calendars*, 38-40, 43-51.

[71] In the OT, the term could mean 'to gain stability, to rely on someone, to give credence to a message or to consider it to be true, to trust in someone'. See also Jepsen, 'אמן', 308. In 1QpHab 2:2, האמין is used in relation to believing in the words of the Teacher of Righteousness. In 2:4 it can be rendered as 'believe in' (García Martínez) or 'be faithful to' (Brownlee). In 2:6 the absolute use has to be rendered 'believe'. In 2:14 the verb is used with reference to the Kittim who do not 'believe in' the precepts of [God].

[72] Barr (*Semantics*, 202) renders בעבור עמלם ואמנתם במורה הצדק 'because of their toil and their faith in the Teacher of Righteousness' against 'because of their toil and their faithfulness to the Teacher of Righteousness' (his own translations) on the grounds of the presence of ב. According to Brownlee (*Midrash*, 128), the *Targum Habakkuk* interprets אמונה of the MT in Hab 2:4 as 'an affirmation of the prophetic message', whereas 1QpHab interprets it in terms of 'faith in the Teacher' due to the rightness of his teaching. However, Gordon, while translating the verb in the *Pesher* as 'faith in' and 'fidelity to', rejects Brownlee's developmental perspective (*Midrash*, 29). See Gordon, *Studies in the Targum to the Twelve Prophets, From Nahum to Malachi*, 87-88. See also Fitzmyer, 'Paul', 606.

of Righteousness might represent Jonathan and someone who belonged to
בני צדוק (the sons of Zadok who had occupied the high priestly office)[73]
or figures who belonged to the Essene movement but whose disagreements
over ideological and legal issues (including eschatological imminence, and
calendrical, Temple and cultic laws) brought about the antipathy and sepa-
ration.[74] Third, one could suggest that the community that was loyal to the
Teacher of Righteousness might have viewed this figure as a messianic
leader in the eschatological age. For one thing, the *Pesher* seems to interpret and appropriate Hab 2:3-4 in such a way that the Teacher of Righteousness is regarded as a divinely appointed ideal figure through whom
and whose teaching the deliverance of 'the men of truth' in the final age is
guaranteed. Scholars have rightly pointed out that differing eschatological
views played a major part in causing the antagonism between the two figures.[75] But we would also suggest that the pesherist's antithetically framed

---

[73] Vermes (*TDSS*, 130f; *CDSSE*, 49f) first advocated this. For him, Jonathan (160-142
BCE) appoints himself as the high priest, which offends בני צדוק, leading to the
emergence of a dissident clerical group led by the Teacher, whose death and the appearance of the Kittim (1QpHab 1:12; 3:5; 6:1, 10; 9:7) (Romans [63 BCE]) form the
terminus a quo and the *terminus ad quem* of the Qumran history respectively (1QpHab
2:2-3; CD 1:5-11; cf. 4QpPsᵃ 3:15-17; Dan 9-11; *1 En* 90:6-7; *Jub* 23:14-19, *T Lev* 17; *As
Mos* 4-5). Vermes' theory is followed partly by Baumgarten and Schiffman, who have
understood the Qumran community as Sadducean on the grounds that the legal matters in
4QMMT show a link between the conservative view of the Sadducees (cf. Josephus: *Ant*
13:297) and the Qumran covenanters, and that *Sadducee* derives from the name צדוק,
hence בני צדוק being the Sadducees (Zadokites). Baumgarten, 'The Pharisaic-Sadducean
Controversies about Purity, and the Qumran Texts', *JJS* (1980) 157-170; Schiffman,
*Reclaiming the Dead Sea Scrolls: The History of Judaism, the Background of Christian-
ity, the Lost Library of Qumran*, 83-145; 'The Qumran Scrolls and Rabbinic Judaism', in
Flint & VanderKam (eds), *Scrolls*, 552-571.

[74] For García Martínez, Essenism is a Palestinian phenomenon rooted in the
'apocalyptic' tradition (e.g. the Enochic Book of the Watchers) and therefore predating
the Antiochene crisis, so the origins of the Qumran sect must be traced to the Essene
movement, whose central ideas are preserved in some of the Qumran writings such as
1QS and CD. The Temple Scroll and 4QMMT also indicate that the opponent of the
Teacher of Righteousness was not from amongst the political powers in Jerusalem but
was a figure within the Essene movement; those who accepted the Teacher's teaching as
revealed broke away from the movement and withdrew to Qumran. García Martínez,
'Qumran Origins and Early History: A Groningen Hypothesis', *Folia Orientalia* 25
(1988) 113-136; *The People of the Dead Sea Scrolls*, 86-96; *Qumran and Apocalyptic:
Studies on the Aramaic Texts from Qumran*, 163-179.

[75] There are examples in Qumran that parallel the sort of antagonism that existed between the Teacher of Righteousness and the Wicked Priest: the Teacher of Righteousness
versus the 'Scoffer' or 'Liar' (CD 1:5-11, 20; cf. 4QpPSᵃ 4:8-9), Belial versus a figure of
a positive character in 4QTestimonia (4Q175:14-30), Melchizedek versus Belial (and 'all
the gods') (11QMelch 13-14), Melki-reshá versus Melchizedek (4Q'Amram), heathen
kings (the kings of Assyria and Egypt) versus the Son of God (4Q246) and 'Wickedness'

characterisation of the figures in relation to their destinies and indeed that of their followers may have been informed by the prophetic oracles of Habakkuk, where the antagonism between the two figures, namely 'the wicked one' and 'the righteous one', seems to us to be evident.

4. The Nahal Hever Text (8HevXIIgr)

The Greek fragments of Habakkuk are part of the scroll of the Greek Minor Prophets discovered in the 'Cave of Horror' in Nahal Hever in 1952 and 1961, hence the siglum 8HevXIIgr.[76] The date of the scroll is uncertain. On the basis of palaeographic evidence, varying suggestions have been made: 50 BCE to 50 CE, mid first century CE, or end of the first century CE. Examination of styles of script and similarities between different scribal personal styles, and comparison with Egyptian, Greek (Herculaneum) and Judean papyri seem to indicate that the material in question may have belonged to the late Ptolemaic or early Roman period. So, as no feature of the manuscript recommends the later date, a date in the late first century BCE has been suggested.[77]

The reconstructors of the text of the scroll accepted that the Greek fragments of Habakkuk from Nahal Hever betray a rabbinic Jewish revisional activity of the LXX before the turn of the Christian Era.[78] They also supposed that the translation followed the MT as closely as possible. However, limited knowledge on the vocabulary and translation technique of the translators of the scroll and the fact that the scroll sometimes agrees with the LXX even where it could have found a literal rendering for an MT word or phrase have led them to follow the LXX text.[79] In any case, the reconstructed text of Hab 2:3-4 in 8HevXIIgr reads as follows:

Verse 3: ὅτι ἔτ]ι [ὅρασις εἰς κ]αιρὸν καὶ ἐνφανήσετ[αι εἰς πέρας]
[καὶ οὐ δ]ιαψεύσεται· Ἐὰν στραγ[γεύσηται προσδέ-]
[χου αὐ]τόν, ὅτι ἐρχόμενος ἥ[ξει καὶ οὐ   ]

---

versus a 'Marvellous Mighty Counsellor' (1QH 3:9-10, 12 and 18). For critical discussions of these texts and messianism in Judaism, see García Martínez, *Qumran and Apocalyptic*, 163-179; and Knibb, 'Messianism', 165-184.

[76] Tov, *Greek*, 1. See also Greenspoon, 'Dead Sea', 104-106. But see Fitzmyer ('Habakkuk', 241), who says that 8HevXIIgr 'seems to be independent of the so-called LXX'.

[77] Parsons, 'The Scripts and their Date', in Tov, *Greek*, 19-26; *Scribal Practices and Approaches Reflected in the Texts from the Judean Desert*, 301.

[78] Tov, Greek, 103; 'The Biblical Texts from the Judean Desert', in Herbert and Tov, *The Bible as Book: the Hebrew Bible and the Judean Desert Discoveries*, 157, 139-166.

[79] Tov, *Greek*, 84.

[.] Verse 4: ἰδ[οὺ] σκοτία, οὐκ εὐθεῖα ψυχὴ αὐτοῦ [ἐν]
[αὐτῷ· καὶ δί]καιος ἐν πίστει αὐτοῦ ζήσετ[αι].[80]

Can we notice any messianic elements in this reading? To start with verse 3, the reviser has used ἐνφανήσετ[αι] for יפח. The rendering of the former ('it or he will appea[r]') obviously does not agree with that of the latter ('it will testify'). Nor does ἐνφανήσετ[αι] fully agree with the LXX's ἀνατελεῖ, although both verbs express a more or less similar conception ('appearance' and 'rising' of something or someone respectively). This poses difficulty to the view that 8HevXIIgr is a later proto-rabbinic revision of the LXX towards MT. But more pertinent to our purpose here, 8HevXIIgr is not clear as to whose appearance is implied in ἐνφανήσετ[αι]; that of [ὅρασις] or ἐρχόμενος? Grammatically, the masculine [αὐ]τόν suggests that ἐνφανήσετ[αι] expresses the 'appearance' of ἐρχόμενος rather than the feminine ὅρασις. This means that the one who rises in the end for the LXX translator is the same figure as the one who will appear for the producer of 8HevXIIgr. However, this does not immediately suggest that the producer of the Nahal Hever text adopted a messianic notion that seems to exist in the LXX.

In verse 4, our scroll complicates the matter by using σκοτία for עפלה of the MT and the ὑποστείληται of the LXX. This obviously fits neither and on the face of it makes little sense. The replacement or, better, embellishment of the MT's לא־ישרה ('not smooth') by οὐκ εὐθεῖα ('not upright') – which is completely unrelated to the LXX's οὐκ εὐδοκεῖ ('not pleases')[81] – seems to suggest that the reviser may have wanted to use σκοτία as a representation of something that characterises 'the arrogant man' (ἀνὴρ ἀλαζών) in verse 5. This obviously is speculative, but the 'arrogant man' is clearly contrasted with the 'righteous one' in 8HevXIIgr. Our scroll does not have the articular ὁ δὲ δίκαιος as in the majority reading of the LXX. In the reconstruction of the original orthography of what is preserved of Hab 2:4b (ΚΑΙΟΣΕΝΠΙΣΤΕΙΑΥΤΟΥΖΗΣΕΤ),[82] the text has καί before [δί]καιος as the adaptation to the MT's וצדיק. This adaptation obviously differs from the LXX's δέ (preceded by ὁ) and, as

---

[80] '[Because the vision is set for] time, and he (or it) will appear and [will not] lie. If he (or it) tar[ries, wait for h]im, because he will surely co[me and not...] [.] Be[hold] the darkness, his soul is not upright [in him; and the] righteous one shall live by his faithfulness.'

[81] Here the Greek εὐθεῖα appears to follow the Hebrew root ישר although, as Tov (*Greek*, 152) points out, the LXX may have followed the MT's vocalisation יָשְׁרָה.

[82] Tov, *Greek*, 52-53. The reconstruction in Tov takes the first five letters as part of δίκαιος, hence [δί]καιος. But see Fitzmyer ('Habakkuk', 241) whose reconstruction differs from Tov's: [δίκ]αιος ἐν πίστει αὐτοῦ ζήσετ[αι]. It also differs from the orthography.

Tov points out, occurs elsewhere in the scroll, e.g. καί replaces the LXX's δέ in Joel 3:3, Hab 2:20 and Mic 4:5.[83]

The reconstruction does not include the article before [δί]καιος either, because, as Tov suggests, the fact that the scroll omits the article before πνεῦμα (LXX: τὸ πνεῦμα) in Hab 1:11 and ἀναγεινώσκων (LXX: ὁ ἀναγινώσκων) in Hab 2:2 suggests that the reviser may have dropped the LXX's article. But Tov also shows that the author of 8HevXIIgr follows the LXX in adding the article against MT three times more than the amount of time he omits the article against the LXX.[84] This and the space before ΚΑΙΟΣ... in the unreconstructed text make us wonder whether the text could not have had the article in its original autograph. But the available evidence will never enable us to know whether the reviser followed the LXX. As we cannot base anything on a conjecture, there is no point in raising the question as to whether the implied referent of the adjective for the reviser was generic or specific.

But it is worth pointing out that the rendering in Hab 2:4b as a whole is closer to the MT than all preserved LXX forms. Particularly notable is ἐν πίστει αὐτοῦ, which is a direct rendering of באמונתו. The reviser, who probably belonged to scribal circles in Palestine towards the end of the first century BCE, may have understood πίστις here as the 'fidelity' not of God or the figure that is said to come in verse 3 but of the 'righteous one'. This is determined by the apparent contrast between οὐκ εὐθεῖα ψυχὴ αὐτοῦ and ἐν πίστει αὐτοῦ. That is to say, the reviser contrasts a person whose soul is not upright and a person who is faithful. So, while there is a possibility to suggest that a messianic reading of 2:3-4 in the LXX is somewhat consistent with that of 8HevXIIgr, the evidence as a whole does not show that the latter bears sufficient contextual and textual indicators of messianic conception.

5. Hebrews 10:37-38: Christological or Anthropological?

The quotation of Hab 2:3-4 in Heb 10:37-38 is part of the author's encouragement to his readers not to wilfully persist in sin, to continue to do the will of God and maintain the initial confidence they displayed even in the

---

[83] Tov, *Greek*, 93.
[84] Tov, *Greek*, 106-108.

face of being publicly exposed to abuse and enduring much suffering and persecution. The author's words are uttered within the eschatological framework of judgement and reward that follows the day of the coming of the Messiah. The readers are told that that day is approaching (10:25) and what was promised will soon materialise (10:36). Then the author quotes Hab 2:3-4:

ἔτι γὰρ μικρὸν ὅσον ὅσον,
ὁ ἐρχόμενος ἥξει καὶ οὐ χρονίσει·
ὁ δὲ δίκαιός μου ἐκ πίστεως ζήσεται,
καὶ ἐάν ὑποστείληται, οὐκ εὐδοκεῖ ἡ ψυχή μου ἐν αὐτῷ.[85]

As will be noticed below, the majority of scholars understand the first two lines (Heb 10:37 = Hab 2:3) christologically and the second two lines (Heb 10:38 = Hab 2:4) anthropologically. So far, only Hanson has proposed a christological interpretation for Hab 10:38 but without any exegetical justification. In what follows, we shall evaluate these perspectives through exegetically analysing Heb 10:37-38 in relation to the immediate and wider textual contexts.

The author of Hebrews conflates Hab 2:3 with Isa 26:20. He derives ἔτι ('still') from Hab 2:3 and adds to the Isaianic phrase μικρὸν ὅσον ὅσον, which is difficult to translate.[86] That our author uses Isa 26:20 is not unusual, because it is one of the passages appended in the Psalter in the LXX and was used for liturgy in synagogues and early church meetings.[87] The reason for such a conflation probably is the commonality of the central concern both prophets express in the contexts of their passages, namely the eschatological coming of the Lord. This can be noticed particularly when Isa 26:20 is read along with 26:21. The conflation seems to enable the author, as Gordon says, to 'heighten the sense of imminent fulfilment attaching to Habakkuk's prophecy'.[88] That is to say, the author of Hebrews uses the spirit of the context of the Isaianic passage to encourage his readers to endure suffering because in a little while ὁ ἐρχόμενος will come and the eagerly awaited salvation will materialise. The author's replacing of the LXX's ὅτι with ὁ (probably by omitting the syllable τι) appears to be an adaptation and adoption of the LXX's probably already messianic idea

---

[85] NRSV translates: 'For yet "in a very little while, the one who is coming will come and will not delay; but my righteous one will live by faith. My soul takes no pleasure in anyone who shrinks back"'.

[86] Fitzmyer, 'Habakkuk', 243.

[87] See Lane, *Hebrews 9-13* (WBC 47b), 305. Isa 26:20 and Hab 2:3-4 may even have been already combined in a pre-Christian *testimonium*, but no conclusive evidence can be found. See also Ellingworth, *The Epistle to the Hebrews*, 555.

[88] Gordon, *Hebrews*, 126.

to his christological concerns by removing ambiguity the absence of the article could potentially cause.[89] Thus whether ὁ ἐρχόμενος in Heb 10:37 is Christ is beyond dispute, but whether ὁ δίκαιός μου in 10:38 is a reference to Christ requires a considered answer.[90] Before venturing that answer, however, the citation must be set in context.

The author uses Hab 2:3-4 not only as a justification for what is said in 10:36 but also as scriptural evidence of what is said in 10:39. That is, the author emphasises the importance of endurance in the face of suffering and persecution because as prophesied by Habakkuk Christ will be coming without delay and resurrection life will be achieved by the faithful Christians thereafter. Then, being well aware of the intensity of suffering and persecution and, as a result, the real possibility of drawing back from the new religious understanding that centres on Christ, the author more or less patronises his readers by telling them that they are not from among those who shrink back and stand to suffer destruction but from among the faithful who stand to gain salvation (10:39). Hence the issue is twofold. First, should ἡμεῖς δὲ ... ἐσμεν ... πίστεως εἰς περιποίησιν ψυχῆς in 10:39 be connected with ὁ δὲ δίκαιός μου ἐκ πίστεως ζήσεται in the citation so that 'my righteous one' is part of the ἡμεῖς (Christians) who will not shrink back (10:39) and for whom a string of biblical characters serve as models and witnesses (11:1ff; 12:1)? Second, should the citation of Hab 2:4 as a whole be understood along with the citation of Hab 2:3 so that ὁ δίκαιός μου is Christ?

The unanimous view of commentators on Hebrews so far is that the phrase ὁ δίκαιός μου refers to a generic individual Christian.[91] This, it can be argued, is shown by the striking reading where the author switches the order of clauses in the LXX reading of Hab 2:4a and 2:4b.[92] The author has already rendered Hab 2:3 in terms of a prediction of one 'who is coming' in order to facilitate the text as a prediction of Christ's coming.[93] So it

---

[89] *Contra* Fitzmyer ('Habakkuk', 243).

[90] As far as the text of Heb 10:38 is concerned, ὁ δὲ δίκαιός μου ἐκ πίστεως (attested in P⁴⁶, ℵ, A, H*, 33, 1739, etc), as against δίκαιος ἐκ πίστεώς μου (D*, 1518, 1611, etc), is favoured, because it has a vastly superior textual support and the phrase δικαιούς μου is more difficult to explain than πίστεώς μου (hence the principle of *difficilior lectio potior*). See also Gheorghita, *Role*, 177. Cf. also UBS 3ʳᵈ with UBS 4ᵗʰ where the committee has upgraded δίκαιός μου from {C} in the former to {B} in the latter.

[91] See, for example, Moffatt, *Hebrews*, 157-158; Attridge, *The Epistle to the Hebrews*, 555; Buchanan, *To the Hebrews*, 175; Koester, *Hebrews*, 467-468; Lane, *Hebrews 9-13*, 305-306.

[92] Such a reading has no support amongst extant textual traditions, so the work may be attributed solely to our author.

[93] For early Christian use of ἐρχόμενος *vis-à-vis* Christ, see Matt 3:11; 11:3; 21:9; Mark 11:9; Luke 7:19; 19:38; Jn 1:15, 27; 11:27.

seems clear that by inverting the clauses the author not only avoids the suggestion of ὁ ἐρχόμενος shrinking back (ὑποστείληται), which appears to be evident in the LXX reading,[94] he also makes ὁ δίκαιός μου the subject of both clauses so that the contrast is between preservation of soul or acquisition of life (περιποίησις) that results from πίστις and destruction or loss [of soul] (ἀπώλεια) that results from shrinking back (v 39). The author thus presents 'my righteous one' as a generic individual Christian who is warned not to shrink back, i.e. not to become apostate,[95] or not to engage in withdrawal and concealment as a mode of endurance.[96] That the author cites μικρὸν ὅσον ὅσον from Isa 26:20 implies that the Isaianic mode of endurance is being advocated amongst the readers of Hebrews. So the alternative standing underscored before any Christian (ὁ δίκαιός μου) during the interim before the *parousia* is fidelity that leads to life (ἐκ πίστεως ζήσεται) or shrinking back (ὑποστείληται) that leads to destruction.[97]

Another argument is that the author of Hebrews contrasts the idea expressed in the LXX, which is to do with the righteous Israelite living through God's faithfulness to his covenant, with the idea of the righteous person of God (the Christian) living by her own loyalty, as she holds on and holds out till the end.[98] If one wishes to take the author of Hebrews as linking ἐκ πίστεως with ὁ δίκαιός [μου] rather than ζήσεται, as many also think Paul in Rom 1:17 and Gal 3:11 does (we will discuss this later in the book), one can argue that like Paul the author of Hebrews understands πίστις as the way a person becomes 'righteous' (11:4, 6) and the way that righteous person 'lives' (11:13-16).[99] This means that the author parallels ζήσεται with περιποίησιν ψυχῆς ('preservation of soul' [cf. Ezek 13:19]), both of which are one and the same thing achieved through πίστις. The reason for the author's confidence is the knowledge of his readers' foun-

---

[94] So also Gordon (*Hebrews*, 126).

[95] Lane, *Hebrews 9-13*, 305

[96] Wilcox, '... AND IF HE SHRINKS BACK', *NTS* 22 (1976) 88-94.

[97] Wilcox, '...AND IF HE SHRINKS BACK', 91-93. Central to the anthropological argument, as Wilcox argues, is that the verb ὑποστείληται in the inverted reading of the Habakkuk citation appears to refer to something that might be done by ὁ δίκαιος. What the verb refers to in Habakkuk, of course, affects how it is understood in Hebrews. Wilcox argues that it is improbable that in Habakkuk the verb refers to the 'he' of the 'coming, he shall come'. He argues that the one who shrinks back is someone who is *not* ὁ δίκαιος. The referent is the Jewish-Christian. For Wilcox, the author conflates Isa 26:20 with Hab 2:3-4 in order to allude to the opposite of the mode of endurance unfolded in Heb 10:32-36. As this mode of endurance is characterised by 'boldness' (v 35), the opposite of it is the one that can be noticed in Isa 26:20 as a whole, namely withdrawal and concealment.

[98] Moffatt, *Hebrews*, 157.

[99] So Koester (*Hebrews*, 467-468).

dational faith in God and commitment to serve him by abandoning what he calls 'dead works' (6:1; 9:13). Along this line, the Christians implied in Hebrews are now righteous, but their acquisition of resurrection life is dependent on their πίστις that models after that of Christ. In short, the subject of ἐκ πίστεως ζήσεται and ὑποστείληται is ὁ δίκαιός μου, who is the generic individual Christian.

However, ὁ δίκαιός μου could equally be understood as Christ for several reasons. First, as the syntax of the LXX reading of Hab 2:3-4 showed, the one whose shrinking back would displease God probably is ἐρχόμενος, however improbable it may seem theologically. Our exegesis of Hab 2:4 in the LXX also showed that ἐρχόμενος can be understood as ὁ δίκαιός [μου], a chosen messiah who will be faithful to God and his task. It seems to be beyond doubt that the author of Hebrews understands Hab 2:3 messianically. The same is not evident in his quotation of Hab 2:4b, but when he penned ὁ δίκαιός μου ἐκ πίστεως ζήσεται the author could also have had the same messianic conception in mind. As ὁ δίκαιός μου has a similar sense to the messianic υἱός μου in Heb 1:5 (cf. Ps 2:7; 89:3, 20; Isa 53:11), the equivalence (if there is one) between 'the coming one' and 'my righteous one' cannot be regarded as farfetched.

Second, the author switches the order of Hab 2:4a and 2:4b probably to parallel ὁ δίκαιός μου with ὁ ἐρχόμενος and, in so doing, to depict the former as christological. The plasticity of the biblical *lemma* in the author's hands is seen not only in the way in which he titularises ἐρχόμενος but also in the way in which he inverts Hab 2:4a and 2:4b, thus making 'my righteous one' the subject of ἐκ πίστεως ζήσεται and ἐὰν ὑποστείληται. Such an inversion can be taken as something that enables our author to strengthen his understanding of 'my righteous one' as a Christian and to avoid any suggestion of 'the coming one' shrinking back as could easily be inferred from the Septuagintal text. However, our author's inversion can equally be understood as an attempt to bring 'my righteous one' in line with 'the coming one'. Along this line, one could argue, switching the order of Hab 2:4a and 2:4b enables the author to claim that despite the immensity of the suffering Jesus faced, he showed loyalty to God marked by his steadfast refusal to shrink back from his task, as the Gethsemane narrative shows (Mk 14:32-50). Consequently, Jesus was glorified at the right hand of the throne of God (cf. 10:38 with 12:2). The author seems to go further by claiming that since Jesus will be coming soon as God's Messiah (10:38),[100] Christians who are from among those who faithfully follow in his footsteps (rather than from among those who

---

[100] It is to be noted here that our author strengthens the idea of the coming of the Messiah by using the future οὐ χρονίσει instead of the LXX's subjunctive οὐ μὴ χρονίσῃ.

shrink back) will attain salvation upon his coming. In short, by aligning 'my righteous one' with 'the coming one', the author of Hebrews presents Jesus as the one who was faithful to God, who now lives in heaven and will come as God's Messiah or Righteous One. That obviously means that, pursuant with an LXX reading discussed earlier, 'the coming one', like 'my righteous one', is the subject of ὑποστείληται and ἐκ πίστεως ζήσεται.[101]

Third, the reason why our author develops ὁ δίκαιος in length by out-lining the heroes and heroines of πίστις[102] in chapter 11 can be argued to be christological rather than anthropological. That is to say, the purpose of our author's argument in chapter 11 is in order to compare Jesus with bib-lical heroes and heroines and then present him as the supreme *exemplar* whose faithfulness, rather than that of those heroes and heroines, achieves the promise of salvation (resurrection life in the heavenly realm). Our author starts his argument with Abel, who is referred to as δίκαιος,[103] whose sacrifice is said to be more acceptable than his brother Cain's and through whose πίστις he continues to speak even after his death (11:4).[104] While the author says here that Abel speaks through his πίστις, in 12:24 he compares Abel with Jesus by saying that Jesus' blood 'speaks a better word than the blood of Abel'. The cry of Abel in Gen 4:10 is certainly the source of our author's expressions in 11:4 and 12:24.[105] But more perti-

---

[101] The question as to whether ἐκ πίστεως is to be connected with the adjective (the one who is righteous by faith will live) or the verb ζήσεται (the one who is righteous will live by faith) becomes irrelevant in this reading. For one thing, since ὁ δίκαιός μου is the subject of the inverted reading of Hab 2:4 as a whole, the focus is both on the faithful-ness and the resurrection life God's 'righteous one' won not only for himself but also for his brothers and sisters. *Contra* Moffatt (*Hebrews*, 157), therefore, when our author cites Hab 2:4 he is as interested in ζωή as in πίστις.

[102] In Hebrews, πίστις is used in terms of 'a certainty of the uncertain, a seeing of the invisible' (Koester, *Hebrews*, 125), hearing and accepting the gospel message (4:2), abandoning 'dead works' and trusting in God (6:1), a means through which the promise is received (6:12), approaching God with confidence (10:22), and the opposite of shrink-ing back (10:39). In some of these places, πίστις can mean 'trust, faith' (4:2; 6:1) while in other places 'faithfulness, fidelity' (6:1; 10:22, 39). The term, in Hebrews in general and in the Habakkuk citation in particular, seems to be understood as encompassing both 'trust in God' and 'fidelity to God'. See also Koester, *Hebrews*, 125-127, 463.

[103] In presenting Abel as δίκαιος, our author goes beyond the Genesis account. But see *1 En* 22:7; *Test Abr* 13:2-3; Matt 23:35; 1 Jn 3:12.

[104] In 11:4, αὐτῆς can be understood as referring back to τοῖς δώροις or πίστει. As the former is plural, the latter is an obvious choice from a grammatical and contextual point of view. No tradition, not even Genesis, connects Abel's sacrifice with πίστις, however.

[105] Gen 4:10 seems to serve as a source of other Jewish and Christian traditions as well. For example, in *1 En* 22:5-7, the spirit of Abel is depicted as making suit. Philo says 'Abel is found quite manifestly using his voice and crying out the wrongs which he has suffered' (*Det. Pot. Ins* 48; cf. 70). Unlike other Jewish traditions, Hebrews does not

nent, while the author understands Abel's sacrifice as superior to Cain's in 11:4,[106] in 12:24 he depicts Christ's blood as speaking in a better fashion than Abel's. The way in which Christ's blood is superior is not specified,[107] but if the point of the comparison is to show that Abel's death, like that of the Maccabean martyrs, for example, has an atoning significance, then Christ's blood that effects lasting remission and true forgiveness of sin speaks not in a different but in a superior way (Heb 7:27-28; 9:13-14; 12:24). Strange though it may seem, the author of Hebrews presents Abel as someone who still lives through his πίστις and blood.[108] As our author talks about Christ's blood speaking in a superior way to Abel's, we can deduce that Christ's πίστις speaks in a superior way to Abel's as well. This leads us to construe Heb 10:38a in terms of Jesus living through his faithfulness, in the sense not only of his eschatological life in the heavenly court but also his example still speaking powerfully to later generations of Christians.

The reading in Heb 12:1-2 appears to support the view that πίστεως in Heb 10:38 is the faithfulness of 'my righteous one'. In 12:1-2, the biblical heroes are presented as 'a cloud of witnesses', while Christ is presented as the pioneer and perfecter of πίστις (12:2). Unlike the biblical characters, who, despite all their suffering and hardship and their being attested διὰ τῆς πίστεως, did not receive τὴν ἐπαγγελίαν (presumably resurrection [v 35]), Jesus is seated ἐν δεξιᾷ τε τοῦ θρόνου τοῦ θεοῦ.[109] Jesus' πίστις is superior to that of the biblical characters outlined in chapter 11, because it results in resurrection life. Not only is he seated at the right hand of God (8:1; 10:12; 12:2), he will also appear the second time to save those who are enduring suffering and hardship (9:28) so that they too will become

---

reflect any interest in the act of fratricide nor in Abel as the proto-martyr (cf. *Jub* 4:2-3; *4 Macc* 18:11).

[106] For a discussion of the Jewish background on this, see Attridge, *Epistle*, 316 and n. 134.

[107] Attridge (*Epistle*, 377) suggests that there may be a distinction between the cry for vengeance of Abel's blood and the redemptive effects of Christ's bloodshed.

[108] Buchanan (*To the Hebrews*, 185) explains Abel's speaking πίστις here in terms of doctrinal confession rather than trust or faithfulness. That is, πίστις is the report of God's judgement that became part of the doctrinal confession; the record of God's judgement that is still on record for those who will read Gen 4:4. Lane (*Hebrews 9-11*, 335) also understands the πίστις that speaks as the record of God's approval of his integrity and his sacrifice in Gen 4:4. That is, Abel's faith continues to speak to us through the written record of his action in Genesis, which transmits to us the exemplary character of his offering. See also Moffatt, *Hebrews*, 164.

[109] In agreement with Lane (*Hebrews 9-13*, 520), that the biblical heroes and heroines did not receive what God promised does not necessarily diminish the significance of their πίστις. The author also knows that Jesus was not the first person to have shown πίστις in or to God.

Chapter 2

part of the heavenly community where God is the Judge (12:21-22). The author's presentation of Jesus here is consistent with his earlier portrayal of him. There he is the 'son of man' to whom the world is subjected. He is also the pioneer of salvation who will bring many children to glory (2:5-10).[110] Furthermore, Jesus is the 'faithful high priest before God' (2:17) and, compared with Moses, he is faithful (πιστός) over God's house as a *son*, while Moses was faithful in all God's house as a *servant* (3:2-6; cf. Ps 89:3, 19-20).[111] All this shows that our author's purpose in comparing and contrasting Jesus with biblical heroes and heroines probably is in order to depict the superiority of the faithfulness of Jesus the Messiah. But this is perhaps encapsulated more clearly in what we would call contrastive *inclusio* in 10:36 and 11:39. In the former, Christians are urged to do the will of God and endure suffering so that they may receive the promise (τὴν ἐπαγγελίαν). In the latter, however, despite being attested διὰ τῆς πίστεως, the biblical heroes and heroines did not receive the promise (cf. 11:13). They may be witnesses of the πίστις that should be shown by Christians, but they are not prime models of πίστις and means of attaining the promise.

In conclusion, although Jesus is not directly referred to as ὁ δίκαιος anywhere in Hebrews, the author's presentation of him as the superior example of πίστις in comparison with other biblical heroes and heroines seems consistent with reading 'my righteous one' as Christ who sets an example of faithfulness for Christians (10:38-39).

---

[110] It is to be noted that Jesus is ἀρχηγὸς τῆς σωτηρίας here, while he is ἀρχηγὸς τῆς πίστεως in 12:2. As Goulder ('Hebrews and the Ebionites', *NTS* 49 [2003] 393-406) also points out, the first two chapters of Hebrews, where OT messianic texts are cited (2 Sam 7:14 and Pss 2:7; 8:4-6; and 110:1), appear to be designed to show the inferiority of angels to Jesus, the Son of God.

[111] The adjective πιστός in relation to Christ could diversely mean Christ's fidelity in temptation, obedience to the Father or trustworthiness in his high-priestly role, but that Christ's faithfulness is presented as superior to that of Moses seems to be clear. See also Hamm, 'Faith in the Epistle to the Hebrews: the Jesus Factor', *CBQ* 52 (1990) 270-291, 281.

6. Conclusions

Our discussion in this chapter showed that there is not a uniform answer to the question as to whether the LXX translators, the Qumran pesherist, the producer or reviser of the Nahal Hever text and the author of Hebrews interpreted Hab 2:3-4 messianically. The LXX translator in Hab 2:3, it seems, gives a messianic interpretation to Habakkuk's idea of YHWH's eschatological coming in the Masoretic text. This is evidenced by the grammatical and conceptual agreement between καὶ ἀνατελεῖ εἰς πέρας in 2:3a and ἐρχόμενος ἥξει in 2:3b and by the personalised expressions such as ὑπόμεινον αὐτόν. Issues are much more complicated in Hab 2:4, not least because the minority reading of LXX MSS has μου after ὁ δίκαιος rather than ἐκ πίστεως. In either translation, the 'righteous one' can be understood as a generic individual. However, since the one who is not expected to ὑποστείλασθαι in 2:4a can be the figure implied in 2:3ab and there seems to be a parallel between what is said in 2:4a and what follows in 2:4b, ἐρχόμενος and ὁ δίκαιός μου can also refer to the same figure. If the Deutero-Isaianic Servant has any messianic significance, 'my righteous one' in the minority reading and in Hebrews may have been informed by Isa 53:11 ('my righteous servant'). YHWH's soul is delighted (Ιακωβ ὁ παῖς μου ... προσεδέξατο αὐτὸν ἡ ψυχή μου [42:1]) in the Servant. In Habakkuk, the 'righteous one' [of God] (δίκαιος) is not expected to shrink back because that would displease YHWH's soul (οὐκ εὐδοκεῖ ἡ ψυχή μου ἐν αὐτῷ).

A similar interpretative pattern cannot be noticed in the *Pesher* Habakkuk. In this composition, the eschatological coming of God in Hab 2:3 is understood in terms of the coming of the final age and the 'righteous one' in Hab 2:4 is interpreted collectively rather than particularly. The *Pesher* as a whole centres on the conflict between the Teacher of Righteousness and the Wicked Priest within an eschatological framework, which appears to betray the influence of Habakkuk, in which the conflict between 'the righteous one' and 'the wicked one' is apparent. The Teacher of Righteousness, for the pesherist, is a divinely appointed ideal figure through whom divine mysteries are disclosed and the eschatological deliverance of his devotees is ensured. Like the pesherist, the producer or reviser of the Nahal Hever text understands the 'righteous one' as a generic individual. Unlike the pesherist and indeed the LXX translator, however, he translates the MT's באמונתו as ἐν πίστει αὐτοῦ, thereby making the 'righteous one' the subject of πίστις. Although there appear to be some indications of a messianic understanding particularly of Hab 2:3 in the fragments, it is safe to conclude that that is not the prevailing view of the text.

When we come to Hebrews 10:37-38, the author here conflates Hab 2:3-4 with Isa 26:20 probably because of the corresponding motif of the coming of the Lord in both prophetic books. Then he titularises ἐρχόμενος in Hab 2:3b and speaks of the coming of Christ. While it is obvious that the author applied Hab 2:3b to his christological concerns, the same cannot be said with certainty about his application of Hab 2:4. In fact, the unanimous scholarly position, particularly as far as the commentaries on Hebrews are concerned, is that the latter is cited in order to address his concerns about the real possibility of some Jewish-Christians lapsing from their faith. That means that ὁ δίκαιός μου is a Jewish-Christian who gains life through her loyalty to God and steadfast refusal to shrink back at the face of suffering and persecution. This seems to be reinforced by the contextual signals and the author's inversion of Hab 2:4a and 2:4b, as the former coheres with the reading in Heb 10:39.

However, our exegesis also showed that the whole citation could be read christologically for several reasons. First, there is no doubt that the author of Hebrews identifies ὁ ἐρχόμενος as Christ. Although the same is not evident in relation to ὁ δίκαιός μου, our author appears to be equating ὁ ἐρχόμενος with ὁ δίκαιός μου. That ἐρχόμενος can be understood as ὁ δίκαιός [μου] in the LXX and ὁ δίκαιός μου has a similar sense to the messianic υἱός μου in Heb 1:5 (cf. Ps 2:7; Isa 53:11) appear to support this. Second, the author inverts Hab 2:4a and 2:4b probably in order to bring ὁ δίκαιός μου in line with ὁ ἐρχόμενος. The Messiah who acquired eschatological life through his faithfulness is the one who will come to save the faithful. Third, the reason behind the author's comparison of Jesus with Abel and other biblical heroes and heroines is probably to show that the prime model of faith/faithfulness and means of attaining the promise of salvation is Christ (cf. 10:36 with 11:39). This is probably reinforced by the author's presentation of Jesus as the pioneer and perfecter of faith/faithfulness in 12:1-2. In short, a christological reading of ὁ δίκαιός μου ἐκ πίστεως ζήσεται is as valid as an anthropological reading.

As indicated in the introduction of this chapter, our reason for studying scriptural and non-scriptural interpretations of Hab 2:3-4 is to set up a backdrop that might inform and illumine our attempt to understand whether Paul cited Hab 2:4b in Rom 1:17 (and Gal 3:11) with a messianic or generic meaning. We saw that the LXX translators probably interpreted Hab 2:3-4 messianically, while messianic and generic arguments are more or less balanced in Heb 10:37-38. On the other hand, the passage is interpreted generically in 1QpHab, and a messianic reading does not seem to be prevalent in the Nahal Hever text. These findings on the whole appear to support the anthropological reading of Paul's citation in Rom 1:17b (and Gal 3:11) more strongly than they do the christological reading. So more positive evidence from Rom 1:17 and related and relevant texts needs to be provided in order to justify the christological argument. As part of that attempt, we now turn to our exegesis of Paul's declarations in the immediate context of Rom 1:17b.

Chapter 3

Christology in the Immediate Context of Rom 1:17b?

1. Introduction

The ways in which we expound issues in Rom 1:16 and 1:17a partly determine whether the double prepositional phrase ἐκ πίστεως εἰς πίστιν and the Habakkuk citation should be understood anthropologically or christologically. So this chapter will be concerned with analysing Rom 1:16 and 1:17a with a particular focus on the hitherto neglected question as to whether or the extent to which Paul was thinking christologically in these verses. But since our understanding of the relationship between Rom 1:17 and its immediate context is dependent in part on the role attributed to γάρ, we will start the chapter with a brief treatment of the particle. Subsequent to that, we will deal with issues relating to δύναμις θεοῦ ('power of God') and the revelation of δικαιοσύνη θεοῦ ('righteousness of God').

In order to answer adequately the question as to whether Paul used the power of God with christology in mind, we will first attempt to determine the grammatical standing of the power of God in relation to εὐαγγέλιον. The result will help us to decide whether Paul thought of the power of God as the content or subject matter of the proclaimed gospel or the gospel as the power of God. This decision will prove crucial when we come to consider the significance of Paul's use of the power of God in relation to Christ or as a linguistic image for Christ. The decision will also pave the way for our next discussion, which is to do with the meaning and significance of the revelation of the righteousness of God in Rom 1:17a.

Rom 1:17a is traditionally interpreted in terms of the gospel revealing righteousness from or by faith. Against this, however, we shall argue that *Rom 1:17a is probably about the revelation of the righteousness of God that designates God's saving power and presence.* But this section will adjudicate between these two readings as thoroughly as possible. We start that task with Francis Watson's treatment of Rom 1:17a in his recent publication *Paul and the Hermeneutics of Faith.* As his argument represents a refined and fresh defence of the traditional reading of Rom 1:17, our analysis of his views on the first half of our passage will set a stage and provide dialogical points for subsequent examination of issues relating to the grammatical standing and meaning of ἀποκαλύπτεται and the questions as to what Paul means by the revelation of the righteousness of God and how that meaning relates to Paul's understanding of Christ. In the course of dealing with these issues, we will also consider relevant textual evidence from OT and Jewish backgrounds and from within Romans.

2. The Role of Γάρ

Γάρ is one of the most common particles in the NT. Although its relation with sentence structure is remote or tenuous in some contexts, the particle often has a causal role between sentences ('for', 'because') or may function as a simple conjunction ('and'), or as a conjunctive adverb ('then').[1] In our passage, it seems to furnish grammatical subordination between 1:15 and 1:16, and 1:17 and 1:18.[2] In 1:16 in particular, the particle can be understood either epexegetically, where it has an explanatory function for Paul's preceding statement in 1:15,[3] or argumentatively, where it has a causal co-ordinating function.[4] The latter view may be preferable because in 1:16a γάρ most probably expresses the reason for Paul's eagerness or readiness (πρόθυμον) to proclaim the gospel to his readers in Rome (1:15), and in verses 16b, 17a and 18 the particle seems to express three different but exegetically and theologically interrelated reasons for Paul's confidence in the εὐαγγέλιον.

The role of γάρ in 1:18 is not immediately clear, however, as it can be taken at least in four ways: 1) as a transitional particle with no logical function;[5] 2) as a connecting element with verse 16 and a further explanation why Paul claims that he is not ashamed of the gospel;[6] 3) as

---

[1] See Blass, F. and Debrunner, A., *A Greek Grammar of the New Testament and Other Early Christian Literature* (trans. and rev. R. W. Funk) (BDF), 235-236; Louw-Nida, *Greek–English Lexicon of the New Testament Based on Semantic Domains.*

[2] P. Achtemeier, 'Righteousness in the New Testament', *IDB* IV, 91-96. For Dunn, on the other hand, γάρ denotes lighter connections than Achtemeier has credited. Dunn, *Romans 1-8*, 38.

[3] See, for example, Fitzmyer, *Romans*, 3 ('Now I am not ashamed of the gospel'); Stuhlmacher, *Letter*, 25 ('I am, namely, not ashamed of the gospel').

[4] See Käsemann, *Commentary*, 21; Cranfield, *Romans 1-8*, 74. In Hellenistic Greek, the particle can have different functions such as *argumentative* (where it introduces the reason for what precedes), *epexegetical* (where it is used to begin a promised narration) and *strengthening* (where it is used along with τίς, τί etc. in questions or with εἰ, πῶς etc. in wishes). For examples of this, see Liddell and Scott, *Lexicon*; BDF, *Greek*, 236.

[5] Lietzmann, *Einführung in die Textgeschichte des Paulusbriefe an die Römer*, 31.

[6] E.g. Barth, *Commentary*, 25f.

explanatory of verse 17 and an indicator of the relation of the whole section of 1:18-3:20;[7] or 4) as an adversative particle signalling the contrast
between δικαιοσύνη θεοῦ and ὀργὴ θεοῦ, and between that which is under
δικαιοσύνη θεοῦ ἐκ πίστεως εἰς πίστιν and the human condition as expressed in 1:18-3:20.[8] Detailed discussion of these options will fall outside
the scope of our purpose in this section. It suffices to say here that γάρ in
1:18 seems to play a significant role as a logical and/or causal connector of
Paul's statement in 1:17 with what is expressed in 1:18ff. Thematic
comparisons and contrasts that exhibit a logical transition from one line of
thought to another by means of γάρ, something not marked in Nestle-
Aland's edition, appear to confirm this. That obviously means that the
sentence in 1:18 is part of what precedes it. From a text-critical perspective, of course, such a view may even be considered as 'anachronistic since
the text was to be read aloud and the original handwriting did not set the
paragraphs off from one another'.[9] Be that as it may, the two statements in
1:17-18, centring on δικαιοσύνη θεοῦ and ὀργὴ θεοῦ, stand in parallelism
and are spelled out in reverse order, i.e. the revelation of δικαιοσύνη θεοῦ
is dealt with in 3:21ff, and the revelation of ὀργὴ θεοῦ in 1:18-3:20.[10]
Along this line, it can be said that while Paul's declaration regarding the
revelation of δικαιοσύνη θεοῦ ἐκ πίστεως εἰς πίστιν – corroborated by the
prophetic text from Habakkuk – is one justifying and affirming reason for
his claim in 1:16, the revelation of ὀργὴ θεοῦ ἐπὶ πᾶσαν ἀσέβειαν καὶ
ἀδικίαν ἀνθρώπων is another reason of a different kind for the same
claim.[11] Thus, Rom 1:16-18 may be structured as follows:

---

[7] Sanday and Headlam, *Epistle*, 40; Cranfield, *Romans 1-8*, 108.

[8] Dodd, *Epistle*, 18; Dunn, *Romans 1-8*, 54; Wilckens, *Brief I*, 101; Fitzmyer, *Romans*, 257, 277.

[9] Dahl, *Studies in Paul: Theology for the Early Christian Mission*, 79. Dahl, in the
same page, goes on to say '[i]n many manuscripts not even the words are separated from
one another. As the text was to be heard, rather than seen, the transition from one unit of
thought to another had to be indicated by other means than by typographical or scribal
arrangement...Greek prose style was in general closer to oral speech than are modern
literary products. In order to follow the flow of thought in the Pauline letter, one should
pay more attention to thematic statements, gradual transitions, and "ring composition"
than to the division into chapter and verse or to headings and systematised outlines supplied by modern translations and commentaries.'

[10] So Dahl (*Studies*, 79f, 135f, 161, 169, 171, 177), but in his attempt to demonstrate
the logical, albeit antithetical, connection between 1:17 and 1:18, he brings into 1:17-18
the 'faith' versus 'law' theology which Paul does not seem to hint at. See also Bassler
(*Divine Impartiality: Paul and a Theological Axiom*, 203-204 [Appendix F]) who also
does not see Paul developing the 'faith' versus 'law' idea here in the same way as he
does in the context of Gal 3:11.

[11] See also Bockmuehl, *Revelation and Mystery in Ancient Judaism and Pauline
Christianity*, 138-139; Schreiner, *Romans*, 77-78.

Οὐ γὰρ ἐπαισχύνομαι τὸ εὐαγγέλιον
1) δύναμις γὰρ θεοῦ ἐστιν εἰς σωτηρίαν κτλ
2) δικαιοσύνη γὰρ θεοῦ ἐν αὐτῷ ἀποκαλύπτεται κτλ
3) ἀποκαλύπτεται γὰρ ὀργὴ θεοῦ ἀπ' οὐρανοῦ κτλ

We do not need to discuss how each proposition explains Paul's lack of shame in the gospel here, as that will be part of our subsequent considerations which now start with an exegesis of Rom 1:16 in general and issues relating to δύναμις θεοῦ in particular.

3. Δύναμις Θεοῦ: Linguistic Image for Christ?

It is important to point out from the outset that δύναμις θεοῦ as a linguistic image for Christ is not an idea that can be detected immediately as the text of Rom 1:16 stands. Indeed, at first glance, the grammatical position of δύναμις θεοῦ in relation to εὐαγγέλιον and the fact that Christ is not mentioned in Rom 1:16-17 seem to rule out any possibility of the genitival substantive being some kind of short hand for Christ. However, dealing with the question as to whether δύναμις θεοῦ should be taken as subject or predicate and determining the nature of its relationship with the gospel might facilitate a christological construal of δύναμις θεοῦ.

3.1. Δύναμις Θεοῦ: Subject or Predicate?

The reason why εὐαγγέλιον is universally taken as the unexpressed subject of 1:16b and δύναμις θεοῦ[12] is placed in the predicate very probably is twofold. First, grammatically the subject may be implied in the ending of ἐστιν and that implied subject in the form of the English 'it' is most naturally understood as referring back to εὐαγγέλιον, which is predicated by ἐστιν/δύναμις θεοῦ/εἰς σωτηρίαν. Secondly, Paul's expressions in 1 Cor 1:18, which does not betray much grammatical or conceptual difference from Rom 1:16 and where ὁ λόγος τοῦ σταυροῦ *is* δύναμις θεοῦ,[13] appear

---

[12] In Romans, δύναμις is a term employed to describe the manner in which Jesus was appointed as the Son of God (1:4), and to designate certain cosmic 'forces' (8:38), and to characterise signs and wonders (δυνάμει σημείων καὶ τεράτων, 15:19) and the working of the Spirit (δυνάμει πνεύματος ἁγίου or [θεοῦ], 15:13, 19). Paul's association of δύναμις with πνεύματος [θεοῦ] is somewhat peculiar. But the power of the 'spirit of God' can be equated with the power of God on the grounds that the 'spirit of God' denotes the extension of God's own personality or identity manifested in his action. For a general understanding of δύναμις in the NT, see Lk 1:51; Acts 1:8; 2:22; 1 Cor 14:11; 2 Cor 1:8. See also Gräbe (*The Power of God in Paul's Letters*, 177f) for detailed exegetical discussion.

[13] Thiselton (*The First Epistle to the Corinthians*, 172; cf. 153-158) defines δύναμις

to influence the way Rom 1:16 is understood.[14] Both views are reasonable.
It is obvious that the Corinthian passage rhetorically equates the
proclamation of the cross with both μωρία and δύναμις θεοῦ and, in so
doing, expresses the paradoxical nature of the message of the gospel, for
those on their way to ruin it represents 'human folly' and for those on their
way to salvation 'divine power'.[15] One question should, however, be
asked: while ὁ λόγος τοῦ σταυροῦ is an unambiguous subject and δύναμις
θεοῦ the predicate in the Corinthians passage, is that also necessarily the
case with εὐαγγέλιον vis-à-vis δύναμις θεοῦ in the Romans passage?

It should be noted here that the traditional reading of Rom 1:16, where
εὐαγγέλιον is the unexpressed subject of 1:16b and δύναμις θεοῦ the predicate (and where the antecedent of ἐν αὐτῷ in 1:17a is also commonly understood to be τὸ εὐαγγέλιον in 1:16a), potentially threatens the validity of
the Käsemannian reading of δικαιοσύνη θεοῦ as the saving power of God.
For to suggest that 'the saving power of God' (δικαιοσύνη θεοῦ) is
revealed 'in the power of God' (the gospel) appears to be a tautology and
even nonsensical. Williams, Byrne and Schreiner have pointed out this
problem. Williams, for example, argues: 'It is not the "righteousness of
God" which he [Paul] describes as God's power; rather, the *gospel* is
God's *dynamis* for salvation because the righteousness of God is being revealed through it.'[16] But while reading εὐαγγέλιον as the implied subject
of 1:16b and δύναμις θεοῦ as predicate is not grammatically impossible,
such a reading should not be regarded as the only available option that is
suitable to the context. For we can also take the genitival substantive as the
subject of the second part of 1:16, much as δικαιοσύνη θεοῦ is the subject
of 1:17a.[17] When this reading is adopted, εἰς σωτηρίαν,[18] one of the three

---

θεοῦ in 1 Cor 1:18 as 'the effective operation of a power-in-weakness which operates
under chosen and accepted constraints, namely, those of the cross, reflected in the cruci-
form lifestyle of apostolic hardships in 4:9-13'.

[14] See, for example, Sanday and Headlam, *Epistle*, 22; Nygren, *Commentary*, 65;
Käsemann, *Commentary*, 21; Stuhlmacher, *Letter*, 28; Dunn, *Romans 1-8*, 39; Moo,
Epistle, 65-66; Cranfield, *Romans 1-8*, 87; Lohse, *Der Brief*, 77; Schreiner, *Romans*, 60;
Gräbe, *Power*, 176-182.

[15] See, for example, Cranfield, *Romans 1-8*, 87; Fitzmyer, *Romans*, 255. For a recent
treatment of 1 Cor 1:18, see Thiselton, *Epistle*, 153-159. This does not necessarily merit
a distinction between the gospel and the proclamation of the cross, because both, as
Thiselton (*Epistle*, 174) argues, are shorthand instances of συνεκδοχή (a technical term in
Greco-Roman rhetoric for an expression that succinctly describes and summarises the
whole) '*for the whole story of God's purposes which lead up to the cross and follow it*'
(italics his).

[16] Williams, '"Righteousness"', 258. Like Williams, Byrne (*Romans*, 60) and
Schreiner (*Romans*, 59; see also 60-61) also argue that εὐαγγέλιον is δύναμις θεοῦ in
which 'the righteousness of God is revealed'.

[17] It is interesting that in the Amharic (the *lingua franca* of Ethiopia) translation, such

uses in Romans (10:1, 10), serves as a predicate. This reading may not be grammatically peculiar, because in the NT in general and in the Pauline letters in particular εἰς with the accusative is sometimes used for the predicate accusative as for the predicate nominative (e.g. Rom 4:3; 9:8; cf. *1 Macc* 2:52).[19] Also, Paul himself employs the prepositional accusative εἰς σωτηρίαν (along with ὑπὲρ αὐτῶν) in Rom 10:1 with the predicate role (ἡ μὲν εὐδοκία τῆς καρδίας καὶ ἡ δέησις πρὸς τὸν θεὸν ὑπὲρ αὐτῶν εἰς σωτηρίαν).

To read δύναμις θεοῦ as the subject of 1:16b may not necessarily invalidate the universally accepted reading that occurs where the phrase is taken as predicate, but it has advantages for the subjective genitive reading of δικαιοσύνη θεοῦ, not least because such an interpretation not only takes δύναμις θεοῦ in close juxtaposition with δικαιοσύνη θεοῦ, but also it assumes shared meaning and significance for both constructions. The new reading also avoids the tautology that, as rightly pointed out by Williams, Byrne and Schreiner (see above), is created when the syntax that takes ἐν αὐτῷ in 1:17a as referring back to 'the gospel' is combined with the Käsemannian reading of δικαιοσύνη θεοῦ (this would obviously lead to the absurd statement that 'the saving activity/power of God [i.e. δικαιοσύνη θεοῦ] is revealed in the power of God [i.e. the gospel]'). But the relationship between the power of God and the gospel in Rom 1:16-17 should be explained in the light of the new reading.

3.2. Δύναμις Θεοῦ *and the Gospel*

However one defines εὐαγγέλιον, the difference between taking δύναμις θεοῦ as subject and taking it as predicate is that in the former the power of God as the content of the proclaimed gospel brings about salvation while in the latter the proclaimed gospel itself is the power of God that brings about salvation.[20] This leaves us with the question as to how εὐαγγέλιον

---

a reading is carefully maintained: *b^ewengel alafrmina; asqedimo l^eaihoodawee degmom l^egreek sew – y^eegziabiher hyle l^emadan newina* (lit. 'I am not ashamed of the gospel. For the power of God is for salvation to all who believe – first for the Jew, then for the Greek.')

[18] The omission of εἰς σωτηρίαν in Codex Boernerianus (G) is probably rightly rejected by Fitzmyer (*Romans*, 256).

[19] BDF, *Greek*, 80, 86.

[20] Käsemann (*Commentary*, 22) defines εὐαγγέλιον as both 'the epiphany of God's eschatological power' and his 'declaration of salvation to the world'. Fitzmyer (*Romans*, 253f) defines it as the 'powerful source of salvation' where the emphasis is on the 'word as a force or power unleashed in human history'. See also Ziesler (*Pauline Christianity*, 83; *Paul's Letter to the Romans*, 68f) who suggests that the gospel is the power of God for salvation and salvation is 'liberation from other powers to enable life to be henceforth under the power of God'. Mason ('"For I am not ashamed of the gospel": The Gospel

would function in relation to δύναμις θεοῦ if the latter is understood as the subject of the second part of 1:16. The obvious answer would be that δύναμις θεοῦ ἐστιν εἰς σωτηρίαν in Rom 1:16b independently forms a justification for Paul's rhetorical statement in 1:16a, where δύναμις θεοῦ is presented as the content of εὐαγγέλιον in the same way as δικαιοσύνη θεοῦ is presented in 1:17a.[21] In other words, the relationship between εὐαγγέλιον and δύναμις θεοῦ in 1:16 can be understood as paralleling the relationship between εὐαγγέλιον and δικαιοσύνη θεοῦ in 1:17. But how we understand ἐν αὐτῷ is important here.[22]

Although it is syntactically possible to understand the antecedent of αὐτῷ as referring back to either παντὶ τῷ πιστεύοντι or τὸ εὐαγγέλιον,[23] perhaps the most probable, if not incontrovertible, antecedent of the dative pronoun is τὸ εὐαγγέλιον (neuter) in 1:16a.[24] In the light of 1:9, τὸ εὐαγγέλιον in 1:16 is τὸ εὐαγγέλιον τοῦ υἱοῦ αὐτοῦ [θεοῦ], so for a puzzled reader, Paul would most probably rephrase 1:17a as follows: δικαιοσύνη γὰρ θεοῦ ἐν τῷ εὐαγγελίῳ τοῦ υἱοῦ τοῦ θεοῦ/τοῦ Χριστοῦ (cf. 1:9; 15:19) ἀποκαλύπτεται ἐκ πίστεως εἰς πίστιν. Syntactically, the phrase ἐν αὐτῷ can be taken with either ἀποκαλύπτεται (δικαιοσύνη θεοῦ is revealed in the 'gospel')[25] or δικαιοσύνη θεοῦ (δικαιοσύνη θεοῦ in the

---

and the First Readers of Romans', 1ff) attempts to shy away from *a priori* interpretations of the term εὐαγγέλιον but appears to suggest implicitly that it has to do with 'the programmatic statement [in 1:3-4] that sets the pace for what will follow from v. 16' (p. 281).

[21] Gräbe (*Power*, 180-182), on the other hand, takes δικαιοσύνη θεοῦ as the content of δύναμις θεοῦ.

[22] The preposition ἐν can be locative ('in'), distributional ('within', 'among'), spherical ('in', 'in the realm of'), temporal ('in', 'on'), or instrumental ('by', 'through', 'with'). The locative sense of the preposition has been a popular and perhaps plausible choice. See also Porter, *Idioms of the Greek New Testament*, 156-159. Leenhardt, *Epistle*, 42; Cranfield, *Romans 1-8*, 87; Schlier, *Der Römerbrief*, 43-44; Wilckens, *Brief I*, 76; Dunn, *Romans 1-8*, 43; Fitzmyer, *Romans*, 257; Schreiner, *Romans*, 59.

[23] The former option is grammatically impossible if αὐτῷ is taken as a dative neuter pronoun, which does not agree with παντί (dative masculine adjective); but if it is read as a dative masculine pronoun, it is possible. This means that the antecedent is a believer. Such an option is difficult to sustain because it makes the believer the revealer of the righteousness of God, which does not agree with Rom 3:21-22. Alternatively, αὐτῷ can be taken as signifying Jesus. In the face of it, this suggestion makes sense because to speak of Jesus as the means through which or the domain within which δικαιοσύνη θεοῦ is revealed can be consistent with Paul's thinking in 3:21f and his ἐν Χριστῷ language. But since Jesus is not clearly used in Rom 1:16-17, this argument cannot be sustained.

[24] See, for example, Leenhardt, *Epistle*, 49-55; Nygren, *Commentary*, 76; Cranfield, *Romans 1-8*, 91; Schlier, *Römerbrief*, 44; Wilckens, *Brief I*, 86; Dunn, *Romans 1-8*, 43-48; Fitzmyer, *Romans*, 257; Schreiner, *Romans*, 62.

[25] Cf. Schlier, *Römerbrief*, 34, 42-43; Käsemann, *Commentary*, 21; Dunn, *Romans 1-8*, 37; Schreiner, *Romans*, 59.

'gospel' is revealed). In the former, the prepositional dative is understood adverbially ('by it [the gospel]'), where it functions as the agent or instrument of ἀποκαλύπτεται and affords the gospel a decisive role in the process of the revelation of δικαιοσύνη θεοῦ,[26] whereas in the latter, the phrase is understood adjectivally ('in it'), which should not necessarily mean that the gospel is something within whose domain δικαιοσύνη θεοῦ is located, but rather the proclaimed message whose main subject matter is δικαιοσύνη θεοῦ. Both readings are grammatically possible,[27] but which is suitable is dependent partly on whether δικαιοσύνη θεοῦ is interpreted as a genitive of origin or a subjective genitive.

Clearly, the adverbial reading of ἐν αὐτῷ suits the former,[28] while the adjectival reading of the preposition suits the latter. When δικαιοσύνη θεοῦ is understood as a genitive of origin, the σωτηρία that is achieved by δύναμις θεοῦ for the believing individual in 1:16 is the same thing as δικαιοσύνη θεοῦ, human righteousness. However, as will be argued later, while Paul would equate 'righteousness' with 'salvation' in Romans, nowhere does he equate God's righteousness with human salvation. To equate δικαιοσύνη θεοῦ with σωτηρία in our context is tantamount to saying that the righteousness of God is brought about by the power of God, which appears to be a doubtful proposition, to say the least. But one could still take ἐν αὐτῷ instrumentally whereby ἐκ πίστεως refers to human faith from which (taking ἐκ with the sense of origin) δικαιοσύνη θεοῦ is revealed. In other words, the individual, through faith as her distinguishing mark, becomes the displayer of δικαιοσύνη θεοῦ in her relation to fellow humans. This certainly is a possible reading. Its problem, however, is that δικαιοσύνη θεοῦ must be understood as the gift of righteousness to a hu-

---

[26] So Campbell ('Romans 1:17', 272-277). Campbell rejects what he calls the 'anthropocentric' reading where the prepositional phrase is taken adjectivally, in which case the 'righteousness of God' is *within* the gospel and the revelation takes place as the gospel offers salvation, which is mediated by faith, an act of apprehension.

[27] We will encounter a similar sort of ambiguity regarding the question as to whether δικαιοσύνη θεοῦ should be modified by ἐκ πίστεως or ἀποκαλύπτεται. This grammatical phenomenon is known as *structural ambiguity*, which is briefly discussed by Palmer ('How Do We Know a Phrase is a Phrase? A Plea for Procedural Clarity in the Application of Linguistics to Biblical Greek', in Porter and Carson [eds.], *Biblical Greek and Linguistics: Open Questions in Current Linguistic Research*, 152-186, 167-185). Palmer's example from Rom 8:2 (ὁ γὰρ νόμος τοῦ πνεύματος τῆς ζωῆς ἐν Χριστῷ Ἰησοῦ κτλ) where ἐν Χριστῷ Ἰησοῦ can be taken either adjectivally or adverbially, is instructive, albeit that the 'phrase levels' (in Palmer's words) in Rom 8:2 are longer than in Rom 1:17a.

[28] Cranfield (*Romans 1-8*, 91-92, 97-99) and Fitzmyer (*Romans*, 257; *According to Paul*, 109) differ on the interpretation of δικαιοσύνη θεοῦ, the former adopting a genitive of origin reading while the latter a subjective genitive, but the comments both make in relation to ἐν αὐτῷ appear to be akin to an adverbial reading of the prepositional phrase.

man person. Although δικαιοσύνη is portrayed as a gift in 5:17, there is hardly anything in the context of Rom 1:17 that suggests that δικαιοσύνη θεοῦ is proffered to a person as a status or ethical quality so as to become her possession.

When δικαιοσύνη θεοῦ is understood as subjective genitive with a power sense, however, ἐν αὐτῷ can appropriately modify the subject so that δικαιοσύνη θεοῦ as God's power in creative and salvific activity can be regarded as the core of Paul's unabashed proclamation of the gospel to the Jews, Greeks and barbarians.[29] Given δύναμις θεοῦ probably has a denotative equivalence to δικαιοσύνη θεοῦ, this syntax further supports the view that δύναμις θεοῦ is the content of εὐαγγέλιον in 1:16b. If valid, all this means is that when Paul proclaims the gospel in Rome, as the term εὐαγγέλιον in 1:16 most probably echoes εὐαγγελίζομαι in 1:15, he proclaims about the power of God, which is *the subject matter* of his gospel. We shall come back to this and related issues after examining how the argument that δύναμις θεοῦ is the content of the gospel contributes to a christological understanding of δύναμις θεοῦ.

3.3. Δύναμις Θεοῦ and Christ

Having pointed out a grammatical possibility that δύναμις θεοῦ can be taken as the subject of 1:16b and argued that the genitival substantive is a content of the gospel, we now ask how Paul would have understood the linguistic image δύναμις θεοῦ in relation to Christ. When we say that Paul presents δύναμις θεοῦ as the content of the gospel, we do not mean that the power of God resides in the proclaimed word *per se*. For to suggest such would undermine the idea that δύναμις θεοῦ as a power manifested in God's creative, forensic and salvific operations is embodied and expressed in Jesus,[30] who features prominently in the exordium. He is the Son of God, Christ and Lord (1:4; cf. 1 Cor 2:5; 6:14; 2 Cor 13:4; Phil 3:10). Paul's readers and many among the Gentiles have established allegiance to him (1:5-6). Paul thanks God through him (1:8) and Paul's brand of εὐαγγέλιον is unambiguously associated with him (1:9). Given that

---

[29] It is important to note here that Paul's confidence to proclaim this gospel in the *princeps urbium* may have derived from a combination of different factors: his belief that δικαιοσύνη θεοῦ is a continuing reality in the world (3:21-26; 10:3-4), the success in his mission to the Gentiles, what he knows about the early happenings amongst the followers of Jesus (cf. 1 Cor 15:1ff), his own experience of the apocalypse of the risen Jesus (cf. Gal 1:12, 16; 3:23-24), his understanding of the effects of Jesus' death and resurrection (1:2-4, 16-17; 3:21-26; 4:23-5:8), and his christologically undergirded eschatological perspective (5:9-11; 8:18-39).

[30] For extended discussions of the relationship between the gospel and Jesus, see Stuhlmacher, 'The Pauline Gospel', in Stuhlmacher (ed.), *The Gospel and the Gospels*, 149-172; Kim, *The Origin of Paul's Gospel*, 67-74.

εὐαγγέλιον for Paul is τὸ εὐαγγέλιον θεοῦ concerning 'his [God's] Son' (1:3), who is set with power (1:4) at the right hand of God (8:34) and whom God revealed 'in' or 'to' Paul (ἐν ἐμοί) in Damascus in order that he may proclaim Jesus to the Gentiles (Gal 1:16; cf. 1 Cor 9:1; 15:8), and, therefore, τὸ εὐαγγέλιον τοῦ υἱοῦ [θεοῦ] (1:9), one may even say that Jesus could have been in Paul's mind when he formulated Rom 1:16 as well.[31] That is to say, Paul might be thinking of δύναμις θεοῦ as something that is embodied in Jesus.[32]

In the exordium, between setting out his credentials (1:1-2) and expressing what is globally known about the πίστις of his readers, his constant desire and indeed attempts to come to Rome with his rather puzzling intention to proclaim τὸ εὐαγγέλιον to the recipients of his letter whose πίστις is proclaimed in the whole world (1:8-15; cf. 15:22-24),[33] Paul puts forward his christological views in 1:3-7, where he uses the phrase τοῦ ὁρισθέντος υἱοῦ θεοῦ ἐν δυνάμει (1:4). Grammatically, one could allow the prepositional phrase ἐν δυνάμει to modify the verb adverbially, in which case τοῦ ὁρισθέντος υἱοῦ θεοῦ ἐν δυνάμει could mean that Jesus is decisively set as Son of God, i.e. by a mighty act; but if the phrase is associated with the title adjectivally, it could mean that Jesus is set as Son of God with power, i.e. Jesus is set as a source of power or enthroned with power in the heavenly sphere. Both readings are possible, but the latter is more congenial to the context because Paul refers to Jesus as Lord and Christ and as someone who gives grace and apostleship, both of which imply possession of power (1:4, 5, 7).[34] As far as the meaning of ἐν δυνάμει is concerned, the prepositional phrase could be understood as describing the idea of God endowing Jesus 'with a source of life to energize human

---

[31] It is most likely that this contextual hint led the copiers of the Majority Texts, the Athos and the Leningrad (copied from Codex Claromontanus [6th century CE]) manuscripts to insert τοῦ Χριστοῦ after τὸ εὐαγγέλιον in 1:16 in order to understand the gospel as the gospel *of Christ* (cf. 15:19). Despite the apparent slenderness of the authority of these manuscripts, they reflect a view that is consistent with what can be noticed from the context, namely that the gospel's content is Christ.

[32] Paul occasionally refers to the 'power of the holy spirit' or the 'power of the spirit of God' in Romans (15:13, 19) and uses δύναμις and πνεῦμα as hendiadys (1 Cor 2:4; 1 Thess 1:5 [πνεύματι ἁγίῳ]). This appears to have a bearing on his use of δύναμις θεοῦ in Romans (1:16) and 1 Corinthians (2:5 and 6:14). It may, therefore, be said that δύναμις θεοῦ equals πνεῦμα θεοῦ (see also Käsemann, *Commentary*, 22; Gräbe, *Power*, 65-66). This does not negate the supreme centrality of Christ, as also recognised by Cranfield (*Romans*, 89) and Fitzmyer (*Romans*, 256).

[33] Does Paul want to replace the πίστις of his Roman audience with another kind of πίστις? If he does not, why does he want to proclaim to them the gospel since the whole point of his proclamation concerns winning others for Christ through allegiance to his movement? See also Cranfield, *Romans 1-8*, 86.

[34] See Käsemann, *Commentary*, 12; Barrett, *Epistle*, 20; Cranfield, *Romans 1-8*, 62.

beings who turn to him as the risen Lord',[35] or depicting Jesus' life as a
messianic king in the age that is characterised by power as opposed to
weakness,[36] or partly expressing Jesus' 'new position as the Son *in power*,
appointed to rule on God's behalf'.[37] Whatever the case, ἐν δυνάμει
signals the power that the Son of God is afforded to exercise his
eschatological role beyond resurrection. But for Paul, the present identity
of Jesus cannot be divorced from his identity as the crucified redeemer.
Nor can it be divorced from the power he possesses as the glorified Son of
God with power and authority (Rom 3:25; 6:1-7; 8:34; cf. Gal 2:20; 6:14).

That probably is why he refers to Jesus as δύναμις θεοῦ in 1 Cor 1:24
(αὐτοῖς δὲ τοῖς κλητοῖς, 'Ιουδαίοις τε καὶ "Ελλησιν, Χριστὸν θεοῦ
δύναμιν καὶ θεοῦ σοφίαν[38]). This passage shares similarities with Rom
1:16: the former has 'Ιουδαίοις τε καὶ "Ελλησιν while the latter has
'Ιουδαίῳ τε πρῶτον καὶ "Ελληνι; the former has θεοῦ δύναμιν while the
latter has δύναμις θεοῦ; and generally in the preceding verses of the former
the form and content of Paul's proclamation is prominent, while that is
also the case in the context of the latter, as εὐαγγέλιον θεοῦ in 1:1,
εὐαγγελίῳ τοῦ υἱοῦ αὐτοῦ in 1:9, εὐαγγελίσασθαι in 1:15 and εὐαγγέλιον
in 1:16a clearly demonstrate.[39] Admittedly, Paul's rhetoric in referring to
Jesus as δύναμις θεοῦ is unusual, but he once uses δύναμις in association
with the genitives κυριοῦ ἡμῶν 'Ιησοῦ (1 Cor 5:4) to say that 'the power
of our Lord Jesus' is something that can be present among his Corinthian
converts when they gather to pronounce judgement upon the man with il-
licit behaviour. It seems that Paul's understanding of Jesus as the embodiment of God's own power in action or, as Thiselton suggests, someone *in*,
through or *as* whom God's power becomes actualised,[40] probably leads
him to speak of δύναμις κυριοῦ ἡμῶν 'Ιησοῦ and refer to Jesus as δύναμις
θεοῦ.[41] Paul strengthens this claim in 1 Cor 1:30 by referring to Christ as

---

[35] Fitzmyer, *Romans*, 235.

[36] Schreiner, *Romans*, 44.

[37] Hurtado, 'Divine', 228.

[38] P[46] and Clement of Alexandria have Χριστὸς θεοῦ δύναμις καὶ θεοῦ σοφία instead
of Χριστὸν θεοῦ δύναμιν καὶ θεοῦ σοφίαν.

[39] These striking similarities have, unusually for him, not been noted by Thiselton
(*Epistle*, 170-172).

[40] Thiselton, *Epistle*, 172.

[41] See Käsemann (*Commentary*, 27), who takes the genitive construction in δύναμις
θεοῦ in parallel with δικαιοσύνη θεοῦ and ὀργὴ θεοῦ in 1:17-18 and gives all three constructions a subjective genitive reading, the power *of God*. See also Gräbe (*Power*, 176-
177), who, like many others, assumes a subjective genitive construction for δύναμις θεοῦ
but does not follow Käsemann.

someone who became σοφία ἀπὸ θεοῦ and δικαιοσύνη [ἀπὸ θεοῦ] 'for us'.[42]

Rom 1:16 does not make it unambiguously clear that Paul describes δύναμις θεοῦ that is directed towards the salvation of Jew and Greek alike as something embodied in Jesus in the same way as he does in 1 Corinthians.[43] But when the use of the phrase in the Romans passage is interpreted in the light of the Corinthians passage, Rom 1:16b seems to contain the idea that salvation is dependent on who Jesus is and what he does as the personification of God's power. For Paul, there is no distinction between Jesus the crucified redeemer and Jesus the risen and glorified Lord and Christ. Paul seems to portray Jesus as someone who represents and embodies God's creative and salvific power in both crucifixion and resurrection states.

4. Revelation of Δικαιοσύνη Θεοῦ

The validity of a christologically orientated interpretation of Rom 1:16b in part depends on whether or not it coheres with how we understand Paul's claim concerning the revelation of δικαιοσύνη θεοῦ in 1:17a. The cumulative understanding of both in turn affects the way we read the double prepositional phrase ἐκ πίστεως εἰς πίστιν and the Habakkuk citation, which we will consider in the following chapters. As indicated above, we will start our discussion here by analysing Francis Watson's views on Paul's declarations in Rom 1:17a. Although we will engage with other scholarly views in the course of our discussion, we have chosen Watson as our dialogue partner mainly because his work is the most recent and representative of the traditional reading, in which Rom 1:17a is explicated in

---

[42] It is to be noted here that Paul's terminology in Rom 1:19-20 parallels the terminology of *Wis Sol* 7:25-26, where δύναμις τοῦ Θεοῦ is paralleled with παντοκράτορος δόξης, φωτὸς ἀϊδίου and ἐνέργεια Θεοῦ. Whether Paul is echoing the *Wisdom* text or simply reflecting an existing linguistic domain cannot be determined with complete certainty, but terminological and conceptual similarities between Rom 1:19-20 and the *Wisdom* text cited above were probably not accidental. Dunn (*Romans 1-8*, 56-57) is right in saying that '[t]he parallel between *Wis* 12-15 and [Rom 1:19-32] is too close to be accidental', although he does not refer to *Wis* 7:25f (but see Cranfield, *Romans 1-8*, 115). For the author of *Wisdom*, σοφία is 'a breath' of δύναμις τοῦ Θεοῦ, 'the fashioner of all things' (7:21-22) and 'the cause of all things' (8:5). In other words, σοφία is an extension and/or expression of δύναμις τοῦ Θεοῦ that causes creation and ensures its order. Like the author of *Wisdom*, we would suggest, Paul in Romans seems to understand δύναμις [θεοῦ] in terms of God's creative activity embodied in Jesus, albeit without making reference to σοφία.

[43] See also Dunn, *Theology*, 177-179.

terms of the revelation of righteousness from or by faith. In this reading, δικαιοσύνη θεοῦ is understood to be the same as both salvation (Rom 1:16b) and the righteousness of the person of the Habakkuk citation (Rom 1:17b). Since the Reformation, such a reading has been seen as natural for Rom 1:17a. Even those who understand Rom 1:17b christologically have not asked whether Rom 1:17a as a whole can be interpreted christologically. We wish to ask precisely that question in this section. But we do that through examining critically the factors that constitute the anthropological reading. We shall identify those factors after analysing Watson's arguments, to which we now turn.

4.1. Francis Watson on Rom 1:17a

Watson, in his recent work *Paul and the Hermeneutics of Faith*, discusses issues in Rom 1:17 and related passages with the main aim of presenting Paul's language of righteousness and faith as the language of scriptural interpretation that arises out of the prior prophetic testimony. Scriptural interpretation, for Watson, is 'constitutive' of the doctrine of 'justification' or 'righteousness by faith' rather than being a secondary addition to the latter.[44] So 'Paul's proclamation of the righteousness of God in Romans 1:17a and 3:21-31 is nothing more nor less than commentary on [Habakkuk 2:4].'[45] Within this framework, several things can be outlined.

First, in Rom 1:17, the Habakkuk citation generates its antecedent, i.e. δικαιοσύνη θεοῦ ἐν αὐτῷ κτλ, which in turn amplifies the prophetic text as an expository gloss.[46] Since the citation is connected with its antecedent by the conventional formula καθὼς γέγραπται, the citation and its antecedent should be understood as interdependent expressions. One of the three arguments Watson outlines is particularly relevant here.[47] He contends that the 'standard' formula introduced by 'as' implies a different relationship between the citation and its context from the 'alternative' formula, which introduces a text as 'a spoken utterance'. For one thing, while the latter is integral to the discourse to the extent that the discourse would be incoherent without it (e.g. Rom 4:3, 6-8, 9, 18, 22, 23),[48] the former

---

[44] Watson, *Paul and the Hermeneutics of Faith*, 43, 53.

[45] Watson, *Paul*, 42.

[46] Watson, *Paul*, 43.

[47] The other two arguments are as follows. First, καθὼς γέγραπται as a standard formula refers to the scripture as a whole. So the words of Hab 2:4 in Rom 1:17b are attributed to scripture as a whole, which speaks in these words (pp 44-45). Second, 'the standard introductory formula emphasizes the written character of the text cited, whereas the alternative formulae normally introduce a text as a spoken utterance – whether the speaker in question is a prophet, God or scripture itself' (p 45).

[48] Watson, *Paul*, 45.

'implies a correspondence between citation and antecedent that entails a degree of repetition, and so, at the level of discourse, of redundancy'.[49] This means that in Rom 1:17, καθὼς γέγραπται plays a role of increasing the argumentative and rhetorical force of Hab 2:4, which, though in different words, repeats Paul's proclamation made up of Paul's own words in the antecedent.

In connection with this, second, Watson argues that there is a harmony between the role of Paul's gospel in Rom 1:17a and that of the prophetic assertion in 1:17b. That is to say, both the gospel and the scripture disclose the righteousness that is by faith.[50] Here the introductory formula καθὼς γέγραπται is taken as a functional equivalent of ἐν αὐτῷ ἀποκαλύπτεται in 1:17a. Watson argues that the 'revelation that occurs *viva voce* in the proclamation of the apostle is at one with the revelation that occurs through the prophetic writing.'[51] One could understand δικαιοσύνη θεοῦ ἐν αὐτῷ κτλ as speaking of a revelation that occurs by faith and for faith only if there was no citation that speaks about the one who is righteous by faith. 'But if the citation speaks of the one who is righteous by faith, the interpretative gloss must also speak of righteousness by faith, rather than revelation by faith'.[52]

Third, Watson further points out that Paul's assertion of God's righteousness revealed ἐκ πίστεως εἰς πίστιν is not only dependent on the Habakkuk citation, but equally interprets that passage into the present situation, as is also the case, for example, in Rom 9:32-33.[53] So, in Watson's view, in the antecedent Paul paraphrases Hab 2:4b as follows: '*The one who is righteous* (that is, with a *righteousness* of God, revealed in the gospel) *by faith* (since the righteousness is received *by faith* and intended for faith) *will live*.'[54] On the basis that δικαιοσύνη θεοῦ cannot be understood in abstraction from the human figure of ὁ δίκαιος, Watson argues: 'Paul's point is surely that the righteousness of Habakkuk's "righteous person" is a righteousness approved by God'.[55] Watson does not deny that the righteousness Paul speaks about is 'of God',[56] but he argues that Paul's concern here is 'to establish an initial correlation' of 'righteousness' and 'faith'. This is suggested by Hab 2:4, which speaks 'simply of a

---

[49] Watson, *Paul*, 46.
[50] Watson, *Paul*, 52-53.
[51] Watson, *Paul*, 53.
[52] Watson, *Paul*, 51.
[53] Watson, *Paul*, 46.
[54] Watson, *Paul*, 48.
[55] Watson, *Paul*, 48.
[56] Watson, *Paul*, 48-49.

righteous status and identifies the means (i.e. faith) by which this righteousness can be attained'.[57]

This seems to lead Watson to reject Käsemann's argument that Paul does not prove his point in 1:17a from Hab 2:4.[58] Watson also rejects Käsemann's interpretation of δικαιοσύνη θεοῦ with a power sense on the basis of scriptural and non-scriptural Second Temple Jewish texts. He argues that Paul's declaration in Rom 1:17a is not an allusion, for example, to Ps 97:2 [LXX]. Had that been the case, Paul would have written: '... for in it the righteousness of God is revealed by faith for faith – as it is written: "The Lord has made known his salvation [*to sōtērion autou*], before the Gentiles he has revealed his righteousness [*apekalupsen tēn dikaiosunēn autou*]."'[59] This enables Watson to understand salvation and righteousness as the outcome of God's power. The correlation, for Watson, is not between δικαιοσύνη θεοῦ and δύναμις θεοῦ, as Käsemann would have, but rather between δικαιοσύνη θεοῦ and σωτηρία, because in verse 16 δύναμις θεοῦ brings about the salvation of everyone who has 'faith' and in verse 17a the 'righteousness [of God]' is 'by faith'. If Paul is not saying this, Watson concludes, the scriptural text he selected to support his declaration is the wrong one.[60]

Watson is right in pointing out the interdependence between Rom 1:17a and 1:17b, because both halves of Rom 1:17 are informed by each other and ἐκ πίστεως in 1:17a in particular is informed by Paul's knowledge of Hab 2:4, part of which is cited in 1:17b. We would also agree with Watson's view on Rom 1:17a which takes ἐκ πίστεως as scriptural and εἰς πίστιν as a Pauline interpretative gloss. Further, we accept Watson's overall assumption that Pauline theology is *intertextual* in form. This would not be disputed, because intertextuality can be commonly noticed in other Jewish writings in the Second Temple period and scholars such as Hays have already recognised this. What is fresh and helpful in Watson's approach, though, is that he seeks to show us that when we talk about the intertextuality of Paul's theology we are talking about Paul's theology being constituted by its relation to an earlier corpus of texts that functions as communally normative scripture, of which Habakkuk is a part. It is within this general framework that Watson defends and advances his overarching case that Rom 1:17a, which is an explanatory gloss of Hab 2:4, is about *the revelation of righteousness from or by faith*. In order to sustain this case, Watson espouses several exegetical arguments. 1) He argues that ἀποκαλύπτεται ἐν αὐτῷ has the same meaning as καθὼς γέγραπται. This

---

[57] Watson, *Paul*, 49.
[58] Cf. Käsemann, *Commentary*, 31.
[59] Watson, *Paul*, 50.
[60] Watson, *Paul*, 50.

enables him to take both the proclaimed gospel and the scripture as reve-latory. 2) He assumes tacitly that ἐν αὐτῷ is adverbial and argues that the gospel is instrumental for the revelation of righteousness from or by faith. 3) He argues that the righteousness of God, like salvation, is brought about by the power of God. 4) He rejects the contribution of Ps 98:2 and some Second Temple Jewish material to our understanding of Rom 1:17a, as he also does the Käsemannian reading of the righteousness of God with a power sense.

However, as our discussion in section 4.3 will show, Watson's rejection of the Käsemannian interpretation is based on a wrong dismissal of the il-luminative contribution of OT and Jewish background texts to an interpre-tation of Rom 1:17a (and 3:21-22). We would argue that Paul's view of the revelation of the righteousness of God is probably informed by Pss 98 and 143. These two psalms, along with other Second Temple Jewish texts, can provide interpretative guidance when we attempt to understand the mean-ing of the phrase in question. Our analysis of the background material and other exegetical factors will lead us to concur with the Käsemannian interpretation and argue that the revelation of the righteousness of God means *the revelation of God's saving power and presence* to those who accept the gospel. We will then attempt to show how this meaning can be consistent with Paul's christology and contribute to a christologically orientated interpretation of Rom 1:17a. All this will be done in sub-section 4.3. Before that, however, in sub-section 4.2, we will critique Watson's central contention: Rom 1:17a is about the revelation of righteousness from or by faith. Our critique will be based mainly on the abovementioned exegetical components of Watson's argument. As component (4) will be examined in 4.3, our focus in 4.2 will be on (1), (2) and (3). As (2) and (3) significantly overlap, we shall deal with both components under the same question whether what Paul says is revealed in Rom 1:17a is *righteousness by faith* or *the righteousness of God*. This is precisely the question that will dominate what follows.

4.2. Revelation of Righteousness by Faith?

As indicated at the beginning of this book, our study is examining the possibility that Paul took 'the righteous one who lives through faith/fulness' in Romans 1:17b to refer to Christ – especially to Jesus' faithful submission to death on the cross – not as a generic reference to believers. Watson's argument, if upheld, would present a potentially fatal obstacle to such a reading. For him, Romans 1:17a asserts that the right-eousness of God (= righteousness) in question is one that 'is revealed' in the gospel; that is, (emphasising the present tense of ἀποκαλύπτεται) it is revealed precisely in or by the *proclamation* of the gospel, rather than in the Christ-event. When taken with the mutually interpretative 1:17b, this would mean that 'the righteous person' of Habakkuk 2:4 must be the one(s) of faith: the believer of 1:16. In what follows, we cross-examine the three components of Watson's argument identified above, to test the security of his case.

We start with the first component, where he relates ἀποκαλύπτεται ἐν αὐτῷ with καθὼς γέγραπται. This relation, as we noted above, results in the argument that while the gospel reveals to the hearer that righteousness is acquired by faith (Rom 1:17a), the scripture reveals that the 'righteous one' shall live by faith (1:17b). As Rom 1:17a and 1:17b express the same idea, the righteousness Paul talks about in Rom 1:17a is the righteousness of the person of the Habakkuk citation. In short, Habakkuk 2:4 as a prophetic text is as revelatory as the gospel is. But Watson's assertions raise significant questions. First, *is* the gospel revelation which Paul talks about really the same as that mediated by Habakkuk? Second, *is* it the case that the 'is revealed' (of 1.17a) points exclusively to a revelation of God's righteousness that occurs in the oral announcement of the gospel, *rather than* in the Christ-event itself? These are the questions which dominate the discussion in this subsection.

Rom 1:1-2, 3:21 and 16:25-26 appear to confirm that 'prophetic writings' can be understood to have revelatory function in as much as they enable the reader to understand about the content of Paul's proclamation. In Rom 16:25-26[61] in particular, not only does Paul seem to equate the gospel with 'the revelation of the mystery that was kept for long ages', he also appears to present the 'prophetic writings' as a means through which that mystery is made known.[62] It is then legitimate to argue, as Watson does,

---

[61] On the textual problem of Rom 16:1-26, see Murphy-O'Connor (*Paul: A Critical Life*, 324-328) who, as shall be argued later, rightly takes the section as an integral part of the letter.

[62] Two things seem to support this. First, when τε in verse 26 is taken as a conjunctive particle, γνωρισθέντος stands as explanatory of φανερωθέντος. Second, φανερόω ('reveal') can be understood as synonymous with γνωρίζω ('make known') (e.g. Rom 9:22-23). It is to be noted here that while some scholars take τε as a conjunctive particle (e.g. Barrett, *Epistle*, 286-287; Käsemann, *Commentary*, 421; Stuhlmacher, *Letter*, 256; Fitzmyer, *Romans*, 753), some do not (e.g. Wilckens, *Brief I*, 147; Dunn, *Romans 9-16*, 912, 915). The main result of reading τε as a conjunctive particle is that it separates φανερωθέντος δὲ νῦν from διὰ γραφῶν προφητικῶν, so that γνωρισθέντος with an elaborative force is linked with the latter. To this effect, Cranfield (*Romans 9-16*, 751; see also pp 811-812) translates v 26 as follows: '... but has now been manifested and, in accordance with the command of the eternal God, has been clarified through the scriptures for the purpose of bringing about obedience of faith among all the Gentiles'. This more or less agrees with the translation of NRSV: 'but is now disclosed, and through the prophetic writings is made known to all the Gentiles, according to the command of the eternal God, to bring about the obedience of faith... .' One further thing that needs to be

that by using καθὼς γέγραπται in Rom 1:17a as the formulaic transition between Rom 1:17a and 1:17b, Paul is presenting both the gospel and the scripture as revelatory. In order to claim that the gospel is revelatory, of course, one has to take ἐν αὐτῷ adverbially. This is grammatically correct, but as shown earlier ἐν αὐτῷ can also be taken adjectivally. If the latter syntax is chosen, ἐν is to be taken as locative rather than instrumental. Such syntactical decision obviously puts a different complexion on one's interpretation of Rom 1:17a in the sense that the gospel is the *centre* in Paul's mission rather than the *means* of the revelation of the righteousness of God, but we will come back to that later in our discussion.

Here we should ask whether there is any problem with Watson's claim that 'revelation that occurs *viva voce* in the proclamation of the apostle is at one with the revelation that occurs through the prophetic writing' (see above). If the 'righteous one' in the Habakkuk citation is understood as the generic believer and the 'righteousness of God' is understood as the righteousness of that believer, there would be no problem with this reading. But as will be argued below, taking the righteousness of God as the righteousness of any human person is not sufficiently warranted. Even more so, Watson's aforementioned claim seems to be problematic because it is based on construing ἀποκαλύπτεται in such a way that the verb refers to a revelation that occurs during oral proclamation *only*. This means that the verb denotes epistemological disclosure of a righteousness that originates from or is mediated by faith but is hidden *from the minds* of the unbelieving Jews and Gentiles. To be sure, that ἀποκαλύπτεται in Rom 1:17 denotes epistemological disclosure of a hidden reality is probably right, because the ἀποκαλύπτω/ἀποκάλυψις[63] language (and related forms, particularly

---

noted here is that most of the uses of φανερόω in Paul denote one's perception of something. Cf. 1 Cor 4:5; 2 Cor 2:14; 3:3; 4:2, 10, 11; 5:10, 11 (2x); 7:12; 11:6; cf. also Eph 5:13, 14; Col 1:26; 3:4 (2x); 4:4; 1 Tim 3:16; 2 Tim 1:10; Tit 1:3; Heb 9:8, 26; 1 Pet 1:20; 5:4; 1 Jn 1:2 (2x); 2:19, 28; 3:2 (2x); 3:5, 8; 4:9; Rev 3:18; 15:4. See also Best, 'The Revelation to Evangelize the Gentiles', *JTS* (1984) 1-30, 23-26. But there is an overall pattern in Paul's terminological employment in the sense that φανερόω and ἀποκαλύπτω are used as synonyms in some places, while the meaning of the former is much closer to that of γνωρίζω in other places. Γνωρίζω is used in Ephesians (1:9; 3:1, 3; 6:19) and Colossians (1:27) in relation to μυστήριον. In Ephesians, it is even used in relation to ἀποκάλυψις (3:3) and ἀποκαλύπτω (3:5), blurring the denotative difference between ἀποκάλυψις/ἀποκαλύπτω and γνωρίζω.

[63] The noun ἀποκάλυψις appears three times in Romans in relation to δικαιοκρισίας τοῦ θεοῦ (2:5), the 'sons of God' (8:19), and the μυστήριον (Rom 16:25). Elsewhere in the Pauline Seven Letter Corpus, it is used with reference to the appearance of the 'Lord Jesus Christ' to the Corinthian believers (1 Cor 1:7) and Paul (Gal 1:12), to the revealing of insightful thoughts (1 Cor 14:6, 26), to describe Paul's reception of guidance to go to Jerusalem (Gal 2:2) and as hendiadys of ὀπτασίαι in 2 Cor 12 – probably both the revela-

φανερόω)[64] supposedly contrasts the hiddenness of something or someone.[65] And *revealing secrets* remains the core idea in much of Paul's ἀποκαλύπτω/ἀποκάλυψις language.[66] But Watson's understanding of revelation as something that 'occurs *viva voce* in the proclamation' does not seem to leave any room for the view that ἀποκαλύπτεται probably expresses the ongoing disclosure of the righteousness of God that had formerly been hidden but was now revealed in the gospel events.[67] Such a

---

tion of the 'Lord' *to* Paul (v 1) and the in- or out-of-body experience of 'the man' Paul knows (v 7).

[64] Although both the substantive ἀποκάλυψις and the verb ἀποκαλύπτω are used in the Gospels (cf. Matt 10:26; 11:25, 27; 16:17; Lk 2:32, 35; 10:21, 22; 12:2; 17:30; Jn 12:38), the Deutero-Pauline letters, 1 Peter and the Apocalypse (cf. Eph 1:17; 3:3, 5; 2 Thess 1:7; 2:3, 6, 8; 1 Pet 1:5, 7, 12, 13; 4:13; 5:1; Rev 1:1), Paul is the main NT user of ἀποκαλύπτω/ἀποκάλυψις. For φανερόω and related terms, see Rom 1:19; 2:28; 3:21; 16:26; cf. Deut 29:29; Jer 33(40):6 (it appears to render נלה); Sir 6:22; Acts 4:16; 7:13; 1 Cor 3:13; 4:5; 11:19; 14:25; 2 Cor 2:14; 3:3; 4:10; 5:10, 11; 11:6; Gal 5:19; Phil 1:13; Eph 5:13; Col 1:26; 3:4; 4:4. For additional discussions, see Campbell, 'Romans 1:17', 275f. See also Snodgrass, 'The Gospel in Romans: A Theology of Revelation', in Jervis *et al* (eds), *Gospel in Paul, Studies on Corinthians, Galatians and Romans for Richard Longenecker*, 288-314. Snodgrass enumerates a catalogue of at least thirty different words, which, he thinks, refer to 'revelation'. Not only are many of the words unrelated to ἀποκαλύπτω, they are also not found in Romans. Sturm does the same in his doctoral dissertation: *An Exegetical Study of the Apostle Paul's Use of the Word Apocalypto/Apokalypsis: The Gospel as God's Apokalypse* (Unpublished PhD Dissertation, Union Theological Seminary, 1985). However, his approach is helpful in that since ἀποκαλύπτω/ἀποκάλυψις does not constitute one concept of revelation, he studies it in relation to other word groups without which, in his view, the term in question could not have a meaningful significance and convey the gospel as God's apocalypse. In doing so, Sturm (e.g. 246-247) finds three clusterings: words of disclosure (e.g. φανερόω, ἀποκαλύπτω, δηλόω, εὑρίσκω, προγράφω, ἔνδειξις, etc.), words of judgement/salvation (κρίνω, ἡμέρα κυρίου, δικαιοσύνη θεοῦ, δικαιοκρισία θεοῦ, σῳζω, δόξα, etc.), and words of perception, apprehension, or understanding (ὁράω, καθοράω, βλέπω, ἀτενίζω, οἶδα, γινώσκω, φρονέω, πνεῦμα, etc.). Space and the limited purpose of this study do not allow us to examine these categories in detail.

[65] Its English rendering ('uncover', 'take out of hiding', 'reveal', 'disclose', 'make fully known') suggests this. See also Louw-Nida, *Lexicon*; Oepke, 'καλύπτω κτλ', *TDNT III*, 556-592.

[66] This does not seem to cohere with the term's root meaning, which (up to the first century BCE and beyond) *in the main* had to do with simply 'uncovering' something. See also Smith, 'On the History of ΑΠΟΚΑΛΥΠΤΩ and ΑΠΟΚΑΛΥΨΙΣ', in Hellholm (ed.), *Apocalypticism in the Mediterranean World and the Near East*, 9-20. See also Bockmuehl, *Revelation*, 32-33; Adler, 'Introduction', in VanderKam and Adler, *Jewish Apocalyptic Heritage in the Early Christianity*, 1-31, 8-10.

[67] Smith ('History', 15-17) even suggests that Paul's idea of revelation in Rom 1:17-18 is expressed not in terms of revealing secrets but in terms of the revelation of God's future purposes for the wicked (wrath) and the righteous (justice). See also Sturm, *Study*, 194ff.

perspective is positively suggested by the connection of 1:17 with 3:21-26, to which we now turn.

In Rom 3:21-26, which will be considered in more detail later in chapter 5, Paul develops his earlier statements in 1:17. In 3:21-22 in particular, Paul talks about the revelation of the righteousness of God. As Paul uses πεφανέρωται rather than ἀποκαλύπτεται, however, how the present passive ἀποκαλύπτεται is understood in relation to the perfect passive πεφανέρωται must be explained. The question is: do the differing temporal elements in both verbs refer to two different times and events of revelation? Watson does not answer this question directly. Nor does he deal with the syntactical issues in Rom 1:17a. But his tacit acceptance of the syntax where ἀποκαλύπτεται is qualified by ἐν αὐτῷ (rather than ἐκ πίστεως, which he takes with δικαιοσύνη θεοῦ) enables him to understand the proclaimed gospel as instrumental for the revelation of the righteousness of God as a righteousness acquired by or on the basis of faith.[68] Consequently, Watson, probably rightly, understands revelation in Rom 1:17 as a present event. But his reading does not seem to appreciate the relationship between ἀποκαλύπτεται (Rom 1:17) and πεφανέρωται (3:21-22). This relationship must recognise that both verbs refer to different times.

One could, of course, argue that neither of them denotes a specific time in the present or past.[69] This argument would be valid if the revelation of the righteousness of God had nothing to do with the gospel events that are historically specific and objective. That certainly is not the case in Paul's thinking (Rom 5:6; Gal 4:4-5). More specifically, such an argument is inconsistent with Rom 3:21-26, where Jesus' death is central and linked with (the revelation of) the righteousness of God. To be sure, the *means* by which God's righteousness is *revealed* is not directly related to the cross in 3:21, but the cross is clearly part of the content, and certainly the basis, for the revelation of that righteousness. This is the case particularly when the meaning of πίστις Ἰησοῦ Χριστοῦ is understood as Christ's faithfulness-to-death in 3:22 and when this meaning is related to Paul's declaration in 3:25, where, as will be shown later in chapter 5, Christ is said to be set forth publicly as a ἱλαστήριον *so that he may become* the ἔνδειξις of the righteousness of God. The verb πεφανέρωται in 3:21, like the noun ἔνδειξις in 3:25-26, appears to express the disclosure of God's righteousness as

---

[68] See also Cranfield, *Romans 1-8*, 92, 100.

[69] See, for example, Lührmann, *Das Offenbarungsverständis bei Paulus und in paulinischen Gemeinden*, 78-80; 'φαίνω κτλ', *TDNT IX*, 4. In Lührmann's view, 'the reference is to a once and for all: the justification grounded in the Christ event (cf. R. 3:24-26; 1:3f) is now a reality for πίστις' (Lührmann, 'φαίνω κτλ', 4; see also his *Offenbarungsverständis*, 160). This means that both verbs denote a subjective appropriation of the Christ event within an existential framework. But Paul would also have understood the Christ event as historical.

something that took place in the Christ-event.[70] The νυνὶ δέ in 3:21 also suggests that the revelation of the formerly hidden righteousness of God was revealed *in the past*. That revelation in the Christ-event (πεφανέρωται) clearly has an impact on the revelation in and through the gospel (ἀποκαλύπτεται).[71] In short, God's revelatory act in Christ's death cannot be understood apart from the revelation of that divine act in the proclamation and *vice versa*.

A similar scenario may be noticed in Rom 16:25-26, because in this passage and Rom 3:21, for example, the use of φανερόω presupposes the revelation of what was formerly hidden. And in both instances, the revelation appears to be a past event with a present impact communicated through Paul's gospel and prophetic writings.[72] So, although ἀποκαλύπτεται in 1:17 refers to an ongoing revelation in Paul's gospel in the present while πεφανέρωται in 3:21 expresses the past revelation in and through Jesus' death,[73] that the latter has an ongoing impact on the former cannot be denied. We would even say: the revelation in Paul's mission is an extension of the revelation in the gospel events. This can be supported further by a comparison between Rom 1:18 and 3:25-26. When Paul talks about the wrath of God being revealed against sinful humanity that is in opposition to the gospel whose subject matter is the formerly hidden but now revealed righteousness of God (Rom 1:17-18), he does not seem to be

---

[70] Blackman ('Romans 3:26b: A Question of Translation', *JBL* 87 [1968] 203-204) argues that the 'noun ἔνδειξις is used in preference to ἀποκαλύπτεται (1:17) and πεφανέρωται (3:21) no doubt because it seemed stronger evidentially and logically'. In his discussion of the relationship between 3:21-22 and 3:25-26, Campbell (*Rhetoric*, 157-159) has also pointed out the semantic correspondence between φανερόω and ἔνδειξις.

[71] See also the use of ἀποκαλύπτεται in 1:18, where the verb expresses God's present act of revealing his judgement against idolatry and immorality (cf. vv 24-26), in relation to the use of ἐφανέρωσεν in 1:19, where Paul talks about God's past act in uncovering what is knowable about himself since or from the creation of the world.

[72] It could even be said that Paul's flexible, albeit probably unwitting, use of ἀποκαλύπτεται to express a future happening in 1 Cor 3:14 also suggests that the grammar of ἀποκαλύπτεται in our passage does not necessarily require a rigid attribution of the events described in δικαιοσύνη θεοῦ ἐν αὐτῷ ἀποκαλύπτεται and ἀποκαλύπτεται ὀργὴ θεοῦ to Paul's lifetime and mission only. For grammatical theories proposed on the use of the present tense, see Porter, *Verbal Aspect in the Greek of the New Testament, with Reference to Tense and Mood*, 106-107; *Idioms*, 30-34. Porter argues that 'in Greek the temporal ordering of events is not measured in relation to a fixed point (absolute time), but by the relations established among the involved events with regard to each other and to the context' (*Idioms*, 25). This may apply to the use of ἀποκαλύπτεται in Rom 1:17.

[73] So Bockmuehl. See his 'Das Verb φανερόω im Neuen Testament', *BZ* 32 (1988) 87-99; *Revelation*, 133-141. See also Barrett, *Epistle*, 33-34; Snodgrass, 'Gospel', 298; Käsemann, *Commentary*, 91f; Dunn, *Romans 1-8*, 161f; Fitzmyer, *Romans*, 257, 279-280, 341, 344. See also Campbell's survey of previous syntactical analyses of 3:21-26 by scholars from across the board (*Rhetoric*, 22-69).

limiting the revelation of the wrath of God to the present sinful state of the pagan world.[74] For when he formulated Rom 1:18f Paul could also have had in mind the divine ἀνοχή before Christ, as in 3:25-26.[75] If so, while the point of Rom 3:25-26 is that God showed his righteousness by judging in the gospel events the sins that were previously 'passed over' or deliberately 'overlooked', the point of Rom 1:18 is that that divine judgement continues to be revealed in the proclamation – one could hardly make sense of one without the other. Similarly, for Paul, the righteousness of God that was revealed in Christ's death is being revealed in his preaching. In sum, the verb ἀποκαλύπτεται signifies the idea that what was revealed at the eschatological event (Christ's death) has now been *kerygmatised* and communicated orally.[76]

We should now ask whether the subject matter of the revelation in Christ's death is the righteousness of God or righteousness by faith. We attempt to answer this question through engaging with the second and third components of Watson's argument we isolated above. We start with the second component, where *he assumes tacitly that ἐν αὐτῷ is adverbial and argues that the gospel is instrumental for the revelation of righteousness by faith*. By 'righteousness by faith', Watson, like other anthropological readers, means a righteous status revealed by the gospel and received by faith. This interpretative option works well when one limits, as Watson seems to do, Paul's idea of revelation in Rom 1:17 to something occa-

---

[74] *Contra* Fitzmyer, *Romans*, 277-278. But see Cranfield, *Romans 1-8*, 109-110; Bockmuehl, *Revelation*, 140. The question as to how Paul could refer to the revelation of the 'wrath of God' and the 'righteousness of God' in one breath is a difficult one. Barth (*Commentary*, 43) answers this question by saying 'the wrath of God is the righteousness of God – apart from and without Christ'. For Cranfield (*Romans 1-8*, 109), ὀργὴ θεοῦ also is being revealed in the gospel, that is, in the on-going proclamation of the gospel ... [and] behind, and basic to, this revelation of the wrath of God in the preaching, is the prior revelation of the wrath of God in the gospel events'. For Barrett (*Epistle*, 29-34), the revelation of wrath is inextricably linked with the revelation of righteousness, because if the former can be demonstrated (as Paul believes), the latter is demonstrated as well. See also Bockmuehl, *Revelation*, 138-139; Oepke, 'καλύπτω κτλ', 583; Snodgrass, 'Gospel', 302.

[75] So Käsemann (*Commentary*, 35).

[76] Bockmuehl (*Revelation*, 226) is probably right in saying that what was revealed in the past with Christ's resurrection 'has now been "kerygmatized" in that the present preaching of the gospel continues to reveal the eschatological righteousness and wrath of God, and the apostolic ministry constitutes a living demonstration of the truth and knowledge of God'. Campbell ('Romans 1:17', 272) also speaks of a previous revelation that is of cosmic nature, although Campbell's distinction between 'the disclosure of the previously unseen righteousness of God to the world within the gospel' and 'the disclosure of salvation from the gospel to the individual' is not clear from the syntax itself. For Campbell, the prepositional phrase ἐν αὐτῷ modifies ἀποκαλύπτεται and functions as the agent or instrument of the verb.

sioned by the orally proclaimed gospel. Watson might protest that he does not deny that revelation is a past as well as a present event. That may well be true, but nowhere in his discussions in his work cited above does he link the revelation of the righteousness of God as something that first took place in the gospel events. Such a link within the framework of his argument would be unsustainable anyway, because once the righteousness of God is understood as that righteousness (a status) which is acquired by faith,[77] it is hardly possible to talk about the revelation of a gift of status in the gospel events. We do not deny that Paul thought that ungodly Jews and Gentiles were endowed with a righteous status (see below). Our contention is that this righteous status given to believers is different from the righteousness of God revealed ἐκ πίστεως εἰς πίστιν and hence to read Rom 1:17a in terms of the gospel revealing righteousness by faith is probably wrong.

Against this, one might say that Paul's use of ἀποκαλύπτω in relation to 'righteousness by faith' in Rom 1:17a parallels his use of φανερόω in relation to the revelation of 'righteousness by faith' in 3:21-22. Although 'revelation of righteousness by faith' cannot be noticed in any of the nine instances where the verb ἀποκαλύπτω appears in Paul's Seven Letter Corpus,[78] this can be argued to be the case particularly when πίστις 'Ιησοῦ Χριστοῦ in 3:22 is understood as the believer's faith in Jesus Christ. So if what Paul says is revealed is righteousness by faith, then the revelation Paul is talking about is to do with an epistemological disclosure of the hidden reality about a new status that God endows to those who accept the gospel message and believe in Christ. According to this interpretation, the righteousness of God = righteousness = a status. This new status that is acquired by faith is disclosed to an individual upon Paul's preaching. On the other hand, if what Paul says is revealed is the righteousness of God, the revelation in both passages must be understood as a past and present event. As we argued earlier, Paul's idea of revelation in Rom 1:17a and 3:21-22 is understood as an event in the Christ-event and in the proclamation. According to this reading, the righteousness of God carries a meaning and significance that is primarily universalistic rather than individualistic.

---

[77] See Watson, *Paul*, 49.

[78] Paul talks about the revelation (ἀποκαλύπτεται) of the wrath of God from heaven upon human injustice and wickedness (Rom 1:18), the revelation (ἀπεκάλυψεν) of a hidden [mystery] (1 Cor 2:10) – presumably the truth about the crucified Lord (vv 7-8), a disclosure (ἀποκαλύπτεται) of the work of each Corinthian Christian on the Day of Judgement (1 Cor 3:13), a revelation (ἀπεκαλυφθῇ) of prophetic words to someone at a meeting (1 Cor 14:30), a revelation (ἀποκαλύψαι) of the Son of God ἐν Paul (Gal 1:16), a revelation (ἀποκαλυφθῆναι) of πίστις (Gal 3:23), and a revelation (ἀποκαλύψει) of a new thought (Phil 3:15). Obviously, none of these refers to the revelation of righteousness by faith.

Watson's construal of the term as a *human status* seems to deprive it of that meaning and significance.

But since one's righteous status means one's standing before God as a saved person and that, according to Rom 1:16, is achieved by the power of God, Watson's argument can still be sustained through equating the meaning of δικαιοσύνη θεοῦ with that of σωτηρία and δικαιοσύνη. This brings us to the third component of his argument mentioned above: *the righteousness of God is brought about by the power of God*. Watson, by his own admission, does not fully engage with the δικαιοσύνη θεοῦ debate, but the disclosure Paul talks about, in his view, is not that of God's saving power (Käsemann, Stuhlmacher), nor of God's covenant faithfulness (Wright, Dunn), but that of the righteousness (or salvation) approved by God, revealed and/or effected by the power of God (the gospel) and acquired by the person of Habakkuk 2:4. The text and context are clear about salvation being effected by the power of God. As the preposition εἰς, which, with an accusative noun, generally expresses entrance, purpose, direction or limit, appears to have been employed with a purpose sense or a metaphorical sense of direction in Rom 1:16b and 1:17a,[79] the power of God is directed towards the salvation of Jews and Greeks who believe.[80] The temporal significance of εἰς σωτηρίαν in 1:16 is ambiguous, which is also the case in 10:1, 11,[81] so when σωτηρία will be brought about is unclear.[82] But nonetheless it is evident that σωτηρία, a political and military

---

[79] See also Oepke, 'εἰς', *TDNT II*, 420-434; Porter, *Idioms*, 152-153.

[80] The dative participle in παντὶ τῷ πιστεύοντι is understood here as a dative of advantage or respect as it is preceded by εἰς σωτηρίαν.

[81] NRSV adopts a verbal rendering to the prepositional phrase here ('my heart's desire and prayer to God for them is that they may be saved' [10:1]; 'one confesses with the mouth and so is saved' [10:10]).

[82] Several passages appear to betray Paul's tendency to attach, albeit vaguely, a present as well as futuristic eschatological significance to the term. This is evident especially in his expressions in 11:11 ('by their transgression salvation [has come] to the Gentiles so as to make them [Jews] jealous') and 13:11 ('our salvation is nearer than when we believed'). So one might be inclined to take εἰς σωτηρίαν both ways in Rom 1:16 too. However, the use of the verb in Romans is much less ambiguous, with 'salvation' designating a future event (5:9, 10; 8:24; 9:27; 19, 13; 11:26). Perhaps the only ambiguous passage is 8:24: τῇ γὰρ ἐλπίδι ἐσώθημεν ('in hope we were saved'). Since 'hope' is to do with some desired ideal that is expected to materialise at some point in time, Paul's expression cannot be taken as a strictly past event. The context itself is overwhelmingly futuristic. See also Bockmuehl (*Revelation*, 145-147), who suggests that Paul's 'salvation' language 'appears to be implemented largely in the future'. This can also be noticed by and large in Paul's uses of both σῴζω and σωτηρία in his Seven Letter Corpus: 1 Cor 1:18, 21; 3:15; 5:5; 7:16; 9:22; 10:33; 15:2; 2 Cor 1:6; 2:15; 6:2; 7:10; Phil 1:19, 28; 2:12; 1 Thess 2:16; 5:8, 9. See also Käsemann, *Commentary*, 22; Fitzmyer, *Romans*, 119; Dunn, *Theology*, 317ff. Cranfield (*On Romans*, 89) understands σωτηρία in

image in the OT[83] and Greco-Roman world,[84] in our passage is something that is brought about by the power of God.[85] There is a similar idea in the two closest constructions in Romans, namely αὐτοῦ δύναμις and δύναμίν μου in 1:20 and 9:17 respectively.[86] In 1:20, God's eternal power is part of what Paul describes as invisible but knowable about God ἀπὸ κτίσεως κόσμου ('from[87] or since[88] the creation of the world') and which God revealed to 'persons' (vv 18-20).[89] In Rom 9:17, where Paul cites Ex 9:16, God's power demonstrated (or shown forth) in/through Pharaoh (ἐνδείξωμαι ἐν σοὶ τὴν δύναμίν μου) is God's judging and saving power, in keeping with the rest of the OT tradition where divine power is often associated with YHWH's military might and sovereign authority that ensure Israel's salvation and victory or defeat and punishment (e.g. Deut 3:22-24; Jer 16:21). In the former, God's power is creative, while in the latter it is salvific. But both express basically the same notion and correspond to Rom 1:16b, where the power of God is said to effect salvation.[90]

Rom 1:16 in terms of 'an eschatological salvation which reflects its splendour back into the present of those who are to share it'.

[83] See, for example, Ps 98:2; Isa 51:5; Hab 3:18; cf. Judg 3:9; Isa 45:15.

[84] In the Greco-Roman world, δύναμις and σωτηρία are closely related. Gods such as Zeus, Apollo, Artemis and Asclepius were often called 'saviours', and were believed to intervene in time of need and save from illnesses, sea storms and other disasters. As the Imuthes-Asclepius papyrus in particular shows, Asclepius is identified with the salvific power of god ('...ἡ τοῦ θεοῦ δύναμις σωτήριος'). The term σωτηρία is also associated with Caesar Augustus according to the inscription in *Cos* 81: ὁ δᾶμος τὰς αὐτοκράτορος Καίσαρος Θεοῦ υἱοῦ Σεβαστοῦ σωτηρίας θεοῖς ἱλαστήριον ('The people [offer this] as an oblation to the gods for the salvation of Imperator Caesar Augustus, son of God' [W. R. Paton and E. L. Hicks, *The Inscriptions of Cos* , 81, cited in Fitzmyer, *Romans*, 350]). See also Cranfield, *Romans 1-8*, 88; Fitzmyer, *Romans*, 119; Gräbe, *Power*, 11-16.

[85] Jesus as σωτήρ is used once by Paul in Phil 3:20. But see, for example, Lk 2:11; Acts 5:31; 13:23.

[86] In the Corinthian correspondence, δύναμις θεοῦ is a divine action manifested in Paul's mission (1 Cor 1:18; 2:5; 2 Cor 6:7) and the divine force that raised Jesus from the dead or became the origin or source of Jesus' life (1 Cor 6:14; 2 Cor 13:4). See also Gräbe, *Power*, 177.

[87] Käsemann, *Commentary*, 36f; Stuhlmacher, *Letter*, 33 ('For that which...becomes visible for the eye of reason from the creation of the world'); Dunn, *Romans 1-8*, 57 ('for his invisible characteristics from the creation of the world are perceived intellectually in the things which have been made'); Schreiner, *Romans*, 84.

[88] Nygren, *Commentary*, 107; Cranfield, *Romans 1-8*, 114; Fitzmyer, *Romans*, 269.

[89] See also Käsemann, *Commentary*, 36; Cranfield, *Romans 1-8*, 114. On issues of natural theology, see Dunn (*Romans 1-8*, 57) who advocates that a type of natural theology is involved in 1:18f. Campbell ('Natural Theology in Paul? Reading Romans 1:19-20', *IJST* 1:3 [1999] 231-252) controverts this and argues that natural revelation is subverted by Paul in 1:19-20. But see Bockmuehl, *Revelation*, 141-142; *Jewish Law in Gentile Churches: Halakhah and the Beginning of Christian Public Ethics*, 129-131.

[90] Josephus also speaks of δύναμις θεοῦ in relation to θεοκρατίαν ἀπέδειξε τὸ

However, the argument that the righteousness of God is brought about by the power of God in the same way as salvation is brought about by the power of God is less certain. First, as shown in the second chapter, the grammar suggests that Rom 1:16b and 1:17a independently but interrelatedly stand as justifying and affirming reasons for Paul's claim in 1:16a. According to this syntactical structure, the gospel can be understood as the *centre* rather than the *means*, in which case both the power of God (1:16b) and the righteousness of God (1:17a) are contents of the gospel. So, in 1:16b Paul declares that *he is not ashamed of the gospel*, because the power of God, which is the content of the gospel, is directed towards the salvation of the Jew and Greek who believe. In 1:17a, he declares that *he is not ashamed of the gospel*, because the righteousness of God, which is the subject matter of the gospel, is being revealed ἐκ πίστεως εἰς πίστιν. So, *pace* Watson, on the basis that ἐκ πίστεως can be understood as a reference to the process that causes the revelation of the righteousness of God, while εἰς πίστιν is a reference to the process that is caused by the revelation of the righteousness of God, the correlation appears to be between εἰς σωτηρίαν and εἰς πίστιν rather than εἰς σωτηρίαν and δικαιοσύνη θεοῦ. The believing Jews and Greeks for whom salvation is effected by the power of God in 1:16b are probably implied in 1:17a as those for whom πίστις is effected by the righteousness of God. We shall come back to this in chapter 5.

Second, Watson's argument probably wrongly treats the righteousness of God as 'righteousness' (δικαιοσύνη) and, in so doing, equates it with 'salvation' (σωτηρία). It cannot be denied that the English rendering of δικαιοσύνη ('righteousness') is deemed to have the same sense as the English rendering of δικαίωσις ('justification'), which is widely understood as having a similar meaning and significance to 'salvation' (e.g. 4:25; 5:18). Also, in Romans Paul seems to equate 'justification' with 'salvation' (5:9) or 'righteousness' with 'salvation' (10:1, 10). But the righteousness of God and 'righteousness' do not seem to have the same meaning in Romans, because the latter almost always carries a meaning that signifies one's ethical standard (righteousness of moral character) or even one's status, while the former does not.[91] It can still be argued, however, that since Rom 5:17, 9:30, 1 Cor 1:30 and Phil 3:9 suggest that

---

πολίτευμα (Moses 'ordained the [Jewish] government to be a Theocracy') (*Ap* 2:165) and God's creative activity (*Ap* 2:166f). *Ap* 2:167 reads: 'He [Moses] represented Him as One, uncreated and immutable to all eternity; in beauty surpassing all mortal thought, made known to us by His power (δυνάμει μὲν ἡμῖν γνώριμον), although the nature of His real being passes knowledge.'

[91] For example, cf. Rom 1:17; 3:3, 21, 22, 25 with Rom 5:17, 18, 21; 6:16, 18; 8:10; 9:30; 14:17.

'righteousness' is something that comes from God it is legitimate to understand the righteousness of God as a divinely given status. Most of these
passages could indeed be construed to present 'righteousness' as a gift of a
righteous status (Rom 5:17; 9:30; Phil 3:9). 1 Cor 1:30 too can be read as
saying that the righteousness that is [given] from God is Christ. But Christ
obviously cannot be a status. As indicated earlier, it would probably be
more congenial to understand 1 Cor 1:30 in line with our earlier equation
of the meaning of the power of God with that of the righteousness of God
in Rom 1:16-17, because in 1 Cor 1:24 Christ is referred to as the power of
God. One could then argue that if 'righteousness' is a status that is given to
Christians from God, it should only be because Christ, as bearer of that
'righteousness', is *the* gift from God. Christians owe their status to God's
salvific act through Christ (who embodies God's saving power).

But the issue is complicated in 2 Cor 5:21, because here Christ is said to
be made 'sin' in order that Paul and other Christians (ἡμεῖς) may become
the 'righteousness of God' in him. As space will not permit us to consider
all the complex issues involved in this declaration, our concern here will
be with the question as to whether the traditional understanding of the
righteousness of God in 2 Cor 5:21 as *righteous status*, as against *God's
saving power*,[92] is sustainable. Thrall and Harris, for example, argue that
the term in this passage means 'being justified by God' or sinners being
given a 'righteous status before God'.[93] In order to sustain this, δικαιοσύνη
θεοῦ is taken to mean δικαιοσύνη whereby the latter stands for
δικαιωθέντες.[94] If δικαιοσύνη (= δικαιοσύνη θεοῦ?) means one's status as a
justified person, what does ἁμαρτία mean? It can mean 'sin offering'
(Christ was treated as sin offering in the cultic sense), 'sinner' (Christ was
treated as if he were a sinner) or 'sin' (Christ was treated as the personifi-

---

[92] There is another option proposed by Wright, namely *God's covenant faithfulness*.
This is argued in his article 'On Becoming the Righteousness of God: 2 Corinthians
5:21', in Hay and Johnson, *Pauline Theology II: 1 and 2 Corinthians*, 200-208. This
reading must assume that ἁμαρτία is infidelity to God's covenant with Israel. But Paul's
concept of ἁμαρτία is much wider than this. As will be argued later in chapter 5, this
covenantal interpretation of the the righteousness of God is exegetically implausible in
Rom 1:17 and its immediate and wider contexts.

[93] See, for example, Thrall, *A Critical and Exegetical Commentary on the Second
Epistle to the Corinthians*, 442-443; Harris, *The Second Epistle to the Corinthians: A
Commentary on the Greek Text*, 455 (but see pages 449-456 for his commentary on the
passage as a whole). It is to be noted here that the verb γίνομαι is interpreted in three
ways: participation ('share'), action ('do') and change ('become'). All three are suitable,
but the last one is preferable, because γενώμεθα ... ἐν Χριστῷ is almost equivalent to
'being in Christ'. See Thrall, *Commentary*, 442-443; Harris, *Epistle*, 455; Martin, *2 Corinthians* (WBC 40), 157.

[94] Harris, *Epistle*, 455.

cation of sin).[95] To defend the sense 'sin offering', appeal has been made to the Hebrew חַטָּאת ('sin', 'sin offering' [Lev 16:5-10]), Isa 53:10 (περὶ ἁμαρτίας) and Paul's own statements in Rom 8:3 and Gal 3:13.[96] Although it is probably the case that Paul had Isa 53:9-11 in mind when he penned 2 Cor 5:21, there are several arguments against taking ἁμαρτία to mean 'sin offering'.[97] As a result, while Thrall appears to prefer the meaning 'sinner',[98] Harris adopts the sense 'sin'.[99] But both Thrall and Harris want to avoid defining δικαιοσύνη θεοῦ ('justification') as 'moral righteousness' because such a definition would demand understanding Christ as sinful.[100] For both, those who were formerly sinners acquired a righteous status (or were justified) as a result of being 'in Christ'. As to why Paul would use the notion of 'becoming the righteousness of God' if he meant to say 'being justified by God', Thrall answers, 'δικαιοσύνη is written for the sake of literary symmetry, to correspond with the previous ἁμαρτία'.[101] And this literary symmetry of juxtaposed opposites infers what Harris calls a 'double imputation': ἁμαρτία is reckoned to Christ's account so that δικαιοσύνη is reckoned to our account.[102] The notion of imputation, however, is rejected by Thrall.[103]

In any case, as Harris himself recognises, the argument of 'double imputation' is undermined by the fact that λογίζομαι is not used in the passage.[104] The existence of this verb would justify Paul's use of δικαιοσύνη as antithetical to ἁμαρτία (had he used this here as in Rom 5:17-21, for example). But as the text stands now, we should ask whether the abstract

---

[95] See Thrall, *Commentary*, 439-443; Harris, *Epistle*, 452-454.

[96] Thrall, *Commentary*, 440; Harris, *Epistle*, 452.

[97] Some of the arguments are as follows. 1) Paul fails to use περὶ ἁμαρτίας (as he does in Rom 8:3). 2) ἁμαρτία does not mean 'sin offering' anywhere in Paul's Seven Letter Corpus. 3) The term in 2 Cor 5:21 probably is more personal (a radical change in divine-human relationship) than what 'sin offering' signifies (objective neutralising or removal of sins). 4) Paul would have used, for example, προέθετο ἁμαρτία had he meant 'sin offering'. See Thrall, *Commentary*, 440-442; Harris, *Epistle*, 453.

[98] Thrall (*Commentary*, 442) basically accepts Barrett's definition (Barrett, *A Commentary on the Second Epistle to the Corinthians*, 180): 'Christ was made "sin" means that "he came to stand in that relation with God which normally is the result of sin, estranged from God and the object of his wrath"'.

[99] Harris (*Epistle*, 454) concludes: 'In a sense beyond human comprehension, God treated Christ as "sin", aligning him so tatally with sin and its dire consequences that from God's viewpoint he became indistinguishable from sin itself'.

[100] Thrall, *Commentary*, 443; Harris, *Epistle*, 452, 455.

[101] Thrall, *Commentary*, 443.

[102] Harris, *Epistle*, 455.

[103] Thrall (*Commentary*, 444) argues that 'since it is ἐν αὐτῷ, i.e. "in Christ" that believers are endowed with this status of righteousness, any notion of an imputed 'alien righteousness' is out of place. To be "in Christ" is to be united with his personal being'.

[104] Harris, *Epistle*, 455.

noun δικαιοσύνη should be treated as having the same meaning as the genitival substantive δικαιοσύνη θεοῦ. This, as indicated above, means that δικαιοσύνη θεοῦ = δικαιωθέντες, thus, the second clause reads: 'we may become justified in him'. It is puzzling, however, as to why Paul did not write ἵνα ἡμεῖς γενώμεθα δίκαιοι ἐν αὐτῷ or ἵνα δικαιωθῆμεν ἐν αὐτῷ [Χριστῷ] if he meant this. It would indeed have been easier for him to use the verb δικαιόω in the same way as he does καταλλάσσω in verse 18 (τὰ δὲ πάντα ἐκ τοῦ θεοῦ τοῦ καταλλάξαντος ἡμᾶς ἑαυτῷ διὰ Χριστοῦ κτλ). But that he does not should caution us against interpreting δικαιοσύνη θεοῦ as 'being justified'. It could be argued, of course, that since Paul is concerned here with the concept of exchange, i.e. atonement through identification or interchange, rather than how people are justified, he does not need to use the verb in verse 21. The question then is: if Paul meant that the symmetry should be understood as it stands, why do commentators construe δικαιοσύνη θεοῦ with the verbal form? Such an attempt, in our view, adds to (rather than lessens) the confusion. Moreover, while Christ's death is clearly in view here, that ἁμαρτία does not seem to mean 'sin offering' (in the sense of the removal of sin through Christ suffering the penalty for sin) and that the context is concerned with the theme of reconciliation appear to be against the view that the notion of atonement (in the sense of Christ suffering the fate of the sinners) is dominant here.[105] This is not to deny the existence of the concept of exchange in the passage. Indeed, by using ἐν αὐτῷ Paul clearly is saying that through their identification with Christ, people exchange ἁμαρτία for δικαιοσύνη θεοῦ. Our disagreement is on the meaning afforded concerning δικαιοσύνη θεοῦ.

We would suggest that the term δικαιοσύνη θεοῦ should be understood primarily with reference to Christ. For one thing, Paul constructs the passage in such a way that δικαιοσύνη θεοῦ replaces ἁμαρτία and *vice versa*: Christ, who is the righteousness of God, was made 'sin' so that we (ἡμεῖς), who were 'sin', may become the righteousness of God. In other words, Christ became what people were and should be in order that they may become what he was and is. That Paul would refer to Christ as the righteousness of God is not a problem, because in his earlier correspondence he depicts Christ as the one who became δικαιοσύνη ἀπὸ θεοῦ for 'us' (1 Cor 1:30). But to suggest that 'we' become δικαιοσύνη θεοῦ (2 Cor 5:21) seems problematic, because the resulting proposition could be: 'we' become Christ. Such a proposition would go further than Paul's claim that he imitates Christ (1 Cor 11:1) and that he and his colleagues are ambassadors for Christ (2 Cor 5:20). To avoid this pitfall, whether ἡμεῖς in 2 Cor 5:21 refers to Paul and his colleagues or believers in general, we propose that what Paul says in the second clause be explained on the basis of ἐν αὐτῷ.

---

[105] See also Thrall, *Commentary*, 441-442.

Paul's concept of ἐν αὐτῷ is based on his belief that Christ in some way dwells in Christians through his Spirit (Rom 8:9-10), is formed within them (Gal 4:19) or lives in them (Gal 2:20). So the ἐν Χριστῷ signifies that the Christian community is the earthly locus of Christ's being. Christ's being, in a sense, is extended and 'corporatised'.[106] This enables Paul to claim in the context of our passage that being 'in Christ' results in being a new creation (v 17) and God reconciled humanity 'through Christ' (v 18). It is the same concept of identification or participation that Paul expresses in the second clause of verse 21: 'so that we may become the righteousness of God *in* or *through him*'.[107]

But how does understanding the righteousness of God *primarily* as Christ explain this complex statement any better than conventional readings? This question can be answered on the basis of this premise: Christ is depicted as the righteousness of God, because he was vindicated as *righteous* through his resurrection. Christ was vindicated not only as someone who possessed a righteous attribute before his death. He was vindicated as the Son of God who had been invested with a messianic power (cf. Rom 1:4; 8:34 with Acts 3:14; 7:52, 55-56; 22:14; Jer 23:5-6). In Paul's thinking, Christians are constituted as 'righteous' through Christ (Rom 5:19), who, as will be shown later, can be referred to as *the suffering righteous one who was vindicated*. As indicated above, however, that Christians are constituted as 'righteous' through Christ does not necessarily mean that they have become Christ. It probably means that they have become sharers of the *extension* of Christ's status and role as a result of their identification with or participation in him. So when Paul claims that people become the 'righteousness of God in Christ', he probably means that they take on Christ-like status and act as agents and instruments of the *extension* of the salvific role that was given to Christ.[108] To say that people

---

[106] So Thrall (*Commentary*, 428).

[107] The phrase ἐν αὐτῷ is flexible in this context. It can either be instrumental or locative. Both are suitable.

[108] We would suggest, albeit tentatively, that this can be explained from Rom 11:26, where Paul speaks of the salvation that 'stands in accord with the Scriptures of Judaism' (Fitzmyer [*Romans*, 624]). In his citation of Isa 59:20-21 in this passage (ἥξει ἐκ Σιὼν ὁ ῥυόμενος ἀποστρέψει ἀσεβείας ἀπὸ 'Ιακώβ), Paul probably consciously departs from both the MT and LXX in that he uses ἐκ instead of the Hebrew ל (גּוֹאֵל לְצִיּוֹן וּבָא ['the deliverer will come *to* Zion']) and the LXX's ἕνεκεν (Καὶ ἥξει ἕνεκεν Σιὼν ὁ ῥυόμενος ['the deliverer will come for the sake of Zion'). In so doing, he adapts what is said about גּוֹאֵל or ὁ ῥυόμενος (YHWH) to Christ. Zion seems to be understood as the community in which Christ dwells. As Israel and her prophets were sometimes identified with their messiah, the new Zion and its apostles can be identified with their messiah. They can also be understood to represent their messiah and carry on his task (cf. Col 1:24-27; 2:6). It seems that it is from this community of faith that Christ is said to come out of. See Käsemann (*Commentary*, 314), who suggests that the reference is to 'the return of the

can possess a Christ-like status, which is sometimes expressed in terms of the gift of righteousness (Rom 5:17), does not amount to accepting that the righteousness of God can primarily mean a human status of righteousness. The symmetry in 2 Cor 5:21 seems to make it clear that the righteousness of God here should be understood as a co-referential term for Christ. Then we can probably talk about people taking on Christ-like status through identifying with Christ the righteousness of (from) God. But conflating the righteousness of God with a gift of righteous status would be conflating Christ with a human status, which is wrong. Alternatively, one might suggest that the righteousness of God should designate *God's saving power*. This is not uncongenial, because Christ is the bearer or embodiment of that divine power (1 Cor 1:24). However, since it is not clear that ἁμαρτία also denotes power in our passage (as it predominantly does in Paul), it would probably be safer to take the righteousness of God as standing *primarily* for Christ.[109]

In any case, our exegetical explanation of 2 Cor 5:21 seems to support the view that Paul does not use the righteousness of God in Rom 1:17 with reference primarily to a divine gift of status. That the term does not mean gift of status in the Romans passage is also conceded by Watson, although he says that the term can refer 'still less' to 'the divine saving action in its entirety'.[110] What Watson means by 'its entirety' is not clear, but for him since Paul paraphrases the Habakkuk citation in Rom 1:17a, the righteousness of God is to be construed not only as the salvation of the person of the Habakkuk citation (i.e. the Christian) but also as 'the pattern of human

---

exalted Christ from the heavenly Jerusalem'. See also Cranfield, *Romans 1-8*, 578. In the Talmud (*bSanhedrin* 98a), Rabbi Yohanan understands גואל in Isa 59:20 as the 'son of David' who will come during the time when a generation is either altogether righteous (Isa 50:21) or altogether wicked (59:16).

[109] That is not to say that one cannot argue that δικαιοσύνη θεοῦ is used as God's power, much as ἁμαρτία can be understood as power. Thrall (*Commentary*, 443) summarises the argument as follows: 'It is suggested that [δικαιοσύνη θεοῦ] denotes God's power. Sin also is power, and the power of sin was concentrated upon Christ. But the result was that sin was itself deprived of power, and that Christ, as bearer of the power (δικαιοσύνη) of God, becomes the power dominating a new world. To "become God's righteousness" then will mean to be granted access to this new world, to have one's existence determined by this power, and to share in it'. Thrall, however, treats such an interpretation as complicated and less convincing, partly because, in her view, ἁμαρτία here is not regarded as power. Interpreting ἁμαρτία with a power sense, for her, would make little sense of ἁμαρτίαν ἐποίησεν. If Paul meant that Christ committed an act of sin, the power sense would indeed make no sense. But if Paul meant that God made Christ 'sin', the power sense could make sense. See also Martin (*2 Corinthians*, 158) who, following Ziesler (*Meaning*, 159), understands δικαιοσύνη θεοῦ here as 'God's whole intervention in Jesus'.

[110] Watson, *Paul*, 49.

conduct that God acknowledges as righteous'.[111] While it is true that ὁ δίκαιος is a person whose identity and actions are characterised by righteousness, to equate this 'pattern of [her] conduct' with the righteousness of God seems overconfident. Rom 1:17a and 1:17b are interdependent declarations. But they should not be collapsed into one, because the former is Paul's scripturally based claim that is contextualised in the light of the gospel events, while the latter is a corroborative proof for Paul's foregoing claim not only in 1:17a but also in 1:16. Put differently, that 'the righteous one' will live ἐκ πίστεως is a scriptural proof that God's power is directed towards the salvation of humanity without distinction (Rom 1:16) and that this divine salvific power is being revealed ἐκ πίστεως εἰς πίστιν (Rom 1:17). So in addition to the syntactical possibilities that would enable us to detect a complementarity between 1:16b and 1:17a, it seems reasonable to maintain that while Paul would equate human righteousness (the justification of believing Jews and Gentiles) with human salvation, it is doubtful that he would equate the salvation of humanity with the righteousness of God. It seems even more doubtful that he would say that the righteousness of God is brought about by the power of God.

In conclusion, our discussions above showed two main things. First, the meaning of the revelation of the righteousness of God in Rom 1:17 should accommodate both *eschatological* and *cognitive* perspectives. That is, it should at once be associated with the gospel events and what is intellectually seen and experienced upon the proclamation of the gospel. Second, while the righteousness of God is a subject matter of Paul's proclamation, it can be neither equated with salvation nor understood to be the righteousness of the person of the Habakkuk citation. Thus, the argument that Rom 1:17a is about the revelation of righteousness that is by faith is implausible.

4.3. Revelation of Δικαιοσύνη Θεοῦ as Divine Coming

Having established that the revelation of the righteousness of God is a past and present event and that the term 'righteousness of God' should be afforded a meaning that is different from the righteousness (or salvation) of the person of the Habakkuk citation, we now come to the question as to how Pss 98:2 (LXX: 97:2) and 143:2 (LXX: 142:2) in relation to Rom 1:17 and 3:21 respectively might contribute to our attempt to determine the meaning of the revelation of the righteousness of God. As summarised in the second chapter of the book, since the late nineteenth century to the present, the righteousness of God in Romans has been interpreted predominantly as (1) the divine quality that proceeds from God to redress

---

[111] Watson, *Paul*, 49.

wrong and save those who believe, (2) the divine (saving) activity or power that excludes evil and establishes the relationship of trust between God and humanity, (3) the righteous status given to believers, or (4) God's faithfulness to his covenant promises.

Space and the limited scope of this study do not permit us to rehearse the strengths and weaknesses of the interpretations of this phrase, but, as our discussions so far have shown, we have, along with many, added our voices to the Käsemannian interpretation (Interpretation [2]) of the term in question. Along that line, we will in the following sub-sections argue that Paul's idea of the revelation of the righteousness of God in Rom 1:17 probably stands for the notion of God's coming in Christ. This notion, in our view, may have been informed by Pss 98 and 143, which we will consider in the first sub-section. In the second sub-section, we will discuss the use of the 'righteousness of God' within Second Temple Judaism, with particular reference to *1 Enoch*. Paul may or may not have had access to Enochic or Qumran writings, but as a sharer of existing ideas and beliefs in the Second Temple period, he may have been aware of the ways in which the term 'righteousness of God' or its equivalent was used in the Second Temple period. The results from our considerations of background material can provide us with interpretative guidance and help us explain how Paul's use of the revelation of the righteousness of God in Rom 1:17 can be christological, the question we will deal with in the last sub-section.

4.3.1. Evidence from Psalms 98 and 143

The Käsemannian reading of the righteousness of God partly depends on the argument that Paul is alluding to Ps 98:2 (LXX: 97:2) in his declaration. As indicated above, Watson contends against this by saying that if Paul is alluding to the Psalm passage, Hab 2:4 is the wrong text for Paul to be citing in Rom 1:17b. That Hab 2:4, possibly along with its context, is an obvious background cannot be disputed. Paul's use of καθὼς γέγραπται before quoting Hab 2:4b in Rom 1:17b and terminological and phraseological correspondences between Rom 1:17a and 1:17b seem to support such a claim. But this should not lead us to reject the view that Paul also used Ps 98:2 as a background to Rom 1:16 and 1:17a. This psalm admittedly is a less obvious background in that there are only two parallel terms between Rom 1:17a and the Psalm text (δικαιοσύνη [θεοῦ] and ἀποκαλύπτω) and that Paul seems to allude to the latter rather than cite it (ἐγνώρισεν κύριος τὸ σωτήριον αὐτοῦ, ἐναντίον τῶν ἐθνῶν ἀπεκάλυψεν τὴν δικαιοσύνην αὐτοῦ).[112] But these parallels and the overall conceptual

---

[112] Elsewhere both MT and LXX have forms very close to δικαιοσύνη θεοῦ, which most probably are based on the belief that YHWH is צדיק /δίκαιος (e.g. Deut 32:6; Ezra

similarity seem to demonstrate that Ps 98:2 is an OT text that Paul could reasonably have been expected to know. Indeed, the specificity of the Pauline idea of the revelation of δικαιοσύνη θεοῦ seems to correspond to ἀπεκάλυψεν τὴν δικαιοσύνην [κύριου] in the Psalm text. This suggests that Paul is non-formally invoking the Psalm text in Rom 1:17.[113]

What is the meaning of Ps 98:2 then? This text deploys ἀποκαλύπτω, which translates the MT's גלה or its equivalent.[114] The term in both Hebrew and Greek assumes 'hiddenness', not least because YHWH in the OT is believed to be 'a God who hides himself' (Isa 45:15) or his face (Ps

---

9:15; Ps 119:137; Jer 12:1; Dan 9:14; Lam 1:18; Zeph 3:5). Those forms, for example, are: צדקת יהוה (δικαιοσύνην Κυρίου) (Deut 33:21) and צדקות יהוה (Κύριε δικαιοσύνας – Jdg 5:11; cf. Mic 6:5 [ἡ δικαιοσύνη τοῦ Κυρίου]). In the Hebrew Bible, צדקה/צדק (יהוה) occurs 276 times (out of 523 occurrences of the צדק word-group). Scholars have given a wide range of meanings to the term: health of soul, community loyalty, salvific order, prosperity, saving gift, YHWH's acts, YHWH's loyalty to the covenant and his activity that befits the covenant, relationship, justice, a process of judging, acquitting and saving, YHWH's saving action that puts the order into effect, and so on. See Scullion, 'Righteousness [OT]', 725ff.

[113] *Pace* Williams ('"Righteousness"', 261), whether Paul expected his readers in Rome to be familiar with this phrase that is distinctly from Jewish scriptures, we cannot be certain. But the issue becomes less of a problem when one treats the recipients of the letter of Romans in terms of what Stowers (*Rereading*, 21-33) calls the 'ideal reader' as opposed to the 'historical reader'. Alternatively, along with Stanley ('"Pearls before Swine": Did Paul's Audience Understand His Biblical Quotations?', *NovT* 41 [1999] 124-144), Paul's recipients could be regarded as illiterate Gentiles who lacked 'hearer competence' to understand Paul's often cryptic scriptural citations and allusions. To deal with either view, one should adopt the so-called audience-orientated approach. This may have merit in establishing the shared assumptions and the level of biblical knowledge that Paul's audience might have had, but it does not seem to provide the proper basis for establishing the author's use of the Old Testament. For methodological issues relating to audience-orientated versus author-orientated approach, see Porter, 'The Use of the Old Testament: A Brief Comment on Method and Terminology', in Evans & Sanders (eds), *Early Christian Interpretation of the Scriptures of Israel*, 79-96. In this article, Porter critically assesses Hays' (*Echoes*, 29-32; cf. '"Righteous"', 207 and Stuhlmacher, *Letter*, 28ff) seven criteria for an intertextual reading of Pauline letters: (1) *availability* of the proposed source of the echo to the author and/or original readers, (2) *volume* of an echo in the sense of explicit repetition of words, (3) *recurrence* of scriptural passage, (4) *thematic coherence* of an echo in relation to Paul's argument, (5) *historical plausibility* of the intended meaning, (6) our predecessors in the *history of interpretation* hearing the same echoes, and (7) *satisfaction* of the reader by the effect of the intertextual relation. For comprehensive reactions to Hays' *Echoes of Scripture*, see the collection of articles in Evans & Sanders (eds), *Paul and the Scriptures of Israel*. For further assessment of Hays' work and interesting discussions of the differentiation between quotations, echoes and allusions (e.g. Qohelet's חבל in Eccl 8:20 in relation to ματαιότης in Rom 8:20), see Moyise, 'Intertextuality', 14-41.

[114] Cf. also Num 24:4, 16; 1 Sam 3:7, 21; Isa 56:1.

143:7).[115] The psalmist in Ps 98:2 does not speak about the hiddenness of YHWH or his face as such, but he speaks of YHWH making known his salvation and revealing τὴν δικαιοσύνην αὐτοῦ in the sight of the nations. In verse 1, the psalmist talks about YHWH's salvific activity on behalf of his own people (rather than YHWH's own salvation[116]). In this psalm and elsewhere, to be sure, YHWH's actions are described with a variety of words whose meanings may not always be identical, and which therefore have many facets. But it is safe to suggest that the revelation of YHWH's 'righteousness' in verse 2 and context is to do with his salvific coming through which he restores order and equity (cf. v 2 with v 9).[117] Thus the notion of revelation here is to be understood within the framework of the Jewish ideology of divine kingship, at the centre of which is YHWH's salvific coming as king, warrior and judge[118] to deal with forces that disrupt order and pose a threat to the life and identity of Israel and, thereby, making himself known to all the nations (cf. 97:2-10).[119] It is not unreasonable to suppose that Paul had such a framework in mind when he constructed Rom 1:16-17.

A similar suggestion can be made in regards to Rom 3:21f, which appears to have been informed by Ps 143:2 (LXX: 142:2). We suggest this on the basis that the Psalm passage (ὅτι οὐ δικαιωθήσεται πᾶς ζῶν ἐνώπιόν

---

[115] Cf. Job 13:24; 34:29; Ps 10:11; 13:1; 30:7; 44:24; 69:17; 88:14; 104:29-30; Is 8:17; 54:8; 59:2; 64:7; Ezek 39:23-24; Mic 3:4; Jer 33:5. See also Balentine, *The Hidden God: The Hiding of the Face of God in the Old Testament*, 1ff, 47-48, 77ff; Bockmuehl, *Revelation*, 1ff, 24-56. For the hidden things (הנסתרות) as opposed to the revealed things (הנגלות) in Qumran, see 1 QS 5:11f (cf. CD 15:13?).

[116] Moo (*Epistle*, 83) speaks of 'the saving righteousness of God', which, he thinks, is pictured as 'God's vindicating his people – his granting to them a deliverance to which they can lay claim, either because of their own righteousness...or because of God's promises' to Israel. Moo applies his interpretation of the 'righteousness of God' as a status enjoyed by a believer to the Psalm text (cf. p 82). For him, 'my righteousness' or 'my salvation' in Ps 35:27-28 and 51:14 means a status received by an Israelite. It is to be noted, however, that in the former the Psalmist speaks of 'your (God's) righteousness' and in the latter he speaks of the 'God of my salvation'. Moo's reading here seems to be influenced by his reading of Paul.

[117] Cf. Ps 5:7; 7:9-10; 22:31; 31:2; 33:4-6; 35:3, 8, 24; 36:2-11; 40:10-12; 50:5-6; 51:16; 69:28; 71:2, 15, 16, 19, 24; 88:12-13; 89:15-17; 99:4; 103:3-6, 14, 17; 111:3; 112:3, 9; 119:142; 143:11-12; 145:7-9. For discussions on the use of the terminology in Psalms and other OT texts, see von Rad, *Old Testament Theology I*, 370-418; Schmid, 'Creation, Righteousness, and Salvation', in Anderson (ed.), *Creation in the Old Testament*, 102-117; Scullion, 'Righteousness (OT)', 731-733; Williams, '"Righteousness"', 263.

[118] Similar patterns can be noticed in Deut 33:21 and Jdg 5:11 where YHWH's צדקה/צדק/δικαιοσύνη carries a sense of the juridical and of military power respectively. Cf. also 1 Sam 12:7; Jer 51:10; Hos 2:21-22; 10:12; Mic 6:5, 8; 7:9; Dan 9:16.

[119] *Contra* Williams ('"Righteousness"', 261-262).

σου) is partially cited in Rom 3:20 (διότι ἐξ ἔργων νόμου οὐ δικαιωθήσεται πᾶσα σάρξ ἐνώπιον αὐτοῦ), which not only brings to a close a major section of Paul's discussion in 3:1-19, but also provides the point of departure for his subsequent discussion. The phrase νυνὶ δέ in 3:21, which sometimes denotes a logical distinction (7:17; 1 Cor 12:18; 13:13) or otherwise has temporal force (15:23, 25; 2 Cor 8:22; Philm 9, 11), serves both as a transitional element that contrasts what precedes with what follows[120] and as a temporal distinguisher between two aeons with a specific focus on the revelation of the righteousness of God.[121] Hence the dependence of an understanding of 3:21f on 3:20 and, indirectly, on the background text (i.e. Ps 143:2 [LXX: 142:2]) from which its language and concept are drawn is necessitated.

Notwithstanding the differences of scholarly opinion on the meaning of the righteousness of God,[122] the genitive construction in 3:21f appears to have been informed by δικαιοσύνη Κυρίου in Ps 143.[123] In the latter part of Ps 143:1, the psalmist cries ἐπάκουσόν μου ἐν τῇ δικαιοσύνῃ σου ('hear me in your righteousness'), as he does in verse 7: Ταχὺ εἰσάκουσόν μου, Κύριε ... μὴ ἀποστρέψῃς τὸ πρόσωπόν σου ἀπ' ἐμοῦ ('Answer me quickly, O Lord, ... Do not hide your face from me'). The psalmist is pur-

---

[120] So Barrett (*Epistle*, 72), Dunn (*Romans 1-8*, 164) and Schreiner, *Romans*, 180. Among the Reformers, Calvin took νυνί adversatively without any temporal sense. See Parker, *Commentaries on the Epistle to the Romans, 1532-1542*, 144; see also Cranfield, *Romans 1-8*, 202.

[121] So Käsemann (*Commentary*, 92).

[122] Sanders, for example, thinks that the phrase here does not bear a power sense as it does in 1:17. While arguing against Käsemann and defining the phrase generally as meaning something like 'salvation and life', 'acquittal in the present for past transgressions', 'future vindication in the judgement', Sanders (*PPJ*, 495) admits that 'Rom 1 does bear the meaning which Käsemann assigns to it'. See also Brauch's article in an appendix of Sanders' *PPJ*. Brauch thinks that '[t]he overwhelming emphasis on God's creative action in the interpretation of Paul, which Stuhlmacher shares with Käsemann, must be seen as an over-emphasis' (p. 542). Seifrid (*Justification by Faith: The Origin and Development of a Central Pauline Theme*, 107-108, 219-225), who interprets δικαιοσύνη θεοῦ as 'forensic justification', objects to the construal of the phrase with a power sense. He (*Justification*, 107) argues that 'the fact that God's covenant faithfulness might be manifested as a saving power does not attest to the *meaning*, "saving power" for the expression δικαιοσύνη θεοῦ'. However, in his recent work *Christ, Our Righteousness: Paul's Theology of Justification*, Seifrid speaks of the 'righteousness of God' as something that signifies *an act of God* in which his 'saving righteousness' is displayed (pp 35-74). This shows that Seifrid has modified his earlier view, which significantly diverged from that of Käsemann and Stuhlmacher. But Seifrid maintains his difference from Stuhlmacher in some ways (p 39 and n. 10). And he holds that δικαιοσύνη θεοῦ in 1:17 is an act of God while in 3:21-22 it is the gift of God mediated 'through the faith of Jesus Christ' (p. 64).

[123] See also Williams, '"Righteousness"', 271.

sued by his enemies, so his salvation could come only if the Lord did not
enter into judgement with him (because no person would be acquitted from
charges against her in the Lord's court [cf. Rom 3:20, 23, 24]), did not
hide his face, and responded in his righteousness (vv 1, 2, 3, 9, 12). The
instrumental sense of ἐν in verse 1 is repeated in verse 11 (ἐν τῇ
δικαιοσύνῃ σου ἐξάξεις ἐκ θλίψεως τὴν ψυχήν μου). It is the righteousness
of the Lord that delivers the psalmist from his suffering. In this Psalm, our
psalmist seems to mix law-court and military metaphors, where the righteousness of the Lord appears to be conceived as the power of the Lord by
which the psalmist is saved.[124] The psalmist's survival depends on the
Lord's response. The Lord's response in his righteousness means *his
appearance* in the realm imagined by the psalmist to deal with some real or
perceived forces that pose a threat to the life of the psalmist, Israel as a
whole and God's righteous rule. It would be wrong to suggest that Paul
transposed such a notion to his declarations in Rom 3:21-22. But it would
equally be wrong to deny that his new thinking could have been informed
and, to an extent, shaped by the psalmist's expression of the presence of
the righteousness of the Lord in terms of the presence of the Lord himself.

4.3.2. Evidence from Enochic and Related Texts

We now come to our study of the Second Temple Jewish background material, particularly *1 En* 71:14 and related texts. But it should be noted here
that as the following chapter will be examining extensively the use of the
epithet 'righteous one' and related issues in the Parables of *1 Enoch*, we
reserve treatment of issues concerning for example, the importance of the
document and the problems of date and text to that chapter.[125] Our concern
in this section is to consider briefly the use of the 'righteousness of God'
or its equivalent in *1 En* 71:14 and related texts. This will hopefully enable
us to see whether or how our interpretation of the righteousness of God in
Rom 1:17 fits into the denotation of the term in Enochic or other Jewish
writings.

---

[124] See also Hays, 'Psalm', 113-114.
Hays' reading of Rom 3:1-21 is set out as follows:
    3:1-8 – Has God abandoned his promises to Israel? Is he inconsistent or unjust?
    3:9-20 – All such objections are invalid: humanity, not God, is guilty of injustice.
    3:21-26 – God has not abandoned his people. He has now revealed his jus-
tice/righteousness in a new way, overcoming human unfaithfulness by his own power and
proving himself faithful/just.
For diverse treatments of Rom 3, see also Dodd, *Epistle*, 46-48; Käsemann, *Commentary*,
78; W. S. Campbell, 'Romans III as a Key to the Structure and Thought of the Letter',
NovT (1981) 22-40.
[125] We hold the view that the Parables were produced probably between the end of the
first century BCE and the destruction of the Second Temple.

In the Parables of *1 Enoch*, the abstract noun 'righteousness' stands for something that is found in the presence of the Lord of Spirits (39:7; 58:4-5) or characterises the figure of the Parables known as the Son of Man, Chosen One, Righteous One or Messiah (cf. 46:3; 71:14 with 38:2, 3; 47:1, 4; 53:6). But it is only in *1 En* 71:14 that 'the righteousness of the Head of Days' is used. The author herein claims that the righteousness of the Head of Days will not leave the Son of Man. Such a link between the term in question and a messianic figure is relevant to our enquiry in this study, thus the question as to what the author means by this claim is appropriate. But in order to answer this question adequately, it might be helpful to consider equivalent uses in earlier Enochic texts, namely *1 En* 99:10 and 101:3.[126]

In *1 En* 99:10,[127] where the Greek has ἐν ὁδοῖς δικαιοσύνης αὐτοῦ [τοῦ ὑψίστου] ('the path of his [Most High's] righteousness'), while the Ethiopic has *befinote tsedq* ('the path of righteousness'),[128] the term δικαιοσύνη [τοῦ ὑψίστου] seems to denote a divine power or activity. For one thing, in

---

[126] Pauline scholars such as Cranfield, Dunn and Moo have attempted to understand the Enochic use of the term in question in the process of explaining Paul's δικαιοσύνη θεοῦ in Romans. But none of them draws his conclusions on the basis of close analyses of the Enochic texts. Cranfield (*Romans 1-8*, 96-97), for example, accepts that Enochic and other Second Temple texts offered a background to Paul's use of δικαιοσύνη θεοῦ, but he insists that Paul must have used what he 'took over with freedom and originality'. Dunn (*Romans 1-8*, 41), on the other hand, refers to *1 En* 71:14 (along with other Second Temple texts) and says that it is 'clearly this concept of God's righteousness which Paul takes over' in Rom 1:17. Moo (*Epistle*, 74) takes not only *1 En* 71:14 but also 99:10 and 101:3 as evidence pertaining to Paul's use of δικαιοσύνη θεοῦ. For him (*Epistle*, 85), 'God's righteousness' in *1 Enoch* 'refers to his faithfulness (71:14)…his moral strictures (99:10), and his merciful works (101:3)'.

[127] The Greek reads: καὶ τότε μακάριοι πάντες οἱ ἀκούσαντες φρονίμων λόγους καὶ μαθήσονται αὐτούς, ποιῆσαι τὰς ἐντολὰς τοῦ ὑψίστου, καὶ πορεύσονται ἐν ὁδοῖς δικαιοσύνης αὐτοῦ καὶ οὐ μὴ πλανήσουσιν μετὰ τῶν πλανώντων καὶ σωθήσονται.

[128] The absence of the possessive pronoun in the Ethiopic is rather surprising, because the phrase in question is immediately preceded by *befinawta l^e'ul* ('the paths of the Most High'). The Greek translators or editors seem to have taken the words that precede the phrase τοῦ ὑψίστου into account, although the Greek again shows slight divergence from the Ethiopic in that it has τὰς ἐντολὰς τοῦ ὑψίστου ('the commandments of the Most High'). But since both the Ethiopic and Greek texts have the Most High as the subject in the immediately preceding phrase, the reading in the Greek seems to us to be original. Knibb seems to follow strictly the Ethiopic reading in his translation: 'And in those days blessed (are) all those who accept the words of wisdom and understand them, and follow the paths of the Most High, and walk in the path of righteousness, and do not act impiously with the impious, for they will be saved.' Isaac, on the other hand, combines the Greek reading: 'In those days, blessed are they all who accept the words of wisdom and understand them, to follow the path of the Most High; they shall walk in the path of his righteousness and not become wicked with the wicked; and they shall be saved' (So also Black).

the context God's execution of great judgement against idolatry, impiety and injustice is contrasted with his salvation of those who 'march' (πορεύομαι) along *the paths* of his 'righteousness'. This is even clearer in 101:3.[129] The Greek has μεγαλωσύνη αὐτοῦ ('his majesty'), while the Ethiopic's *tsedqa z^eahu* ('his righteousness'). Although both translations seem to refer to God's activity, the latter might be preferable on textual grounds.[130] In this text, 'the anger of the Most High' is paralleled with the 'righteousness of the Most High' against which human beings should not utter proud words. In the immediate context, the Most High is also portrayed as the creator of the universe who gives knowledge and wisdom to his creation and maintains its order (vv 6-9). Stuhlmacher may then be right in arguing that the phrase in question does not signify *Eigenschaft des Richters* ('an attribute of the judge'), but rather the Creator's demonstration of power in order to establish *Recht* ('justice', 'law').[131] For him, the phrase is a theological theme that is linked with the question of 'God's justice' (*Gottes Recht*) and him being the Creator in a chaotic world.[132] Although Stuhlmacher does not show how the meaning of the term in question relates to the figure of the Parables in *1 En* 71:14, his interpretation of the righteousness of God in *1 Enoch* with a power sense appears to be valid.

The denotation of the term in question with a similar sense is probably common in other Second Temple Jewish texts as well. To outline the main examples here: 1) In *Psalms of Solomon*, δικαιοσύνη θεοῦ describes the juridical and salvific activity of God (2:15; 8:24f; 9:2f; 17:29f; cf. *Test Dan* 6:10). 2) In 1QM 4:6, אל צדקת is one of the terms that describe God's power or activity.[133] The fact that phrases such as 'God's army',

---

[129] The Greek reads: ἐὰν ἀποστείληται τὸν θυμὸν αὐτοῦ ἐφ᾽ ὑμᾶς καὶ ἐπὶ τὰ ἔργα ὑμῶν, οὐχὶ ἔσεσθε δεόμενοι αὐτοῦ; διά τί ὑμεῖς λαλεῖτε τῷ στόματι ὑμῶν μεγάλα καὶ σκληρὰ ἐπὶ τῇ μεγαλωσύνη αὐ[τοῦ;

[130] The employment of μεγαλωσύνη may have been triggered and, indeed, influenced by μεγάλα, which occurs only several words before μεγαλωσύνη in the sentence, because of which the translators may have overlooked the Aramaic צדקה. So the Ethiopic translation ('his righteousness') is to be preferred. Black, however, prefers to follow the Greek reading ('because you uttered with your mouths proud and harsh words against his majesty, you will have no peace'), while Knibb ('For you speak proud and hard [words] against his righteousness, and you will not have peace') and Isaac ('Because you utter bold and hard [words] against his righteousness, you shall have no peace') follow the Ethiopic reading.

[131] Stuhlmacher, *Gerechtigkeit*, 169. See also Sanders, *PPJ*, 352-362. Although Sanders discusses *1 En* 99 and 101, his focus is not so much on δικαιοσύνη θεοῦ as δίκαιοι.

[132] Stuhlmacher, *Gerechtigkeit*, 175.

[133] 'And when they go to battle, they shall write on their banners: "God's truth", "God's justice" (צדקות אל), "God's glory", "God's judgement" and after these (names) all the ordered list of their names' (García Martínez).

'God's power', 'God's victory' and 'God's salvation' are mentioned in the rest of the column (4:7ff) seems to confirm this.[134] 3) The sense of אל צדקות in 1QS 11:12[135] is not entirely clear, but since the phrase is used as the means through which 'judgement' or 'vindication' is achieved (cf. 11:13), it too probably denotes God's power (cf. 1QS 10:25).[136] 4) The idea of the revelation of צדקות אל, as in Rom 1:17 and 3:21-22, is not common in Qumran, although it is indicated in 1QH 6:15-16.[137]

We now come back to *1 En* 71:14. The author of the Parables closely links the coming of the Head of Days, which is evident in the context of the passage in question (vv 9, 12, 15, 17), with the Son of Man whom 'the righteousness of the Head of Days' (*tsedqu ler^ese mewa^el*) will not leave (71:14). The idea of the coming of God here most probably depends on a similar perspective in the first chapter of the Book of the Watchers (BW). In *1 En* 1:4 in particular, God is said to 'appear with his host' and 'in the strength of his power from heaven' (φανήσεται ἐν τῇ δυνάμει τῆς ἰσχύος αὐτοῦ ἀπὸ τοῦ οὐρανοῦ). The reason is explained later in the chapter: he

---

[134] *Contra* Seifrid (*Justification*, 106). For discussions of points of contact between Pauline letters and Qumran writings, see Trebolle Barrera, *People*, 216-220. See also Sanders (*PPJ*, 305-312) for a discussion of scholarly views until 1977 and his own analysis of the Qumran texts that speak about the 'righteousness of God' or related forms.

[135] 'As for me, if I stumble, the mercies of God (אל חסד) shall be my salvation (ישוע') always; and if I fall in the sin of the flesh, in the justice of God (צדקות אל), which endures eternally, shall my judgement be' (García Martínez).

[136] Käsemann (*NTQT*, 172) is probably right in stressing this, but he readily assumes that Paul adopted the Qumran use of the phrase as *terminus technicus*. For a differing view, see Sanders (*PPJ*, 305-321, 494-495) who argues that the meaning of צדקות אל ('the righteousness of God') in 11:12 is 'mercy' because of the apparent parallelism of the phrase with אל חסד ('mercies of God'). Seifrid (*Justification*, 106) also argues that assigning 'saving power' to צדקות אל is without proof. See also Moo (*Epistle*, 85), who defines the phrase as 'mercy' or 'saving faithfulness'.

[137] The text reads:

וכול יודעיך לא ישנו דבריך כי אתה צדיק ואמת כול בחיריך וכול עולה
[ור]שע תשמיד לעד ונגלתה צדקתך לעיני כול מעשיך

'and everyone who knows you [Lord] does not change your words. For you are just, and all your chosen ones are truth. All injustice [and wick]edness you obliterate for ever, and your justice is revealed to the eyes of all your creatures' [García Martínez and Tigchelaar].
There are other texts that talk about the idea of revelation *per se*. For example, in CD, the Teacher of Righteousness, whom God raises (קום), makes known (ידע) God's dealings with wickedness (1:11-13). In 1QS, what is revealed (גלה) is the interpretation of Torah to the sons of Zadok (5:1-13). In 1QpHab, the revelation is limited to the chosen, and what is revealed to them is not 'righteousness' but the knowledge of YHWH through the Teacher of Righteousness (10:14; 11:1f). For a good survey on revelation in Qumran, see Nickelsburg, 'The Nature and Function of Revelation in 1 Enoch, Jubilees and Some Qumranic Documents', in E. Chason and M. Stone (eds), *Pseudepigraphic Perspectives: The Apocrypha and Pseudepigrapha in Light of the Dead Sea Scrolls*, 91–120.

comes in order to deal with ungodliness and injustice and bring about *peace* for or make *peace* with the righteous (1:8-9). Divine coming in this chapter is not connected with a figure of some significance.[138] In 71:14, however, the emphasis is on the Son of Man. The significance of this figure is partly dependent on the righteousness of God remaining with him. The meaning of the righteousness of God is not clear here. The term can be afforded a *moral* or *power* sense. If the former, the term refers to God's moral or ethical quality with which the Son of Man is also invested. Given that the Son of Man in the passage is described as someone who was born unto righteousness and over whom righteousness abides, this reading can be plausible. But for this reading to be probable, the 'righteousness [of God]' should be treated as having the same meaning as 'righteousness'. In the light of the use of the 'righteousness [of God]' in earlier Enochic passages and other Second Temple Jewish texts, the two terms do not appear to have the same meaning, because in almost all uses the 'righteousness [of God]' signifies divine action or power rather than divine quality in the sense of moral righteousness.

The power sense is probably more akin to the context of 71:14 as well. The key, in our view, is the militaristic overtone. In 71:12, for example, the author talks about the Head of Days coming with the four principal angels Michael and Gabriel, Raphael and Phanuel and 'thousands and ten thousands of angels without number' (cf. 1:9). Why the Head of Days along with his entourage is coming is not specified. When the lost passage in verse 13 is understood in the light of 46:3 (there is verbal similarity between 46:2-3 and 71:13-14),[139] however, the reason for the coming of the Head of Days does not seem to be different from the reason for his coming in the first chapter of BW. What is different is that there is a development in the Parables. That is, while it is God who brings about peace for or makes peace with the righteous in BW, in 71:14-16 it is the Son of Man through whom the chosen and the righteous will enjoy *peace* in the world to come. The graphic description in chapter 46, where the Son of Man is said to remove the kings and the mighty from their thrones, loosen their rein, break their teeth and so on, is not repeated in 71:12-16. But it seems notable that the author identifies the role of the coming God with or as that of the Son of Man, a figure with messianic power and authority.

Black, probably rightly, suggests that *1 En* 71:14 alludes to צמח צדקה ('the branch of righteousness' or 'the Righteous Branch') in Jer 23:5 (cf.

---

[138] But see 1:2 where Enoch is referred to as 'the blessed and righteous man of the Lord'.

[139] In the lost passage (i.e. 71:13), the Son of Man was described as accompanying the Head of Days, and Enoch asked one of the angels (as in 46:3) concerning the Son of Man as to who he was.

33:15)[140] and that a Davidic messianic feature is 'attached to the person of Enoch'.[141] What Black does not point out, however, is that in the context of Jer 23:5, YHWH's action that occasioned the rising of the Righteous Branch is followed by the salvation and safety of Israel. As a result, the Righteous Branch is called יהוה צדקנו (v. 6; cf. 33:6). צדקה here is inextricably linked with YHWH's salvific action through the Righteous Branch. Similarly, the Son of Man in *1 En* 71:14 is described as the embodiment and expression of the righteousness of the Head of Days through whom the installation of eschatological peace is ensured. This figure is portrayed as formerly hidden, but upon his revelation he is set on the celestial throne and acknowledged by the kings and the mighty as someone who possesses divine power and authority (cf. 12:1-2 with 38:2; 42:1-4; 48:2-7; 62:6f; 69:26-29; 71:14). When we combine this observation with our author's juxtaposition or identification between the role of the coming of God and that of the Son of Man, it seems to us to be safe to suggest that the righteousness of the Head of Days that remains with the Son of Man probably means the peace- and justice-installing power of God that the Son of Man embodies.

To conclude, while no certainty is possible as to whether Paul had access to Enochic or any other Second Temple Jewish texts, it cannot be denied that the apostle could have shared ideas and worldviews with those responsible for the use of the term 'righteousness of God' or its equivalent in *1 En* 71:14 and other texts such as *1 En* 99:10, 101:3, 1QM 4:6, 1QS 11:12 and *Ps Sol* 17:29f. These texts in the main seem to use the phrase in question with a power sense. Furthermore, *1 En* 71:14 (and context) portrays a formerly hidden but now revealed divine agent or messianic figure as someone who embodies God's righteousness and carries out *God's task* in the world. We do not know if this was an existing pattern within some Jewish circles. Neither can we rule it out. If it was an existing pattern, Paul could have been aware of it.

4.3.3. Revelation of God in Christ

As we saw earlier, Pss 98 and 143 express a belief that the hiddenness of the righteousness of the Lord as God's saving power or action means the hiddenness of the Lord himself. So the psalmist's cry for the appearance of the righteousness of the Lord obviously is a cry for the appearance of the

---

[140] Jer 23:5 (cf. 33:15) reads: 'Behold, the days are coming, says the Lord, when I will raise up for David a righteous branch (והקמתי לדוד צמח צדיק, καὶ ἀναστήσω τῷ Δαυιδ ἀνατολὴν δικαίαν) and he shall reign as king and deal wisely (ומלך מלך והשכיל, καὶ βασιλεύσει βασιλεὺς, καὶ συνήσει ['a king shall reign and understand']), and he shall execute justice and righteousness upon the earth.'
[141] Black, *Book*, 252.

Lord himself to save his own and judge the enemies of his people. Our consideration of the use of the term 'righteousness of God' in Enochic and other Second Temple Jewish texts seems to reinforce the argument that the revelation of the righteousness of God means the revelation of God's saving power and presence. This section attempts to show how the meaning of the revelation of the righteousness of God in Rom 1:17 can be related to Christ.

Scholars such as Hays and Wright have argued that in Rom 1:16-17, Paul, against the background of the problem of theodicy, saw Jesus' death as the apocalyptic moment in which God's covenant promises with Israel came to their sudden climax and finality.[142] There are not sufficiently unambiguous textual signals in the passage and its immediate context to corroborate this claim, but Hays and Wright may be right in approaching Paul's declarations in Rom 1:16-17 from an 'apocalyptic' perspective that is underpinned by the problem of theodicy. The background for Paul's claim in Rom 1:16-17 would certainly have been the problem of theodicy, because like any thinking first century Jew, Paul probably longed for the appearance of 'God's righteousness' where 'apocalyptic' was the main climate of his thought.

The term 'apocalyptic' has been afforded confusingly diverse meanings, considering which will not serve our purpose here. It suffices rather to say that since Schweitzer and Käsemann, many have understood the term to mean Paul's outlook and epistemology that are characterised by a universalistic conception of two antithetical ages and/or spheres controlled by opposing forces or protagonists.[143] While Schweitzer limited the notion of

---

[142] This is also consistent with Hays' view that in Romans Paul is explicating and defending the story of Israel that finds its coherence in its relation to the scriptural story of 'God's righteousness'. Hays, *Echoes*, 38-41, 157-158; 'Πίστις and Pauline Christology', in Johnson & Hay (eds), *Pauline Theology IV*, 35-60, 46. Wright ('Letter', 398-403; 425-426) explicates Rom 1:17 through a combination of covenant, law-court and apocalyptic metaphors. See also Bockmuehl, *Revelation*, 221-230.

[143] For diverse approaches and definitions, see Beker, *Paul's Apocalyptic Gospel: The Coming Triumph of God*, 68-69; *Paul the Apostle: The Triumph of God in Life and Thought* 144; Rowland, *Christian Origins: An Account of the Setting and Character of the Most Important Sect of Judaism*, 58f; De Boer, *The Defeat of Death: Apocalyptic Eschatology in 1 Corinthians 15 and Romans 5*; 'Paul and Apocalyptic Eschatology', in J. Collins (ed.), *The Encyclopedia of Apocalypticism*, 345-383; A. Y. Collins, *Cosmology and Eschatology in Jewish and Christian Apocalypticism*; Matlock, *Unveiling the Apocalyptic Paul: Paul's Interpreters and the Rhetoric of Criticism*. Matlock's summaries of scholarly ideas from Schweitzer through to the mid 1990s are very informative, but his critique of scholarship would be weightier if his work showed sufficient knowledge of Second Temple Jewish literature upon which most of the subjects of his analytical scrutiny depend.

apocalyptic to the Danielic-Enochic nexus of ideas,[144] Käsemann argued that Paul went beyond that, because for him the hidden and heavenly Son of Man was revealed as the exalted Lord of the world and the success of the Gentile mission had introduced a change of perspective into his thinking.[145] Paul's perspective, for Käsemann, is dualistic where there are two opposed spheres into one or the other of which humanity is integrated.[146] It is within such a model that Käsemann seeks to explain the revelation of the righteousness of God in Rom 1:17: the revelation of the *power* at work in a human being as well as the *gift* of a righteous status granted to a human being. The expression of this power and gift is the Son of God through whom God is revealed or comes to claim his right on the earth.[147] When Paul talks about the revelation of the righteousness of God, then, he is talking about God himself entering the earthly sphere through Christ.[148] Beker and Martyn have concurred with Käsemann's overall thesis: the former speaks of God as the coming one who has already come to his creation,[149] while the latter describes the divine apocalypse as a continuing

---

[144] Schweitzer, *Interpreters*, 177, 244-245; *The Mysticism of Paul the Apostle,* 82, 96-97. As Beker (*Apocalyptic*, 101) rightly notes, within his mystical interpretation of Paul's thinking Schweitzer transposed apocalyptic to his ethical ideal of 'reverence for life' that results from the realisation of the mystical convergence between the natural and supernatural (see also Schweitzer, *My Life and Thought: An Autobiography*; *The Teaching of Reverence for Life*). Schweitzer's interpretation of Jesus' eschatology in terms of the imminent end of the physical world (as opposed to a subjective future with no immediate catastrophes) determined his coinage of Paul's theology as mystical. Such a thesis, as Wright (*The New Testament and the People of God*, 321, 332-334) has complained, is based on construing some of the Second Temple Jewish language as flatly literal, when, in actual fact, it could have been highly figurative. Wright follows Caird (*The Language and Imagery of the Bible*, 243-271), who criticised Weiss and Schweitzer for fostering such a view by 'assuming that the biblical writers had minds as pedestrian as their own' (p. 271). For earlier criticisms of Schweitzer, see Dodd, *The Meaning of Paul for Today*; *The Apostolic Preaching and Its Developments*; Cullmann, *Christ and Time: The Primitive Christian Conception of Time and History*; *Salvation in History*.

[145] Käsemann, *New Testament Questions of Today* (*NTQT*), 102, 115-118, 130.

[146] Käsemann, *NTQT*, 103; 128, 135-136.

[147] Käsemann, *Commentary*, 29; see also Way, *Lordship*, 278. Way's (*Lordship*, 130) outline of Käsemann's identification of particular 'apocalyptic' features is helpful: imminent expectation of the parousia; an orientation to the world (not to the individual) within which a human being is understood as 'a piece of world'; the two-aeons motif; the correspondence of the primal time (*Urzeit*) and end-time (*Endzeit*); a belief in transvaluation of all values at the end; the 'eschatological law' of the correspondence of deed and recompense (*jus talionis*).

[148] Käsemann, *Commentary*, 29.

[149] Beker, *Paul*, 19, 362-363. Differing from Käsemann, Beker (*Paul*, 59ff; *Apocalyptic*, 30) argues that δικαιοσύνη θεοῦ ἀποκαλύπτεται is to do with the appearance of divine 'righteousness' to vindicate God's unswerving faithfulness to his promises to Israel. This cannot be detected in Paul's statement, however.

event or process inaugurated in the coming of Christ and characterised by
God's dynamic invasion of the cosmos.[150] Although Beker and Martyn do
not specifically afford a christological meaning concerning the idea of the
revelation of the righteousness of God in Rom 1:17, like Käsemann they
understand the Pauline idea of revelation in terms of a universalistic
conception of divine revelation in the sense mainly of God's interventional
appearance in and through Christ to alter circumstances in the realm of the
created world.[151]

This conception, we would further argue, can be linked with Paul's own
autobiography that centres on his understanding of the revelation of Christ
in terms of the divine coming into his Pharisaic life (Gal 1:16).[152] As
argued earlier, Christ is the embodiment of the righteousness of God (1
Cor 1:30; 2 Cor 5:21), so the revelation of Christ can mean the revelation
of the righteousness of God (Rom 1:17). The term 'righteousness of God'
denotes God's quality of being righteous, not because he observes and up-
holds an abstract standard of δίκη; nor because righteousness as a static
moral and ethical quality resides in him, but rather because he actively establishes his righteous and divine rule and order in the world by dealing
with evil and vindicating the cause of the wronged. In doing so, he makes
the power he possesses as the supreme Saviour, Judge and Ruler of the
world visible. So when we say that the righteousness of God as the eschatological saving activity or power of God is being revealed, we mean that
God's salvific power that became a reality in the world through Christ is
being disclosed. In other words, the formerly hidden salvific power of God
that was manifested in Christ is being made known to Jews and Gentiles
through the *kerygmatisation* of the gospel events (Rom 1:16-17). But
Paul's idea of the revelation of God's eschatological saving power should
not be divorced from his idea of the revelation of Christ (Gal 1:16; Rom
15:20-21), because Christ is the bearer of God's power that saves and
installs righteousness. In short, the revelation of the righteousness of God
probably stands for the revelation of God in Christ (and, by extension, for
the revelation of Christ himself) both in the gospel events and in proclamation.

---

[150] Martyn, *Theological Issues in the Letters of Paul*, 87.

[151] See also Rowland, *Origins*, 56-64, 316; *The Open Heaven: A Study in Apocalyptic
in Judaism and Early Christianity*, 14ff. It is to be noted here that the concept of apocalyptic can be explained in terms of some vision through which heavenly knowledge concerning historical circumstances is directly disclosed. It can also be explained in terms of
a set of beliefs about the future (i.e. the expectation of an imminent catastrophic end of
the physical world) or a state of mind (i.e. one's otherworldly journey while in a trance,
or revelation through a vision or audition of a supernatural reality in the sphere of a person's existence). But that does not seem to be part of Paul's thinking in Rom 1:17.

[152] See also De Boer, 'Paul', 350, 356, 364-368.

This christological construal of the revelation of the formerly hidden but now revealed divine righteousness can be supported by Paul's talk about the revelation of μυστήριον in the doxological composition in Rom 16:25-27. The authenticity of this passage as an integral part of the letter has been a matter of text-critical debate, which is partly triggered by the fact that the earliest papyrus (P[46]) has the doxology between 15:33 and 16:1. The doxology can be a later addition to a fourteen-chapter form, a ceremonial conclusion appended at a later stage, or an epistolary conclusion original to Paul himself.[153] We cannot consider these proposals here for reasons of space and limited purpose. However, while remaining uncertain about its actual position, on the grounds that many important papyri and parchment manuscripts, and the oldest Latin (e.g. VL, Vg), Coptic, Syriac and Ethiopic texts contain the doxology[154] and that the

---

[153] These possibilities were proposed by Hurtado ('The Doxology at the End of Romans', in Epp & Fee [eds], *New Testament Textual Criticism: Its Significance for Exegesis. Essays in Honor of Bruce M. Metzger*, 185-199) in response to Gamble (*The Textual History of the Letter to the Romans*, 96-124), who, on the basis of stylistic and textual observations (some MSS having the fourteen-chapter text of Romans), argued that the doxology is inauthentic and an editorial product added to the fourteen-chapter form of the letter. Marshall ('Romans 16:25-27 – An Apt Conclusion', in Soderlund & Wright [eds], *Romans*, 170-184) goes a little further than Hurtado in that he concludes that 'the doxology fits aptly at the end of Romans' (the quotation is from page 183).

[154] The following diagram shows that many MSS up to the ninth century CE contained the passage (I am indebted to Nestle-Aland and Fitzmyer [*Romans*, 46-47]).

Manuscript	Date	Name	Contents
P[46]	200CE	Chester Beatty Papyrus II (Dublin): University of Michigan	5:17-6:3; 15:29-33; 16:25-27; 16:1-3; 16:4-13; 16:14-23
ℵ (01)	4th century	C. Sinaiticus (London)	All of Romans
B (03)	4th century	C. Vaticanus (Rome)	All of Romans
A (02)	5th century	C. Alexandrinus (Lond.)	All of Romans
C (04)	5th century	C. Ephraemi (Paris)	All of Romans, except 2:5-3:21; 9:6-10:15; 11:31-13:10
D[p] (06)	6th century	C. Claromontanus (Paris)	All of Romans, except 1:1-7a, 27-30
P[61]	700 CE	? New York University	Only 16:23, 25-27
044	8th/9th century	C. Athous (Mt Athos)	All of Romans
F[p]	9th century	C. Augiensis (Cambridge)	All of Romans, except 1:1-3:19
G[p]	9th century	C. Boernerianus (Dresden)	All of Romans, except 1:1-5; 2:16-25
L (020)	9th century	Bib. Angelica (Rome)	All of Romans
P (025)	9th century	? (Leningrad)	1:1-2:14; 3:6-8:32; 9:12-11:21; 12:2-16:28

paragraph echoes some of the motifs and expressions in other parts of the letter,[155] we wish to base our subsequent discussion on the perspective that Rom 16:25-27 probably belonged to the original Pauline edition of Romans.[156]

Our focal question is: how does a christological interpretation of Rom 1:16-17 fit into the expressions in the doxology? The relevant expression is the revelation of μυστήριον,[157] which 'had been silent or hidden' (σεσιγημένου) for 'eternal ages' (χρόνοις αἰωνίοις). The revelation of μυστήριον has so far been understood in terms of the revelation of 'the salvific decree of God in and through Christ'[158] or the revelation of 'the saving plan of God' in the preaching of the gospel.[159] Both interpretations are valid, but neither of them suggests that the revelation of the formerly hidden μυστήριον could mean the revelation of Christ. There are several things that seem to support this christological construal.

First, a link can be made between the revelation of the formerly hidden 'mystery' that results in ὑπακοὴν πίστεως amongst Jews and Gentiles (16:25-26)[160] and the fact that Paul's prime objective in proclaiming the

---

[155] For example: εὐαγγέλιον (cf. 1:16), ἀποκάλυψις (cf. 2:5; 8:19), φανερωθέντος δὲ νῦν διά τε γραφῶν προφητικῶν (cf. 1:2; 3:21) and εἰς ὑπακοὴν πίστεως (cf. 1:5).

[156] See also Gamble, *Histroy*, 127-129; Donfried, 'A Short Note on Romans 16', in Donfried (ed.), *The Romans Debate*, 44-52; Fitzmyer, *Romans*, 50; Hurtado, 'Doxology', 185-199; Stuhlmacher, *Letter*, 10, 256-258; Marshall, 'Romans 16:25-27', 174-180.

[157] The term μυστήριον is not widespread in Paul's Seven Letter Corpus: Rom 11:25; 1 Cor 2:1 (?); 2:7; 4:1; 13:2; 14:2; 15:51; cf. Eph 1:9; 3:3-4, 9; 5:32; 6:19; Col 1:26-27; 2:2; 4:3. It is to be noted here that in 1 Cor 2:1 some important textual witnesses such as ℵ², B, D, F, G, Ψ, Majority Texts, Vulgate and the Syriac version have τὸ μαρτύριον rather than τὸ μυστήριον.

[158] Stuhlmacher (*Letter*, 257) seems to equate this salvific decree of God with the appearance of Christ, the word of God (cf. Philo: *Plant*, 117). This view is consistent with that of Käsemann (*Commentary*, 425-426) who associates μυστήριον with the divine word that is enwrapped in the divine silence. Such a view is informed by *Wis* 18:13-16, where the story of Ex 12:28ff is philosophically recounted, the all-powerful word of God (ὁ παντοδύναμός σου λόγος) was sent from the throne of the king in heaven (ἀπ᾽ οὐρανῶν ἐκ θρόνων βασιλειῶν) as a warrior during silence (σιγῆς) and struck the Egyptian first-born, which resulted in the Egyptians acknowledging that Israel was the 'son of God' (Θεοῦ υἱόν). In reference to the *Wisdom* text, Käsemann (*Commentary*, 426) suggests that Rom 16:25-26 'is not talking of the divine word which leaps into the silence of the world but of the word which follows the divine silence'.

[159] Marshall, 'Romans 16:25-27', 180, 182.

[160] Grammatically, ὑπακοὴν πίστεως (lit. 'obedience of faith/faithfulness') can be understood in various ways (here I follow Cranfield's classification [*Romans 1-8*, 66]): objective genitive ('obedience to the faith' in the sense of the body of doctrine accepted, 'obedience to faith' in the sense of the authority of 'faith', 'obedience to God's faithfulness attested in the "gospel"'), subjective genitive ('the obedience which faith works', 'the obedience required by faith'), adjectival genitive ('believing obedience'), or genitive of apposition ('the obedience which consists in faith'). Of these interpretations, one can-

gospel in places where Christ has not already been named (15:20; cf. 16:25) was so that "[t]hose who have never been told of [Christ] shall see, and those who have never heard of him shall understand" (15:21). Second, in 1 Corinthians μυστήριον θεοῦ is used in relation to Christ who is identified as the wisdom of God, the power of God and the righteousness from God (1:24, 30; 2:1, 6-10). Third, that Christ, for Paul, is the mystery of God that was once hidden but is now revealed appears to be reflected in the so-called Deutero-Pauline letters, Ephesians (1:9; 3:3-4; 6:19) and Colossians (Col 1:26-27; 2:2-3; 4:3) in particular. Finally, the once/now structure with the christological turn of words can be seen in the writings of Ignatius ('Jesus Christ, who was with the Father before the worlds and appeared at the end of time' [*Mag* 6:1]) and Hermas ('The Son of God is older than all his creation. ... He was made manifest in the last days of the consummation' [*Sim* 9:12]).[161] These texts confirm a continuity of thinking between Paul and the Church Fathers in relation to Christ's eschatological revelation.

In sum, while the revelation of 'mystery' can be understood as God's decree or plan of salvation, the evidence outlined above seems to favour the argument that the revelation of 'mystery' stands for the revelation of Christ. As Christ is the one who embodies the identity and activity of God as the supreme Saviour, Judge and Ruler of the world, we can conclude, albeit deductively, that there is a christologically undergirded conceptual similarity between the meaning of the revelation of the mystery [of God] and that of the revelation of the righteousness of God.

---

not easily choose the interpretation that best suits the structure of Paul's thought. As Black (*Romans*, 38) suggests, however, πίστις in 1:5 seems to be something from which the obedience springs. In ὑπακοὴ πίστεως, the stress is placed on πίστις as an active agent or even the matrix within which obedience is exercised. In 5:19, ὑπακοή is expressed as that of Jesus. For further discussion, see Garlington, *Faith*, 10-31, 108.

[161] Diognetus 8 reads slightly differently from Ignatius and Hermas: 'And having conceived a great and unutterable scheme he communicated it to his Son alone. For so long as he kept and guarded his wise design as a mystery, he seemed to neglect us and to be careless about us. But when he revealed it through his beloved Son, and manifested the purpose which he had prepared from the beginning he gave us all these gifts at once, participation in his benefits, and sight and understanding of (mysteries) which none of us ever would have expected.' Some may take these texts as having a direct influence on the composition of Rom 16:25-27, but as Marshall ('Romans 16:25-27', 182) points out, there is nothing to suggest that the once/now structure in our doxology belongs to a later period.

5. Conclusions

We began this chapter by asking whether and to what extent Rom 1:16 and 1:17a can be understood with christological significance. Having considered Paul's expressions in these verses, it seems to us to be safe to conclude that despite the absence of direct references to Christ or absolutely obvious christological clues, various evidences seem to suggest that δύναμις θεοῦ and the revelation of δικαιοσύνη θεοῦ probably are linguistic images for Christ and God's salvific power and presence in and through Christ respectively. The function of γάρ in Rom 1:15-18 as a causal-coordinating particle seems to facilitate this interpretation, because 1:16b, 1:17a and 1:18a can be taken as independently forming three exegetically interrelated reasons probably intended to justify and affirm Paul's claim that he is not ashamed of the gospel. So our exegetical premise is that the meaning of the power of God that is proclaimed in the gospel and is directed towards the salvation of Jews and Greeks (1:16) is concomitant with that of the righteousness of God (the subject matter of Paul's gospel) that is being revealed ἐκ πίστεως εἰς πίστιν (1:17a).

While accepting the reasonableness of the traditional reading that εὐαγγέλιον is the unexpressed subject of the second half of 1:16 and δύναμις θεοῦ predicate, we argued that it would also be reasonable to take δύναμις θεοῦ as the subject of 1:16b, much as δικαιοσύνη θεοῦ is the subject of 1:17a. This enables us to understand the power of God that is directed towards the salvation of Jews and Greeks as the content of Paul's gospel. It also makes it possible to take the power of God as a co-referential term for Christ. Christological elements in the context and other evidence enable us to maintain this new reading. In Rom 1:4, for example, Christ is depicted as someone who is designated as the Son of God *with power* (ἐν δυνάμει) beyond resurrection. The gospel Paul preaches is a gospel concerning (1:3) or of the Son of God (1:9), who, for him, always remains the crucified but exalted redeemer (6:1-7; 8:34). Paul refers to the crucified Christ as the power of God (1 Cor 1:24). To say that the power of God is the content of Paul's gospel is thus the same thing as saying that Christ is the content of Paul's gospel.

When we come to Rom 1:17a, this half is traditionally understood in terms of the revelation of righteousness that is acquired on the basis of or by faith. In this reading, as argued by Watson in particular, revelation appears to be limited to Paul's oral proclamation, the righteousness of God is equated with the righteousness or salvation of the person of the Habakkuk citation (the believer) and, consequently, the righteousness of God and salvation are understood as the outcome of the power of God. There is no question that Paul equates righteousness and salvation in Romans. The abstract noun 'righteousness' can also be understood to be a righteous status received through Christ (Rom 5:17; Phil 3:9). However, the traditional understanding of Rom 1:17a in terms of the revelation of righteousness-by-faith, where the righteousness of God is construed as gift of status received by faith, cannot be sustained exegetically and syntactically.

First of all, the internal-textual and Second Temple Jewish evidence show that the righteousness of God is generally employed with a power sense. Paul's use of Pss 98 and 143 as backgrounds for Rom 1:17a and 3:21 respectively also suggests that revelation in Rom 1:17a (ἀποκαλύπτεται) and 3:21 (πεφανέρωται) probably denotes the revelation of a formerly hidden divine salvific power in the gospel events and through the *kerygmatisation* of those events in Paul's mission. Furthermore, the juxtaposition between the power of God and the righteousness of God as contents of the gospel also suggests that both terms have the same sense, namely God's saving power. But the divine saving power revealed in the cross and in the proclamation should not be taken as some abstract concept. For Paul, God's identity and saving power are embodied and expressed in Christ (the formerly hidden but revealed mystery of [God]), so he depicts Christ as the righteousness and power of God (1 Cor 1:24, 30; 2 Cor 5:21). Such a depiction is not peculiar, because in Jer 23:5-6 a messiah is called 'the Lord our Righteousness'. This prophetic passage seems to inform the author of the Parables in *1 En* 71:14, where a formerly hidden but revealed messianic figure is understood as the embodiment of 'the righteousness of the Head of Days'. Paul's expressions in Rom 1:17a should thus be understood in the light of the revelation of Christ (Gal 1:12, 16). The righteousness of God revealed in the Christ event and in proclamation is God's salvific power embodied in Christ rather than a righteous status acquired by faith. To talk about a status being revealed in the Christ event makes no sense. Also, to conflate the meaning of righteousness with the meaning of the righteousness of God would be tantamount to conflating human status or salvation with Christ. Our reading is more probable than the conventional interpretation of Rom 1:17a.

Paul seems to have cited Hab 2:4b in Rom 1:17b (ὁ δὲ δίκαιος ἐκ πίστεως ζήσεται) as a *proof* for his *claim* in Rom 1:17a not only because of his extensive interest in the πιστ- word group but also because of the etymological and lexical relationship between δίκαιος and δικαιοσύνη θεοῦ. How we understand *the claim* obviously affects the way we understand *the proof*. Accordingly, attempting to understand the meaning of ὁ δίκαιος will be the focus of our exegetical inquiry in the following chapter.

Ο ΔΙΚΑΙΟΣ: Generic Individual or Messianic?

1. Introduction

As the central aim of this study is to evaluate critically the christological interpretation (over against the anthropological interpretation) of Rom 1:17 in general and the Habakkuk citation in particular, our discussion in this chapter will centre on the question as to whether ὁ δίκαιος in the Habakkuk citation refers to the generic believer or Christ. Before attempting to answer this question by considering issues and arguments based on the citation and related Pauline texts, however, we will discuss the manner in which the epithet is used in some NT passages. After that, we will examine the use of the epithet in the Parables in *1 Enoch* and in shared interpretative traditions within Judaism. Our discussion of the Parables will enable us to answer the question as to whether there is sufficient evidence to claim that the epithet is a messianic designation throughout the Parables. But more importantly, the cumulative result of our treatment of this document, non-Pauline texts of the NT and other Jewish writings of the Second Temple period will hopefully inform and illumine our reading of the same epithet in the Habakkuk citation in Rom 1:17. Finally, we will return to Paul and examine Rom 1:18-3:20 with the view to answering the question as to whether Paul's central idea in the block can be shown to be consistent with a christological construal of ὁ δίκαιος in the Habakkuk citation.

2. Righteous One in Non-Pauline Texts of the New Testament

The singular adjective δίκαιος with or without the definite article is used as a designation for Jesus in some non-Pauline NT texts. We herein examine briefly whether or to what extent the uses in Matt 10:41b, Acts (3:14; 7:52; 22:14) and the so-called Catholic Epistles (1 Pet 3:18; 1 Jn 2:1) can be regarded as messianic.

1) In Matt 10:41b, Jesus says καὶ ὁ δεχόμενος δίκαιον εἰς ὄνομα δικαίου μισθὸν δικαίου λήμψεται. It is not immediately clear that any of

the δίκαιος language here refers to Jesus.[1] As the line in this half clearly reproduces much of the vocabulary of the previous half (ὁ δεχόμενος προφήτην εἰς ὄνομα προφήτου μισθὸν προφήτου λήμψεται [10:41a]), however, the parallelism can thus be understood as 'synonymous' to the effect that the prophet and the righteous one are one and the same.[2] But does the one who is received have the same referent as the one in whose name (εἰς ὄνομα προφήτου) the former is received? Scholars generally understand all uses of προφήτης and δίκαιος in the passage as referring to itinerant Christian missionaries.[3] In order to maintain this reading, the RSV, for example, takes εἰς causally and renders εἰς ὄνομα δικαίου 'because he is a righteous man'. However, that εἰς could be used causally in NT passages has been shown to be unsustainable.[4] Furthermore, the RSV and, indeed, most commentaries do not seem to take into account the connection between εἰς ὄνομα δικαίου ('in the name of the righteous one') and 10:40, where Jesus says '[w]hoever welcomes you welcomes me, and whoever welcomes me welcomes the one who sent me'. As a result, they fail to appreciate that εἰς ὄνομα δικαίου denotes acceptance of Jesus' messengers as prophets and righteous persons.[5] It seems to us to be the case that the prophet/righteous one who is received and the prophet/righteous one in whose name the former is received have different referents: Christian missionary and Christ, the sent and the sender. Jesus the teacher and the master (10:24-25) is also Jesus *the sending prophet and righteous one*.[6] The question, then, is whether δίκαιος with reference to Jesus in 10:41 is messianic. No straightforward answer is possible from 10:40-42, but since 11:2 concludes the preceding accounts in 10:40-42,[7] a connection between the 'righteous one' with reference to Jesus in 10:41 and τὰ ἔργα τοῦ Χριστοῦ in 11:2 could suggest that the former is indirectly messianic. As ὁ Χριστός most probably is a messianic title for Jesus ὁ ἐρχόμενος (11:3; cf. 3:11), the phrase τὰ ἔργα τοῦ Χριστοῦ refers back to Jesus' 'authoritative

---

[1] The adjective is also used in Matt 9:13; 13:43, 49. In all these references, δίκαιος is generic. It is to be noted that the use in 9:13 on the literal level is in tension with the use in 10:41.

[2] So Davies and Allison, *The Gospel according to Matthew* (vol 2), 227.

[3] See, for example, Davies and Allison, *Gospel*, 227; Hagner, *Matthew 1-13*, 295-296; Harrington, *The Gospel of Matthew*, 153; Descamps, *Les justes et la justice dans les évangiles et le christianisme primitif hormis la doctrine proprement paulinienne*, 213-219.

[4] See, for example, Wallace, *Greek*, 369-371.

[5] See Gundry, *Matthew: A Commentary on His Literary and Theological Art*, 202.

[6] Davies and Allison (*Gospel*, 227) accept that Jesus is the prophet and the righteous one, but they do not refer to him as the 'righteous one' who sends the righteous ones.

[7] Davies and Allison (*Gospel*, 240), probably rightly, argue that 11:2 brings closure to 4:23-11:1.

words and his mighty deeds as messianic'.[8] In brief, while Matthew's use
of δίκαιος with reference to Jesus in 10:41 may not be directly messianic,
that Jesus the *sending righteous one* in this verse is Jesus the Messiah in
11:2 cannot be denied.

2) In Acts, Jesus is referred to as ὁ δίκαιος by Peter, Stephen and Paul
in three different contexts. In 3:14, Peter before the Sanhedrin accuses the
Jews of denying τὸν ἅγιον καὶ δίκαιον. Here the two adjectives bound
together by one article are contrasted with ἄνδρα φονέα, which makes the
verse an allusion to the Barabbas episode in Luke 23:18-19. Since they appear to be merely descriptive in contrast with the 'murderer' and the designation δίκαιος in particular recalls the acclamation of the centurion about
Jesus when he was on the cross (Lk 23:47), one might even suggest that
both adjectives designate Jesus' attribute or moral character as a dedicated
and righteous agent sent by God to his people. This may be valid, but ὁ
δίκαιος (and ὁ ἅγιος) in 3:14 is unambiguously messianic, because in the
context Jesus is referred to as the glorified 'servant' (or 'child') of God
(3:13, 26), the suffering messiah (3:18) and the messiah appointed for
Israel (3:20).[9] This is also the case in Acts 7:52, where Jesus is presented
as ὁ δίκαιος who is persecuted and martyred (v 52) and as ὁ υἱὸς τοῦ
ἀνθρώπου who is standing ἐκ δεξιῶν τοῦ θεοῦ (vv 55-56).[10] In the narrative of the trial of Stephen in Acts 7, in short, Jesus' role as an appointed
judge (Acts 10:42; 17:31) in his post-resurrection life seems to correlate
with the description of his present position in the heavenly court.[11] Finally,
in Acts 22:14, Paul, from the step of the Antonian fortress, tells the
Jerusalem crowd that he was someone who was chosen to know God's will
and 'to see the Righteous One'. In this verse, Paul is referring to what
Ananias in Acts 9:17 said to him after his experience on the road to
Damascus. The fact that the reference in the latter is to ὁ κύριος (who appeared to Paul) rather than to ὁ δίκαιος (whom Paul is divinely chosen to

---

[8] Davies and Allison, *Gospel*, 240. See also Harrington, *Matthew*, 159.

[9] See also Descamps (*Les justes*, 76-79), who argues that depicting ὁ δίκαιος in Acts
3:14 as a suffering messiah is not sufficient. For him, both ὁ δίκαιος and ὁ ἅγιος are
honorific titles reserved for a prophet. They designate here the power of the messiah,
who saves his people through 'mighty justice'.

[10] In *1 Enoch*, the Son of Man/Chosen One is described as both standing before the
Lord (49:2; cf. 48:2-3) and sitting on the celestial throne as judge, having been appointed
or glorified by the Lord (51:3; 55:4; 61:8; 62:2; 69:27). Cf. Ps 110:1 and Dan 7:13-14
with Lk 22:69, and *1 En* 69:27 with Matt 19:28; 25:31; Jn 5:22, 27. See also Rowland,
Heaven, 368-370; Fletcher-Louis, *Luke-Acts: Angels, Christology and Soteriology*, 246-
247; Descamps, *Les justes*, 79-81.

[11] There are only five uses of ὁρίζω in the whole of the NT: in Acts 10:42, 17:31; Heb
4:7 (with the sense of God appointing or setting a 'day'), and Rom 1:4.

see) does not diminish the messianic significance of ὁ δίκαιος in 22:14.[12] For one thing, in his recounting of the Damascus event, Paul refers to Christ as ὁ κύριος in 22:10. In short, the Acts evidence shows sufficiently clearly that for Luke the term ὁ δίκαιος is messianic.

3) The term 'righteous one' with or without the definite article is used with reference to Christ in some so-called Catholic Epistles as well. In 1 Pet 3:18, for example, the substantive δίκαιος recalls the earlier christological statements in 2:21-25. Both passages express Christ's innocence or sinlessness. But both passages appear to be reliant on Isa 53:11, which formed the concept of the *suffering righteous one* within a broader Jewish tradition where it eventually assumed messianic import (cf. *Wis* 2:18; 4:10-16 with *1 En* 38:2, 3; 53:6). As we saw above, Acts clearly shows that such a concept was subsequently applied as a messianic designation to Jesus by Peter, Stephen and Paul.[13] While δίκαιος in 1 Pet 3:18 appears to serve primarily as an attribute of Jesus, it seems the case that the term is specifically used with reference to the one who suffered for many. The same may be true in 1 Jn 2:1, where δίκαιος is used along with Jesus Christ (Ἰησοῦν Χριστὸν δίκαιον). Two things can be noticed here. First, the use of the adjective corresponds to 1:9 where God is referred to as δίκαιος and πιστός, which suggests that the author adds the 'righteous one' to present Jesus not only as an innocent sufferer (2:2) but also as someone who represents God the Righteous One (cf. Rom 3:26).[14] Second, the term seems to be intended to show how Jesus became the *Paraclete* in the divine court.[15] To be sure, the term does not seem to carry primarily a messianic sense, because in verse 29, Jesus is again referred to as δίκαιος and anyone who does δικαιοσύνη is born of him or, as in 3:7, is δίκαιος – such particular and generic reference can be observed in James 5:6 as well, although in the latter the term is used arthrously. However, it should be stressed again that there is a traditional background to the description in 1 Jn 2:1, probably echoing Isa 53:11[16] and stemming from the Apostolic use of ὁ δίκαιος as a title for Jesus.[17] It is on these grounds that Longenecker argues that 1 Pet 3:18 and 1 Jn 2:1 along with other Jewish-Christian materials employ δίκαιος 'not only as an attribute of Jesus but also in substantival adjective

---

[12] See also Descamps (*Les justes*, 81-84), who argues that ὁ δίκαιος in Acts 22:14 is a messianic epithet.

[13] See also Michaels, *1 Peter* (WBC 49), 202; Elliott, *1 Peter: A New Translation with Introduction and Commentary*, 641.

[14] See Strecker, *The Johannine Letters* (translated by Linda Maloney), 35-36.

[15] So Strecker (*Letters*, 39-40). See also Schnackenburg, *The Johannine Epistles* (translated by Reginald and Ilsa Fuller), 87.

[16] Schnackenburg, *Epistles*, 87.

[17] See also Smalley, *1, 2, 3 John*, 38.

form as a christological title'.[18] Barrett, on the other hand, dismisses them as 'irrelevant' to our messianic understanding.[19] We would generally go along with Longenecker's conclusion, but it ought to be nuanced.

From our discussion above, in the so-called Catholic Epistles there is no arthrous use of δίκαιος with reference to Christ; nor is there any clear reference where the adjective is employed with a messianic sense. Christ is referred to as δίκαιος in 1 Pet 3:18 and 1 Jn 2:1, but that does not amount to an assertion that δίκαιος is messianic for the obvious reason that the adjective can simply be construed as a reference to an attribute of any person whose life is characterised by righteousness. Indeed, Peter and John employ δίκαιος primarily as an attribute of Jesus, but they, probably depending on Isa 53:11, seem to do so in order to show that Jesus is *the suffering one*. For John in particular, Jesus represents God the Righteous One and stands as the *Paraclete* before the throne of God. This seems to suggest that the term expresses something more than merely an attribute. We would cautiously propose that δίκαιος in these two passages be understood as referring *indirectly* to Jesus as *the suffering messiah*. Matt 10:41 can also be interpreted as indirectly messianic. But all this means is that in non-Pauline NT texts it is only Acts 3:14, 7:52 and 22:14 that *clearly* use [ὁ] δίκαιος messianically. This brings us to our next question as to how the epithet was used in Second Temple Jewish literature, *1 Enoch* in particular.

3. Righteous One in the Parables of *1 Enoch*

While many now accept the relevance of the Parables for NT christology, the focus has been on comparing the traits of the figure of the Parables with that of Jesus in the Gospels and answering the question whether the epithet Son of Man in the former set a precedent for its use in the latter. Theisohn was one of the earliest scholars to do a detailed study of the traditions of the figure, but he did not go beyond attempting to connect the Son of Man tradition in the Parables and comparative traditions with that of the Synoptic Gospels.[20] It should be recognised here, however, that Theisohn rightly challenged his predecessors, who – using *Religionsgeschichte* – had viewed the figure of the Parables and its origin as foreign

---

[18] Longenecker, *The Christology of Early Jewish Christianity*, 47; cf. also Hays, "'Righteous'", 194-195.

[19] Barrett, *Commentary on Acts*, 196.

[20] Theisohn, *Der auserwählte Richter: Untersuchungen zum traditionsgschichtlichen Ort der Menschensohngestalt der Bilderreden des Äthiopischen Henoch*, 1ff.

to Judaism, and attempted to understand the figure within the framework of Jewish *Traditionsgeschichte*.[21]

With regard to the Parables and Paul, over two decades ago John Collins claimed that the Parables were 'evidently closer to Paul's "pattern of religion" than to any form of "covenantal nomism", the pattern which E. P. Sanders finds to be typical of Palestinian Judaism'.[22] To substantiate this argument, Collins pointed out the significance of the notion of revelation on which the entire Enochic tradition is based, the implicit claims of an authority older than Moses, and the terminology of 'election', 'faith' and 'righteousness'.[23] While Collins' recognition of the relevance of the Enochic ideas in the Parables to Paul's 'pattern of religion' is an important step forward, Collins did not explore how the *messianic* portrayal of the figure of the Parables and the thought pattern and worldview behind that portrayal could inform a study of Paul's christology. Nor have Pauline scholars pursued this, although they recognise the importance of the Parables and indeed use relevant texts from the document. Our discussion below will attempt to remedy that through showing how the idea of the 'righteous one' as a messianic designation developed and was expressed within the Enochic tradition. But before that, we need to pay brief attention to the problem of the date of the Parables.

3.1. The Problem of the Date of the Parables

Some scholars dismiss the relevance of the Parables to NT studies on the grounds that they are too late to have influenced NT thinking. In this section, we ask whether there is not evidence for an earlier dating and we shall briefly assess that evidence. We do that not in order to claim that the Enochic materials had direct influence on Paul but rather because using the Parables as comparative material to a first-century NT writing such as that of Paul would only be justifiable if the Parables could be shown to be prior to or contemporary with that writing.

No consensus has been and is likely to be reached regarding the date of the Parables, however. The disputes have intensified since Milik's hypothesis that the Parables, which were not part of the Enochic fragments discovered in the Dead Sea region, were a fourth century CE Christian

---

[21] Theisohn, *Der auserwählte*, 3, 206 and n. 5. For the *Religionsgeschichte* approach, see Sjöberg, *Der Menschensohn im äthiopischen Henochbuch*; and Kvanvig, *Roots of Apocalyptic: The Mesopotamian Background of the Enoch Figure and of the Son of Man* (esp 571-602).

[22] Collins, 'The Heavenly Representative: The Son of Man in Enoch', in Collins and Nickelsburg, *Ideal Figures in Ancient Judaism*, 125.

[23] Collins, 'Representative', 125.

production.[24] On the basis of a reconstruction of the Qumran Aramaic fragments of the Book of Enoch, Milik claimed that the Book of Parables, unlike other sections of *1 Enoch*, never entered the Qumran library, but that it replaced the Book of Giants, which should follow immediately on the Book of the Watchers. Nowadays the majority of scholars do not date the Parables at such a late period, but many are still reluctant to consider any date before 100 CE. We would argue that absence of the text from Qumran should not lead to an assumption that the material was a Christian production; nor does it negate the view that it was probably first-century BCE or CE material, for several reasons:

First, the Parables are very probably of a Semitic origin and most likely dependent on the Book of the Watchers, so it is most likely that they are a Jewish rather than a Christian production as Milik claimed. Second, a proposed Christian origin of the section is unnecessary since it lacks any reference to the story of Jesus and the fall of Jerusalem.[25] Third, against Milik's theory that the Book of Parables replaced the Book of Giants, no fragments actually establish that the Book of Giants was copied in the same manuscript as any of the Enochic writings.[26] Fourth, the fact that the Book of Parables was not found with the Aramaic fragments at Qumran does not mean that there was no time when it was contained in the Aramaic Book of Enoch; its absence could be accidental, much as the Book of Esther's absence from the OT Dead Sea Scrolls probably is.[27] The document's absence from Qumran can also be explained if it was produced in the latter years of the Qumran sect.[28] But even if it was produced earlier, one might say, the Parables would not have been acceptable in Qumran because of their near equation of the sun and the moon (ch 41),[29] assuming, in view of their adherence to the solar calendar, that the Qumran community viewed the sun as superior to the moon.[30]

---

[24] So according to Milik's reconstruction (*The Books of Enoch*, 58, 89ff), the original Enoch Pentateuch is: *Astronomica, Book of the Watchers, Book of the Giants, Book of Dreams* and *Epistle of Enoch*.

[25] This is not to say that Christians were not capable of producing a text without reference to Jesus. But see Charlesworth, *OTP & NT*, 103, 107, 108-110; Collins, 'The Son of Man in First-century Judaism', *NTS* 38 (1992) 448-466, 452; Sacchi, *Jewish Apocalyptic and its History*, 34 and n.4.

[26] See, for example, Collins, *Apocalypticism in the Dead Sea Scrolls*, 23-24.

[27] There are thousands of unidentified Qumran fragments. Geza Vermes once joked: 'if the word "and" from the Book of Esther can be found among those unidentified fragments, the question of the absence of the book can be settled'. Perhaps not. But what we say about Esther applies to the Book of Parables.

[28] Collins, 'Son', 452.

[29] See Stone and Greenfield, 'The Enochic Pentateuch and the Date of the Similitudes', *HTR* 70 (1977) 51-65.

[30] As Collins ('Son', 452) argues, since a community with a different ideology proba-

It might then be argued that the Parables were written in the late first-century BCE or some time in the first-century CE. Internal evidence could seem to correspond to a historical situation in the late first-century BCE. In *1 En* 67:8, for example, hot springs are said to be used by the kings and the mighty, which are mentioned very frequently in the document. If those hot springs refer to the hot springs at Calirrhoe, east of Dead Sea, which were used by Herod the Great after God inflicted great punishment for his impiety (Josephus: *Ant* 17:171-172; cf. *Wars* 7:186-189), Herod the Great can be understood as one of the referents of the kings and the mighty.[31] On this basis, some dated the Parables at around 40 BCE.[32] But the reference to the 'hot springs' is too general and could have been made retrospectively after the death of Herod, so the argument that the Parables were composed as early as 40 BCE cannot be pressed. It seems the case, however, that the composition came into being some time between the late first-century BCE and 70 CE. This can be argued not only from the absence of any reference in the Parables to Jesus and the destruction of the Second Temple, but also on the grounds that Matt 19:28 and 25:31 probably depended on passages such as *1 En* 69:27, 29 (cf. Jn 5:22; Acts 10:42).[33]

---

bly produced the Parables, it is not surprising that they failed to find their way to the Qumran library. It should be pointed out, however, that more than one calendar is attested in Qumran, and *1 En* 41:5 does say that 'one (probably the sun) is honoured more than the other'. For an extensive discussion on this, see VanderKam, *Calendars in the Dead Sea Scrolls: Measuring Time*, 43-51, 71-90, 110-116.

[31] Generally, the Parables appear to represent and reflect a developed polemical perspective of a Jewish movement that held an ideological framework that centred on an eschatological figure; a polemical perspective against the Jerusalem aristocracy, which was perceived to be nurturing and espousing a corrupt and oppressive ideology.

[32] See, for example, Charles, *The Book of Enoch*, liv-lvi; *The Apocrypha and Pseudepigrapha of the Old Testament, Pseudepigrapha, vol II*, 232; Black, *The Book of Enoch or 1 Enoch*, 242.

[33] This argument is based on the assumption that Matthew was written sometime in the early second half of the first century CE. Knibb ('The Date of the Parables: A Critical Review', *NTS* 25 [1979] 345-359), who had previously suggested a date at the end of the first-century CE, later concedes, probably rightly, that the Parables '*might* [italics his] come from earlier in the first-century in view of the possibility of the dependence of Matt. 19:28; 25:31 on 1 Enoch, and in view of the fact that the fall of Jerusalem in 70 is not obviously reflected in the Parables in the way that it is in 4 Ezra'. See Knibb, 'Messianism in the Pseudepigrapha in the Light of the Scrolls', in *DSD* 2 (1995) 165-184, 171. For the dependence of Matt 19:28 and 25:31 on *1 Enoch*, see also Theisohn, *Der auserwählte*, 79-80, 153f; Black, *Book*, 188; Collins, 'Son', 451-452.

3.2. Textual Problems vis-à-vis Righteous One

The term 'righteous one'[34] is a variant but equivalent form of three other epithets attributed to the figure of the Parables: Son of Man,[35] Chosen One[36] and Messiah.[37] VanderKam has done a detailed study of the terms, their occurrences, and their interrelations and meanings, so there is no need to rehearse that.[38] For our purpose here, we discuss briefly the textual

---

[34] Our author borrowed the form 'Righteous One' from Deutero-Isaiah (Isa 53:11: צדיק עבדי ['the righteous one, my servant']). Deutero-Isaiah uses the root צדק quite widely as well (42:6, 21; 45:8, 13, 21, 23, 24; 48:18; 51:7; 53:11; 54:14).

[35] The term Son of Man comes from Dan 7 (cf. 7:13 with *1 En* 46:1 ['one like a son of man']), as also do the divine title 'the Head of Days' (cf. 7:9 with *1 En* 46:2), the notion of enthronement (cf. 7:13-14 with *1 En* 69:27, 29) and probably the idea of the kings oppressing the righteous and the Son of Man dealing with the former (cf. 7:9-10, 13, 22-27 with *1 En* 46:1-8; 47:3).

[36] From Deutero-Isaiah again come the term 'Chosen One' (Isa 41:8, 9; 42:1; 43:10, 20; 44:1, 2; 45:4; 49:7; cf. especially Isa 42:1; 43:20 with *1 En* 45:3, 4; 55:4; 61:5), the reference to the Chosen One/Son of Man as 'a light to the nations' (cf. Isa 42:6; 49:6 with *1 En* 48:4), the idea of the naming of the Chosen One (cf. Isa 49:1; cf. 44:21, 24 with *1 En* 48:3, 6), and the motif of the kings and the mighty (cf. Isa 40:23; 41:2, 25; 45:1; 49:7 with *1 En* 46:4f; 62:3f).

[37] The term 'messiah' is used with reference to Cyrus in Deutero-Isaiah (45:1), and 'son of man' (בן אדם) is used in a general sense (51:12). It is doubtful that the author of the Parables derived the terms Messiah and Son of Man from Deutero-Isaiah. But it appears that our author depends on some messianic texts from Psalms (cf. Ps 2:1ff with *1 En* 46:4f; 52:4-6; 62:2f). Our author also relies on Ps 110:1 (cf. *1 En* 45:3; 49:2; 69:27).

[38] See VanderKam, 'Righteous', 169-191; *Revelation*, 413-438; see also Theisohn, *Der auserwählte*, 32-35. The references to and texts for the four epithets are as follows:
1) Son of Man
   walda sabe'
      46:2:   with the Head of Days and has the appearance of man (cf. v 1)
      46:3:   chosen by the Lord, possesses righteousness, revealer of secrets
      46:4:   removes the kings of the earth from their authorities
      48:2:   named in the presence of the Lord before creation
   walda be'esi
      62:5:   sits on the throne of his glory [v 6, the kings and the mighty exalt him]
      69:29: appears, sits on the throne of glory, evil and corruption pass away
      69:29: his word will be strong before the Lord
      71:14: the righteousness of the Head of Days remains with him
   walda egʷuala- emmaheyyāw
      62:7:   hidden from the beginning, preserved and revealed by the Most High
      62:9:   worshipped by the kings and the mighty
      62:14: the righteous and chosen live with him (v 15: glory and garment of life)
      63:11: the kings and the mighty will be driven from before him
      69:26: his name has been revealed to the stars and spirits
      69:27: sits on the throne of his glory, judges the sinners
      70:1:   the name of the Son of Man was raised aloft in the presence of the
      71:17: there will be length of days with him

problems *vis-à-vis* the term 'righteous one' in order to indicate the text on which we base our arguments.

The epithet 'righteous one' (*tsadeq*) occurs in the Parables only in 38:2, 3; 47:1-4 and 53:6. Most of the occurrences are disputed from the text-critical standpoint. In the first occurrence (38:2), the adjectival substantive *tsadeq* ('the righteous one') is attested in BM 491 and Eth II (e.g. BM 490 and Ryl), whereas the abstract noun *tsedq* ('righteousness') is attested in BM 485, Berl, Abb 35, Abb 55 and Tana 9. Despite the apparently stronger attestation of the latter, most translators (Charles, Knibb, Black, Isaac) accept the former because 'the Righteous One' makes better sense in relation to what follows ('and when the Righteous One appears before the chosen righteous...').[39] The second occurrence (38:3) is more difficult because the singular *tsadeq* is attested only in Tana 9 (other MSS have the plural *tsadeqan*). The Tana 9 reading is followed only in Isaac's translation. In the light of 46:3, where the Son of Man/Chosen One is said to reveal that which is secret, i.e. 'the secrets of righteousness' (49:1; 58:5), the reading of Tana 9 ('the secrets of the Righteous One are revealed') is more probable.

---

2) Chosen One (*heruy*)
   39:6:   Enoch sees the Chosen One of righteousness and faith/faithfulness
   40:5:   four figures in the divine court bless the Chosen One and the chosen ones
   45:3-4:   he will sit on the 'throne of glory'; heaven will be transformed
   45:4:   he will be caused to dwell amongst the souls of [the righteous ones?]
   48:6:   the adjective *heruy* describes the Son of Man
   49:2:   he stands before the Lord of Spirits
   51:3:   he will sit on the throne of his glory on the day of salvation
   51:5:   he 'will have arisen' in the days of salvation
   52:6:   mountains will melt like wax before him
   52:9:   different metals will be destroyed upon his appearance
   53:6:   he is referred to as the Righteous One
   55:4:   the kings and the mighty watch him sit on the throne of Lord's glory
   61:5:   the dead and destroyed return and find hope on his day
   61:10:   he is included in the list of angelic powers
   62:1:   the kings and the mighty are ordered to see if they can acknowledge him
3) Righteous One (*tsadeq*)
   38:2:   the Righteous One will appear before the righteous ones
   38:3:   the secrets of the Righteous One are revealed
   47:1:   the blood of the Righteous One ascends to or before the Lord
   47:4:   the blood of the Righteous One is admitted before the Lord
   53:6:   the Righteous One/Chosen One will reveal the house of his congregation
4) Messiah (*maših*)
   48:10:   the kings and the mighty deny the Messiah of the Lord
   52:4:   the Messiah has authority over all (c.f. vv 6f)
[39] Uhlig (*Das äthiopische*, 576 and n. 2b) prefers the abstract noun.

As regards the two other occurrences in 47:1 and 4, whether *demu
lētsadeq* in these verses is an individual or collective reference ('the blood
of the righteous one') is debated. Some scholars have suggested that in the
light of *deme tsadeqan* ('the blood of the righteous ones') in verse 2, *demu
lētsadeq* should be understood as a collective singular as well.[40] This is a
reasonable argument, because *tsadeq* is sometimes used as a collective individual in *1 Enoch*. But it could equally be argued that the author would
have used the plural *tsadeqan* in verse 1 in the same way as he did in verse
2 had he intended *tsadeq* to be understood collectively. In any case, that
demu lētsadeq also means 'the blood of the righteous one' cannot be denied. In short, *tsadeq* in 47:1, 4 can be understood either as a singular epithetical reference, hence an allusion to the same epithet in 38:2 and 53:6,
or a collective reference.[41]

3.3. The Righteous One as Eschatological Figure

Like many Second Temple Jewish writers, the author of the Parables seems
to attempt to express his ideological perspective by transferring to his own
situation ideas, beliefs and worldviews that already existed in the Second
Temple Jewish world. We wish to start our investigation into the ways in
which the 'righteous one' is expressed as a messianic designation with one
interesting feature of the Book of Parables, namely its development of the
framework of the earlier Enochic writings through provision of a new interpretation for existing scriptural traditions so as to present a righteous
figure with messianic and supernatural traits. This is exhibited in *1 En*
71:14: 'And that angel came to me, and greeted me with his voice, and said
to me, You are the Son of Man who was born to righteousness, and righteousness remains over you, and the righteousness of the Head of Days will
not leave you' (Knibb).

The portrayal of Enoch in this passage, as in many other passages, reflects a tradition based on the Book of the Watchers, where, for example,
Enoch is described as 'the blessed and righteous man of the Lord' (1:2), as
'the scribe of righteousness' (ὁ γραμματεὺς τῆς δικαιοσύνης) (12:4; 15:1),
as someone who was taken up to heaven (14:8; cf. 4Q^En 6:21; *1 En* 87:3),
as 'the righteous one/the faithful one' (ὁ δίκαιος/ὁ ἀληθινός) (15:1), and
as someone who reprimands the Watchers (15:2f).[42] In later Enochic writ-

---

[40] For further discussions, see VanderKam, 'Righteous One, Messiah, Chosen One,
and Son of Man', in Charlesworth (ed.), *The Messiah*, 169-191, 170-171 (republished in
his recent book *From Revelation to Canon: Studies in the Hebrew Bible and Second
Temple Literature*, 413-438); Knibb, *Ethiopic II*, 132; Charles, *Pseudepigrapha II*, 90;
Collins, *Apocalyptic*, 181; Theisohn, *Der auserwählte*, 35.

[41] See also Black, *Book*, 209; VanderKam, 'Righteous', 171.

[42] In 15:1, the Ethiopic refers to Enoch as 'the righteous one'. The Greek MS Pan-

ings, Enoch reads and understands the heavenly tablets and teaches his children 'another [astronomical] law' (81:1f), is given 'wisdom' (82:2-3) and is the first [righteous] man born in the first of the seven weeks (93:3). In *Jubilees* too, he is the first-born human being, is the first to learn wisdom from amongst 'the sons of men', is someone who bears witness against the Watchers, and is placed in the Garden of Eden (4:16-26, cf. 10:17; *Pseudo-Jubilees* [4Q227]). It is not possible to ascertain with any degree of certainty the origin of such characterisation.[43] But that the tradition of the figure of Enoch was a circulating tradition is beyond dispute.[44] Pertinent to our purpose here, as in the Book of the Watchers, the term ὁ δίκαιος or ὁ γραμματεὺς τῆς δικαιοσύνης is employed in the *Testaments of the Twelve Patriarchs* (e.g. *Test Lev* 10:5; *Test Jud* 18:1; *Test Dan* 5:6) and the *Testament of Abraham II* (11:3). Interestingly, in the *Testament of Abraham II*, it is Abel who is described as the first witness (ὁ πρῶτος μαρτυρήσας) and judge (κρίτης) while Enoch is described as a scribe (γραμματεύς) and the one who declares sentence (ὁ ἀποφαινόμενος) (11:3).[45] And Abel (not Enoch) is the 'son of Adam' who sits on the throne to judge all human beings and the creation as a whole (13:1f).[46]

---

apolitanus reads:ʾΟ ἄνθρωπος ὁ ἀληθινός, ἄνθρωπος τῆς ἀληθείας, ὁ γραμματεύς. In iconographic and literary sources Enoch appears as the heavenly scribe with a quasi-angelic role in the judgement. Excavations of two Byzantine (tenth century) monasteries have disclosed chapels with images of 'Enoch the Scribe' holding a tome identified as 'The Book of Life'; and in one case Enoch is presiding over a judgement scene. See Frankfurter, 'The Legacy of Jewish Apocalypses in Early Christianity: Regional Trajectories', in VanderKam & Adler (eds), *The Jewish Apocalyptic Heritage in Early Christianity*, 129-200.

[43] Nor can we be sure about the relationship between the Enochic traditions mentioned above and the Genesis tradition (5:21-24) in the sense of whether the Book of the Watchers used Genesis as its source for this particular tradition. It is to be noted that in the MT Enoch 'walked with God' and 'God had taken him', while in the LXX he 'was pleasing to God' and 'God had transferred him'.

[44] Cf. *Genesis Apocryphon* 2:20-21; 5:9-10, 24; *Aramaic Levi* (4Q213) 5, *Sir* 44:16; 49:14; *Wis* 4:10-16; *2 En* 22:8; 33:5-9; 68:1-2; Philo: *Mut* 38; *Abr* 17; *Pseudo-Philo* 1:15-16; Josephus: *Ant* 1:85; 9:28; Heb 11:5; Jude 14-15; *Targum Onqelos* Gen 5:24; *Book of Giants* 8; *Targum Pseudo-Jonathan* Gen 5:24. The figure of Enoch could be regarded as a Jewish equivalent of such primordial legendary heroes as Enmeduranki and Utnapishtim/Atrahasis who were taken up to gods, glorified (or given a changed status) and shown secrets of heaven as some Babylonian and Mesopotamian traditions show. See VanderKam, *Enoch and the Growth of an Apocalyptic Tradition*, 33ff; Collins, *The Apocalyptic Imagination: An Introduction to Jewish Apocalyptic Literature*, 44ff.

[45] Later in the composition, Enoch does not even qualify to remain ὁ ἀποφαινόμενος as his task is limited to writing alone. The reason for this apparent relegation probably is the popular and circulating tradition that Enoch did not see death (13:8). It is the fact that he was murdered by his brother that qualifies Abel to act as judge.

[46] Nickelsburg and Stone have suggested that there may be some connection between

The Parables obviously diverge from this, as they present Enoch as the 'son of Adam' (37:1) and represent a belief where an Enochic figure is identified as/with an enthroned eschatological figure, which is particularly apparent in 71:14. Here, the figure is conspicuously described as 'the Son of Man' and associated with 'the righteousness of the Head of Days'. This is seen as creating complications, because Enoch and the Son of Man appear to be separate figures in the main body of the Parables. The argument that the Righteous One as an eschatological figure is a development of an earlier Enochic tradition, where the figure of Enoch is referred to as ὁ δίκαιος/ὁ ἀληθινός, will only stand if these complications are resolved and it can be shown that the author of the Parables presents a single eschatological figure in 71:14 and indeed throughout the Parables. Since Charles, many attempts have been made either to see both as two separate figures throughout the Parables, or to confine the identification to 71:14 (or chs 70-71?), or to maintain the identification throughout the Parables while, in doing so, seeing its ideological significance for the producers of the document.[47]

One of the earliest solutions was offered through answering a grammatical question: does the demonstrative *we'etu* (*'anta we'etu walda be'esi* ['you are *this* Son of Man']) serve as a demonstrative adjective in 71:14? It was argued that *we'etu*, like another demonstrative *zeku* ('that'), can be understood as representing the definite article in the Greek *Vorlage* ὁ υἱὸς τοῦ ἀνθρώπου.[48] One could argue, as Collins does, that *we'etu* does not function as a demonstrative in *1 En* 71:14 and, therefore, the term 'son of man' in the passage is simply generic.[49] But this is simply unconvincing,

---

the judgement scene here and that described in the Parables, as there may be a connection between the Son of Adam and the Son of Man (cf. *1 En* 37:1). This connection is by no means clear, because for the producers of the *Testament of Abraham* Abel (not Enoch) is an eschatological judge. See Nickelsburg and Stone, *Faith and Piety in Early Judaism: Texts and Documents*, 144, and 158 and n. 8.

[47] On this, see Casey, *Son of Man: The Interpretation and Influence of Daniel 7*, 100-101. See also Moule, *Origin*, 11-22; Hooker, *The Son of Man in Mark*, 30-48; VanderKam, 'Righteous', 413ff.

[48] So Charles (*Book*, 86-88). Charles' view was echoed by Ullendorff in his 'An Aramaic "Vorlage" of the Ethiopic Text of Enoch?', *Atti del Convegno Internazionale di Studi Etiopici*, 259-268, 265. There, he argued that the Parables were translated from Aramaic to Ethiopic whereby the Ethiopic translators understood the Aramaic בֶּן אָדָם or בַּר אֱנָשׁ as titular. But he later changed his view by saying that 'the Ethiopic evidence has little or nothing to contribute and it remains essentially an Aramaic (Hebrew) issue' (Ullendorff, *Ethiopia and the Bible*, 61 and n. 2).

[49] Collins ('Son', 456-457) argues that since Ethiopic does not have a definite or indefinite article and the word *we'etu* in 71:14 'functions as a copula rather than a demonstrative', *'anta we'etu walda be'esi* in the text could simply mean 'you are *a* son of man', referring to human Enoch, with no identification of Enoch as/with the Son of Man.

because *we'etu* clearly is a demonstrative that could be understood to represent the definite article. The term Son of Man in *1 En* 71:14, therefore, is titular on the basis of *we'etu*. The question must be whether the significance of the presence or absence of the demonstrative adjective with the figure of the Parables should be emphasised at all.[50] Knibb has recently shown that in the Ethiopic translation of Ezekiel 9 and 10 the demonstrative *zeku* or *we'etu* is inserted on four occasions before a figure seen by the prophet, i.e. 'son of man' (9:11; 10:3, 6, 7) and on two occasions it is not (9:3; 10:2), but in all cases the meaning is 'the son of man'. On this basis, he concludes that the presence or absence of the demonstrative is insignificant.[51] Knibb's suggestion seems to be plausible. As the same can be said regarding the Parables, our decision as to whether the figure of Enoch is identified as/with the Son of Man in *1 En* 71:14 should not rely entirely on the presence or absence of *we'etu*. Furthermore, if emphasis is placed on the presence or absence of the demonstrative, 'Chosen One' (*heruy*) should have less significance (in terms of its role of designating the figure of the Parables) than 'Son of Man' on the basis that it is never preceded by *zeku* or *we'etu* despite being used almost as many times as 'Son of Man' (*walda sab'e/walda be'esi/walda 'eg^wuala-'emmaheyyāw*) – which is often preceded by *zeku* or *we'etu*. That obviously is absurd. The debate is better shifted from the arthrous/anarthrous question to internal textual and external contextual issues.

Along these lines, the arguments against the idea that the author is referring to a single eschatological figure are as follows. First, inasmuch as the Son of Man is said to be pre-existent, i.e. he existed before all other creatures including the human Enoch (*1 En* 48:3, 6; 62:7; cf. 39:6-7; 40:5; 46:3 and 70:1), then to understand the primordial man who is described as the son of Jared, seventh from Adam, as the same being as the pre-existent Son of Man/Chosen One would be an attempt to reconcile two irreconcilable notions.[52] Therefore, second, 71:14 cannot have been part of the original Parables, but a different tradition to which chs 70-71 (a later appendix) belong.[53] Third, in 70:1 there is a clear distinction between Enoch and the Son of Man because there Enoch's name rises to the presence of the Son of Man.[54] Fourth, although there is a real identification between Enoch and the Son of Man in 71:14 (cf. 46:3 with 71:14, and 62:14 with 71:16),

---

[50] Black (*Book*, 206) and Collins ('Son', 456) think so.

[51] Knibb, *Translating the Bible, The Ethiopic Version of the Old Testament*, 73-74.

[52] Knibb, 'Messianism', 170ff; see also Vanderkam, 'Righteous', 179f.

[53] Knibb, 'Messianism', 180.

[54] Collins, 'Son', 453f. In answer to the obvious question as to why the author failed to bring 71:14 in line with 70:1, Knibb ('Messianism', 172) suggests that 70:1-2 is a redactional link inserted between chs 37-69 and chs 70-71: there is a noticeably harsh shift from the third person in 70:1-2 to the first person in 70:3-71:16.

Knibb insists that in the Parables there is 'a real belief in the pre-existence of the son of man', which militates against applying such an identification to the rest of the Parables.[55] Fifth, in 39:6, the Chosen One is viewed as the pre-existent figure because Enoch sees him in his dwelling.[56] Sixth, if Enoch had been the same person as the Son of Man he would not have failed to recognise himself (46:2; 71:14).[57] Finally, there is no reference to Enoch's earthly life in *1 Enoch* that would suggest that he was viewed as an exalted figure in his heavenly life.[58] The Parables thus show a real belief that the Chosen One/Son of Man/Righteous One/Messiah and the figure of Enoch are two distinct figures (transcendental and human) who exist in two distinct spheres (heavenly and earthly) throughout the Parables (Collins) or in chs 37-69 (Knibb).

However, there are arguments in favour of taking the figure of the Parables as a single figure. First, the logical difficulty created by Enoch's failure to recognise himself in 39:6 and 71:14 is one of a series of unusual phenomena, but it can be resolved through viewing the Son of Man as the heavenly double of the earthly Enoch,[59] which can be supported by the *Prayer of Joseph Fragment A* where Jacob the man and angel Israel probably are the same being.[60] Second, the intimate connection between chapters 37-69 and 70-71 suggests that the latter could not have been a later addition. In 39:1-3, the author recapitulates the story of Enoch's earthly life and his translation, which is repeated in 70:1-2. Both texts appear to contain a summary of events during Enoch's life of 365 years and his life

---

[55] Knibb, Messianism', 178, 180.

[56] Collins, 'Son', 454-455; Knibb, 'Messianism', 178; VanderKam, 'Righteous', 184.

[57] Collins, 'Representative', 122.

[58] Collins, 'Representative', 123.

[59] This can be said on the basis that 'a creature of flesh and blood could have a heavenly double or counterpart', which means that Enoch 'was viewing his supernatural double who had existed before being embodied in the person of Enoch'. VanderKam, 'Righteous', 182-183; see also Collins, 'Representative', 116.

[60] In this Fragment, Jacob (Israel) is presented as 'an angel of God and a ruling spirit', 'the *first born of every living thing to whom* God gives life' (A: 1-3), the 'chief captain among the sons of God', and 'first minister before the face of God' (A: 7-8). Both references are from the translation of Smith, 'Prayer of Joseph', in Charlesworth, *OTP II*, 699-700. Knibb ('Messianism', 180) and VanderKam ('Righteous', 183) agree that the *Fragment* offers a parallel to *1 En* 71:14, although they predictably differ in that while Knibb understands that Jacob identifies himself with angel Israel, who is conceived as being pre-existent, VanderKam argues that Jacob is conceived as having a celestial counterpart and existing 'before other creatures'. Collins ('Son', 456) does not see the *Fragment* offering any parallel at all, because it is not apparent that Jacob is unaware of his identity in the *Prayer of Joseph*, as Enoch is in the Parables. But Collins' view does not seem to weaken the case for seeing parallels between the two figures.

of post-365 years.[61] Chapters 37-69 fit into the former, while chapters 70-71 fit into the latter. In both sections, however, the author is concerned with a developed view of an Enochic figure.[62] Third, as VanderKam argues, 'the notion that Enoch was the son of man [in 71:14] was an inference that a member of the Enoch[ic] circle(s) might have drawn by juxtaposing *1 En* 14 (the earlier text), where Enoch is at the centre, with Daniel 7 (a later document)'.[63] Thus, the Son of Man is a title that may have been appropriated to a charismatic figure (i.e. pseudo-Enoch) in Enochic circles.[64] Fourth, as will be discussed later, the tradition of the figure of the Parables is closely paralleled in the *Wisdom of Solomon* where Enoch, albeit implicitly, is referred to as the Righteous One *par excellence* (4:10-16).[65] Finally, as far as the literary issue regarding the apparent shift from the third person singular in 70:1-2 to the first person singular in 70:3ff is concerned, there is no need to take the former as a later redactional layer intended to make a smooth transition between chs 69 and 70 (*contra* Knibb and Collins).[66] For one thing, 70:1f probably reflects the author's literary

---

[61] Sjöberg (*Menschensohn*, 161) and VanderKam ('Righteous', 178-179) even propose, probably rightly, that Gen 5:22 is understood as about Enoch's pre-translation life where he sojourns with the angels (האלהים) and Gen 5:24 about his post-translation life where he sojourns with God (אלהים).

[62] This development in a different form continues in later pseudepigraphal writings attributed to Enoch. The image of the patriarch as 'the Scribe', 'the Prince or Governor of the World' and the like in the Slavonic Enoch (*2 Enoch*), for example, is developed into the image of the angel Metatron in *Sefer Hekhalot/3 Enoch* (e.g. 4:3-5; 9:2; 10:1). In *3 En*, Metatron is the Prince of the World, the leader of 72 princes of the kingdom of the world and speaks in favour of (pleads for) the world before the Holy One. See also Orlov, 'The Origin of the Name "Metatron" and the Text of 2 (Slavonic Apocalypse of) Enoch', *JSP* 21 (2000) 19-26.

[63] VanderKam, 'Righteous', 182.

[64] Nickelsburg ('Nature', 117) also suggests that behind the Enochic texts some people called scribes or 'the wise' can be seen, and they can be related to the משכילים of Daniel who 'led many to righteousness'. See also Boccaccini (*Beyond the Essene Hypothesis: The Parting of the Ways between Qumran and Enochic Judaism*, 188f), who has attempted to go beyond García Martínez's 'Groningen Hypothesis' by locating the ideological roots of Essenism and Qumran Judaism within Enochic Judaism. He argues that main-stream Essenism through its influence by the ideology of Enochic Judaism, which centres on the *notion of reversal* through a superhuman figure, provides a context for Christian origins.

[65] Nickelsburg, 'Salvation without and with a Messiah: Developing Beliefs in Writings Ascribed to Enoch', in Neusner *et al* (eds), *Judaisms and their Messiahs at the Turn of the Christian Era*, 49-68, 64; *Jewish*, 177.

[66] Knibb's and Collins' redactional arguments are in keeping with Charles' translation: 'And it came to pass after this that his name during his lifetime was raised aloft to that Son of Man and to the Lord of Spirits from amongst those who dwell on the earth'. Charles, *Book*, 141; see also *Pseudepigrapha II*, 235; Knibb, *The Ethiopic Book of Enoch II*, 165; and Collins' discussion, 'Representative', 119-122. However, as VanderKam

pattern, not least in 39:1f.[67] In the latter Enoch was carried off from the earth to the end of heaven, where he sees the Chosen One (BM 486) or the place of the Chosen One (Ryl),[68] while in the former Enoch's name is 'raised aloft'.[69] That, of course, poses the question as to whether the name of Enoch parallels the Chosen One. But 48:3 and 69:27 show that the name of the Son of Man is not different from the Son of Man himself, suggesting that the name of Enoch before and after its elevation in 70:1-2 can be correlated with the hidden and revealed name of the Son of Man/Chosen One in 69:27. Thus there is no distinction between the elevated name of Enoch and the Son of Man even in 70:1-2.[70]

Furthermore, when the text of Abbadianus (Abb) 55 (a 15th or 16th century Ethiopic manuscript), which, unlike the majority of MSS, omits *baxabehu* ('unto him' – Enoch's name was elevated 'unto him [the Son of Man]'), is accepted as the original reading, the distinction between Enoch

---

('Righteous', 184) put it: 'What the author appears to have intended in 70:1 was that Enoch's name was elevated to the place where those characters whom he had seen in his visions were to be found, namely in the throne-room of the celestial palace. That is, he does not see the son of man here but begins his ascent to the place where he himself will perform that eschatological role.' See also Casey, *Son*, 100-102; Hays, '"Righteous"', 193-194.

[67] In both passages, the author recapitulates Enoch's translation. In both, there is a similar abrupt shift from a third person (39:2; 70:1-2) to a first person (39:3f; 70:3f; cf. 1:2). In both, that abrupt shift makes it difficult to understand whether the person in the third person is the same as (or different from) the one in the first person.

[68] There are 15 or 16 instances where *heruy* ('the chosen'), an adjectival form, is used as a substantive ('the chosen one') to designate a single individual. 39:6 is one of those texts. Some Ethiopic MSS, including BM485, employ the singular while in others, including Ryl, the plural *heruyan* is used. On text-critical grounds, the reading of BM 485 appears preferable. So the reading goes: 'And in that place my eyes saw the Chosen One of righteousness and faith/faithfulness; and there will be righteousness in his days' (Knibb, *Ethiopic II*, 126). See also Black (*Book*, 196f) for the explanation of the discrepancy between the singular and the plural.

[69] See Collins, 'Representative', 121. In 70:1-2, Knibb renders $w^e w^e ts$ 'a s'moo bama'kalomoo 'and his name vanished among them', while Olson ('Enoch and the Son of Man in the Epilogue of the Parables', *JSP* 18 (1998) 27-38, 32) renders it 'his name went in their midst'. The latter rendering better explains the idiom, because it could mean that Enoch's name frequently went forth from people's lips, i.e. it became the most talked about name, probably owing to his hiddenness (cf. *1 En* 12:1). But Olson renders of *tala'āla* in verse 1 as 'exalted' and in verse 2 as 'raised aloft' because the former refers to Enoch's name while the latter to Enoch the man (p. 33). This is unnecessary, because the verb in both its occurrences seems to describe the translation of Enoch, which may well involve exaltation (cf. *1 En* 87:3; Eth. Isa 53:11). As Charles (*Book*, 141) points out, it is related to the account of Elijah in 2 Kgs 2:11. See also VanderKam, 'Righteous', 178.

[70] The syllogism goes as follows: A (Enoch's name) equals B (Enoch); B (Enoch) equals C (the Son of Man); therefore, A is C.

and the Son of Man in the passage disappears. Olson has argued that *baxabehu* is omitted in at least four or possibly five new MSS from the Ethiopian Manuscript Microfilm Library (EMML 1768, 2436, 6974, 7584 and most likely 2080), so therefore the reading of Abb 55 probably reflects the original text and is to be preferred against the majority reading.[71] This leads Olson, like Casey before him (although Casey does not refer to EMML), to reject Charles' reading of 70:1-2, which creates a distinction between the patriarch Enoch and the Son of Man.[72] Casey's and Olson's position is supported by the reading in Tana 9, which does not have the third person singular pronoun ending *hu* (*beqedma baxaba* ['before unto'] as opposed to *beqedma baxabehu* ['before unto him]). This evidence alone does not enable us to be certain that the omission of *baxabehu* in Abb 55 is original. But the addition of *baxabehu* does not necessarily prove that the majority reading is original either.

Indeed, it can be argued that the majority reading resulted from the scribal attempt to distinguish between the human Enoch and the divine Son of Man. The reason probably being that the Ethiopic title for the latter, *walda 'eg^wuala- 'emmaheyyāw*, which in the Ethiopic New Testament renders the Greek ὁ υἱὸς τοῦ ἀνθρώπου for Jesus, was deemed inappropriate for human Enoch. This christological motivation could have led the Christian scribes to add *baxabehu* so as to allow *walda 'eg^wuala- 'emmaheyyāw* to represent the heavenly Son of Man. The aim of the scribes in so doing may have been to unambiguously distinguish him from *walda be'esi*.[73] Such a practice should not be surprising, because christologically motivated scribal attempts to alter *walda be'esi* can be noticed, for instance, in 62:5 and 69:29 where it is rendered 'son of a woman', which, though non-christological, is close in meaning to *walda 'eg^wuala- 'emmaheyyāw* ('son of the offspring of the mother of the living'). *walda be'esi* was never employed for Jesus in the Ethiopic New Testament, probably because of the sense it carried, i.e. 'son of [any] man/male', which could have been seen as incompatible with the significance attached

---

[71] Olson, 'Enoch', 27-38. EMML 1768 and 7584 are dated at late fifteenth century CE, while EMML 2436 and 6974 at seventeenth and eighteenth centuries respectively. The date of EMML manuscripts has been controversial, however, as some date at twelfth to fifteenth century, while others have dated at fifteenth century. See Isaac, *OTP I*, 6; Olson, 'Enoch', 31 and n. 17.

[72] Olson ('Enoch', 33) provides an alternative rendering: 'And it happened afterwards that the immortal name of that Son of Man was exalted in the presence of the Lord of Spirits beyond all those who live on the earth. He was raised aloft on a chariot of wind, and his name was often spoken among them.' Casey (*Son*, 102) does not render *semu heyāw* as 'immortal name': 'Now it came to pass after this that the name of that son of man was raised aloft while he was still alive to the Lord of the Spirits' (70:1).

[73] See Black, *Book*, 250; VanderKam, 'Righteous', 183-184; Olson, 'Enoch', 34-35.

to the term (in 69:29, for example, *walda be'esi* is enthroned in the celestial court). Of all the uses of *walda be'esi* ('the Son of Man'), that in 71:14 is the only one that has survived unscathed,[74] but this unscathed state of *walda be'esi* in comparison with the scribal attempt to make the phrase non-christological in 62:5 and 69:29 is extremely suggestive.[75] On that basis, it is probably safe to suggest that the description of the elevation of the patriarch/his name, the Son of Man, to the Lord of Spirits in 70:1-2 and his exaltation or celestial enthronement for an eschatological role in 71:14, is consistent with the reading without *baxabehu*.

So neither the christologically motivated insertion of *baxabehu* in 70:1-2 in order to distinguish between *walda 'eg^wuala- 'emmaheyyāw* (the exalted Son of Man = Jesus) and human Enoch nor the argument that the figure of the Parables and Enoch are two different beings (throughout the Parables [Collins] or in chs 37-69 [Knibb]) takes seriously a development of thinking that resulted, by and large, from a process of interpretation of the Danielic figure of the Son of Man[76] and transferred messianic ideas to a primordial hero. That is to say, the author of the Parables associates the portrayal of Enoch as ὁ δίκαιος/ὁ ἀληθινός/ὁ γραμματεύς τῆς δικαιοσύνης in the Book of the Watchers with the Danielic Son of Man tradition to express an ideological perspective that is eschatologically and messianically orientated.

The author seems to go even further, in that he brings the identity and role of the eschatological figure in line with that of God. In the first chapter of the Book of the Watchers, there is the idea of divine epiphany, where God comes out of his dwelling, treads on Mt Sinai with his company or army, judges *hatēan werasēan* (ἁμαρτολοὶ καὶ ἀσεβεῖς), and brings salvation to *tsadqan weheruyan* (δίκαιοι καὶ ἐκλεκτοί) (1:3-9; cf. 25:1f).[77] This idea, which is also expressed in 91:7 and is in keeping with not only the Danielic tradition (cf. Dan 7:21-22 with 7:9, 13-14, 26-27) but also with that of, for example, Habakkuk (2:20; 3:3, 12-13), Zephaniah (1:14-18; cf. Dan 8:19) and Malachi (3:1-5), is developed in the Book of Parables,

---

[74] As Olson ('Enoch', 36) perhaps rightly suggests, the Ezekielic reading of 71:14 that prevailed in the Ethiopian Christian tradition probably safeguarded the text from scribal alteration there. In 62:5, BM 491 and Eth II have Son of Woman, while BM 485, Berl, Abb 35, Abb 55 and Tana 9 have Son of Man. See Knibb, *Ethiopic II,* 151; *Bible*, 73-74; Schweizer, 'The Son of Man Again', *NTS* 10 (1963/64) 256-261. See also Isaac's note ('1 Enoch', *OTP* I, 43) on *walda 'eg^wuala-'emma-heyyāw* and *walda sab'e*.

[75] Since *walda 'eg^wuala- 'emmaheyyāw* (lit. 'son of the offspring of the mother of the living' [cf. Gen 3:20]) is used again in 71:16, as a variant to *walda be'esi* in 71:14, the referent in both 70:1 and 71:14 is an Enochic figure, who is now given, rather surprisingly, a messianic trait.

[76] See also Theisohn, *Der auserwählte*, 51; VanderKam, 'Righteous', 190.

[77] See also Kvanvig, *Roots*, 584-585.

which speaks not of God's epiphany but of the revelation or appearance of the Righteous One/Chosen One/Messiah/Son of Man with an eschatological role (38:2; 48:7; 52:9). The parallel between Zeph 1:18 and *1 En* 52:7, which is unnoticed so far, is particularly striking:

> Zeph 1:18: Neither their silver nor their gold will be able to save them on the day of the Lord's wrath; in the fire of his passion the whole earth shall be consumed ...

> *1 En* 52:7: And it will come to pass in those days that neither by gold, nor by silver, will men save themselves; they will be unable to save themselves or to flee.

The main difference between the two texts is that in the immediate context of the Parables salvation comes through an eschatological figure (cf. 62:13);[78] in Zephaniah judgement comes through the Lord. The author of the Parables seems to depend on Zephaniah's eschatology and adds a messianic edge to what is said about the Lord. Elsewhere in the Parables, the appearance of the Righteous One/Chosen One is followed by his role as a fearsome warrior-judge who removes the kings and the mighty from their political and judicial positions, judges Azazel and his associates, liberates the downtrodden and sits on the throne (38:2-3; 46:3-5; 52:4-9; 53:1-7[79]; 55:4 [cf. 56:1ff]; 62:1; 69:26).[80] The figure's court action is inextricably linked with his salvific action (51:1-5; cf. Isa 42:1, 6; 49:6-7).

In sum, the Danielic tradition coupled with other traditions such as Zephaniah enabled the author of the Parables to transfer messianic traits and eschatological functions to an Enochic figure via earlier Enochic traditions where God's salvific coming is expressed. Indeed, the author takes a portrait of the patriarch, who was 'born to righteousness' and with whom 'the righteousness of the Head of Days' will remain (71:14), and speaks of it in terms of a messianic/eschatological figure: 'the Chosen One of righteousness and faith/faithfulness' (39:6), the Righteous One (38:2; 53:6), the

---

[78] For instance, *1 En* 52:9 reads: 'All these (mountains of silver and gold – referring to the mighty kings) will be wiped out and destroyed from the face of the earth, when the Chosen One appears before the Lord of the Spirits.'

[79] Translators differ on 53:6: 'And after this the Righteous and Chosen One will cause the house of his congregation to appear' (Knibb); 'And after this the Righteous and Elect One shall appear...' (Black); 'After this, the Righteous and Elect One will reveal the house of his congregation' (Isaac).

[80] See Bauckham, ('Throne', 43-69) on the figures enthronement. He thinks that the sitting of the figure on the throne signifies his inclusion in the unique divine identity (p. 60). It is also to be noted here that chs 55 and 56 are reminiscent of ch 10 where the judgement of God against Azazel and Semyaza was carried out by Raphael and Michael. Kvanvig (*Roots*, 583f), albeit without making direct reference to the texts in question, perhaps wrongly argues that such ideas are applications of the Mesopotamian rebel kings imagery.

Son of Man 'with whom righteousness dwells' (46:3), or the Messiah with
power and authority (52:4-5).[81]

3.4. Righteous One in Shared Interpretative Traditions

The epithet 'righteous one' obviously finds its root in the OT's use of the
term צדיק or δίκαιος ascribed to God.[82] The term is also associated with
some individuals in their relation to God, but expressing different ideas:
moral and religious rightness (Job 1:1; 2:3; 9:15), an atoning role (cf. Gen
6:9 [6:10, LXX]; 7:1 with *Jub* 5-7; Isa 53:11),[83] and a messianic role of
executing 'justice' (משפט) and 'righteousness' (צדקה) (Isa 11:1-5; Jer
23:5-6). In this sub-section, we wish to provide an overview of how the
Deutero-Isaianic Servant tradition, the Proto-Isaianic messianic tradition
(Isa 11:1-5) and the messianic tradition of Jer 23:5-6 were shared by various Jewish (and Christian) writings. The result will enable us to demonstrate that the Enochic use of 'righteous one' (or its equivalent) with a
messianic sense was something that was shared by others within some
Jewish and Christian traditions in the Second Temple period.

We start with *Wisdom of Solomon*. *Wisdom* depends on a common
Deutero-Isaianic Servant tradition from Isa 53:11.[84] In chs 2-5, for example, the term δίκαιος with or without the article is used ten times (2:10, 12,
16 [δικαίων], 18; 3:1 [δικαίων], 10; 4:7, 16; 5:1, 15 [δίκαιοι]). None of
these uses appear to be messianic, but we should explore a bit further. In
the story, the 'righteous man' is presented as vulnerable to the oppressive
acts of the rulers/judges (οἱ κρίνοντες [1:1]) or kings (βασιλεῖς [6:1]) of
the earth (2:10). And yet, he opposes their actions and reproaches them for
the way in which they handle νόμος (2:12). As a result, it seems, they are
not impressed by his claims to knowledge of God and being παῖς κυρίου or
ὁ δίκαιος υἱὸς Θεοῦ[85] and, even more so, his theology of divine intervention and post-mortem existence (2:2-5, 10, 13-18). They persecute him and

---

[81] In the light of all this, Casey's (*Son*, 111) argument, that the author of the Parables
does not attribute messianic role to the Son of Man because Enoch is not a king or because of a deliberate rejection of the Davidic line, is to be rejected. As Theisohn (*Der
auserwählte*, 68) points out, scripturally based associations of messianic traits to figures
such as Enoch was part and parcel of the Jewish messianic conceptual framework.

[82] Deut 32:4; 2 Chr 12:6; Ezra 9:15; Neh 9:8; Ps 119:137; Isa 45:21; 58:2; 64:5; Jer
12:1; Lam 1:18; Dan 9:14; Zeph 3:5.

[83] The Servant can also be (or represent) the community (i.e. Israel).

[84] See also Nickelsburg, *Resurrection, Immortality, and Eternal Life in Intertestamental Judaism*, 62-66, 83-90; 'Salvation', 64; *Jewish Literature Between the Bible and
Mishnah: A Historical and Literary Introduction*, 175-185, 214-223.

[85] As Nickelsburg (*Resurrection*, 91) suggests, the 'son of God' language here may
also be dependent on the Deutero-Isaianic tradition rather than *3 Maccabees* (6:23),
which has an affinity with *Wisdom*.

condemn (καταδικάσωμεν) him to a shameful death (2:20), but since he belongs to the company of the obedient and the faithful, rather than the company of διάβολος (2:21-24), his life is in the hands of God (3:1-3, 9, 14).

As the story develops in 4:10-16 the author seems to describe, albeit implicitly, an Enochic figure. The figure of Enoch does not clearly feature in the earlier uses of δίκαιος,[86] but in this passage, the figure's faithfulness in the midst of wickedness and his consequent translation by God can be noticed. This translation motif in *Wisdom* is consistent with Gen 5:24[87] and the so-called Astronomical Book and the Animal Apocalypse in *1 Enoch*. None of these specifically describes Enoch's role in heaven.[88] In the Book of the Watchers (*1 En* 12-15) and *Jubilees* (4:19-22), however, Enoch's translation is followed by his eschatological role.[89] The same appears to be the case in *Wis* 4:10-16.[90] In short, while the 'righteous one' is portrayed as a paradigm of fidelity and suffering in the earlier passages, in

---

[86] See Cheon ('Three Characters in the Wisdom of Solomon', *JSP* 12 [2001] 105-113) who sees three characters in *Wis* 3 and 4 (the sterile woman [3:3], the eunuch [3:14] and the just youth [4:7]) but fails to recognise the influence of an Enochic tradition even in 4:10-16.

[87] *Wisdom* uses εὐάρεστος θεῷ while Genesis εὑρέστησεν Ενωχ τῷ θεῷ; the former employs μετετέθη while the latter μετέθηκεν. The use of the verbs μετατίθημι ('to place among', 'to place differently', 'to change') and ἁρπάζω ('to ravish away', 'to carry off hastily') in the *Wisdom* passage shows that the figure was translated from one location and placed in another.

[88] In *1 En* 81:1-4, the translation is not mentioned but is simply assumed, as Enoch is already in heaven. Subsequently in verse 5, three men bring him back to earth so that he shows for one year the children of Adam (v 4) that 'no flesh is righteous before the Lord'. And in the second year, he is taken away again (v 6). There is a similar story in the Animal Apocalypse where Enoch is 'raised' by three men from the midst of oppression and set 'in a high place' (cf. *Sir* 44:16; 49:14) where he remains for some time (87:1-4). Then afterwards, he is brought back to the midst of the sheep (the oppressed people of God) before the final events take place (90:31). Although there is a seeming contradiction between the two stories as far as the temporal sequence is concerned, this does not affect the core assumption, i.e. the translation of Enoch from the midst of wickedness.

[89] After his 365 years on earth, the angels escorted Enoch to the Garden of Eden so that he may be 'a sign' and 'bear witness against all of the children of men' (4:23-24). As VanderKam suggests, 'Enoch carried out the role of a witness both during and after his time on earth. His testifying role continues until the final judgement' ('1 Enoch, 33-104, 98). A motif that describes his eschatological role is reinforced by 4Q227. The text copied in the early Herodian period reads: ויעד על כולם [וגם על העירים: 'And he [Enoch] testified against them all] and also against the Watchers'.

[90] 4:16, for example, reads: 'And the righteous [one] who has died (or has finished his labour) will condemn the unfaithful who are living; and youth that is quickly perfected will condemn the aged who are unrighteous'. NRSV's pluralising of the reading should be rejected because the text unambiguously uses ὁ δίκαιος.

Wis 4:10-16 our author seems to adapt the Enochic translation myth to his own context probably via the Deutero-Isaianic Servant tradition and presents the 'righteous one' with a role in the heavenly courtroom.

The Parables too depend on the Deutero-Isaianic Servant tradition. Indeed, Deutero-Isaiah is one of the main sources from which the author of the Parables borrowed such forms as 'Righteous One' (Isa 53:11: עבדי צדיק ['the righteous one, my servant'])[91] and 'Chosen One' (Isa 41:8, 9; 42:1; 43:10, 20; 44:1, 2; 45:4; 49:7; cf. especially Isa 42:1; 43:20 with *1 En* 45:3, 4; 55:4; 61:5), the reference to the Chosen One/Son of Man as 'a light to the nations' (cf. Isa 42:6; 49:6 with *1 En* 48:4), the idea of the naming of the Chosen One (cf. Isa 49:1; cf. 44:21, 24 with *1 En* 48:3, 6) and so on. Incidentally, a Deutero-Isaianic tradition is shared by Luke and the author of the Parables as well. For example, while Luke presents Jesus as ὁ δίκαιος who suffered death (Acts 7:52) and as ὁ υἱὸς τοῦ ἀνθρώπου who is standing ἐκ δεξιῶν τοῦ θεοῦ (Acts 7:55-56), the author of the Parables describes the Son of Man/Chosen One as both standing before the Lord (49:2; cf. 48:2-3) and sitting on the celestial throne as judge (51:3; 55:4; 61:8; 62:2; 69:27).

The portrayal of the figure of the Parables with a messianic role is informed by not only the Deutero-Isaianic Servant tradition but also the Proto-Isaianic messianic tradition, Isa 11:1-5 in particular. In *1 En* 49:1-4, for example, the passage as a whole is alluded to. But it is the verbal similarity between Isa 11:2 and *1 En* 49:3 that is more striking.[92] Furthermore, Isa 11:5, where צדק (δικαιοσύνη) and אמונה (ἀλήθεια) are used in relation to the Shoot of Jesse, seems to have been alluded to in *1 En* 39:6, in which the identity of the figure of the Parables is distinctively described as 'the Chosen One of righteousness and faithfulness' – the phrase 'the plant of righteousness and fidelity' (τὸ φυτὸν τῆς δικαιοσύνης καὶ τῆς ἀληθείας) in *1 En* 10:16 also seems to have been borrowed from the Isaianic reference to the Shoot and Branch of Jesse.

---

[91] Deutero-Isaiah uses the root צדק quite widely as well (42:6, 21; 45:8, 13, 21, 23, 24; 48:18; 51:7; 53:11; 54:14).

[92] Isa 11:2: 'The Spirit of the Lord shall rest upon him, the spirit of wisdom and understanding, the spirit of counsel and might, the spirit of knowledge and the fear of the Lord.'

1 En 49:3: 'And in him dwells the spirit of wisdom, and the spirit which gives understanding (some MSS: and the spirit of the one who gives understanding), and the spirit of knowledge and of power, and the spirit of those who sleep in righteousness.' For similar influences cf., for example, Gen 49:10 and Isa 49:6 (cf. 42:6) with *1 En* 48:4. It is to be noted here the Spirit of the Lord that rests on the 'Shoot of Jesse' (whose identity is characterised by 'faithfulness') in Isa 11:1-5 is said to be put on the 'Chosen Servant of the Lord' in Isa 42:1b.

This Isaianic tradition is also shared by *Ps Sol* 17, in which a messianic figure is described as a 'righteous king' and 'anointed Lord' (v 36), the one who exercises his power in δικαιοσύνη (vv 26-31) and who shepherds the flock ἐν πίστει καὶ δικαιοσύνη (v 40).[93] The content of Isa 11:1-5 is similar to that of Jer 23:5-6 (cf. 33:15-16) and both texts are interpreted and appropriated messianically in some Qumran scrolls.[94] An interpretation of the Isaianic text is contained in a fragmentary text of 4QpIsaᵃ (4Q161): in Fragments 8-10 (col iii): 17-25 the 'shoot of Jesse' or, as the text reads, '[the shoot] of David', is understood to be a messianic liberator and judge. 4Q161 may be paralleled with 4QSefer ha-Milhamah (4Q285), in which Jeremiah's 'righteous branch' seems to be interpreted in line with Isaiah's prophecy, as 'the branch of David' (צמח דויד) is identified with the Prince of the Congregation (Frag 5:1-6). The term 'righteous' is obviously not used in 4Q161 and 4Q285, but in reflection on Jeremiah's 'righteous branch' again 4QpGenᵃ (4Q252) refers to the coming messianic figure as 'the messiah of righteousness' or 'the righteous messiah' (הצדק משיח) and 'the branch of David' (צמח דויד).[95] Despite the differing contexts, these texts and the Parables appear to have shared the thought world of common textual traditions and viewed a messianic figure as someone whose identity is characterised by 'righteousness'.

To conclude, in the Parables of *1 Enoch*, the Righteous One as an eschatological figure is a development of an earlier Enochic tradition, where the figure of Enoch is referred to as ὁ δίκαιος/ὁ ἀληθινός. The use of biblical motifs and a variety of epithetical designations for the figure of the Parables betray that this development took place through the author's dependence, for example, on the Danielic Son of Man tradition, Deutero-Isaianic Servant tradition and the messianic traditions of Proto-Isaiah and Jeremiah. Most of the traditions mentioned here are shared by other Jewish and Christian writers, many of whom do not explicitly refer to a messianic or eschatological figure as the 'righteous one' but refer to him as 'right-

---

[93] See also Winninge, *Sinners and the Righteous: A Comparative Study of the Psalms of Solomon and Paul's Letters*, 89-109.

[94] For full discussion of this and related issues, see Collins, *The Scepter and the Star: The Messiahs of the Dead Sea Scrolls and Other Ancient Literature*, 53ff; García Martínez and Trebolle Barrera, *People*, 160ff; and Atkinson, 'On the Herodian Origin of Militant Davidic Messianism at Qumran: New Light from *Psalms of Solomon* 17', *JBL* 118 (1999) 435-460.

[95] Cf. 4Q*Florilegium* (4Q174) 1:10-13 (צמח דויד [line 11]); and 4QAramaic Apocalypse or Pseudo-Danielᵈ (4Q246) (אל די ברה ['Son of God']); see also Allegro, 'Further Messianic References in Qumran Literature', *JBL* 75 (1956) 174-176; Collins, *Scepter*, 62; 'Messiahs in Context: Method in the Study of Messianism in the Dead Sea Scrolls', in Wise *et al* (eds), *Methods of Investigation of the Dead Sea Scrolls and the Khirbet Qumran Site*, 213-227; and Atkinson, 'Herodian', 455.

eous king', 'righteous messiah' or someone whose life is characterised by righteousness and faithfulness. Thus the 'righteous one' or its equivalent as a messianic designation probably is a shared (directly or indirectly) idea in the Second Temple period. Whether this evidence informs and provides interpretative guidance for our reading of the epithet ὁ δίκαιος in Rom 1:17 will be seen in our subsequent discussions.

4. Righteous One in the Habakkuk Citation: Believer or Christ?

Commentators of Romans are unanimous in taking ὁ δίκαιος in the Habakkuk citation of Rom 1:17 as an epithet that signifies the person who belongs to Christ and so to those who belong to the new age through or on the basis of faith rather than fulfilling the law. There are, to be sure, differences of opinion over the syntactical question whether ἐκ πίστεως should be related to the subject ὁ δίκαιος or the verb ζήσεται. That is to say, if ἐκ πίστεως is taken with the subject, the means through or the basis on which a person is righteous before God is πίστις,[96] whereas if it is taken with the verb, the manner in which the believer should continue to live or conduct her daily existence is πίστις.[97] Despite these differences, the majority of scholars on either side of the syntactical choice understand ὁ δίκαιος as the generic believer. As surveyed in the first chapter of this book, however, scholars such as Hanson, Hays, Campbell and Wallis have proposed a christological reading for the epithet. But their interpretation continues to encounter strong resistance. We wish to examine below the extent to which such an interpretation can be supported by internal and external evidence. We will do that by considering the merits and demerits of the arguments for and against the christological construal of ὁ δίκαιος.

Against reading ὁ δίκαιος with reference to Christ, it has been argued that *there are no contextual signals that enable us to understand ὁ δίκαιος as a messianic title in Rom 1:17* (italics mine).[98] The absence of contextual signals coupled with the reading of 1:17a in terms of righteousness with which human beings are endowed through or on the basis of faith suggests

---

[96] E.g. Käsemann, *Commentary*, 32; Stuhlmacher, *Letter*, 29, 76-77; Byrne, *Romans*, 60-61.

[97] E.g. Schlatter, *Romans*, 26; Fitzmyer, *Romans*, 256-263. For a thorough defence of this position, see Cavallin, '"The Righteous Shall Live by Faith": A Decisive Argument for the Traditional Interpretation', *ST* 32 (1978) 33-43. See also Haacker, *Der Brief des Paulus an die Römer*, 43-44; Lohse, *Der Brief*, 82.

[98] Watts, '"For I Am Not Ashamed of the Gospel": Romans 1:16-17 and Habakkuk 2:4', Soderlund & Wright (eds), *Romans and the People of God: Essays in Honour of Gordon D. Fee on the Occasion of His 65th Birthday*, 3-25, 16. See also Descamps, *Les Justes*, 221.

that Paul could not have 'expected those who heard his letter read to realize that they were to understand the quotation as referring to Christ'.[99] When one talks about the absence of contextual signals, one needs to be clear whether she is talking about the immediate or wider context of Rom 1:17 or the contextual background of the Jewish or Greco-Roman world. We shall return to this below, but it seems obvious that Paul in his Seven Letter Corpus does not appear to be overtly interested in using ὁ δίκαιος with reference to Jesus. Indeed, the use of the δίκαιος language in Paul's Seven Letter Corpus is very limited, as the term is employed *once* with reference to the commandment/Torah (Rom 7:12), *five* times with reference to a person or persons (Rom 1:17b; 2:13; 3:10; 5:7, 19) and *once* with reference to God (Rom 3:26).[100] Out of the five references to a person or persons, only Rom 1:17b has the term with the definite article. Nowhere in Romans does Paul refer to any Jew or Greek as ὁ δίκαιος,[101] although he embraces the Jewish perspective that no one living can be 'regarded as righteous' in the presence of God (Rom 2:13; 3:10, 20 [cf. Ps 143:2]).[102] Furthermore, since Hab 2:4 is not cited anywhere in pre-Pauline Jewish writings where ὁ δίκαιος can be construed messianically, we are left without any contextual evidence as to how Hab 2:4 was customarily read within some circles of Judaism.

However, Paul's reference in Rom 5:19 to Jesus as [ὁ] δίκαιος can be understood to serve as a contextual signal for a christological construal of ὁ δίκαιος in the Habakkuk citation. The expression regarding the obedience of One Man along with οἱ πολλοί in the text seems to betray the text's dependence on Isa 53:11, where the obedient activity of צדיק/δίκαιος is effective for many. Indeed, it appears that Deutero-Isaiah's 'righteous one' provided a conceptual framework for Paul's ὁ ἑνὸς ἄνθρωπος or, as in 1 Cor 15:47, the Second Man as opposed to the First Man (Adam of the Garden of Eden).[103] But could the hearer or reader in

---

[99] Cranfield, *On Romans*, 88.

[100] Elsewhere in Paul's Seven Letter Corpus, the term occurs only three times: *two* with reference to a thing or a situation where the meaning of the word is related to custom and virtue (Phil 1:7; 4:8) and *one* with reference to a person (Gal 3:11).

[101] Wallis (*Faith*, 80), presumably based on this fact, says that 'it is questionable that Paul would refer to a believer as ὁ δίκαιος'.

[102] The recognition that no human being is 'righteous' was common within some circles of Judaism in the Second Temple period, as *1 En* 81:5 ('…no flesh is righteous before the Lord') and 1 QH 17:14 ('No one is righteous in your judgement, and no one is innocent in a suit before you' [Fitzmyer] – García Martínez: 'for no-one is pronounced just in your judgement, or inno[cent] at your trial') show. See Watts ('"Ashamed"', 16-17), who also argues that Paul nowhere else uses the titular adjective in the same way as he does in Rom 1:17.

[103] See also Dunn, *Romans 1-8*, 284; *Theology*, 236 and n. 4; Moo, *Epistle*, 358; Schreiner, *Romans*, 287.

Rome have worked out that in Rom 5:19 Paul was talking about Jesus in terms of the righteous and obedient one? If we assume she could, could she also have remembered what she heard earlier and related her understanding of 5:19 to the epithet ὁ δίκαιος in the Habakkuk citation? No certainty is possible, because we have no way of knowing how the hearer or reader in Rome would have understood any given epithet or OT citation in Paul's most complex letter.[104] But can the way in which Jesus is depicted in Rom 5:19 provide interpretative guidance for a christological reading of ὁ δίκαιος in Rom 1:17? The answer could be 'yes', because while Paul's reference to Jesus as [ὁ] δίκαιος may be indirect, the expression in the former is almost explicit and logical in the sense that the claim that many will be constituted δίκαιοι through the obedience of One Man would be meaningless if that One Man were not by implication [ὁ] δίκαιος *par excellence*.

Quarles, however, argues that *interpreting Rom 1:17 in the light of 5:18-19 seems to turn Rom 1:16-18 on its head*, because the idea that Christ achieved eschatological life through his faithfulness parallels the Qumran pesherist's interpretation of Hab 2:4. Consequently, not only does this break the connection of Rom 1:17 and 1:18 with verse 16 where the gospel is the power of God for salvation to all who believe, but also it runs counter to Paul's argument in Rom 3:19-4:25 where righteousness is by faith rather than by the law and its works.[105] As argued in the foregoing chapter, however, when Rom 1:16b is understood as an independent justification of Paul's claim in 1:16a that he is not ashamed of the gospel, in which case δύναμις θεοῦ is the content or the subject matter of the gospel in the same way as δικαιοσύνη θεοῦ in 1:17a and ὀργὴ θεοῦ are, the christological reading does not seem to break the connection of verses 17 and 18 with verse 16. On the contrary, it appears to facilitate a more coherent interpretation of the passage in the sense that the power of God that brings about salvation for believing Jews and Greeks is an image for the 'right-

---

[104] For an extensive and helpful study relating to this issue, see Stanley, "'Pearls'", 125-144. Stanley's conclusion is that any analysis of Paul's quotations must take account of the literary capabilities of the hearers and/or readers of Paul's letters. Through such analysis, it is hoped that we will know the level of the literary competence of Paul's audience, for example, in Rome and, consequently, will limit ourselves to interpreting his letters at that level. Such an approach needs exhaustive knowledge of the literary backgrounds and capabilities of the recipients of Romans. Such knowledge is not possible given that we have very little or no access to the background of the recipients and their literary competence. Certainly, attempting to understand Romans on the basis of the level of the literary competence of its recipients can be helpful. This should not, however, be a substitute for attempting to understand the most probable meaning that Paul would have intended in his text.

[105] Quarles, 'From Faith to Faith: A Fresh Examination of the Prepositional Series in Romans 1:17', *NovT* 45 (2003) 1-21, 18.

eous one', Christ. Also, to read Habakkuk's ὁ δίκαιος in the light of Rom 5:19 may not necessarily undermine the significance of believing or accepting the message of the proclaimed gospel whose subject matter is God's salvific power that Jesus embodies in his death, resurrection and exaltation. We shall come to this in the following chapter.

Here at least two arguments can still be put forward against the claim that Habakkuk's ὁ δίκαιος ἐκ πίστεως ζήσεται corresponds to Paul's idea in the second half of Rom 5:19 (διὰ τῆς ὑπακοῆς τοῦ ἑνὸς δίκαιοι κατασταθήσονται οἱ πολλοί). First, in Rom 5:19 the *obedience* of Christ through which many will be constituted as 'righteous' and gain life (cf. v 21) most certainly is Christ's *obedience to death*. If the 'righteous one' who gains life is Christ in Rom 1:17b, there must then be an indication that he dies too. That we cannot find in Rom 1:17 and its immediate context. The result is that *given the conspicuous absence of the idea of the death of Christ in the context of Rom 1:17 interpreting the 'righteous one' as Christ who gains life is uncongenial.* Second, since Paul's concern in the Habakkuk citation is to do with 'the basis on which human beings experience the saving righteousness of God', *the context of Rom 1:17 has nothing to do with the question as to whether Christ shall live.* Paul nowhere says Christ shall gain eschatological life for himself by his faithfulness to God.[106] This is said to be reinforced further by the structural argument that when ἐκ πίστεως as human faith is understood to be expounded in Rom 1-4, ζήσεται as the life that is gained by faith can be understood to be expounded in 5-8.[107]

However, ἐκ πίστεως in the Habakkuk citation can be given a meaning that is equivalent to Christ's obedience and ζήσεται can be argued to be the eschatological life of Christ. To start with issues relating to ἐκ πίστεως, it cannot be denied that Paul's ἐκ πίστεως in particular and πιστ- terminology in general drop out of scene between Rom 5:12 and the end of chapter 8. The block between Rom 5:12 and 8:39 is dominated by Paul's expressions relating to the life of the Christian. But that does not necessarily suggest that Christian life (ζήσεται) is dependent on Christian faith (ἐκ πίστεως). This is not to deny that πίστις in some passages of Rom 1-4 means human faith in the sense of one's believing acceptance of and response to God's saving act in and through Christ. It is simply to say that

---

[106] Schreiner, *Romans*, 74.

[107] Schreiner (*Romans*, 292), for example, says: Romans '1-4 stress that human beings must exercise faith to be justified, while chapters 5-8 insist that those who receive God's grace live a transformed life'. Before him, this structural argument was advanced by Cranfield and Nygren. See Cranfield, *Romans 1-8*, 102; Nygren, *Commentary*, 85ff. But see also Käsemann (*Commentary*, 32) who, against Nygren, comments: 'To make the quotation govern the structure of chs. 1-4 and 5-8…is artificial and does not take the second half of the epistle into account.'

reading ἐκ πίστεως in the Habakkuk citation as human faith should not be seen as an exegetical necessity. The interpretation that takes ἐκ πίστεως as human faith is based on the view that διὰ/ἐκ πίστεως Ἰησοῦ Χριστοῦ (Rom 3:21-26) – an expanded form of ἐκ πίστεως – has an objective genitive meaning (human faith in Jesus Christ). But this construction can also be interpreted as the faith/faithfulness of Christ on which the faith of Christians is based. Thus the δίκαιος who will live ἐκ πίστεως can be argued to be Christ. Such a view, of course, requires showing that the likely referent of ἐκ πίστεως in both halves of Rom 1:17 is Christ, but we will come to all this in the following chapter.

In relation to the issue as to whether or to what extent the meaning of ἐκ πίστεως in Rom 1:17b corresponds to Rom 5:19, it suffices to say the following. Paul understands πίστις as obedience, which appears to be evident in Rom 1:5 and 16:26, where ὑπακοὴν πίστεως can be construed epexegetically. On this basis, it could be argued that the ὑπακοή of the One Man in Rom 5:19, which is another way of saying ὑπακοὴ Χριστοῦ in 2 Cor 10:5, can be loosely connected with the subjective genitive meaning of πίστις Χριστοῦ without claiming terminological synonymity between ὑπακοή and πίστις. Garlington seems to concur with this, as he argues that the obedience of Christ in Rom 5 is 'his fidelity to God the Creator and his perseverance in the course set before him by his Father'.[108] This obviously leads to a suggestion that Paul's implicit reference to Jesus as [ὁ] δίκαιος in his antithetical comparison between the two paradigmatic individuals corresponds to his possible understanding of ὁ δίκαιος in Rom 1:17: the 'righteous one' gains life through his faithfulness or obedience to God and the Adam of the Garden of Eden dies because of his unfaithfulness or disobedience to God. So the Christian life in Rom 5-8 can be understood as something gained as a result of Christ's fidelity to God and his obedient mission. But can we understand ὁ δίκαιος ... ζήσεται in the Habakkuk citation as Jesus' eschatological life?

Obviously, this question cannot be answered on the basis of the citation or its immediate context, because there is no obvious indication in Rom 1:16-18 of Christ and his eschatological life. This is not unusual, because Paul never provides us with a complete picture of a certain aspect of his thought in a given passage. It is through making relevant connections between his scattered ideas that we can attempt to gain (if at all) that complete picture. Along this line, one can perhaps answer the question above from the use of the ζάω/ζῳοποιέω/ζωή language in Romans, in which at least fourteen references show that such language is directly or indirectly linked with the resurrection life of Jesus whereby human beings are the

---

[108] Garlington, *Faith*, 108.

beneficiaries of that life.[109] For Paul, Jesus the Son of God is also Christ and Lord[110] beyond whose resurrection δικαιοσύνη reigns in life through him, eternal life is given to those who live in him and through whose *life* eschatological salvation will be achieved (cf. Rom 1:4 with 5:10, 17). He is someone through whom God's eschatological judgement will be carried out (2:16). Furthermore, Jesus' life/living and his role as the judge of all – a role that would be uniquely attributed to God in the OT (14:9-11; cf. Isa 45:23; 49:18; Jer 22:4; Ezek 5:11; and Phil 2:10-11) – are closely connected.[111] In short, Jesus' eschatological life is Jesus' resurrection life.[112]

---

[109] 5:10: 'we will be saved in his [the Son of God's] life (ἐν τῇ ζωῇ αὐτοῦ)'

5:17: 'righteousness will reign in life (ἐν ζωῇ) through the one *man*, Jesus Christ'

5:18: 'through one *man's* righteousness humanity as a whole *is led* to ... (δικαίωσιν ζωῆς)'

5:21: 'grace reigns through righteousness to eternal life (ζωὴν αἰώνιον) through Jesus Christ our Lord'

6:4: 'just as Christ was raised...so also will we walk in the newness of life (ἐν καινότητι ζωῆς)'

6:10: 'that which he [Jesus] lives (ζῇ), he lives (ζῇ) to God' (cf. v 9)

6:11: 'on the other hand [consider yourselves] as those who live (ζῶντας) to God in Christ Jesus'

6:23: 'but the gift of God *is* eternal life (ζωὴ αἰώνιος) in Christ Jesus our Lord'

8:2: 'for the law of the Spirit of life (τοῦ πνεύματος τῆς ζωῆς) liberated you...'

8:11: 'the one who raised Christ from the dead will make alive (ζωοποιήσει) your mortal bodies...'

14:9: 'Christ died and lived (ἔζησεν), so that he may be Lord of the dead and the living (ζώντων)'

[110] There are a number of references to Jesus as Son of God (and, occasionally, Lord) in Paul: υἱὸς αὐτοῦ (1:3, 9; 5:10; 8:3 [τὸν ἑαυτοῦ υἱὸν], 29, 32 [τοῦ ἰδίου υἱοῦ]; 1 Cor 1:9; Gal 1:16; 1 Thes 1:10; cf. Col 1:13; 1 Cor 15:28); ὁ υἱὸς θεοῦ (1:4; 2 Cor 1:19; Gal 2:20). In both Rom 1:4 and 5:21, Paul uses Ἰησοῦ Χριστοῦ τοῦ κυρίου ἡμῶν.

[111] In his Seven Letter Corpus too, Paul employs the ζάω/ζωή/ζωοποιέω language in relation to δύναμις θεοῦ and to Jesus' role as king. In 2 Cor 13:4, Paul's description of Jesus as someone who was crucified through ἀσθενείας but lives (ζῇ) through δυνάμεως τοῦ θεοῦ points to Jesus' state before and after he was afforded ζωή respectively, further supporting our suggestion that ὁ δίκαιος ... ζήσεται signifies Jesus' role in his resurrection life. Also, in 1 Cor 15:22-25, ζωοποιέω is closely connected with Jesus' role as a powerful βασιλεύς. Moreover, Paul's phrases τὴν δύναμιν τῆς ἀναστάσεως αὐτοῦ in Phil 3:10 – particularly when the genitive is taken as subjective, i.e. the power Jesus possesses as a resurrected One – seem to confirm our construal of ὁ δίκαιος ... ζήσεται in relation to τοῦ ὁρισθέντος υἱοῦ θεοῦ ἐν δυνάμει κτλ. This is the case particularly when ἐξ ἀναστάσεως νεκρῶν in the latter is rendered with a temporal force ('beyond the resurrection from the dead', i.e. *from* the point in time when such an event took place) and the text is construed in terms of the resurrection life of the Son of God defined by his eschatological role (cf. Rom 8:34).

[112] ἀνάστασις in Rom 1:4 is one of the two uses in Romans. The other is in Rom 6:5 where it expresses the possibility for those who are baptised of being united with Jesus in a resurrection like that of his. This resurrection (in relation to believers) may be under-

Then, it could be argued that in referring to the life/living of ὁ δίκαιος,
Paul is probably talking about Jesus' eschatological existence characterised
by his role with power and authority as the Lord, Christ and Son of God.[113]

Given the ambiguity with which the citation is employed in Rom 1:17
and Gal 3:11, however, this argument cannot be regarded as conclusive.
Indeed, one can argue – as Watson does – that *had Paul implied Christ in
the Habakkuk citation, he would have given us an explicit reference to
christology in the antecedent (Rom 1:17a) particularly of Rom 1:17b, for
example, as in 1 Jn 2:1.* In Rom 1:17a, Watson would argue, δικαιοσύνη
θεοῦ should not be understood in abstraction from the human figure of ὁ
δίκαιος, as Paul's point in the citation is to establish the initial correlation
of 'righteousness' and 'faith' in the sense that the righteousness of the person of Hab 2:4 is a righteousness that is approved by God.[114] To be sure,
Paul does not give us explicit reference to christology in Rom 1:17 and
that the epithet ὁ δίκαιος can be interpreted generically is not disputed.
However, our discussion in the foregoing chapter of issues relating to the
immediate context of Rom 1:17b showed that Paul's failure to provide us
with explicit reference to christology may not amount to an absence of
christology in Rom 1:16-17. Indeed, δύναμις θεοῦ and (the revelation of)
δικαιοσύνη θεοῦ can be understood as co-referential terms for Christ and,
if valid, that Paul could also have re-interpreted ὁ δίκαιος with reference
to Christ remains a real option. Hays, as discussed in the first chapter of
this book, has even argued that Gal 3:16, with its messianic exegesis of
Gen 17:8, shows that the seed of Abraham refers to a single individual who
is destined to be the heir of the promise to Abraham, who obviously is the
Messiah, Jesus Christ. Hays wishes to read the christology in Gal 3:16
back into the Habakkuk citation in 3:11, but he does not present us with a
plausible case. We shall come back to issues relating to Gal 3:11 in the
subsequent chapter.

---

stood in terms of the new life, as 6:4 describes. In this verse, however, it is ἐγείρω that
Paul employs. The verb is used ten times in Romans (4:24, 25; 6:4, 9; 7:4; 8:11 [2x], 34;
10:9; 13:11). In two of those uses, Jesus' resurrection is understood as a basis for the life
of those who are baptised or who dwell in Christ (or in whom the Spirit dwells) (6:4;
8:11).

[113] Since Paul is citing a scriptural passage, the sense of ζήσεται should not be limited
to the future only (cf. Gen 15:5 with Rom 4:18). In the NT the ζάω language with a
future form does not have a clearly distinguishable level of time. In 2 Cor 13:4, for
example, the future ζήσομεν does not necessarily express Paul's life exclusively in a future period of time. Also, ζήσεται in Gal 3:11-12 does not appear to indicate exclusively
the future life/living of 'the righteous one' or the one who does the commandments of the
law but rather a general theological principle with no strict limitation to a futuristic level
of time. The same may be true about the citation in Matt 4:4 and Lk 4:4: οὐκ ἐπ' ἄρτῳ
μόνῳ ζήσεται ὁ ἄνθρωπος.

[114] Watson, *Paul*, 48, 52.

Here we should pay attention to one further argument against the christ-ological reading of ὁ δίκαιος in the Habakkuk citation in Rom 1:17. That is that *in Heb 10:37-38 where Hab 2:3-4 is cited it is ὁ ἐρχόμενος who is understood messianically rather than ὁ δίκαιος.* The latter is 'simply the person who has faith in the interim'.[115] As we discussed in chapter 1, Hanson and Hays have argued that ὁ δίκαιος in the Habakkuk citation of Rom 1:17 and Gal 3:11 can be identified with [ὁ] ἐρχόμενος of the Septuagint. Hanson in particular argued that since the author of Hebrews presents ὁ ἐρχόμενος as Jesus, affording ὁ δίκαιος and ὁ ἐρχόμενος the same referent in Hebrews is reasonable, because the 'shrinking back' in Heb 10:38 can be understood as referring to Jesus' Gethsemane experience where there was a real possibility of Jesus running away from his captors and, as a re-sult, being unfaithful to God. Hanson, however, did not show exegetically how ὁ δίκαιος can be understood messianically in Hebrews itself.

Our treatment of the Habakkuk citation of Heb 10:38 and context in the third chapter of this book showed that although the case in favour of an anthropological reading of the citation is strong, the balance of argument could tilt towards the messianic reading of the epithet, particularly when one accepts the main reason behind the author's inversion of Hab 2:4a and 2:4b as one of epithetical juxtaposition. That is to say, the author's reason for inverting the texts is not only in order to bring in line the ὑποστείληται language in 10:38 with what he says in 10:39 (ἡμεῖς δὲ οὐκ ἐσμὲν ὑποστολῆς κτλ), which is the case when the collective reading is taken as the only valid option, but also (perhaps mainly) in order to juxtapose the meaning and significance of ὁ δίκαιός μου with ὁ ἐρχόμενος, Christ. In so doing, the author could be understood as exhorting his readers by saying that they should be steadfast in their faith, because their Messiah who now lives in heaven through his faithfulness-to-death will be coming soon to liberate them from their tribulations. However, although our exegetical analysis of Hab 2:3-4 showed that the LXX translator probably interpreted the Hebrew reading of the passage messianically, we cannot be absolutely certain that Paul understood the Greek text of Hab 2:3-4 as a messianic reading or in the same way as the author of Hebrews did. Nor can we reject the view that Paul's intention behind his declaration in Rom 1:17a and his use of Hab 2:4 as a proof in 1:17b could have been informed by a messi-anic understanding of Hab 2:3-4 and the ways in which the epithet ὁ

---

[115] Watts, "'Ashamed'", 17. For Watts, Paul's choice of Habakkuk is motivated by the question of theodicy rather than Jesus' messianic status. For him, this is what the Habakkuk citation does ("'Ashamed'", 24; cf. 17-18): 'By evoking the question of theodicy, and especially in the context of the ineffectiveness of Torah to restrain sin, it introduces the matter of the mystery of God's ways vis-à-vis Israel, and as such provides a scriptural matrix in which Paul can justify his gospel.'

δίκαιος (or its equivalent) was used in some Second Temple Jewish and early Christian circles.

In conclusion, the final answer (if there is one) to the question as to whether Paul intended a messianic meaning for the epithet in his citation of Hab 2:4 in Rom 1:17 will have to await our examination of ἐκ πίστεως in the following chapter. But our above adjudication between the arguments for and against a messianic reading of ὁ δίκαιος showed that arguments in favour of either position can be maintained exegetically.

5. Righteous One and Romans 1:18-3:20

From our discussions of issues relating to ὁ δίκαιος thus far, it seems clear that the epithet or its equivalent is used with reference to an eschatological or messianic figure in some Jewish writings and to Jesus in some NT texts. But the same degree of certainty is not possible in Rom 1:17. Our purpose in this section is to consider Rom 1:18-3:20 to see if Paul's expressions in this block would lend support to a christological reading of ὁ δίκαιος? Before attempting to understand how Rom 1:17 can be explained in relation to 1:18-3:20, it would be helpful to discuss Francis Watson's views briefly, because in his *Paul and the Hermeneutics of Faith*, he defends the anthropological reading of Rom 1:17 (over against both theocentric or covenantal and christological readings) on the basis of the text's connection with Rom 1:18-3:20.

For Watson, the catena of scriptural citations in 3:10-18 makes it clear that the sphere of the law is universal and its role is pronouncing the divine verdict on transgressing Jews and Gentiles without distinction, which is summed up by verse 10: οὐκ ἔστιν δίκαιος οὐδὲ εἷς (Ps 13:3b [LXX]). The result of the law uttering verdict on the people of the law (Jews) is that they stand in the same position of guilt as the Gentiles.[116] This nomistic testimony corresponds to the prophetic testimony in Rom 1:16-17. For in the latter, the one who is righteous by faith will live, while according to the former, no one is righteous, not even one. The positive assertion in the prophetic text and the corresponding negation, which is drawn as a conclusion from the law's own utterance rather than the prophetic text, can be noticed from the comparison and contrast between 1:17 and 3:20. There is a deep tension within the law, which Paul's antithetical hermeneutic claims to uncover.[117] Throughout Rom 1:16-3:20, the Habakkuk citation provides Paul with a scriptural testimony that the faith spoken in Rom 1:17 serves to

---

[116] Watson, *Paul*, 57-65.
[117] Watson, *Paul*, 66.

establish the law by enabling us to hear the negative but authentic voice of the law and, as a result, to understand that law is making way for faith.[118]

Watson is right in asserting that any attempt to explain Rom 1:17 must take account of 1:18-3:20 for the obvious reasons that 1:17 is syntactically connected with 1:18[119] and the citation in 1:17b is antithetically related to the citation in 3:10. These scriptural citations inform Paul's assertions in 1:17a and 3:20 respectively. Watson is also right in recognising the motif of universality throughout 1:18-3:20.[120] However, in his attempt to argue that the aim of 1:18-3:20 in its antithetical relation to 1:16-17 is to show that 'the law represents not the appointed way to salvation but the definitive disclosure of universal human sinfulness',[121] Watson focuses on issues in 3:10-18 by virtually ignoring exegetical elements in 1:18-32. One ought to take account of the exegetical elements in 1:18-32 in order to appreciate fully that Paul develops his expressions in Rom 1:17 and 1:18 in reverse order in 3:21-5:11 and 1:19-3:20. In the latter, the ἄνθρωποι, upon whose wickedness and unrighteousness ὀργὴ θεοῦ[122] is being revealed, appear to be Jews and Gentiles who are under ἁμαρτία (3:9; cf. 1:16) – a cosmic power as well as a realm in which that power is exercised[123] – and,

---

[118] Watson, *Paul*, 55-57.

[119] Harrison (*Paulines and Pastorals*, 79-85) argues that 1:18-2:2a is an interpolation added by a Paulinist scribe. Recently, Walker ('Romans 1.18-2.29: A Non-Pauline Interpolation?', *NTS* 45 [1999] 533-552) has also insisted that Rom 1:18-2:29 is not only non-Pauline, but also much of it is anti-Pauline. However, the majority of scholars accept the section as Pauline and integral to the original letter (e.g. Käsemann, *Commentary*, 37; Cranfield, *Romans 1-8*, 106f; Dunn, *Romans 1-8*, 53-55; Fitzmyer, *Romans*, 270).

[120] For Watson (*Paul*, 65-71), the theme of the 'universality of sin' runs through Rom 1:18-3:20. See also Bassler, *Impartiality*, 121-170; Davies, *Faith*, 47-52. Davies depends on Bassler, who attempts to see a Christian trajectory akin to the idea of divine impartiality.

[121] Watson, *Paul*, 71.

[122] Cf. 2:5, 8; 3:5; 4:15; 5:9; 9:22; 12:19; 13:4, 5; OT: 2 Kgs 22:13; Ezra 10:14; 2 Chr 12:12; Ps 78:31; Isa 13:13; 26:20.

[123] For a cosmic understanding of ἁμαρτία (and indeed Death), see Louw-Nida, *Lexicon*; Schlier, *Römerbrief*, 180f; Ziesler, *Pauline*, 73ff; *Letter*, 68ff; Murphy-O'Connor, *Paul*, 334-335; Adams, *Constructing the World: A Study in Paul's Cosmological Language*, 173; and B. Longenecker, *The Triumph of Abraham's God: The Transformation of the Identity in Galatians*, 36f, 40-46. Longenecker's discussion is based on Galatians, but it is relevant. He argues that Paul understands the kingdom of Death as a world order characterised by Sin and that Sin is equivalent to what liberation theologians call 'structural evil'. According to Longenecker, both exercise sovereignty over the world by predetermining the manner of human life through setting up a system and society in which God's kingship is not acknowledged and injustice is exercised. Furthermore, an understanding of ἁμαρτία as a realm as well as a power in or under which humanity exists can be noticed in the seventeen uses of the term in Romans 3-8: 3:9 (cf. 1:16) (power), 5:12a (power [?]), 5:12b (power/lord), 5:21 (king), 6:6 (lord), 6:13 (power), 6:14 (lord), 6:16

156

Chapter 4

therefore, cannot achieve salvation through the law and its works (3:10, 20). Rom 1:17 states the means of salvation while 1:18 describes in a nutshell the sort of state humanity is in. These antithetical notions are echoed in reverse order in 3:20 and 3:21-26. The former summarises the state of humanity under Sin while the latter describes how salvation is achieved for humanity under Sin. This seems to suggest that the antithesis in the main is not between two testimonies (prophetic and nomistic) but between two types of humanity, which seems to be represented by ὁ δίκαιος and ἄνθρωποι.[124]

The ἄνθρωπος in 2:1, who probably becomes Paul's imaginary dialogue partner in 3:1-9,[125] could be understood as a Jew who relies on his knowledge of the divine law for whatever reason.[126] It appears that this figure is intended to function as a representative of not only those who are given the written law (Jews) but also those with the natural law (Gentiles) in 1:18-3:20.[127] Both sets of people are accused of exercising wickedness and unrighteousness, obstructing ἀλήθεια (1:18), exchanging the glory of the immortal God for the likeness of mortal humanity (1:23), exchanging what is natural for unnatural (1:24, 26-27) and using their throat, tongue, lips, mouth, feet, eyes, minds and hearts as 'instruments of unrighteousness' (cf. 1:29-31 and 3:10-18 with 6:13). In short, in Rom 1:18-3:20 Paul sees the world through a single pair of spectacles, so to speak. For him, as the scripture witnesses, οὐκ ἔστιν δίκαιος οὐδὲ εἷς.[128]

(lord), 6:17 (lord), 6:18 (power), 6:20 (lord), 7:8 (lord [?]), 7:14 (lord), 7:20 (power [?]), 7:23 (power), 7:25 (lord), 8:2 (power).

[124] The former is the embodiment of πίστις and δικαιοσύνη θεοῦ, while the latter stand for collective humanity whose lives are characterised by ἀσέβεια/ἀδικία and obstruction of ἀλήθεια, which sometimes seems to share the same sense as πίστις (cf. Rom 1:25, 3:7 and 15:8 with 3:3; see also 9:1; 2 Cor 11:10; Gal 2:5, 14).

[125] For structural arrangements of 3:1-9, compare Elliott (Rhetoric, 139-140) with Stowers (Rereading, 165-166). For a text-critical treatment of the text, see Dahl, 'Rom 3:9: Text and Meaning', in M. Hooker (ed.), Paul and Paulinism, Essays in Honour of C.K. Barrett, 184-204, 186-192.

[126] For Fitzmyer (Romans, 296-298) and Dunn (Romans 1-8, 104ff), this Jew relies on his knowledge of the law for his exemption from divine judgement (cf. Wis 11:9-11, 23; 12:22; 15:2-3), while for Stowers (Rereading, 104; see also 83-125) this man is not a Jew at all. He is a pretentious Gentile who judges those Jews who belong to mainstream Judaism for failing to combine Jewish law with following Jesus.

[127] Contra Käsemann (Commentary, 33), who totally rejects the possibility of representative figures in 1:18ff. He is right, however, in espousing the idea that the sections are about humanity in general, i.e. the totality of the cosmos. Fitzmyer (Romans, 269f), on the other hand, limits 1:18-32 to 'pagans'.

[128] This is not to suggest that Paul failed to recognise the unique Jewish situation within a particular history. See also Keck ('Romans?', 24-25); Wright, 'Romans and the Theology of Paul', in Hay & Johnson (eds), Pauline, 30-67.

This citation in Rom 3:10 probably is a combination of memorised texts from Qoheleth and Psalms, as the phrase οὐκ ἔστιν δίκαιος seems to have been drawn from the former and οὐδὲ εἷς from the latter.[129] Paul's replacement of Psalms' οὐκ ἔστιν ἕως ἑνός by οὐδὲ εἷς may be attributed to a memory error or deliberate reproduction of a phrase of his choice in his eagerness to combine both texts for his own purpose. The reason for merging these texts and then preferring δίκαιος (Qoheleth) against ποιῶν χρηστότητα or ἀγαθόν (Psalms) is probably because of the need to stress that one who is δίκαιος is not ὑφ᾽ ἁμαρτίαν (v 9).[130] But in a context where the gospel, whose subject matter is δικαιοσύνη θεοῦ that is being revealed ἐκ πίστεως εἰς πίστιν, is rejected there is no δίκαιος among Jews and Gentiles. This scriptural witness in 3:10 stands in antithetical relationship with Paul's declarations in Rom 1:17 and neatly squares with Paul's assertion in 3:20 ('For no flesh will be justified before God through works of the law'). The assertion here comes from Ps 142:2, which is also shared by other Jews of the Second Temple period, as can be noticed in *1 En* 81:5 ('...no flesh is righteous before the Lord') and 1 QH 17:14 ('No one is righteous in your judgement, and no one is innocent in a suit before you' [Fitzmyer]). But Paul uses this shared concept in order to articulate the idea that Jews and Gentiles exist in a sphere that is permeated by Sin. Indeed, they are under the lordship of Sin. So neither observing 'works of the law' (for the Jew) nor not observing them (for the Gentile) will qualify them for 'justification'.[131] Based on this perspective, it appears, Paul, through citing Hab 2:4, sets ὁ δίκαιος against those who exercise wicked and unjust acts and use their physical, intellectual and emotional faculties as instruments of unrighteousness (1:18-3:20). If our contention that the foci of Paul's antithesis are the person of the Habakkuk citation and the persons in 1:18-3:20 is valid, we should then ask where Paul's antithetical pattern received its framework.

---

[129] Eccl 7:20a (MT): כי אדם אין צדיק בארץ

Eccl 7:21 (LXX): ἄνθρωπος οὐκ ἔστι δίκαιος ἐν τῇ γῇ

Ps 14:3b or 53:4a (MT): נאלחו אין עשה־טוב אין גם אחד

Ps 13:3b or 53:3b (LXX): οὐκ ἔστι ποιῶν χρηστότητα (53:3b: ἀγαθὸν) οὐκ ἔστιν ἕως ἑνός

[130] Stanley (*Language*, 90-91) is right in taking ὑφ᾽ ἁμαρτίαν as the determining factor for the way in which Paul formulates the citation, but probably wrong in limiting the citation to Psalms.

[131] In 2:13, however, Paul asserts that those who will be 'justified' (δικαιωθήσονται) or considered as δίκαιοι παρὰ θεῷ are not the hearers but the doers of the law. As Fitzmyer (*Romans*, 308) notes, Paul's statement in 2:13 might seem to stand in contradiction with what he says in 3:20. But in this context, Paul's main aim is to relativise the distinction between those 'without the law' and those 'in the law' by showing that the law is also operative among Gentiles, although the Mosaic Law is not known in their world.

An Enochic tradition could be suggested as a source of Paul's pattern of thought on the basis that *1 En* 91:7 parallels Rom 1:18f.[132] Notwithstanding the parallel, however, we do not have sufficient internal evidence in Paul that supports the view that Paul's antithetical pattern between Rom 1:17 and 1:18-3:20 received its framework from such a tradition. Rom 1:18-3:20 is about those persons who epitomise humanity in the state where it is under Sin. This draws our attention not to the tradition of Enoch but to Pauline understanding of the tradition of Adam.

To be sure, there is no explicit reference to the Adam tradition in Rom 1, but 1:23 (καὶ ἤλλαξαν τὴν δόξαν τοῦ ἀφθάρτου θεοῦ ἐν ὁμοιώματι εἰκόνος φθαρτοῦ ἀνθρώπου καὶ πετεινῶν τετραπόδων καὶ ἑρπετῶν) is thought to have an implicit reference. Barrett, Hooker, Käsemann and others have pointed out that in Rom 1:23 Paul depends on the creation story of Genesis (particularly 1:26-27) and alludes to Ps 106:20 and Jer 2:11, while having Deut 4:15-18 in mind (and perhaps Isa 44:9-20 as well).[133] The phrases καὶ ἠλλάξαντο τὴν δόξαν and ἐν ὁμοιώματι in Ps 106:20 correspond to Paul's καὶ ἤλλαξαν τὴν δόξαν and ἐν ὁμοιώματι. But εἰκών, which is central in Rom 1:23, is absent in this psalm. His use of εἰκών in our text suggests that Paul had the Genesis account of Adam in mind, however the reduplication ἐν ὁμοιώματι εἰκόνος φθαρτοῦ ἀνθρώπου is understood.[134] This seems to be confirmed by the parallel between the

---

[132] The Enochic text reads: 'And when iniquity and sin and blasphemy and wrong and all kinds of evil deeds increase, and when apostasy and wickedness and uncleanness increase, a great punishment will come from heaven upon all these, and the holy Lord will come in anger and in wrath to execute judgement on the earth' (Knibb). Käsemann (*Commentary*, 37-38) notices the parallel between *1 En* 91:7 and Rom 1:18. See also Dunn, *Romans 1-8*, 54. Some have argued that Paul does not refer to Jews in Rom 1:18-32, because he talks about idolatry, which did not exist amongst Jews of his days. However, some Second Temple Jewish texts suggest a possible existence of idolatry and/or apostasy among some Jews. In *3 Maccabees*, Dosethius apostatises from ancestral traditions (1:1-3; cf. 2:25-30; Josephus: *Ap* 2:49). In a third-century papyrus, Dosethius (Dosetheos) is said to have become a priest of Alexander the Great and the Ptolemaic kings of Egypt (*CPJ* 127e [222 BCE]) – see also Feldman & Reinhold (eds), *Jewish Life and Thought Among Greeks and Romans: Primary Readings*, 57. In Josephus, Jews such as Antiochus of Antioch (*War* 7:50), the children of Alexander and the grandson of Herod the Great (*Ant* 18:141) abandon their religion presumably in favour of other religions. Interest in some form of idolatry is also reflected in *Wisdom* and *1 Enoch*. In the former, the wilderness story regarding the idolatry of Israel (which results in γενέσεως ἐναλλαγή, 'sexual perversion' [14:26; cf. Rom 1:26]) is retold (11:15-16; 12:24), while the latter speaks against the creation of images, astrology and idolatry (8:1ff; 99:7, 9, 10).

[133] Barrett, *From First Adam to Last*, 1-21; *Epistle*, 38f; Hooker, 'Adam in Romans 1', *NTS* 6 (1959/60) 297-306; 'A Further Note on Romans 1', *NTS* 13 (1966/67) 181-183; Käsemann, *Commentary*, 45; see also Dunn, *Romans 1-8,* 61-62; Schreiner, *Romans*, 87.

[134] Hooker ('Adam', 305) understands it in terms of humanity exchanging its own 're-flection of the glory of God for the image of corruption', while Barrett (*Epistle*, 38) takes

events in the creation story of Genesis and Romans 1:18f, such as Adam's knowledge, the creation of the world, Adam's desire to become like God, Adam giving allegiance to the Serpent and Adam being thrown out of the Garden of Eden.[135] To be sure, εἰκών within the text does not specifically refer to humanity as it can also stand for the birds, four-footed animals and creeping things,[136] but given the events from the creation story and the contrast between δόξα θεοῦ and εἰκὼν ἀνθρώπου, this does not necessarily invalidate the argument here.

That Paul depends implicitly on the Adam tradition in Rom 1:23 and its context can be supported further by his expression in Rom 3:23 (πάντες γὰρ ἥμαρτον καὶ ὑστεροῦνται τῆς δόξης τοῦ θεοῦ), which, as Käsemann, Stuhlmacher and Dunn have also argued,[137] probably echoes the tradition of the Adam of the Garden of Eden. Fitzmyer rejects this view, because, for him, 'Paul is not yet expressing himself in the terms he uses in 5:12-21, and even there he corrects the contemporary Jewish understanding of Adam'.[138] Fitzmyer may be right in arguing that Paul was probably correcting or even polemicising the contemporary Jewish understanding of Adam. But as the ensuing discussions will show, he is probably wrong in denying that Rom 3:23 echoes the Adam tradition. Käsemann, Stuhlmacher and Dunn equally fail to notice that there was no homogenous understanding of Adam in Second Temple Judaism and that it is against the backdrop of differing strands of Adam tradition that Rom 1:23 and 3:23 are to be explicated.

To provide an overview of those strands, in the oracle of Ezek 28, which is related to the Genesis tradition (Gen 3:22-24 [LXX: 3:23-25]), the

---

it in terms of 'the inferior, shadowy character of that which is substituted for God' and Käsemann (*Commentary*, 45, 95) in terms of the lost Adamic glory. See also Schreiner (*Romans*, 88), who rejects the proposals of both Hooker and Barrett. But Schreiner himself offers us no better alternative, as he simply argues that ὁμοιώματι εἰκόνος refers to idol worship.

[135] See also Hooker, 'Adam', 300-301; Wedderburn, 'Adam in Paul's Letter to the Romans', in Livingstone (ed.), *Studia Biblica 3: Papers on Paul and Other New Testament Writers*, 413-430; *The Reasons for Romans*, 119.

[136] See Käsemann, *Commentary*, 45; Dunn, *Romans 1-8*, 61-62.

[137] Käsemann, *Commentary*, 95; Stuhlmacher, *Letter*, 58. Dunn (*Romans 1-8*, 168) argues that Paul's use of ἁμαρτάνω and ὑστερέω in relation to δόξα here, and his use of the δόξα motif in Rom 1:23 and 8:18-21, show that he is influenced by Jewish ideas regarding the loss of Adam's glory and its restoration. He cites the following Jewish texts where he thinks the idea of the restoration or enhancement of Adam's glory is mentioned: *Apoc Mos* 39:2; *1 En* 50:1; *4 Ezra* 7:122-125; *2 Apoc Bar* 51:1, 3; 54:15, 21; 1 QS 4:23; CD 3:20; 1QH 17:15. Dunn partly depends on Scroggs (*The Last Adam. A Study in Pauline Anthropology*, 73), who also suggests that Adam's disobedience cannot be far from Paul's mind here even though he does not refer to Adam directly in the text.

[138] Fitzmyer, *Romans*, 283, 347.

King of Tyre, who regarded himself as a god (as opposed to 'a human' [אדם]) and wiser than Daniel (vv 2-3), is driven out of the holy mountain of God, the Garden of God (cf. vv 15-16 [LXX][139] with Rom 3:23; 5:12).[140] This, to a great extent, agrees with *Jubilees* 3, which also talks about Adam and Eve's expulsion from the Garden of Eden, the Temple, Mount Zion (3:12, 15-35; 8:19). 4Q265 (*4QSerek Damesek*) excludes expulsion but elaborates the Genesis narrative of the Garden of Eden (2:11-17 [Lev 12:2-5]) and strikingly parallels the *Jubilees* tradition.[141] The tradition that goes further than expulsion, however, is the *Apocalypse of Moses*. In this composition, Adam and Eve lose the glory of God, which might consist of either immortality or righteousness or both.[142] On the contrary, several Qumran compositions indicate that the glory of Adam (כבוד אדם) – the reflection of divine glory – in the Garden of Eden, the Temple of the Lord, is restored and has become the glory of the faithful and the saved (CD 3:18-20; 1QH 4:13-15; *4QpPs^a* (4Q171) [Ps 37:19] 3:1-2).

---

[139] It is to be noted here that whereas the MT sees the cherub as the object of being driven, the LXX sees the cherub as the subject of driving. See also Noort, 'Gan-Eden in the Hebrew Bible', in Luttikhuizen (ed.), *Paradise Interpreted, Representation of Biblical Paradise in Judaism and Christianity*, 24.

[140] There have been ongoing debates as to whether the oracle in Ezek 28 is a description of the fall of Satan or Lucifer (a heavenly כרוב). It has also been difficult to identify whether Ezekiel is speaking about a single individual or the King of Tyre and a cherub. The latter difficulty is compounded by the fact that the MT's reading seems to describe the King of Tyre as the Cherub, the appointed guardian, whereas the LXX reading describes the Cherub as the companion of the King of Tyre (ἐκτίσθης σὺ μετὰ τοῦ χεροὺβ [v 14]). For discussion of both problems, see Zimmerli, *Ezekiel* (2), 86f; Noort, 'Gan-Eden', 21-36.

[141] The parallel is so striking that García Martínez concludes that 'the author of 4Q265 is using the Eden story precisely in the rewritten form found in *Jubilees* as the source or inspiration of his narrative' ('Man and Woman: Halakah Based upon Eden in the Dead Sea Scrolls', in Luttikhuizen [ed.], *Paradise*, 95-115, 111). He also notes that like *Jubilees*, the new fragment of 4Q265 seems to identify typologically the Garden of Eden with the Temple (2:6, 14) – cf. מקדש אדם in *4QFlorilegium*. See also Wise, '4QFlorilegium and the Temple of Adam', *RevQ* 15 (1991) 103-132; van Ruiten, 'Eden and the Temple: The Rewriting of Genesis 2:4-3:24 in the Book of Jubilees', in Luttikhuizen (ed.), *Paradise*, 63-81; Baumgarten, 'Scripture and Law in 4Q265', in Stone *et al* (eds), *Biblical Perspectives: Early Use and Interpretation of the Bible in the Light of the Dead Sea Scrolls*, 25-33. For the Rabbinic portrayal of Adam as a priestly figure, see Scroggs, *Adam*, 43-44.

[142] Eve recalls: '... at that very moment my eyes were opened and I knew that I was naked of the righteousness with which I had been clothed. And I wept saying, "Why have you done this to me, that I have been estranged from my glory with which I was clothed?"' (20). Later, Adam rebukes Eve saying: 'O evil woman! Why have you wrought destruction among us? You have estranged me from the glory of God' (21). For an extensive analysis of this composition, see Levison, *Portraits of Adam in Early Judaism: from Sirach to 2 Baruch*, 1ff. I followed Levison's translation above (p. 169).

Jubilees and *1 Enoch* present us with a different sort of scenario, how-ever. In *Jubilees* 4:22-24, Adam (with Eve) goes out of the Garden of Eden (3:32-35, cf. v 27) and Enoch is placed in it.[143] In *1 Enoch*, while the Book of the Watchers, after describing the expulsion of Adam and Eve from παράδεισος τῆς δικαιοσύνης (32:3-6), does not tell us whether the Garden of Righteousness was later occupied by anyone, the Parables tell us that the Garden of Righteousness is a place to which Enoch, who is also identi-fied with/as a messianic figure, was taken up (60:8; cf. 60:23; 70:3-4; 71:14; 77:3). For the author of the Parables, it is this figure – Son of Man, Chosen One, Righteous One and Messiah – who sits on the throne of divine glory, not Adam (45:3-4; 46:3; 51:3; 62:5; 69:27, 29; 71:14).[144]

Paul's perspective in Rom 1:23 and 3:23 is not expressed in the graphic language of expulsion from the Garden of Eden or being cast out from the mountain of God. In 1:23, it is described in terms of exchanging the glory of the immortal God for the image of mortal humanity. In 3:23, Paul's use of ἁμαρτάνω and ὑστερέω in connection with δόξα θεοῦ probably shows that humanity has failed to conform to or been robbed of the glory of God.[145] This reminds us of the text in the *Apocalypse of Moses* to which we drew attention earlier. In this composition, [divine] righteousness and the glory of God are paralleled and the loss of the former means the loss of the latter.[146] For Paul too, Adam is no longer the representation of God's

---

[143] Part of 4:23, for example, reads: 'And he [Enoch] was taken away from the sons of men, and we [the angels] conducted him into the garden of Eden in majesty and honour'.

[144] Although it uses the epithet Son of Man, *1 En* 69:27 ('And he sat on the throne of his glory, and the whole judgement [lit. 'and the sum of judgement'] was given to the Son of Man...') is particularly relevant here as it expresses the conception which might have become common in some circles of the first-century world. E.g. Matt 19:28: 'when the Son of Man is seated on the throne of his glory, you who have followed me will also sit on twelve thrones, judging the twelve tribes of Israel'; Matt 25:31: 'When the Son of Man comes in his glory, and all the angels with him, then he will sit on the throne of his glory'; Jn 5:22: 'The Father judges no one but has given all judgement to the Son'; and 5:27: 'and he has given him authority to execute judgement, because he is the Son of Man'. Cf. also, Acts 2:33; 7:52, 55-56.

[145] The use of ἁμαρτάνω in 3:23 is one of the seven uses in the entire letter. All seven uses are, strikingly, confined to the first six chapters (2:12 [2x]; 3:23; 5:12, 14, 16; 6:15). The verb ἁμαρτάνω can be translated as 'miss the mark', 'fail of one's purpose', 'fail of having', 'sin', while the verb ὑστερέω can be translated as 'come short of', 'be robbed of a thing', 'fail to obtain', 'be in want of'. See Liddell-Scott, *Lexicon*. According to Rienecker & Rogers (*Linguistic Key to the Greek New Testament*, 356) ὑστεροῦνται τῆς δόξης τοῦ θεοῦ may be construed in three ways:

   a) objective genitive: failing to give glory to God
   b) subjective genitive: failing to receive the glory of God
   c) possessive genitive: failing to conform to the image of God

[146] Levison (*Portraits*, 187) argues that it 'would be a distortion to discuss the prime-val splendor of Adam in terms of *imago dei*'. For Levison, this 'attribute of Adam re-

glory. Through him, ἁμαρτία seized power (5:12f) and, as a result,
'Ιουδαίους τε καὶ "Ελληνας πάντας ὑφ' ἁμαρτίαν (Rom 3:9; cf. *1 En*
99:3[147]) and οὐκ ἔστιν δίκαιος οὐδὲ εἷς (Rom 3:10). The statements in
Rom 3:9 and 3:10, it seems, are enveloped in the phrase πάντες ἥμαρτον
(in, since, or because of Adam, 5:12[148]) in 3:23. Like the authors of
Jubilees and *1 Enoch*, Paul no longer sees Adam as a paradigmatic figure.
Adam represents humanity without God's glory, the image of mortal humanity. This is consistent with Gen 3:22-24, where the reason why God
drove Adam out of the Garden of Eden was precisely because he wanted to
limit his ability to live forever by eating from the Tree of Life. It can then
be argued, as the true representation of the glory of the immortal God, for
Paul, is Christ, 'righteous one', the man of heaven, those who do not share
in or conform to his image are exchanging the glory of immortal God for
the image of mortal man, the man of dust (Rom 5:18-19; 8:29; 1 Cor
15:49; 2 Cor 3:18; 4:6).[149] From all this, Paul's antithetical pattern in 1:16-
17 and 1:18-3:20 appears to have received its framework from his
understanding of Jesus *vis-à-vis* Adam of the Garden of Eden.

For Paul, it seems, humanity devoid of divine glory represents what
Adam of the Garden of Eden was and did and, therefore, humanity under
the lordship of Sin. If valid, in 1:23 and 3:23, as in 5:12-21, Paul might be
arguing against one contemporary Jewish conception of Adam,[150] while
more or less agreeing with another. That is to say, in some Qumran
traditions, Adam remains paradigmatic, while in *1 Enoch*, for example, he

---

mains after the loss of paradise, etc., and becomes one of the bases for God's mercy toward him' (p. 187). It is true that in the *Apocalypse of Moses* Adam's being the image of
God forms a basis for the angelic intercession after Adam's death (see also Levison,
Portraits, 172). Thus Adam did not lose the image of God upon fall, but the loss of the
glory of God is evident. That Adam did not lose the image of God after fall can be argued
from Gen 9:6 and 1 Cor 11:7-9 as well.

[147] Dahl ('Rom 3:9', 194, 197) argues that *1 En* 99:3 (and its context) is a key for understanding Rom 3:9, and indeed the subsequent catena of scriptural quotations. On the
basis that προέχεσθε in the Enochic passage parallels Paul's use of προεχόμεθα in 3:9, he
may be right – the verb προέχω or the middle προέχομαι means 'to hold before [one-
self]', which could be understood metaphorically as 'to put forward' or 'to hold out as an
excuse'. See also Wilckens, *Brief I*, 172; Dunn, *Romans 1-8*, 146-147.

[148] For various interpretations of ἐφ' ᾧ πάντες ἥμαρτον, see Fitzmyer, *Romans*, 413-
416. There was divergence of opinion among the rabbis. Some argued that if all human
beings die because of Adam's misdeed, it is because all human beings sin through Adam,
while others thought that since there were some who did not die (Enoch and Elijah), it
meant that there were some who did not sin, hence each human being (including Moses
and Aaron) dies through their own sin. The rabbis ultimately agreed that death is God's
decree on human beings because of Adam. For good treatments of this, see Davies, *Paul*,
20-27, and Scroggs, *Adam*, 32-38.

[149] See also Hooker, 'Adam', 304-305.

[150] So Hooker ('Adam', 297-306); see also Scroggs, *Adam*, 73-74, 75 and n. 3.

is replaced by a messianic figure known as the Son of Man, Righteous One, Messiah, Chosen One. Paul appears to have a similar conceptual framework to the latter, although for him it is not the Enochic figure but Christ who is paradigmatic. All this seems to confirm our proposal that the antithesis between Rom 1:16-17 and Rom 1:18-3:20 should be explicated through the antithesis between ὁ δίκαιος in Rom 1:17b and ἄνθρωποι in 1:18. The proposal, however, works for both generic and messianic interpretations of ὁ δίκαιος. That is to say, if ὁ δίκαιος is understood as generic, the believer is contrasted with those Jews and Gentiles under the lordship of Sin, whereas if the epithet is understood as messianic, Christ can be contrasted with the collective humanity under the lordship of Sin. Both construals seem plausible, but if we are right in suggesting that Paul's antithetical pattern in 1:17 and 1:18-3:20 received its framework from the tradition of Adam of the Garden of Eden *vis-à-vis* Jesus, reading ὁ δίκαιος christologically might be consistent not only with the context of 1:16-3:20 but also with that of 3:21-5:11.

5. Conclusions

Our discussion in this chapter showed that Paul in his letters was not that interested in employing the δίκαιος language with reference to Christ. Indeed, the only passage where he could be understood as *implicitly* referring to Christ as the 'righteous one' is Rom 5:19. But that δίκαιος is used with reference to Christ in Paul or elsewhere in the NT in and of itself does not legitimate a christological interpretation of ὁ δίκαιος in Rom 1:17, because the same term with or without the definite article is used with reference to the followers of Jesus in the NT.[151] That is, the term can simply be used with reference to an attribute of any person, including Jesus. So we thought it important to study, albeit briefly, every single NT passage in which the term is used with reference to Christ. Consequently, we noticed that in 1 Pet 3:18 and 1 Jn 2:1 the adjective is used anarthrously and with reference primarily to Jesus' attribute. But both Peter and John seem to use the term in order to show that Jesus is *the suffering one*. For John in particular, Jesus represents God the Righteous One and stands as the *Paraclete* before the throne of God. On these grounds, both passages could be understood as referring *indirectly* to Jesus as *the suffering messiah*. Indirect messianic

---

[151] For example, the δίκαιος language with or without the definite article is used diversely in Deutero-Pauline, other epistles and the Apocalypse: for God (2 Tim 4:8; 1 Jn 1:9; Rev 16:5), for Abel (Heb 11:4; 1 Jn 3:12), for any Christian (2 Thess 1:5; 1 Tim 1:9; Tit 1:8; Heb 10:38; Js 5:6, 16; 1 Pet 3:12; 4:18; 2 Pet 2:7, 8 [2x]; 1 Jn 3:7, 12; Rev 22:11) and for God's judgement (2 Pet 1:13; Rev 19:2) and ways (Rev 15:3).

reference can be noticed in Matt 10:41 as well. Differing from John, Peter and Matthew, however, Luke's use of [ὁ] δίκαιος in Acts is unambiguously messianic (3:14, 7:52 and 22:14).

But no pre-Pauline Jewish writing cites Hab 2:4 in such a way that the citation can be understood messianically; nor does any other NT writer but the author of Hebrews cite Hab 2:4. So, given all this and the strength of internal exegetical arguments in favour of the anthropological reading of ὁ δίκαιος in the Habakkuk citation of Rom 1:17, it may be unwise to arrive at any conclusive judgement at this stage that the christological construal of ὁ δίκαιος is more compelling than the anthropological construal. These factors, however, should not necessarily lead us to reject the legitimacy of reading the epithet in the citation as Christ. For one thing, our analyses of Rom 1:17 and its immediate context in the light of parallel contextual elements in Second Temple Jewish writings showed that the epithet could be understood either generically or specifically. We had noticed a similar situation earlier where ὁ δίκαιος in the Habakkuk citation of Heb 10:38 could be construed either collectively or particularly. For another, if Paul understood ὁ δίκαιος in the Habakkuk citation of Rom 1:17 with a christological meaning, that would not have been completely strange. The reason is that the messianic meaning and significance attached to the term 'righteous one' or its equivalent in Enochic and related Jewish writings of the Second Temple period and the use of [ὁ] δίκαιος with *indirect* reference to Christ by Matthew, 1 Peter and 1 John and *clear* messianic reference by Luke strongly suggest that such an understanding was common within some Jewish and Christian circles. As a sharer of scriptural and interpretative traditions, Paul could well have understood ὁ δίκαιος as a christological designation via Isa 53:11, a passage that appears to have influenced Paul's and early Christians' understanding of the role of Christ and the significance of the gospel events. But our final decision as to whether ὁ δίκαιος in the citation in Rom 1:17 is generic or specific must depend on our exegetical reading of ἐκ πίστεως in relation to the πίστις Χριστοῦ construction in Galatians and Romans, to which we now turn.

Chapter 5

ΕΚ ΠΙΣΤΕΩΣ: Christological or Anthropological?

1. Introduction

What Paul means by πίστις in Rom 1:17 and elsewhere remains contentious. He speaks of πίστις in different ways in his Seven Letter Corpus,[1] but he nowhere gives a specific definition of the term as the writer of Hebrews, for instance, does (11:1). Paul, of course, was not the first Jew to use the πιστ- word-group, for the LXX's rendering of the Hebrew words אמת/אמונה by πίστις (and ἀλήθεια)[2] and the use of the word-group in Ben Sira, Philo and Josephus demonstrate that it was common linguistic currency within Jewish circles.[3] Despite many attempts to understand Paul's use of the term through investigating the religious, cultural and semantic nuances that were given to the πιστ- terminology in these Jewish-Hellenistic writings,[4] however, the distinctions between the meaning of

---

[1] He refers to πίστις in relation to Jesus (Gal 3:23-25), notably connects it with the post-Easter community and its beliefs (Gal 1:23), and couples it as a virtue with others of the same kind, particularly ἀγάπη (1 Cor 13:13; 2 Cor 8:7; Gal 5:6, 22; 1 Thess 1:3; 3:6; 5:8). Paul also contrasts διὰ εἴδους [περιπατεῖν] (as the lower degree) with διὰ πίστεως περιπατεῖν (the higher degree) (2 Cor 5:7) almost in the same way as he contrasts πνεύματι περιπατεῖν with ἐπιθυμίαν σαρκὸς (Gal 5:16). He further speaks of πίστις as a special gift possessed by a select few (1 Cor 12:9) and understands it to be an unquestioning belief (1 Cor 13:2; cf. Rom 12:6).

[2] According to Barr's statistics, אמונה is translated in the LXX by πίστις 20 times, by πιστός 1 time, by ἀλήθεια 22 times and by ἀληθινός 2 times. אמת is translated by πίστις and πιστός 7 times, and by ἀλήθεια and related words 107 times. Barr, *Semantics of Biblical Language*, 198-199.

[3] In Philo, the substantive is used for 'pledge', 'security', 'proof', 'faithfulness' (in the execution of charge), 'faith', 'trust', and as 'conviction' and 'belief'. In Sirach: 'steadfastness', 'faithfulness' and 'obedience' (in religious sense); and 'trust' (in human relationships). In Josephus: 'loyalty', 'faithfulness'. See Lindsay, *Josephus and Faith, Πίστις and Πιστεύειν as Faith Terminology in the Writings of Flavius Josephus and in the New Testament*, 44-46, 51, 56-63, 87.

[4] For example, see Hay ('*Pistis* as "Ground for Faith" in Hellenized Judaism and Paul', *JBL* 108 [1989], 461-476), who argues that πίστις in pagan and Jewish writings means 'pledge' or 'evidence', i.e. 'objective basis for faith'. See also Lindsay (*Josephus*, 98, 148, 163), who argues that unlike Josephus (and others except Sirach) who under-

Treue and *Glaube*, 'faithfulness' and 'faith', continue to trouble scholars.[5] The problem is even more complicated in Rom 1:17 because of the cryptic double prepositional phrase ἐκ πίστεως εἰς πίστιν in 1:17a in relation to παντὶ τῷ πιστεύοντι in 1:16 and the Habakkuk citation in Rom 1:17b (cf. Gal 3:11). Our inquiry in this chapter will be concerned with determining whether ἐκ πίστεως means human faith or Christ's faithfulness in both halves of Rom 1:17.[6]

Out of 55 occurrences of the substantive in Paul's Seven Letter Corpus, more than a third are in the ἐκ πίστεως form. Curiously, the use of this form is exclusively confined to Romans and Galatians.[7] Given such level of distribution in these two letters, which also happen to contain the citation from Hab 2:4b (ὁ δὲ δίκαιος ἐκ πίστεως ζήσεται), it is hardly possible to overlook the significance of the prepositional phrase for understanding Paul's use of πίστις and what it denotes not only in Rom 1:17 but also elsewhere in Romans. The phrase is also significant for understanding the δίκ- language in Romans, because while only two of the twelve uses of ἐκ πίστεως in the letter are indirectly connected with this language (4:16 [2x];

---

stands πίστις in a profane sense, the NT (including Paul) follows the OT use of אמונה and understands πίστις 'exclusively' as religious faith[fulness] and fidelity. For a recent attempt, see also Campbell, *The Quest for Paul's Gospel: A Suggested Strategy*, 178-207.

[5] Haussleiter, 'Der Glaube Jesu Christi und der christliche Glaube', *NKZ* 2 (1891) 109-145.

[6] Paul's expression in Rom 1:17 is part of his wider interest in the πιστ- word group, which he uses much more extensively than any other NT writer. As the statistical diagram below shows, πιστ- terms occur about 161 times in the Pauline Seven Letter Corpus out of which the substantive πίστις alone occurs 91 times, whereas it occurs only 101 times in all the rest of the NT. See also Morris, 'Faith', in Hawthorne, *et al* (eds), *Dictionary of Paul and His Letters*, 285-291, 285.

πιστ- terms	Rom	1 Cor	2 Cor	Gal	Phil	1 Th	Phile	Total
πίστις	21	7	5	9	4	7	2	55
ἐκ πίστεως	12	--	--	11	--	--	--	23
διὰ πίστεως	7	--	1	3	1	1	--	13
πιστός	--	5	2	1	--	1	--	9
πιστεύω	21	9	2	4	1	5	--	42
ἀπιστία/ἄπιστός	4	11	3	--	--	--	--	18
Total	65	32	13	28	6	14	2	160

[7] See also Campbell, *Rhetoric*, 211-213; 'ΠΙΣΤΙΣ', 91-103; 'Romans 1:17', 267, 272-273; 'Presuppositions', 713-719.

cf. v 13) and two are not at all connected (14:23 [2x]), eight uses (over 66%) – two of them in our passage – are directly connected (1:17a, 17b; 3:26, 30; 5:1; 9:30, 32; 10:6).

So, in this chapter, we will consider issues relating to this significant prepositional phrase. We will attempt to show that *although the phrase means human faith in some places and is employed ambiguously in other places, cumulative evidence suggests that in Rom 1:17 it probably denotes the faithfulness of Christ shown in his death on the cross.* To achieve this, we will begin our discussion with a brief textual assessment of the ways in which Paul appropriates Hab 2:4b in Gal 3:11 and Rom 1:17. This introduces us to the interpretative difficulties and possibilities the citation poses. Consequently, we will deal with the question as to whose πίστις Paul is referring to in his ἐκ πίστεως in Rom 1:17. This question has divided scholars, as some have contended that it refers to God's covenant faithfulness (theocentric/covenantal reading), while others have argued that it refers to human faith (anthropological reading), while still others have argued that the phrase refers to Christ's faithfulness (christological reading). We will pay attention to the theocentric/covenantal reading of ἐκ πίστεως, because such an interpretation, according to a number of scholars, is believed to be relevant to the Habakkuk citation in Rom 1:17 in particular. But for the reason that will become clear later our discussion in this chapter will, by and large, concentrate on the christological and anthropological interpretative options. The reason for focussing on these two options is because the obvious choice in terms of the wider textual uses of ἐκ πίστεως vis-à-vis the πίστις Χριστοῦ construction in particular is between human faith [in Christ] and Christ's faithfulness. After considering issues in Gal 3:11 and Rom 1:17 and examining the arguments surrounding the use of ἐκ πίστεως in Rom 9:30-10:13, we will explore how texts on which the πίστις Χριστοῦ debate is based (Gal 2:16 and Rom 3:22 in particular) and the Abraham argument in Romans 4 can help us explain what ἐκ πίστεως means in Rom 1:17.

2. A Textual Conundrum

In what follows, we wish to consider briefly the question as to why Paul failed to or chose not to follow either the MT or LXX when he cited Hab 2:4 in Rom 1:17 and Gal 3:11. Hab 2:4 may have been part of a collection of biblical extracts (previously called a book of testimonies) used by those like Paul in their controversy with other Jews.[8] To be sure, in neither

---

[8] See Dodd (*Scripture*, 26f) for his cautious acceptance of the previous proposals and Lim (*Scripture*, 150-158) for the survey of the scholarship regarding the so-called

Romans nor Galatians is the passage used along with a string of citations, as, for example, in Rom 3:10-18, but that does not invalidate the possibility of the passage in question being part of, using Lim's terms, 'handy collections of biblical passages for reference'.[9] Paul's verbatim citation of Hab 2:4 in Rom 1:17 and Gal 3:11 (ὁ δὲ δίκαιος ἐκ πίστεως ζήσεται) to an extent confirms this. But Paul does not follow fully either the Masoretic text or the LXX variations. Had he followed the former or ἐν πίστει αὐτοῦ, as found in the Nahal Hever text or the Proto-Theodotionic version, his citation would have had αὐτοῦ after πίστεως. Had he followed the latter, the citation would have had μου after πίστεως (א, B, Q, V, W) or, like Heb 10:38, after ὁ δὲ δίκαιος (A, C, 26, 49).[10] Can we view Paul's failure or choice as a misuse of the sacred text he had at his disposal (in Hebrew, Greek or both), a memory error, an exegetical variant deliberately modified and employed, or the outcome of Paul's dependence on a text that is different from both the Masoretic and Septuagintal texts known to us?[11]

It is probably important to note here that it is not absolutely evident that the Habakkuk citation in question is based exclusively on the LXX texts, as some would suggest. It is true that many of the Pauline citations agree almost verbatim with, for instance, the Göttingen edition of the LXX. But this does not necessarily make Hab 2:4b Septuagintal because, as Lim has shown, the main criterion for a Pauline citation to be distinctively Septuagintal cannot just be a word for word agreement between an edition of the LXX and a Pauline reading – which is not even the case in Rom 1:17b – but rather between a Pauline citation and 'the LXX in those passages

---

Testimony Book hypothesis. According this hypothesis, there was 'one lost Testimony Book against the Jews which was first compiled by Matthew, used by Paul and other New Testament writers, attested to in Papias, cited by the Church Fathers (especially Cyprian), and extant in a secondarily redacted, sixteenth-century manuscript found in the monastery of Iveron on Mount Athos' (Lim, *Scripture*, 150). Lim prefers 'biblical extracts' to 'testimony book' and reinforces the hypothesis by using examples from Qumran, which, not surprisingly, include 2 Cor 6:14-7:1 in relation to texts such as 4QFlor (4Q174) and 1QM 4:1-2.

[9] Lim, *Scripture*, 154. For the possible existence of a collection of passages used by Paul and his disciples, see Lk 4:16-19; Acts 17:2-3 and 2 Tim 4:13.

[10] MS C's insertion of the personal pronoun after δίκαιος in Rom 1:17 is peculiar and probably an attempt to make the passage conform to its own reading of Habakkuk.

[11] These, needless to say, are very complex issues but we do not need to deal with them in detail here, not least because much work has already been done in the area. See, for example, Hays, *Echoes*, 1ff; Moyise, 'Intertextuality', 14-41; Stanley, *Language*, 1ff; 'The Social Environment of "Free" Biblical Quotations in the New Testament', Evans & Sanders (eds), *Early Christian Interpretation of the Scriptures of Israel*, 19-27. See also Lim (*Scripture*, 123-160) for the questions and possible answers with regard to the complexities of identifying Pauline modifications of biblical quotations.

where the Septuagint differs from all other text-types'.[12] This means that even if a Pauline citation looks as though it has been drawn from the LXX without material change, that verbal similarity alone does not make the citation especially Septuagintal unless otherwise it betrays a clear and unambiguous distinction from the MT or 1QpHab etc. Thus one's categorisation of our text as either Hebrew- or Greek-based can only be partially true. This makes it difficult to argue that Paul was unaware that he was not following the Greek or Hebrew *Vorlage* of Hab 2:4. He may have depended on both LXX and MT.

As to why Paul failed or chose not to follow either the LXX or MT, it can be argued, as Dunn has done, that the apostle intentionally left out the first person singular pronoun μου and the third person singular pronoun αὐτοῦ respectively. In doing so, he was introducing a deliberate ambiguity into the meaning of ἐκ πίστεως so that it could be read either with God as in the majority readings of the LXX variations or with the believer as in the MT.[13] As someone who was conversant in Greek, 'in the Hebrew dialect' (Acts 21:37-22:21) and probably in Aramaic, Paul could have known the text in question from both the Hebrew biblical texts and excerpts and Greek editions available at the time.[14] It can therefore be assumed that he knew Hab 2:4 very well, so the omission of μου could only have resulted from design rather than accident. But such a theory is difficult to prove or disprove. Alternative theories may not shed much light either. For example, it could be said that Paul may be quoting from a text that is no longer extant. It could also be said that the Greek text of Rom 1:17b is a citation by memory of the Hebrew text, in which case the discrepancy in question is accounted for by Paul's misremembering.[15] The latter theory assumes that Paul's memory was so bad that he experienced arbitrary memory lapses twice, i.e. in Galatians and Romans. This seems unlikely. However, it is difficult, if not impossible, to prove or disprove either of these theories.

One other explanation for this textual conundrum is that Paul may have been 'working consciously but unreflectively within the bounds of contemporary literary conventions that shaped the way quotations might be handled'.[16] Issues relating to literary conventions in the first century world

---

[12] Lim, *Scripture*, 141-142.

[13] Dunn, *Romans 1-8*, 45, 148. Robinson (*Wrestling with Romans*, 15) goes even further and accuses Paul of misusing the scripture.

[14] On Paul's linguistic background and exegetical training, see Lim, *Scripture*, 161ff.

[15] So Schlatter (*Romans*, 26).

[16] Stanley, 'Social', 27. By 'literary conventions', Stanley (p. 20) is referring to the practice that existed in the Greco-Roman world where the Greeks and Jews were trained from childhood to quote from memory basic texts from Homer and the Hebrew Bible respectively.

fall beyond the scope of our present concern, but one thing must be said here. Even if Paul is judged to have lacked reflection on the exegetical or hermeneutical issues embedded in Rom 1:17b, the question as to whether he was conscious of quoting the Habakkuk text without μου or αὐτοῦ can be explained from his omission of the first or third person singular pronoun with ἐκ πίστεως in Romans. That is to say, the fact that ten out of twelve uses of ἐκ πίστεως in the letter do not have a personal pronoun suggests that the absence of μου or αὐτοῦ probably was simply habitual or common practice rather than an attempt to make a significant theological point. However, this does not necessarily mean that Paul did not have the personal pronoun in his mind at all. For in his omission of the pronoun, he may have been following a Greek literary style where the possessive pronoun becomes unnecessary and is omitted if the referent is clear enough and is employed with the definite article.[17] In the case of Rom 1:17b and Gal 3:11, then, the referent of ἐκ πίστεως can be ὁ δίκαιος, hence the use of αὐτοῦ might have been judged unnecessary.

However, we have no way of knowing whether or not Paul followed such a Greek literary style. It would have been easier for him to add either the first or third personal pronoun. Adding μου after ὁ δὲ δίκαιος would even have been more congenial to him, but he fails to do that too. So from a textual standpoint, we cannot determine why Paul in both Rom 1:17 and Gal 3:11 fails to or chooses not to use the third person singular pronoun αὐτοῦ after ἐκ πίστεως (in keeping with the Hebrew באמונתו and the Nahal Hever text) or the first person singular pronoun μου after ὁ δὲ δίκαιος (in keeping with LXX's minority reading) or after ἐκ πίστεως (in keeping with LXX's majority reading). It remains possible, however, that Paul quoted Hab 2:4 from memory, or from a text that existed at the time but was later lost, or from either a Hebrew or Greek text but by deliberately modifying it. The result of this conclusion in relation to our main question of this chapter is that at this stage we cannot claim or disclaim that Paul understood Hab 2:4b in Rom 1:17 and Gal 3:11 as messianic or generic individual believer. An attempt to answer this question must be made through considering the citations in their own contexts. To that we now turn.

---

[17] See Sollamo, 'The Koine Background for the Repetition and Non-Repetition of the Possessive Pronoun in Co-ordinate Items', in Fraenkel and Wevers (eds), *Studien zur Septuaginta: Robert Hanhart zu Ehren*, 52-63; 'Repetition of Possessive Pronouns in the Greek Psalter: The Use and Non-Use of Possessive Pronouns in Renderings of Hebrew Coordinate Items with Possessive Pronouns', in Hiebert et al (eds), *The Old Greek Psalter: Studies in Honour of Albert Pietersma*, 44-53.

3. Ἐκ Πίστεως: God's Covenant Faithfulness?

As indicated above, there are some scholars who argue that ἐκ πίστεως in Rom 1:17 refers to God's covenant faithfulness. If this reading is valid, it has the potential to undermine both the christological and anthropological arguments. But is it valid? And would it necessarily do so? This section will seek to answer these questions.

Since E. P. Sanders, the approach to Romans in the light of God's covenantal relationship with Israel has gained strength.[18] To describe the argument in a nutshell; as God's covenant relationship with Israel was the central focus of Paul's thinking, his formulation of the thematic statement of Romans must also have been influenced by a covenantal perspective. Crucial in this argument is the definition of δικαιοσύνη θεοῦ as God's covenant faithfulness.[19] No explanation, to be sure, is given in our passage as to the way in which Paul and his readers related the term's usage to a covenantal perspective, but, in Dunn's view, the fact that the term is employed here and elsewhere in itself shows that 'Paul is drawing directly upon Christianity's heritage of Israel's covenant faith' in response to God's faithfulness.[20] A basis for defining δικαιοσύνη θεοῦ as God's covenant faithfulness is the supposed equation between the term in question and πίστις/ἀλήθεια θεοῦ in Rom 3:3-7.[21] Hence Rom 1:16-17 demonstrates a 'dynamic interaction between "the righteousness of God" as God's saving action for *all* who believe and "the righteousness of God" as God's

---

[18] See, for example, Dunn, *Romans 1-8*, 42-49; *Theology*, 334ff, 499ff; 'Paul', 85-100; Wright, *The Climax of the Covenant*, 1ff; 'Romans', 30-67; 'Letter', 395ff; Hays, 'ΠΙΣΤΙΣ', 35-60; B. Longenecker, *Eschatology and Covenant*, 1ff; 'Contours of Covenant Theology in Post-Conversion Paul', in R. Longenecker (ed.), *Road*, 125-146.

[19] Dunn argues that in Hebraic thought δικαιοσύνη is a concept that expresses mutual obligations within divine-human and human-human relationships. Along this line, the term δικαιοσύνη θεοῦ is taken to denote God's fulfilment of the obligations he took upon himself in creating humanity, in the calling of Abraham and in the choosing of Israel. See Dunn, *Theology*, 342; cf. *Romans 1-8*, 44. But it is interesting that Dunn almost agrees with the Käsemannian view by arguing that Paul took it for granted that those familiar with Jewish scriptures would understand δικαιοσύνη θεοῦ as 'the power of God' put forth to effect God's part in saving not only Israel but also the whole world. Gentile God-worshippers as well as Jews would recognise the equation between δικαιοσύνη θεοῦ and δύναμις θεοῦ εἰς σωτηρίαν, because they could understand the former as God's action on behalf of human beings. See Dunn, *Romans 1-8*, 47; *Theology*, 343-344.

[20] Dunn, *Theology*, 344.

[21] Dunn seeks to demonstrate this by structuring chs 1-8 under δικαιοσύνη θεοῦ εἰς πίστιν (ὁ δίκαιος ἐκ πίστεως – 'the righteous by faith' [1:18-5:21] and ζήσεται [6-8]) and chs 9-11 under δικαιοσύνη θεοῦ ἐκ πίστεως (ὁ δίκαιος ἐκ πίστεως – 'the righteous by God's faithfulness'). Dunn, *Romans 1-8*, 37-38. See also Williams, '"Righteousness", 263; Hays, 'ΠΙΣΤΙΣ', 41-47, 55.

faithfulness to *Israel*, his chosen people'[22] or, as Wright puts it, between God's faithfulness to Israel and his justice to creation as a whole.[23]

It appears that behind the pervasive employment of the term 'covenantal' in the course of explaining Rom 1:17 is a desire to establish Paul's theology on a particular coherent basis, i.e. Paul's redefinition and application of the idea of God's faithfulness to his covenant with his chosen people and his obligations to his creation as a whole.[24] This desire seems to originate from the view that focusing on a small picture might stifle distinctive contributions of other passages that can be discovered through a big picture approach.[25] Certainly, one should not allow a reading of Rom 1:17, for example, to stifle or squash distinctive contributions of other passages. Equally, one should not allow the distinctive contributions Rom 1:17 can make to an understanding of the whole letter to be pre-determined by an attempt to establish a coherent solution for the suppos-edly coherent problem that Paul seeks to address in the letter.[26] In short, one could argue for the legitimacy of the covenantal reading so long as it does not overlook some distinct contributions that Rom 1:17 can make to the letter as a whole.

The absence of overt covenantal language in the first half of Romans might be a problem for the reading, however. The issue of 'covenant' no doubt is important in Paul's thinking, but Paul fails to use the term διαθήκη in our passage and its immediate and wider contexts. In fact, the term first appears in Romans in 9:4, one of the two references in the letter and eight in Paul's Seven Letter Corpus.[27] It can be argued, of course, that the notion of covenant is implied in the passage in question and indeed in the first five chapters of Romans, as is shown by the high concentration of the term Ἰουδαῖος in the first three chapters,[28] references in 1:2 and 3:21 (cf. 16:26) to Jewish scripture as a record of promises or a witness to the gospel, Paul's interest in the significance of God's dealings with Abraham in

---

[22] Dunn, *Romans 1-8*, 43-44; *Theology*, 344.

[23] Wright, 'Romans', 36-42, 64-65; 'Letter', 398ff.

[24] See, for example, Dunn, 'Romans', 88-89; 95-100.

[25] So Wright ('Romans', 31), for example, argues: '[u]ltimately, the best argument for any exegesis ought to be the overall and detailed sense it makes of the letter, the co-herence it achieves. Solutions that leave the letter in bits all over the exegetical floor do not have the same compelling force, as hypotheses, as does a solution that offers a clear line of thought all through, without squashing or stifling the unique and distinctive con-tribution of the various parts.'

[26] These contributions are obviously conveyed through the use of certain terminology, a good example of which is the high concentration in Rom 1:1-5:11 of the πιστ- word group, without which Paul's distinctive thought in the block as well as in the letter cannot be established.

[27] Rom 11:27; 1 Cor 11:25; 2 Cor 3:6, 14; Gal 3:15, 17; 4:24. Cf. Eph 2:12.

[28] Rom 1:16; 2:9, 10, 17, 28, 29; 3:1, 9, 29; 9:24; 10:12.

chapter 4, and his reference to νόμος 24 times in the first five chapters.[29] To this can be added numerous uses of 'Ισραήλ in chs 9-11[30] and Paul's extensive interest in alluding to or citing from the Jewish scripture throughout the letter. On the basis of this evidence, one may concede that use of these terms directly denote covenantal concerns and therefore the use of the term 'covenantal' is legitimate in the discussion of the passage in question in the same way as the use of the term 'eschatological' is (the latter is not directly used in Rom 1-5 but clearly implied in various expressions).

It is, however, still questionable that God's covenant faithfulness is an appropriate notion to explain δικαιοσύνη θεοῦ. This rendering, as indicated above, is based on the equation between πίστις θεοῦ and δικαιοσύνη θεοῦ in Rom 3:3-5. But without demonstrating the existence of a generally recurring dynamic equivalence between the implied meaning of ἐκ πίστεως and πίστις θεοῦ, one may wonder whether it is exegetically valid to allow the equation between πίστις θεοῦ and δικαιοσύνη θεοῦ to influence the way ἐκ πίστεως is understood in relation to δικαιοσύνη θεοῦ. Were the phrase ἐκ πίστεως θεοῦ used or were ἐκ πίστεως and πίστις θεοῦ customarily equated in Romans and Paul's Seven Letter Corpus, this question would already be settled, but neither usage is found in Paul.

One may nevertheless be persistent in holding the view that the equation between πίστις θεοῦ and δικαιοσύνη θεοῦ in Rom 3 determines the way in which Rom 1:17a is to be understood. That is to say, God's faithfulness (ἐκ πίστεως) is the source from which δικαιοσύνη θεοῦ is revealed towards [human] faith (εἰς πίστιν). But the covenantal readers themselves do not speak with the same voice and therefore have left us with a great deal of confusion here. For example, Dunn sees an intentional ambiguity in the use of ἐκ πίστεως in the Habakkuk citation where the phrase could be taken with 'both ὁ δίκαιος and ζήσεται and stand for both 'God's faithfulness' and 'human faith'.[31] Hays agrees with Dunn that ἐκ πίστεως in 1:17a refers to God's faithfulness and δικαιοσύνη θεοῦ to God's covenant faithfulness, but he interprets ἐκ πίστεως in the citation as Christ's faithfulness.[32] Hays,

---

[29] Rom 2:12, 13, 14, 15, 17, 18, 20, 23, 25, 26, 27; 3:19, 20 (2x), 21, 27, 28, 31; 4:13, 14, 15, 16; 5:13, 20.

[30] Rom 9:6, 27, 31; 10:19, 21; 11:2, 7, 25, 26.

[31] This view, as discussed above, is based on the conjecture that Paul deliberately departed from both the Masoretic and Septuagintal reading of Hab 2:4 in order that ἐκ πίστεως could be taken as both divine faithfulness and human faith. In Dunn's view, it should be noted here, human faith as *unconditional trust* is contrasted with *faithfulness*, which is equivalent to 'works of the law' or covenant loyalty demonstrated in strict adherence to the boundary markers of Jewish particularism. See Dunn, *Romans 1-8*, 44-45, 48. See also Robinson, *Romans*, 15-16, 42.

[32] Hays ('ΠΙΣΤΙΣ', 41-42) takes the double prepositional phrase in Rom 1:17a as 'a

unlike Dunn, also sees a positive correlation between Paul's defence of
God's faithfulness to Israel and the christological (or subjective genitive)
understanding of πίστις 'Ιησοῦ Χριστοῦ.[33] But he neither develops this
sufficiently clearly nor explains the logic of God's faithfulness (ἐκ
πίστεως) being the source of God's covenant-faithfulness (δικαιοσύνη
θεοῦ).[34] In any case, to say that God's faithfulness is the source of God's
covenant faithfulness does not appear to be an appropriate explanation
with regard to δικαιοσύνη θεοῦ in particular. Indeed, to render δικαιοσύνη
θεοῦ ἀποκαλύπτεται ἐκ πίστεως '"God's covenant faithfulness" is revealed
from "God's faithfulness"' leaves one with a tautology.

We would argue that to render ἐκ πίστεως 'from faith/faithfulness' is
probably incompatible with the meaning of Rom 1:17a and its context.[35]
Grammatically, the preposition ἐκ can have instrumental, causal, spatial
and temporal forces, a characteristic which it shares in common with διά.[36]

---

rhetorically effective slogan to summarize the gospel message of a salvation that originates in God's power and is received trustingly by the beneficiaries of that power'. But,
as will be seen elsewhere, he differs from Dunn in his overall understanding of πίστις.
However, Campbell ('Romans 1:17', 269 and n.16) criticises Hays, though only in a
footnote, for prematurely surrendering a crucial point. Hays ('ΠΙΣΤΙΣ', 41 and n. 12)
takes this as an overstatement. See also Dunn, *Theology*, 354-385; 'Once More, ΠΙΣΤΙΣ
ΧΡΙΣΤΟΥ', in Johnson & Hay (eds), *Pauline Theology IV*, 61-81, 74f; and Hays,
'ΠΙΣΤΙΣ', 47-48; 59.

[33] Hays, 'ΠΙΣΤΙΣ', 56.

[34] His surmise in any case agrees with that of Wright, who regards Romans as a defence of God's covenant faithfulness to Israel shown through his acceptance of Gentiles
through the representative of Israel, i.e. Jesus Christ. Wright ('Letter', 425) explicates
Rom 1:17a as follows: 'When God's action in fulfillment of the covenant is unveiled, it
is because God is faithful to what has been promised; when it is received, it is received
by that human faith that answers to the revelation of God in Jesus Christ, that human
faith that is also faith*fulness* to the call of God in Jesus the Messiah.' He had previously
argued that rendering δικαιοσύνη θεοῦ as 'God's covenant faithfulness' is 'the most
compelling reason for reading some if not all of Paul's linguistically ambiguous references to *pistis Christou* as denoting "the faithfulness of the Messiah"' ('New Exodus,
New Inheritance: The Narrative Substructure of Romans 3-8', in Soderlund and Wright
[eds], *Romans and the People of God*, 26-35, 32 and n. 10).

[35] In this reading, ἐκ πίστεως is taken as the source of the revelation of this covenant-
based divine action (δικαιοσύνη θεοῦ). The role of ἀποκαλύπτεται is also deemed central
for such an interpretation. As Dunn has argued, for example, the fact that the verb
precedes the prepositional phrase 'naturally' leads one to understand ἐκ as denoting the
source of the revelation, while εἰς denotes that to which the revelation is directed, hence
ἐκ πίστεως εἰς πίστιν is rendered 'from (God's) faithfulness to (man's) faith'. See Dunn,
Romans 1-8, 43-44; 'Once', 76f; *Theology*, 340-345; see also Gaston, *Paul and the Torah*, 118-119.

[36] See BDF, *Greek*, 113-114, 119-120; and Wallace, *Greek Grammar Beyond the Basics: An Exegetical Syntax of the New Testament with Scripture, Subject and Greek Word
Indexes*, 368-372.

Although ἐκ plus genitive is often used with reference to source or origin while διά plus genitive with reference to instrument or agent in Paul's Seven Letter Corpus, exceptions and flexibilities can be noticed in the apostle's use of both prepositions. For example, ἐκ πίστεως and διὰ τῆς πίστεως in Rom 3:30 probably are, to use Campbell's words, 'stylistic variations of the same basic idea', i.e. the sense of instrumentality or agency carried in the phrases.[37] There are numerous interchangeable uses in Romans and elsewhere of both ἐκ and διά with an instrumental sense, making ἐκ πίστεως in 1:17 with the sense of origin doubtful.[38] Further-more, the source-sense for the prepositional phrase in the second half of the passage will not work, because in the citation ἐκ – in line with both the Hebrew's ב and Septuagint's ἐκ – is to be rendered instrumentally ('by' or 'through'). If the meaning of the prepositional phrase is understood to be informed by the meaning of the same preposition in the citation, the source-sense of ἐκ in the first half of Rom 1:17 does not work either.[39] It seems unlikely that Paul would have given one meaning in the first half of the verse and then a different meaning in the second half, although to sug-gest that Paul had Hab 2:4 in his mind every time he used the phrase in Romans (and Galatians), so that the phrase carries the same significance everywhere it occurs in the letter as in Rom 1:17, would be to overstate the case.[40] In short, the reading of Rom 1:17 that takes ἐκ πίστεως in 1:17a as God's faithfulness and in 1:17b as Christ's faithfulness (Hays)[41] or at once

---

[37] Campbell, 'ΠΙΣΤΙΣ', 96.

[38] (1) In Rom 2:27, Paul uses ἐκ and διά in relation to two hypothetical persons, Gentile and Jew: the one, who, ἐκ φύσεως (lit. 'through/by nature'), is uncircumcision or Gentile but fulfils the law judges the one, who, διὰ γράμματος καὶ περιτομῆς, [is circumcision or Jew] but transgresses the law. (2) In Rom 3:22, δικαιοσύνη θεοῦ is [revealed] διὰ πίστεως Ἰησοῦ Χριστοῦ, while in 3:26 ἐκ πίστεως Ἰησοῦ is used arguably as the means through which God is [seen] to be δίκαιος and the one who 'justifies'. (3) In 3:30, the One God will 'justify' the Jew ἐκ πίστεως and the Gentile διὰ τῆς πίστεως. (4) In Gal 3:22, Paul declares that the promise ἐκ πίστεως Ἰησοῦ Χριστοῦ is given to those who will trust, while in 3:26 he says that 'all' (πάντες) are 'sons of God' διὰ τῆς πίστεως ἐν Χριστῷ Ἰησοῦ. (5) In Phil 3:9, Paul confesses about not having his own δικαιοσύνη that is ἐκ νόμου but rather διὰ πίστεως Χριστοῦ.

[39] Nygren (*Commentary*, 81) also argues that ἐκ πίστεως in 1:17a and 1:17b must have the same sense.

[40] However, Campbell ('Romans 1:17', 278-279) probably rightly criticises an approach that affords differing meanings to ἐκ πίστεως in Rom 1:17:
If the phrase in v. 17a and the text in v. 17b are interpreted diversely, the verse is actually fractured into separate and unrelated statements. Not only is this puzzling in its own right, but it cuts across the apparent function of Hab 2:4, which is to support scripturally *what has just been said*. Why would Paul cite a supporting text that does not in fact support anything but makes a different statement – *and that with an identical phrase*? Such a procedure is simply incoherent (italics his).

[41] Hays at the same time appears to support his argument with regard to πίστις and

God's faithfulness and the believer's faith in both halves of the passage (Dunn) is as problematic as it is implausible.[42]

4. Ἐκ Πίστεως: Human Faith or Christ's Faithfulness?

Romans and Galatians have much in common, as the use of ἐκ πίστεως is confined to the two letters, the 'justification' language is highly concentrated in them and Paul quotes Hab 2:4 in both. If Pauline scholarship is right in holding the view that Galatians was written before Romans, it is probable that in the latter Paul drew upon arguments that he had set forth in the former (cf., for example, Rom 3:20 with Gal 2:16). Hence, ἐκ πίστεως in the Habakkuk citation in Gal 3:11 along with Paul's expressions in the immediate context needs to be examined before considering the use of the phrase in Rom 1:17 and context. Such a procedure should not, however, be taken as an attempt to harmonise Paul's expressions in both letters, because such would undermine the significance of the differing circumstances in Galatia and Rome upon which Paul's assertions are contingent.[43] After discussing Gal 3:11 and Rom 1:17, we shall explore the meaning of ἐκ πίστεως in Rom 9:30-10:13.

4.1. Galatians 3:11

Our consideration of the question as to whether ἐκ πίστεως in Gal 3:11 refers to human faith or Christ's faithfulness must start with the ongoing debate over the syntax of the Habakkuk citation, after which we will outline several textual and exegetical observations that might help us answer the question. As is well-known, some take ἐκ πίστεως with ὁ δίκαιος, while others take it with ζήσεται. Some do not see any material distinction between the two syntaxes, because the identity of the righteous person derives and is determined by faith, which includes her living as someone who is righteous,[44] and in either syntactical reading the focus is the manner in

---

Paul's christology by saying that Rom 1:17 provides decisive evidence that Paul's use of 'the peculiar locution ἐκ πίστεως is derived from Hab 2:4' ('ΠΙΣΤΙΣ', 35-60, 42) and has become an 'exegetical catchphrase' in Romans ('ΠΙΣΤΙΣ', 42; see also *Faith*, 150-157). The fact that Hays affords two different meaning to the prepositional phrase in 1:17a and 1:17b puzzles Campbell, who otherwise agrees with Hays that the deployment of ἐκ πίστεως in Romans and Galatians is an intertextually motivated allusion to Hab 2:4. See Campbell, *Rhetoric*, 211-213; 'ΠΙΣΤΙΣ', 100-101; 'Romans 1:17', 277f; 'Presuppositions', 713-719.

[42] Dunn, *Romans 1-8*, 44-48. For Wright ('Letter', 426), 'Paul does not need to say' whether the reference is to divine faithfulness, human faithfulness or both.

[43] Betz, *Galatians: A Commentary on Paul's Letter to the Churches in Galatia*, 176.

[44] Dunn, *The Epistle to the Galatians*, 174.

which ὁ δίκαιος finds life.[45] However, scholars on the whole are divided over these syntaxes: some take ὁ δίκαιος as the justified ungodly and ἐκ πίστεως as the means through which that justification takes place, while others take ὁ δίκαιος as the Christian and ἐκ πίστεως as her way of life.[46] In both syntaxes, ἐκ πίστεως is contrasted with the law or works of the law.[47] Both readings seem to be plausible, but neither of them takes ἐκ πίστεως christologically. But can a christological reading of ἐκ πίστεως in the citation be proposed at all?

As far as the immediate context is concerned, in verse 10 Paul (through citing Deut 27:26 as a proof text) claims that the reliance on the works of the law brings a curse as opposed to a blessing.[48] Verses 10 and 11 together show that righteousness associated with πίστις is contrasted with righteousness associated with ἔργα νόμου.[49] This suggests that both ἔργα νόμου and πίστις are exercised by human persons, so it seems unlikely that ἐκ πίστεως refers to Christ's faithfulness. The citation of Lev 18:5 in 3:12 appears to further strengthen this argument in the sense that living by faith (if ἐκ πίστεως modifies ζήσεται) for the justified person (v 11) leaves no room for living by observing works of the law (v 12). Moreover, if the law by which one is not justified before God in verse 11a is contrasted with ἐκ πίστεως in 3:12a, nothing seems to suggest in 3:10-12 in particular that ἐκ πίστεως can be understood in terms of Christ's faithfulness.[50] Whether or not this renders a christological reading of the prepositional phrase in the Habakkuk citation uncongenial partly depends on how we understand the use of ἐκ πίστεως and the πίστις language in general within Paul's argument in the context. We wish to outline several observations that might help us in that process.

1) Paul sees ἐν Χριστῷ ᾽Ιησοῦ, διὰ τῆς πίστεως and ἐκ πίστεως ᾽Ιησοῦ Χριστοῦ as instrumentally equivalent. In 3:13, Christ is presented as the one who redeemed us from the curse of the law, the result of which, ac-

---

[45] Hays, *Faith*, 134.

[46] For a thorough study concerning this syntactical question, see Cavallin, '"The Righteous Shall Live by Faith": A Decisive Argument for the Traditional Interpretation', *ST* 32 (1978) 33-43.

[47] The reading that takes the prepositional phrase with the adjective associates righteousness with faith and subtly emphasises the clear distinction between the ways in which Judaism and Paul could have understood Hab 2:4b. This, one would say, is demonstrated by the juxtaposition of Hab 2:4 and Lev 18:5, whether the former can be taken as 'a restatement' of the latter ('a classical covenantal nomism' [Dunn *Theology*, 373; see also his *Epistle*, 174f]) or a contradiction to the Levitical text (Martyn, *Issues*, 185-186; see also 183-190).

[48] Why Paul thinks the works of the law bring curse can be answered in different ways. See, for example, Dunn (*Epistle*, 174f) and Martyn (*Galatians*, 313f).

[49] See also R. Longenecker, *Galatians*, 119; Koch, 'Text', 83.

[50] See also Silva, 'Faith', 242.

cording to verse 14, is the blessing of Abraham that came ἐν Χριστῷ
'Ιησοῦ (this is juxtaposed with the promise of the Spirit received by Gentiles διὰ τῆς πίστεως). Then, in 3:15-18, Paul rejects the accepted meaning
of Gen 17:8 as a reference to the promise given to Abraham and the generations of his descendants and takes τὸ σπέρμα as a reference to one person, namely Christ. The point he wants to make in so doing is that the inheritance of the blessing of Abraham did not come through the law but
through the promises that were given to Abraham and his offspring, Christ.
Rather paradoxically, he later denies that he is pitting the promises against
the law, for the law was not something that had an ability to make one
alive anyway (v 21). One's acquisition of life, for Paul, is concomitant
with one's existence in the sphere of δικαιοσύνη (rather than ἁμαρτία),[51]
which depends on the reception of the promise (v 22). Earlier, Paul had
said that the blessing of Abraham came ἐν Χριστῷ 'Ιησοῦ and the promise
of the Spirit was received διὰ τῆς πίστεως. Now in 3:22, the promise is
given ἐκ πίστεως 'Ιησοῦ Χριστοῦ to those who believe (τοῖς πιστεύουσιν).
Thus, Paul seems to treat ἐν Χριστῷ 'Ιησοῦ, διὰ τῆς πίστεως and ἐκ
πίστεως 'Ιησοῦ Χριστοῦ as being instrumental for the giving and reception
of the Abrahamic promise.

2) The phrase ἐκ πίστεως probably is an abbreviated form of ἐκ πίστεως
'Ιησοῦ Χριστοῦ. While Paul's claim that the law is unable to make one
alive and thus bring about δικαιοσύνη in 3:21 is contrasted with the giving
of the promise ἐκ πίστεως 'Ιησοῦ Χριστοῦ in 3:22, his claim in 3:11 that
no one would be justified before God through the law is contrasted with
the prophetic testimony that declares ὁ δίκαιος ἐκ πίστεως ζήσεται.[52] So
is ἐκ πίστεως in the citation a shorthand for ἐκ πίστεως 'Ιησοῦ Χριστοῦ?
In the light of ἵνα ἐκ πίστεως δικαιωθῶμεν in 3:24, where the phrase is not
followed by a pronoun that signifies the subject or object of πίστις, the
answer could be 'yes'. To be sure, it may equally be said that Paul could
easily have put the genitive 'Ιησοῦ Χριστοῦ between ἐκ πίστεως and
δικαιωθῶμεν had he thought that ἐκ πίστεως meant the same thing as ἐκ
πίστεως 'Ιησοῦ Χριστοῦ. However, that Paul is not so consistent is shown
by ἵνα δικαιωθῶμεν ἐκ πίστεως Χριστοῦ in 2:16, which must surely carry
the same meaning as ἵνα ἐκ πίστεως δικαιωθῶμεν in 3:24. We can therefore cautiously conclude that ἐκ πίστεως in the citation probably is an ab-

---

[51] See also Martyn, *Galatians*, 313f.

[52] It is to be noted that of the eleven occurrences of ἐκ πίστεως in Galatians (2:16;
3:2, 5, 7, 8, 9, 11, 12, 22, 24; 5:5), five are connected with δίκ- language:

2:16: ἵνα δικαιωθῶμεν ἐκ πίστεως Χριστοῦ
3:8: ὅτι ἐκ πίστεως δικαιοῖ τὰ ἔθνη ὁ θεός
3:11: ὅτι ὁ δίκαιος ἐκ πίστεως ζήσεται
3:24: ἵνα ἐκ πίστεως δικαιωθῶμεν
5:5: ἡμεῖς γὰρ πνεύματι ἐκ πίστεως ἐλπίδα δικαιοσύνης ἀπεκδεχόμεθα

breviated form of ἐκ πίστεως 'Ιησοῦ Χριστοῦ. This should not, however, mean that all uses of ἐκ πίστεως must be supplied with 'Ιησοῦ Χριστου, but the close link between the δικ- language and ἐκ πίστεως in 2:16 justifies the question as to whether or not Paul implied a genitive pronoun not only in 3:11 but also in passages such as 3:8 and 3:24. How we understand ἐκ πίστεως Χριστοῦ in 2:16 thus determines the meaning of ἐκ πίστεως in the Habakkuk citation, because Paul seems to have used the Habakkuk quotation as a supporting evidence of his belief that Christians have been justified ἐκ πίστεως Χριστοῦ, although the language and perhaps theology of the latter would certainly have been informed by the former.

3) The meaning of ἐκ πίστεως in 3:11 can include human action. This issue must again be linked with the meaning of πίστις Χριστοῦ, which we shall deal with later in the chapter. But it is worth mentioning here that due to the ambiguity in Gal 3:11 and the multivalent significance that the use of πίστις has in the letter, even if the genitive Χριστοῦ is understood as subjective, it would be wise to couple or complement that understanding with a construal of πίστις as a human action. This has been recognised by Hanson, who argues that the citation along with the context expresses the idea not only of Christ (as someone who is always destined to live by faith) being vindicated or justified by God but also Christians being justified by faith in Christ.[53] Such a reading makes sense when Paul's argument in Gal 3:1-20 is understood in terms of the antithesis between the way of the law and the way of faith. The law put Christ to death, but God vindicated or justified him through his faith/faithfulness. Christians' justification by faith is then dependent on the vindication of Christ on the basis of his faith/faithfulness. Hays, who equates ὁ δίκαιος in the citation with Χριστὸς 'Ιησοῦς in 3:14 and τὸ σπέρμα in 3:16, also concedes that the fact that Paul does not follow either the MT or any of the LXX readings results in three translational possibilities of the citation: 'The Messiah will live by (his own) faith(fullness)'; 'The righteous person will live as a result of the Messiah's faith(fullness)'; or 'The righteous person will live by (his own) faith (in the Messiah)'.[54] In the first translation, both ὁ δίκαιος and ἐκ πίστεως are christological. In the second, the adjective is anthropological while the prepositional phrase is christological. But in the third translation, both the adjective and the preposition are anthropological. The decision as to whether one translational option is more appropriate to the context than the other or whether all translational options should be given equal cre-

---

[53] Hanson, *Studies*, 51.

[54] Hays, *Faith*, 140. See also Martyn, *Galatians*, 313. For him, it is unlikely that Paul speaks of ὁ δίκαιος in terms of Christ (that leads one to speak of the 'rectification of Christ himself'), but he argues that in the citation ἐκ πίστεως refers simultaneously to Christ's faith and the faith that it kindles in human beings.

dence should await our discussion of the prepositional phrase vis-à-vis the
πίστις Χριστοῦ formulation.

4) But whether the parallel between the coming or apocalypse of πίστις
and the coming of Christ in 3:23 supports a christological construal of ἐκ
πίστεως in 3:11, as it might support that of ἐκ πίστεως δικαιωθῶμεν in
3:24, must be explored. As Silva observes, a simple equation between the
act of believing and the coming of πίστις will not work, because Abraham
is described as having exercised believing before the coming of πίστις and
to say that the act of believing 'has come' is nonsensical.[55] The parallelism
between ἐλθεῖν τὴν πίστιν in 3:23 and γέγονεν εἰς Χριστόν in 3:24
strongly suggests that when he talks about the coming of πίστις Paul is referring to Christ. This is supported by the instrumental equivalence that
seems to exist between ἐν Χριστῷ 'Ιησοῦ, διὰ τῆς πίστεως (3:14) and ἐκ
πίστεως 'Ιησοῦ Χριστοῦ (3:22).[56] In Gal 3:23, in short, πίστις is hyposta-
tised in such a way that it can be understood as being synonymous with
Christ.[57] Silva concurs with this argument but takes the term 'as a simple
metonymy whereby the word stands for the object of faith', i.e. Christ.[58]
One can equally argue that πίστις here stands for the subject of πίστις,
because that 'justification' has been/will be achieved through πίστις
appears to mean the same as that it will be achieved through Christ, the
Revealed (Gal 1:12, 16) or Coming One (cf. Gal 3:23 [τὴν μέλλουσαν =
πίστις] with Rom 5:14 [τοῦ μέλλοντος = Second Adam]).[59] Whether the
juxtaposition between the coming of πίστις and the apocalypse of Christ
can be understood to support (indirectly and metaphorically) a christologi-

---

[55] Silva, 'Faith', 240.

[56] All of them serve as the means through which the Abrahamic promise was given
and received; that is, if ἐν is taken as instrumental rather than locative.

[57] Georgi (Theocracy, 43f, 83f), after noting the parallelism, says: 'One may therefore
ask, with respect to the two exceptional passages where πίστις appears with a genitive,
whether the genitive should not be interpreted as subjective or even explicative – in other
words, whether the phrase does not mean "the faith of Jesus", or even "the faith that is
Jesus". If so, in 2:16 and 3:22 the term πίστις would denote the trust (or even better
"loyalty") of Jesus, indeed the trust and loyalty Jesus stands for, and this establishes and
preserves social solidarity. This interpretation would agree with what is said about Jesus
in chaps. 3 and 4' (43). Hay ('Pistis', 472), on the other hand, argues that 'Paul
conceived of Jesus as the basis of faith especially in the epistemological sense that he is
the basis of Christian faith-knowledge of God'.

[58] Silva, 'Faith', 240.

[59] As Betz (Galatians, 119) perhaps rightly recognises, δικαιωθήσεται in 2:16 is
taken to refer to an eschatological action. However, he probably wrongly interprets ἐξ
ἔργων νόμου οὐ δικαιωθήσεται πᾶσα σάρξ (cf. Rom 3:20): 'The flesh cannot be justified
on its own terms and through its own efforts, because that would be "through the works
of the Torah".'

cal reading of ἐκ πίστεως in the citation should, however, await the wider discussion of the πίστις Χριστοῦ debate later.

4.2. Romans 1:17

As in Gal 3:11, it is not immediately clear if ἐκ πίστεως in Rom 1:17 can be read christologically, partly because Paul fails to or chooses not to follow either an MT- or LXX-inspired option. In this section, we shall attempt to examine various exegetical issues with the view to establishing exegetical foundations for understanding ἐκ πίστεως either anthropologically or christologically. We will start our discussion with the question of the appropriateness of interpreting ἐκ πίστεως in Rom 1:17 as human faith [in Christ] on the basis of the πίστις – ἔργα antithesis in the context of Gal 3:11 and the meaning of πιστεύοντι in Rom 1:16. Then we will attempt to determine what ἐκ πίστεως means through scrutinising the legitimacy of the anthropological reading that is based, by and large, on the syntactical relationship between δικαιοσύνη θεοῦ (rather than ἀποκαλύπτεται) and ἐκ πίστεως in Rom 1:17a and between ὁ δίκαιος and ἐκ πίστεως in 1:17b.

In the light of Gal 3:11, Rom 1:17 is traditionally interpreted from the perspective of the Law-Gospel antithesis, which means that ἐκ πίστεως is to be interpreted with an anthropological subject.[60] The Pauline meaning of πίστις in Rom 1:17b must then be different from that of the prophet in the sense that while Paul saw it as something through which one is declared righteous and acquires life, Habakkuk saw it as the fidelity, trustworthiness or integrity by which the righteous preserve their lives (whether that be escaping threatening destruction or saving their souls in spite of the worst that might happen). The way the prophet is understood to have seen πίστις, for Paul, might be thought of as a meritorious act that cannot be fulfilled. In other words, the prophet's πίστις is equivalent to Paul's understanding of the law and its works. The same citation in Gal 3:11, in whose context Paul seems to use the law or works of law over against ἐκ πίστεως, can be used to support this antithesis.[61] The meaning of ἐκ πίστεως could then be 'faith in Christ', not in the sense of accepting the claims of Jesus he had rejected before, or passing from 'faith' in the One God to 'faith in Christ', but rather in the sense of having faith, which leaves no place for

---

[60] Nygren (*Commentary*, 90-92), for example, argues that Hab 2:4 had played a role in the historical world of Habakkuk and later in Jewish Synagogues in terms of giving significance to righteousness by faithful devotion to God and by the law (and its works), but now it enables Paul to articulate the antithesis between 'the righteousness of the law' and 'the righteousness of faith'. It is the same passage that enables Luther to see the difference between the Law and the Gospel. See also Morris (*The Epistle to the Romans*, 69-72), who follows Nygren's interpretation of Rom 1:17.

[61] See also Dodd, *Epistle*, 14-15, 18.

182

human merit that is achieved through complying with a code of commandments.[62] As an antithesis between ἐκ πίστεως and the law or works of the law cannot be detected in Rom 1:17 or its immediate context, however, it would be methodologically wrong to insist on understanding the phrase in the light of the πίστις – ἔργα antithesis in the context of Gal 3:11.

But one can argue that ἐκ πίστεως stands for 'faith in Christ' on the basis of aligning the meaning of the phrase with that of τῷ πιστεύοντι in Rom 1:16 where the believing of Jews and Gentiles can be understood as faith in Christ. According to this view, Paul thought that salvation was not closely tied to distinctive prerogatives such as circumcision and law, but rather it had a universal and inclusive scope where the only condition would be the response of 'faith' (παντὶ τῷ πιστεύοντι), which would involve, as Byrne puts, both 'perception' and 'commitment'.[63] That response of 'faith', of course, is 'faith in Jesus' as Son of God, Messiah, Saviour and Lord. But opinions differ, as some take the implied object of τῷ πιστεύοντι as at once the gospel, Jesus and God,[64] while others take it as Jesus.[65] Jesus obviously is central in the exordium of the letter, but no reference is made to him in 1:16-17 while God is used twice and two references (once implicitly) are also made to the gospel, although neither God nor the gospel is referred to as an explicit object of πιστεύοντι. The absence of an object *vis-à-vis* πιστεύω is not surprising, however. For out of the 21 uses of πιστεύω in Romans (which constitutes half of the 42 occurrences in Paul's Seven Letter Corpus), *eleven* references do not have an object at all (1:16; 3:22; 4:11, 18; 6:8; 10:4, 14 (2x), 13:11; 14:2; 15:13); *one* has τὰ λόγια τοῦ θεοῦ as its object (3:2), *five* God (4:3, 5, 17, 24; 10:14 [slightly ambiguous]), *one* λίθος – an OT reference to God perhaps transposed to Jesus here (9:33), *two* God's act of raising Jesus (10:9, 10 [slightly ambiguous]) and *one* the message of the 'gospel' (10:16). In the contexts of those eleven references without an object, three uses do not require an object and while God and the gospel can be possible candidates to be implied objects at least in five of the remaining references, κύριος, which can arguably be understood as Christ, is a probable candidate in two of them.[66] This data on the whole shows that Paul is not interested in using

---

[62] So Dodd (*Epistle*, 17).

[63] Byrne (*Romans*, 52) defines 'faith' as follows: 'that attitude which discerns God acting creatively (that is, as Creator) in the world and in one's own life, urging the surrender of one's life project to that perception in trust and obedience'.

[64] See, for example, Cranfield, *Romans 1-8*, 89 ('faith in the message, and so faith in Jesus Christ who is its content and in God who has acted in Him and whose power the message is'); Fitzmyer, *Romans*, 256 ('faith in its [the gospel's] message, faith in Christ Jesus whom it announces, and faith in God from whom it comes').

[65] For example, Wilckens, *Brief I*, 85, Gräbe, *Power*, 179.

[66] 1:16b: the 'gospel' prominently features in the immediately preceding clause.

the verb πιστεύω where Jesus is the object of human believing in the same way as, for example, John in his Gospel clearly does. The data may not enable us to make a firm conclusion that the object of πιστεύοντι in Rom 1:16 is or is not Jesus, the gospel or God, but it should make us hesitant about cheerfully applying the idea of 'faith in Christ' to Rom 1:16-17.[67]

From our discussion so far, reading ἐκ πίστεως in Rom 1:17 as human faith in Christ on the basis of the πίστις – ἔργα antithesis in the context of Gal 3:11 and the meaning of πιστεύοντι in Rom 1:16 does not have sufficient methodological or exegetical support to be absolutely secure. But the reading can still be pushed on the grounds of the syntactical relationship between δικαιοσύνη θεοῦ (rather than ἀποκαλύπτεται) and ἐκ πίστεως in Rom 1:17a and between ὁ δίκαιος and ἐκ πίστεως in 1:17b. As discussed elsewhere, in this reading ἐν αὐτῷ, rather than ἐκ πίστεως, is taken instrumentally. So, as Watson, for example, would argue, the gospel reveals that the righteousness is acquired by or on the basis of faith.[68] But Watson, perhaps rightly, shies away from referring to ἐκ πίστεως as 'faith in Christ' and prefers to talk about the phrase in terms of something a community or an individual does in reaction to the message of the gospel. This is matched by divine action, as represented in εἰς πίστιν, which is intended to draw out a further implication of the scriptural ἐκ πίστεως with its in-

---

3:22: Jesus, God or the gospel could be the object here.

4:11: the use of πιστεύω is influenced by Gen 15:6: 'Abraham trusted in God'.

4:18: in the preceding verse and the context as a whole God is the object.

6:8:   πιστεύομεν here does not seem to require an object.

10:4: the 'gospel' is a possible object because in the context proclaiming
       Jesus' death and resurrection is prominent (e.g. vv 8-11).

10:14: κύριος (2x) from verse 13 is an object in both uses.

13:11: the object is not clear, but it could either be God or the 'gospel'.

14:2: the term denotes a conviction about dietary laws, thus no object is required.

15:13: the object is not clear, perhaps not necessary.

Elsewhere in Paul's Seven Letter Corpus, there is one unambiguous reference where Paul speaks about either trusting in or being entrusted with the gospel (1 Thess 2:4) and two references where proclamation is connected with believing (1 Cor 15:11; 2 Cor 4:13), while we have a single increasingly beleaguered reference in Galatians in which Paul says καὶ ἡμεῖς εἰς Χριστὸν Ἰησοῦν ἐπιστεύσαμεν (2:16). Cf. also Eph 1:13 where, it appears, believing in Jesus follows hearing the gospel.

[67] What Wilckens (*Brief I*, 85), for example, writes epitomises such a cheerful application: 'Dass Gottes heilschaffende Gerechtigkeit den Sünder "ohne das Gesetz" allein aufgrund des Glaubens an Christus zum Gerechten macht [3, 21f], das ist der Charakter des Evangeliums, der dieses von jüdischer Gottesverkündigung trennt und so christlichen Glauben von jüdischem unterscheidet' (trans. 'The fact that God's-salvation-creating-righteousness 'without the law' solely on the basis of faith in Christ makes the sinner righteous (3:21f) is the character of the gospel, which separates it from Jewish proclamations about God thus differentiating Christian belief from Jewish belief').

[68] Watson, *Paul*, 51.

strumental relationship with δικαιοσύνη θεοῦ. The divine action here is actually divine reaction to that fact which takes place as a form of 'faith' and thus a divine acknowledgement of one's righteousness that is by faith. So, for Watson, the Habakkuk righteous person is the person whose righteousness is acknowledged by God or, as in 3:22 and 4:3, the person to whose believing God reacts by justifying her.[69]

This argument clearly reinforces the syntax that takes ἐκ πίστεως with ὁ δίκαιος ('He that is righteous by faith shall live'),[70] rather than ζήσεται ('The righteous one shall live by faith'),[71] in the Habakkuk citation and ἐκ πίστεως with δικαιοσύνη θεοῦ in Rom 1:17a. The structure of Rom 1-8 – where 1:18-4:25 expounds the meaning of ὁ δίκαιος ἐκ πίστεως, while 5:1-8:39 expounds the meaning of the promise that the person who is righteous by faith shall live – and that the connection between 'righteousness' and 'faith' is made explicitly in 5:1 (cf. also 4:11, 9:30 and 10:6) seem to support this reading. But such a reading cannot be taken for granted, because ἐκ πίστεως can equally be taken with ζήσεται. That Paul keeps the citation close to Habakkuk and has not written ὁ δὲ ἐκ πίστεως δίκαιος ζήσεται, which would otherwise conform to his phrase ἡ δὲ ἐκ πίστεως δικαιοσύνη in 10:6 (cf. 9:32), confirms this. Paul could also have known that in the MT and LXX of Habakkuk באמונתו was connected with יחיה and ἐκ πίστεώς [μου] with ζήσεται respectively. Furthermore, in Gal 2:20, Paul describes the life he lives in the flesh as the life he lives 'by faith in the Son of God'. In short, to take ἐκ πίστεως with ζήσεται and understand the citation as talking about a Christian whose daily existence is characterised

---

[69] Watson, *Paul*, 51. As discussed in the preceding chapter, according to Watson (*Paul*, 55-57), throughout Rom 1:16-3:20 the Habakkuk citation provides Paul with a scriptural testimony that the faith spoken in Rom 1:17 serves to establish the law by enabling us to hear its negative but authentic voice (3:10) and, as a result, to understand that law is making way for faith (3:20).

[70] See, for example, NRSV; Nygren, *Commentary*, 85f; Barrett, *Epistle*, 27, 32; Käsemann, *Commentary*, 32; Wilckens, *Brief I*, 76, 89-90 ('Der Gerechte aber aufgrund des Glaubens wird leben'); Cranfield, *Romans 1-8*, 102.

[71] See, for example, NIV; Murray, *Epistle*, 33; Sanday and Headlam, *Epistle*, 28f; Schlatter, *Romans*, 27; Schlier, *Römerbrief*, 34, 44-46 ('Der Gerechte wird aus Glauben leben'); Moody, 'The Habakkuk Quotation in Romans 1:17', *ExpT* (1981) 205-208, 208; Fitzmyer, *Romans*, 264-265; Hanson, *Studies*, 41f; Wallis, *Faith*, 79-81. Wright (*Messiah*, 74-75, 126-127) not only argues that the prepositional genitive can be understood as modifying the verb, he also suggests that the opposite of ἐκ πίστεως εἰς πίστιν might be ἐξ ἔργων νόμου'Ιουδαίους, which means that the double phrase in our text looks forward to 10:5-8. But see also Dunn (*Romans 1-8*, 45-46), who wishes to have it both ways because, in his view, 'the continuing sharp division between translators and commentators who insist on "either-or exegesis" underlines its unreality...'. Schreiner (*Romans*, 74) agrees with Dunn.

by faith or whose faithfulness is rewarded with (eschatological) life[72] is as valid as taking ἐκ πίστεως with ὁ δίκαιος and understanding the citation as talking about an implied pagan or sinner who through faith is declared righteous and receives the promise of life. So the syntactical parallelism between Rom 1:17a and Rom 1:17b may not be sufficient to sustain the traditional reading of Rom 1:17 in terms of righteousness by faith [in Christ].

One could even argue that severing the syntactical connection between ἐκ πίστεως and ἀποκαλύπτεται and taking the former with δικαιοσύνη θεοῦ in 1:17a, as Schlatter observed, may wrongly require the revelatory meaning to be more or less assimilated by a pedagogical meaning. That is, the righteousness of God as the righteousness that is given from God is taught in the gospel and received by faith, by which one is freed from sin and guilt and led to rest and comfort.[73] That Paul sees 'righteousness' as a gift can certainly be noticed, for example, in Rom 5:17 and Phil 3:9, but the idea that 'righteousness is received by faith through the teaching of the gospel' seems to make 'faith' mean one's intellectual assent. So Rom 1:17 should be understood in terms of ὁ δίκαιος signifying the person to whom a set of religious truths (εὐαγγέλιον) formerly hidden (including righteousness by or from faith) are intellectually communicated (ἀποκαλύπτεται) leading to her agreement to or acceptance of those truths in the form of 'faith in Christ' (πίστις).[74] For Lutherans such as Nygren, of course, such a meritorious inference, which originates mainly from understanding πίστις as believing the articles of the faith, would be unacceptable, because πίστις is a divine gift and salvation is by grace alone.[75]

---

[72] So the JPS translation of Hab 2:4b: 'But the righteous man is rewarded with life [for] his fidelity'.

[73] Schlatter, *Romans*, 25.

[74] Indeed, it has been argued that ἐκ πίστεως in the first instance means the affirmation of Jesus of Nazareth as Messiah and Son of God whereby πίστις here represents the beginning of an act of mental assent to the gospel message and/or ecclesiastical doctrines regarded as timeless religious truths. See, for example, Sanday and Headlam, *Epistle*, 33-34. For interpretations with a more modern spin, see Hay '*Pistis*', 472f; Schreiner, *Romans*, 64ff, 72-73.

[75] Schlatter (*Romans*, 21-22) calls this 'synergistic theology' in which one's relationship is not ordered in keeping with what God does and makes one to be but rather in keeping with one's ability to fulfil God's will, which inevitably results in failure, guilt and fear. It is not human faith that gives the gospel its saving power. On the contrary, as Nygren (*Commentary*, 71) would argue, 'it is the power of the gospel that makes it possible for one to believe, Jew and Greek alike. Faith is only another word for the fact that one belongs to Christ and through Him participates in the new age.' Since πίστις is not something that is demanded of a person as a *condition* for the gospel to become 'the power of God unto salvation', to suggest otherwise is a fateful distortion of the Pauline view on which Luther's *sola fide* is based. Such a suggestion makes the sufficiency of

Be that as it may, taking the preposition with δικαιοσύνη θεοῦ requires one to take the righteousness of God as the righteousness of the person of the Habakkuk citation. This, as argued earlier, is unsustainable. While the English rendering of the Pauline δικαιοσύνη ('righteousness') is deemed to have the same sense as that of δικαίωσις ('justification') and there are places in Romans where Paul uses 'justification' or 'righteousness' and 'salvation' (5:9; 10:1, 10) in synthetic parallelism, in Paul's Seven Letter Corpus the righteousness of God and righteousness cannot be taken as having the same meaning, because the latter almost always carries a meaning that is to do with human standing (whether that is to do with the status of a person or her ethical standing), while the former does not. Indeed, as Pss 98 and 143 and some Second Temple Jewish texts show, the righteousness of God represents God's power and presence amongst his people. God's hiddenness from his people meant the absence of his right-eousness and *vice versa*. It is likely that Paul, during his Pharisaic life, could have understood the righteousness of God in the same way. The righteousness of God, for him, probably was a hidden affair. But as Rom 1:17 and 3:21-26 show, we would argue, Paul's encounter with Christ led him to believe that the righteousness of God had now been revealed in and through Christ's death. It is maintaining the link between ἐκ πίστεως and ἀποκαλύπτεται that enables one to uphold such an understanding. But we ought to establish this syntax before exploring the question whether such a syntax will help us to determine the subject of ἐκ πίστεως: any human person or Christ?

If ἀποκαλύπτεται is not modified by ἐν αὐτῷ and does not primarily de-note what the person learns and knows, it can be taken with ἐκ πίστεως while δικαιοσύνη θεοῦ is connected with εἰς πίστιν. This can be achieved, firstly, by paralleling the meaning of εἰς πίστιν to that of παντὶ τῷ πιστεύοντι in 1:16 on the basis that πιστεύω and πίστις are *sometimes* taken as correlative in Romans (e.g. 4:5, 11, 18, 19; 10:8-9; 14:1, 2).[76] The parallel is also punctuated by the preposition εἰς, which, in both 1:16b and 1:17a, seems to refer to a purpose, goal or end-state.[77] Secondly, the

---

faith for salvation a legalistic notion. Nygren does not deny that the πιστ- language in Rom 1:17 refers to human faith, but he rejects the view that the language has anything to do with one's contribution to her salvation or acquisition of life in the same way as the law is traditionally believed to do within Judaism. See also Nygren, *Commentary*, 90-92; Morris, *The Epistle to the Romans*, 69-72.

[76] See also Gaston, *Paul and the Torah*, 119; Cranfield, *On Romans*, 88.

[77] In the exordium, the preposition εἰς indicates a similar idea: Paul is set apart for the purpose of the 'gospel of God' (εἰς εὐαγγέλιον θεοῦ) (1:2), he received grace and apostleship so that the obedience of 'faith/faithfulness' (εἰς ὑπακοὴν πίστεως) will be achieved among the nations (1:5), and he longs to see his Roman readers to share spiri-tual gifts so that they may be strengthened (εἰς τὸ στηριχθῆναι) (1:11). And in ch 10,

suggested syntactical reading can be achieved partly by modifying the double prepositional phrase through inserting a simple conjunction (ἐκ πίστεως [καὶ] εἰς πίστιν) and then reading ἐκ instrumentally as a reference to the process that causes the revelation of δικαιοσύνη θεοῦ, while εἰς purposively as a reference to the process that is caused by the revelation of δικαιοσύνη θεοῦ.[78] This is in keeping with Rom 1:16 where the dative construction παντὶ τῷ πιστεύοντι preceded by εἰς σωτηρίαν seems to express the target towards which the power of God is directed and the goal it achieves. The result of such a reading in Rom 1:17 is that the righteousness of God, which is a subject matter of Paul's gospel, is being revealed ἐκ πίστεως so that Jews and Greeks would have πίστις. In this case, ἐκ πίστεως carries a causal or instrumental significance for the gospel whereby one is made to believe and, thus, live in the domain characterised by the righteousness of God, while εἰς πίστιν suggests a teleological dimension in the gospel whereby the believer becomes someone whose existence is shaped by the values of Christ.[79] This syntax enables us to avoid assuming emphatic equivalence between ἐκ πίστεως and εἰς πίστιν, which results in understanding the meaning of the former in terms of both cause and effect or means and end.[80] Since ἐκ is related to εἰς as an antonym in the NT Greek,[81] emphatic equivalence between ἐκ πίστεως and εἰς πίστιν does not seem to be correct in strictly grammatical terms. For Paul could not have had both prepositional phrases purposively at once. Nor could he have had them instrumentally at once.

That is, of course, if the double preposition is not understood as an idiomatic expression in its own terms. Recently, Charles Quarles[82] and John Taylor[83] have argued in favour of this understanding based on the ἐκ+A+εἰς+A formulaic construction where a given idiom indicates movement, extended time, and progression. But they arrive at slightly different conclusions. Quarles, who rejects the traditional interpretation of the construction as an idiom of emphasis on the basis that there is no evidence

---

πιστεύω is used as something that is to be demonstrated by Jew and Greek alike and the preposition εἰς marks the goal of that action, i.e. σωτηρία or δικαιοσύνη (vv 1, 4, 10, 12).

[78] See also Fitzmyer, *Romans*, 263.

[79] See also Schlatter, *Romans*, 23-25.

[80] Campbell (*Rhetoric*, 207 [Appendix 1]) probably rightly complains that interpreting ἐκ πίστεως as both means and goal 'seems unusual, and even contradictory, for if faith is the goal, how can it be a means? – can it function before it is created? But if faith is the means, why then is it also a goal? Has it already been introduced? Thus the phrase's causality seems fundamentally disjointed'.

[81] See also Porter, *Idioms*, 154-155.

[82] Quarles, 'Faith', 1-21.

[83] Taylor, 'From Faith to Faith: Romans 1.17 in the Light of Greek Idiom', *NTS* 50 (2004) 337-348.

where 'the combination of the two prepositional phrases drastically altered or cancelled the normal sense of the individual prepositional phrases',[84] favours John Chrysostom's interpretation, namely 'the faith of the Old Testament believer to the faith of the New Testament believer'.[85] Taylor argues that the construction is to be understood as an idiom of growth, progress or advance not in the sense of growth in personal faith but in the sense of the progress of the gospel and the growing number of believers among the Gentiles. The double preposition refers to the growth of faith among the Gentiles by means of which the righteousness of God is revealed.[86]

Although Taylor tentatively entertains the idea that the referent or the implied subject of πίστις in ἐκ πίστεως might be the faith of the Jews among whom the church originated, while in εἰς πίστιν it might be the growing response of faith among the Gentiles,[87] his main thesis that the righteousness of God is revealed by the faith of the Gentiles seems to collapse the meaning of each preposition into one. There are, to be sure, numerous biblical examples that seem to support Taylor's contention that the construction should be read as an idiom of growth or progression, as, for example, ἐκ δυνάμεως εἰς δύναμιν (Ps 83:8 – 84:7 [LXX]), ἐκ κακῶν εἰς κακά (Jer 9:2), ἐκ θανάτου εἰς θάνατον ... ἐκ ζωῆς εἰς ζωήν (2 Cor 2:16), ἀπὸ δόξης εἰς δόξαν (2 Cor 3:18), καθ᾽ ὑπερβολὴν εἰς ὑπερβολήν (2 Cor 4:17) and χάριν ἀντὶ χάριτος (Jn 1:16) show.[88] But Taylor's interpretation does not appear to accommodate fully even the notion of *origin* and *destination* which some of these examples here seem to contain. Furthermore, as Quarles has shown, in Greek literature the object of εἰς is sometimes modified by the adjective ἕτερος, which is implied even when it is not stated. So, for example, when ἐκ θαλάττης εἰς θάλατταν is used, the referent in each preposition is different, whether it be two different seas or the sea at two opposite shores. In Rom 1:17 too, as Taylor would also accept, the referent of ἐκ πίστεως could be different from that of εἰς πίστιν.[89] If valid, we can take ἐκ πίστεως with ἀποκαλύπτεται and εἰς πιότιν with δικαιοσύνη θεοῦ. Consequently, ἐκ πίστεως can be understood as the means through which the righteousness of God, the subject matter of Paul's gospel, is being revealed to those Jews and Greeks who believe.

---

[84] Quarles, 'Faith', 8.

[85] Quarles, 'Faith', 18-21.

[86] Taylor, 'Faith', 344-346.

[87] Taylor, 'Faith', 344-348.

[88] This is corroborated by the oft quoted non-biblical grave inscription ἐκ γῆς εἰς γῆν ὁ βίος οὗτός ('dust is the beginning and the end of this [human] life'). See also Bauer, Arndt, Gingrich and Danker (BAGD), *A Greek-English Lexicon of the New Testament*, 663; Käsemann, *Commentary*, 31.

[89] Quarles, 'Faith', 8, 19; Taylor, 'Faith', 347.

This brings us back to the central question of this sub-section, which is whether ἐκ πίστεως means human faith or Christ's faithfulness.

The main obstacle to answering this question straightforwardly is Paul's failure to or choice not to follow either an MT- or LXX-inspired option. Since he uses ἐκ πίστεως or διὰ πίστεως without any personal pronoun, for example, in Rom 3:25, 3:30, 5:1 and Gal 3:24, however, such a failure is not untypical. This could lead one to suggest that a personal pronoun may have been implied in each of these passages. Indeed, Dunn argues that a personal pronoun is implied in, for example, Rom 1:17 and 3:25. In both, the subject is God on the basis of Rom 3:3.[90] But we have already argued that assuming an equivalence between πίστις θεοῦ and ἐκ πίστεως is implausible, as Paul never uses ἐκ πίστεως θεοῦ anywhere in his Seven Letter Corpus. Also, to read Rom 1:17a as saying that the righteousness of God is being revealed in the 'gospel' ἐκ πίστεως [θεοῦ] would have no parallel anywhere in Romans, while there is one strong example in 3:22, where the righteousness of God is said to have been revealed διὰ πίστεως Ἰησοῦ Χριστοῦ, a variant of ἐκ πίστεως Ἰησοῦ in 3:26. Furthermore, that Paul employs the cryptic phrase διὰ [τῆς] πίστεως in Rom 3:25 only two verses after using διὰ πίστεως Ἰησοῦ Χριστοῦ in 3:22 suggests that the former is an abbreviation of the latter. Paul does the same in Gal 3:24, where he simply writes ἵνα ἐκ πίστεως δικαιωθῶμεν, although in 3:22 he had already employed ἐκ πίστεως Ἰησοῦ Χριστοῦ and in 2:16 ἵνα δικαιωθῶμεν ἐκ πίστεως Χριστοῦ.

Since Rom 1:17 probably anticipates 3:21-26, it seems reasonable to suggest that ἐκ πίστεως could have prepared Paul's readers for the introduction of διὰ πίστεως Ἰησοῦ Χριστοῦ and ἐκ πίστεως Ἰησοῦ in 3:22 and 26 respectively. It may also be suggested that the hearer of the letter, which may have been read several times over at meetings (presupposing that such a practice existed among the addressees of Paul), could have understood ἐκ πίστεως in 1:17 in the light of ἐκ πίστεως Ἰησοῦ in 3:26, and also perhaps of διὰ πίστεως Ἰησοῦ Χριστοῦ in 3:22. But would that have enabled the hearer or reader to construe ἐκ πίστεως in terms of Christ's faithfulness?[91] The answer could be 'yes', if she understood Rom 1:16-17

---

[90] Dunn, 'Once', 76-77.

[91] The christological readers render the double prepositional phrase, for example, 'from the faith [of Jesus] to the faith [of the Christian] ('Ramaroson, 'La justification par la foi *du* Christ Jésus', *ScEspr* 39 [1987], 81-92, cited in Fitzmyer, *Romans*, 263); 'by means of [Jesus'] faithfulness resulting in [others'] faithfulness' (Stowers, *Rereading*, 202); '*through* the faithfulness of Christ's own death and *to* or *for the purpose of* those who trust God and believe these events' (Campbell, 'Presuppositions', 714; italics his); '*through the faithfulness of the Messiah*, for the benefit of all who believe' (Wright, 'Exodus', 32; italics his). Wallis (*Faith*, 82) argues that Paul draws on Hab 2:4 to explain his declaration in 1:17a: 'It [δικαιοσύνη θεοῦ] is initially revealed in Jesus the Righteous

in the light of the Christ event and in relation to 1:2-4. But we cannot be certain about the competence of the hearer to say confidently that, on the basis of her general knowledge of Christ and what she heard 13 verses earlier,[92] she added in her mind ' Ιησοῦ Χριστοῦ after ἐκ πίστεως when she heard Rom 1:17 read and then understood the prepositional phrase as a short hand for ἐκ πίστεως ' Ιησοῦ or διὰ πίστεως ' Ιησοῦ Χριστοῦ. The same uncertainty applies to Rom 3:30 where Paul uses ἐκ πίστεως and διὰ τῆς πίστεως with reference to God's act of justifying the circumcision and the uncircumcision respectively, which looks forward to the Abraham argument in Romans 4.[93]

What appears to be evident from our discussion so far, however, is that there is an instrumental relationship between the *revelation of the righteousness of God* and ἐκ πίστεως and that the latter probably is an abbreviation of διὰ πίστεως ' Ιησοῦ Χριστοῦ and ἐκ πίστεως ' Ιησοῦ in 3:22, 26. This is based on the relationship between Rom 1:16-17 and 3:21-26, because it seems obvious that πάντας τοὺς πιστεύοντας in 3:22 is reminiscent of παντὶ τῷ πιστεύοντι in 1:16 and that δικαιοσύνη θεοῦ πεφανέρωται and

---

One, whose life of faith (ἐκ πίστεως) provides the basis for the righteousness and faith (εἰς πίστιν) of all the people – Jew and Gentile alike.' With a different emphasis, Georgi (*Theocracy*, 88) also suggests: 'the soteria of the God Jesus has made loyalty a two-way street (ek pisteos eis pistin 1:17): it demonstrates and creates loyalty, but demands loyalty as well (1:16-17)'.

[92] That 'general knowledge' could include what Paul's readers in Rome knew about Christ. One suspects that there were some Jewish Christians who, like Stephen and Apollos in Jerusalem and Ephesus respectively (Acts 6:8-9; 7:51-57; 18:24-26), argued strongly in synagogues for the messiahship of Jesus, leading to disturbances and the fateful imperial edict during Claudius. Claudius' expulsion (49 CE) is reported by Luke (Acts 18:2), Suetonius (*Claudius* 25:4), Dio Cassius (60.6.6) and Paulus Orosius (5th century CE Christian historian). The cause was *Chrestus*, probably a misspelling of *Christus* (Christ). See also Fitzmyer, *Romans*, 31; Levinskaya, *The Book of Acts in Its First-century Setting: Diaspora Setting*, 176; and Bruce, 'The Romans Debate – Continued', in Donfried (ed.), *Debate*, 175-194.

[93] Stowers ('ΕΚ ΠΙΣΤΕΩΣ and ΔΙΑ ΤΗΣ ΠΙΣΤΕΩΣ in Romans 3:30', *JBL* 108 [1989] 665-674, 674), however, surmises that '[t]he phrases with ἐκ πίστεως express the "vicarious" benefits of Abraham's and Jesus' heroic faithfulness toward God…while [t]he phrase διὰ πίστεως refers specifically to Jesus' atoning life and death for the redemption of the Gentiles'. But Stowers seems to overstate the case, because, first, given the universal outlook of the context of 3:22, it is highly unlikely that Paul would speak of διὰ πίστεως ' Ιησοῦ Χριστοῦ there as exclusively referring to the atoning significance of Jesus' faithful death to the Gentiles. Second, even though the use of the prepositions in 3:30 appears to have material significance because of περιτομή (Jews) and ἀκροβυστία (Gentiles) in the context, the construction can still be understood to be a rhetorical one, where both prepositions have the same meaning. In any case, we cannot be sure (at least at this stage) if both prepositions refer to Jesus' faithful death in either an inclusive (to the Jews and Gentiles) or exclusive sense (to the Gentiles).

δικαιοσύνη θεοῦ διὰ πίστεως Ἰησοῦ Χριστοῦ in 3:21-22 most probably are used interchangeably with δικαιοσύνη θεοῦ ἀποκαλύπτεται ἐκ πίστεως in 1:17a. It is also based on the view that the phrases διὰ πίστεως Ἰησοῦ Χριστοῦ (3:22), (probably) διὰ τῆς πίστεως (3:25) and ἐκ πίστεως Ἰησοῦ (3:26) appear to have been developed from ἐκ πίστεως in 1:17. If it is valid to take ἐκ πίστεως in Rom 1:17 as equivalent to the πίστις (Ἰησοῦ) Χριστοῦ construction, it should be on the basis of our decision on the meaning of this construction in Rom 3:21-26 and elsewhere in Paul (Galatians in particular)[94] that we should determine whether the subject of ἐκ πίστεως is any human person or Christ. But before that, it would be helpful to consider the use of ἐκ πίστεως in Rom 9:30-10:13.

4.3. *Ἐκ Πίστεως in Romans 9:30-10:13*

It may not be an exaggeration to claim that Rom 9:30-10:13 is an expanded and explicated version of Rom 1:16-17, not least because the former contains some unambiguous anticipations of the latter passage such as (δικαιοσύνη) ἐκ πίστεως (9:30; 10:5, 6), δικαιοσύνη θεοῦ (10:3 [2x]), εἰς σωτηρίαν (10:1, 4 [εἰς δικαιοσύνην], 10), παντὶ τῷ πιστεύοντι (10:4), and (οὐ γάρ ἐστιν διαστολὴ) Ἰουδαίου τε καὶ Ἕλληνος (10:12). Given the limited purpose of our chapter, however, our discussion here will concentrate on whether or how the meaning of the πίστ- terminology in general and ἐκ πίστεως in particular will contribute to an interpretation of ἐκ πίστεως in Rom 1:17. The specific question we would like to explore here is whether Paul is thinking in terms of the faithfulness of Christ (christological) or faith in Christ (anthropological) when he uses the phrase ἐκ πίστεως in 9:30-10:13.

There are at least three arguments in favour of the anthropological reading of this block. First, in 9:30-32, Paul seems to summarise his preceding assertions regarding God's act of showing forth his power (ἐνδείξωμαι ἐν σοὶ τὴν δύναμίν μου) in or through Pharaoh (9:17; cf. Ex 9:16) and making known his power (γνωρίσαι τὸ δυνατὸν αὐτοῦ) to the Gentiles (9:22-29)[95] in terms of Gentiles pursuing or attaining (κατέλαβεν)

---

[94] The πίστις [Ἰησοῦ] Χριστοῦ texts in Paul are: Rom 3:22, 26; Gal 2:16a, 16b, 20; 3:22; Phil 3:9a (cf. Eph 3:12; Js 2:1; Rev 14:12). Recently, Ulrichs (*Christusglaube: Studien zum Syntagma πίστις Χριστοῦ und zum paulinischen Verständnis von Glaube und Rechtfertigung*, 71-76, 253) has argued that 1 Thess 1:3 contains the earliest πίστις Χριστοῦ reference in Paul. This is not impossible, but the complexity of the textual construction does not allow us to claim confidently that Paul used πίστις Χριστοῦ here. Ulrichs' thesis is also based on the view that goes against the widely accepted dating of Galatians as the earliest of Pauline correspondences.

[95] In εἰ δὲ θέλων ὁ θεὸς ἐνδείξασθαι τὴν ὀργήν in 9:22, the participle θέλων is debated. Some take it causally, 'because he [God] wished' (e.g. Barrett, *Epistle*, 172, 176f; Cranfield, *Romans 9-16*, 494-497 ['because he willed' it), while others have taken it con-

δικαιοσύνην ἐκ πίστεως. The Gentiles who pursue righteousness ἐκ
πίστεως are contrasted with Israel who pursue righteousness ἐξ ἔργων
νόμου. Israel's pursuit of righteousness ends in failure because of the
stumbling rock. Paul cites Isa 28:16, part of which reads 'whoever trusts *in
him* will not be ashamed'. The rock (λίθος) then is the object of one's trust
and, in the light of 1 Pet 2:4-6, a reference to Christ. Thus ἐκ πίστεως
means faith/trust in Christ by which righteousness is attained.

The second argument comes from 10:3-4. Israel's pursuit of righteousness through works and their failure in 9:30-32 is described in terms of
their attempt to establish their 'own righteousness' because of their ignorance of the righteousness of God in 10:3-4. While scholars such as Käsemann and Stuhlmacher construe the righteousness of God here with a
power sense,[96] commentators such as Nygren, Barrett and Cranfield interpret the genitive θεοῦ in the phrase in 10:3 as a genitive of origin.[97] According to the latter interpretation, the phrase denotes the righteousness
that comes from God, which appears to be consistent with the meaning of
τὴν ἐκ θεοῦ δικαιοσύνην in Phil 3:9.[98] This interpretation seems to be
clarified further in Rom 10:4 (we shall come back to this below) in the
sense that when the phrase εἰς δικαιοσύνην is taken with νόμος, the verse
can be understood as saying that Christ is the τέλος of the law as a way of
righteousness for everyone who believes. Whether this means Christ is the
τέλος of the law to those who believe 'in him' is not entirely clear but the
foregoing reading seems to suggest that the object of believing is Christ.

Finally, 10:5-13. Whether verse 5 should be understood as a continuation and explanatory of verse 4 or a contrast to verses 6-8 has been de-

---

cessively, 'though he wished' (Dunn, *Romans 9-16*, 566-568; Fitzmyer, *Romans*, 569). If
the former is taken, God 'endured' (ἤνεγκεν) 'with much patience' (ἐν πολλῇ
μακροθυμίᾳ) 'the objects of wrath that are prepared for destruction' (σκεύη ὀργῆς
κατηρισμένα εἰς ἀπώλειαν) in order to reveal his wrathful judgement and his saving
power to both Jews and Gentiles (so Barrett, *Epistle*, 177-178; cf. Isa 54:16; Jer 1:25;
27:25 [LXX]). If the latter is taken, however, δύναμις [θεοῦ] is understood as something
undesirable and the emphasis is put on 'with much patience': 'though wrath might have
led God to make known his power, his loving-kindness restrained him' (so Fitzmyer,
Romans, 569). The former interpretation is more suited to Paul's ideas, particularly
where he uses δύναμις θεοῦ and δικαιοσύνη θεοῦ (1:16-20; 3:26).

[96] Käsemann, *Commentary*, 281; Stuhlmacher, *Gerechtigkeit*, 93; *Letter*, 154. See also
Fitzmyer, *Romans*, 583; Byrne, *Romans*, 311, 314; Haacker, *Der Brief*, 204-206.

[97] Nygren, *Commentary*, 379; Barrett, *Epistle*, 183; Cranfield, *Romans 9-16*, 515.

[98] Barrett (*Epistle*, 196) puts: 'There is a close parallel to this verse in Phil. iii. 9
('righteousness from God", ἐκ θεοῦ), which strongly suggests that, in Romans, the genitive "of God", and the genitive substitute "their own" (τὴν ἰδίαν), denote *origin* rather
than *possession*. There is a righteousness which comes from God as his gift, and there is
(or, at least, there may be thought to be) a righteousness which men evolve out of themselves by works done in obedience to the law.' So Bultmann (*Theology I*, 285).

bated. In the latter understanding, the contrast underlines the futility of the quest after righteousness ('justification') through 'works' (v 5) and the usefulness of the way of 'justification by faith' (vv 6-8). The former represents the Jewish way (γράμμα), while the latter the way of 'righteousness' proclaimed by Paul (πνεῦμα). That the contrastive δέ in verse 6 separates the quotation of Lev 18:5 (10:5) from that of Deut 30:11-14 (10:6-8) and that Moses (who *writes* 'justification by works') is set against the personified ἡ ἐκ πίστεως δικαιοσύνη (who *speaks* 'justification by faith') seem to confirm this.[99] The point then is that Paul contrasts the witness of Moses in Lev 18:5 to the righteousness of the law with what the voice of the personified ἡ ἐκ πίστεως δικαιοσύνη instructs one as to what she should not say in her heart. By citing Deut 30:12, Paul argues that what a person needs to do to be saved is confess in her mouth that Jesus is Lord and believe in her heart that God raised him from the dead. The second part of Isa 28:16 can be used to support this, because it says 'whoever trusts *in him* will not be put to shame'. Κύριος in verse 12 probably is a reference to Christ, hence the object of trust in the Isaianic quotation. We offer below a critical response to each argument.

As far as the first argument is concerned, Paul, in Rom 9:30-32, seems to set Gentiles' attainment of righteousness through faith in Christ over against Israel's *failure* to attain righteousness through works. This can be supported by the meaning of λίθος in the citation of Isa 28:16 in 9:33 and part-citation of the same passage in Rom 10:11. This scriptural term is probably employed with reference to Christ. The object of faith or trust in 10:11 can be argued to be God or Christ, but that it is Christ is supported by what Paul says in verse 9 about one's confession in his mouth of Jesus as Lord, which seems to correspond to the idea of 'calling upon him' or, as the citation from Joel 3:5 in verse 13 says, 'calling upon the name of the Lord'. The anthropological reading of ἐκ πίστεως in the block in question is, therefore, valid. But there is an issue as to how Paul understood ἔργα and πίστις in relation to Israel in particular.

Gathercole argues that ἔργα here are 'neither solely concerned with legalistic "achievement" nor simply identificatory'. They are orientated towards 'righteous status in the present' and 'eschatological vindication in the future'.[100] Gathercole's argument is based on his study that combines a comparative analysis of Second Temple Jewish writings with an exegesis of Romans 1-5.[101] Central to this study is Paul's dialogue with a Jewish interlocutor in Rom 2:1ff. Gathercole argues that Paul's dialogue partner,

---

[99] Schlier, *Römerbrief*, 311-312; Käsemann, *Commentary*, 286-288; Dunn, *Romans 9-16*, 602.

[100] Gathercole, *Boasting*, 229.

[101] Gathercole, *Boasting*, 197-262.

who represents the nation,[102] held a theology of final salvation or vindication for the righteous that obediently fulfil the Torah.[103] Through this argument, Gathercole seeks to correct both the traditional and New Perspective approaches. In his view, the basis for the confidence of Paul's dialogue partner is both the fulfilment of legalistic requirements and national righteousness based on election.[104] This is not without a precedent, because in certain circles of Second Temple Judaism both obedience and election were believed to be the basis of eschatological salvation of God's people.[105] Gathercole goes on to argue that it is against such doctrine that Paul is trying to show his Jewish interlocutor in Rom 2:1ff that obedience to Torah will not be comprehensive enough for justification. Paul's point is that the interlocutor should repent in order to qualify for atonement.[106] The interlocutor's unrepentance results in failure to attain righteousness. His failure represents Israel's failure (Rom 9:31).[107] Thus Israel's error is not exclusivism through focusing on certain commandments, as Dunn has argued.[108] Her error is 'focusing on the commandments at the expense of faith in the promises',[109] i.e. understanding the law 'as *centred* around works to the exclusion of faith'.[110]

So is Paul saying that Israel should abandon works altogether? Although Gathercole does not pose this question, his statement here could be taken as an answer to it: 'the view that doing works is a path that is in itself wrong is misguided'.[111] Gathercole may be right in this, because, according to Paul, the law demands works (Rom 2:13; 10:5) and circumcision remains important for the Jew (Rom 3:1-2, cf. 3:30; 4:12). But what is not abundantly clear in Rom 9:30-10:13 in particular is whether Paul is arguing against Israel's view of ultimate vindication through works. This is not to deny that some Second Temple Jews believed that their qualification for resurrection life or the vindication of their righteousness in the end will be linked to their fulfilment of divine commandments (4QMMT), their willingness to lay their lives for the sake of the law (2 Maccabees), their fidelity to their leader/teacher or the causes of the group to which they be-

---

[102] Gathercole, *Boasting*, 199.

[103] Gathercole, *Boasting*, 197-215.

[104] Gathercole, *Boasting*, 215.

[105] Gathercole, *Boasting*, 37-90.

[106] Gathercole, *Boasting*, 215.

[107] Gathercole, *Boasting*, 207.

[108] Dunn, *Romans 9-16*, 587-588.

[109] Gathercole, *Boasting*, 229.

[110] Gathercole, *Boasting*, 227 (italics his).

[111] Gathercole, *Boasting*, 227. But Westerholm (*Perspectives*, 400) suggests that Paul excludes 'works' for Israel, because no one is righteous by them (Rom 3:20, 28).

longed (1QpHab, *1 Enoch*), etc.[112] Despite such belief, which was often coupled with critical self-assessment and consciousness of sin, however, these Jews still saw themselves as righteous over against the unrighteous (probably the majority). This makes us wonder whether their obedience or faithfulness was to gain righteous status. But we will come back to this below when we discuss Paul's apparent contrast between πίστις Χριστοῦ and ἔργα νόμου in Gal 2:16. For our purpose here, it should be said that the extent to which the Jewish evidence mentioned above provides interpretative guidance for Rom 9:30-10:13 cannot be overemphasised, because in the Romans text future attainment of righteousness is not evident. Indeed, except σωθήσῃ in 10:9, it is difficult or even impossible to find unambiguous futuristic elements in Rom 9:30-10:13.

Another problem with Gathercole's argument is that he plays down the universal scope of righteousness (or salvation). The main reason for this appears to be his confusion of the righteousness of God with human righteousness that, in his view, is possessed by faith.[113] In Rom 9:30-33, it seems clear that the error of the referents of 'Israel' (probably non-Christian Jews) is their misguided *pursuit* of righteousness through works to the exclusion of πίστις that is associated with Christ. The origin of that error is not only their failure to recognise that the divine grace, through which God entered into covenant with Abraham and continued to fulfil his promises in spite of Israel's unrighteousness and stubbornness (Deut 9:4-5), is now universally mediated through Christ. It is also their *ignorance* of the righteousness of God (10:3), which, according to Rom 1:17 and 3:22, is revealed ἐκ πίστεως or διὰ πίστεως Ἰησοῦ Χριστοῦ to those who believe (or have πίστις), Jews and Gentiles without distinction. As the righteousness of God has taken on this universal dimension, righteousness is to be understood within this universal dimension too, because, as argued in chapter 3 earlier, righteousness is occasioned by the righteousness of God, God's saving action in and through Christ. Christ has become the embodiment of God's righteousness or, in Jeremiah's language, 'the Lord our Righteousness' (Jer 23:6; 1 Cor 1:30; 2 Cor 5:21). So although Paul would accept that doing works enabled Jews to participate in the national righteousness on the grounds of election (Deut 6:25; 7:6, 11), he can now say that doing works to the exclusion of πίστις does not enable them to enter into the universal righteousness created by Christ. But this

---

[112] See also Gathercole, *Boasting*, 214. Elliott (*Survivors*, 515-573, 634-637) also argues that the faithful remnant of Israel will be vindicated within the world of men, that is, their message and teachings of righteousness will be vindicated by the 'elect' nation, in which the majority are currently apostates.

[113] Gathercole, *Boasting*, 228.

understanding needs to be related to the meaning of πίστις. So does πίστις mean faith/believing or faithfulness?

As discussed above, the verb πιστεύω in 9:33; 10:4, 9, 10 is conventionally understood to have the same meaning as πίστις in 9:30-32 and 10:6. Thus Israel's problem is its failure to have faith in Christ. Whether one takes this failure as resulting from focusing on obedience to Torah as the basis of justification (Gathercole)[114] or misguidedly using Sabbath, food-laws and circumcision to exclude Gentiles (Dunn), there appears to be a case for faith in Christ in 9:30-33. But there is a question whether the same can be said in 10:6. We will consider that below. It is important to emphasise here, however, that in Rom 10:9-10, faith/believing is directly linked with not only God's act of raising Jesus from the dead but also righteousness. This righteousness is *a sphere or order of relations* which is created and characterised by Christ and into which Jews and Gentiles must enter. The error of the referents of Israel is not doing works of the law as such, but failing to demonstrate their entrance into this sphere of relations by professing Jesus' lordship and acknowledging God's salvific action in and through him. The root of this error, as indicated above, is Israel's ignorance of the righteousness of God. This is linked to the second argument above, to which we now turn.

The anthropological argument that the genitive in δικαιοσύνη θεοῦ (10:3-4) denotes origin rather than possession so that the righteousness that comes from God is contrasted with the righteousness that human beings possess through obedience to the law is plausible.[115] However, as indicated above and extensively argued in chapter 3 of this book, the phrase can also be interpreted in the light of Rom 1:16-17, 3:21-26 and 9:22ff, where, according to the Käsemannian reading, it probably denotes the saving power of God revealed or made known to Jews and Gentiles. If valid, Paul's central point in 10:3 is that while the referents of 'Israel' have remained ignorant about the righteousness of God that became a reality in the Christ event and is now being revealed, (some) Gentiles have acknowledged the righteousness of God that was made known in and through Christ. Notwithstanding their fervent and tenacious zeal for God, Israel's ignorance means failure to come under the authority of the righteousness of God whose revelation constitutes the coming of God himself as Lord

---

[114] Gathercole does not argue that πίστις or πιστεύω in the block in the question stands for faith in Christ. He simply uses the term 'faith'. But see Sanders' comment on Rom 9:3-10:13. He (*PLJP*, 37-38) says: 'Israel's failure is not that they do not obey that law in the correct way, but that they do not have faith in Christ ... The argument is christological and is orientated around the principle of equality of Jew and Gentile.' See also Räisänen, *Paul*, 175-176; Badenas, *Christ*, 116.

[115] See also Gathercole, *Boasting*, 228-229.

and Creator in Christ. Such an understanding brings together the bipolar sense of the righteousness of God whereby Christ embodies God's salvific power and functions as the sphere within which that power occasions salvation and order.[116]

It is important to link this understanding with the statement in Rom 10:4: τέλος γὰρ νόμου Χριστὸς εἰς δικαιοσύνην παντὶ τῷ πιστεύοντι. This axiomatic statement has been studied in great detail by Robert Badenas in his *Christ the End of the Law: Romans 10:4 in Pauline Perspective*. So we do not need to engage in any detailed study of it here. Nor does our purpose require us to do so. For our limited purpose here, it suffices to note that Χριστός probably is the subject of the first half of the statement in question, thus 'Christ is the τέλος of (the) law'.[117] And the term τέλος seems to denote purpose or goal (end-goal rather than end-termination) particularly when εἰς in εἰς δικαιοσύνην is taken with the whole clause and given a directional or purposive sense (as in 1:16).[118] So 'Christ is the goal of the law' can mean that Christ put an end to the manner and mechanism by which the law is defined. Christ not only brought to an end the old order of relations, he also introduced the age to come by establishing righteousness that has a universal and inclusive character (10:12).[119] Paul goes further in 10:5, which contains a quotation from Lev

---

[116] Here we agree with Byrne (*Romans*, 60, 314) who holds a similar bipolar approach, but we disagree with him on his reading of δικαιοσύνη θεοῦ as the faithfulness of God and a righteous status before God.

[117] That is, when the phrase τέλος νόμου, which is a biblical *hapax legomenon*, is taken as a predicate. What 'Christ is the τέλος of (the) law' means, of course, depends largely on what τέλος is understood to mean. The term has received extraordinarily diverse meanings, which are organised largely under either teleological (end-goal) or temporal (end-termination) categories. While it cannot be denied that the term could mean end-termination, the purposive sense of εἰς coupled with external evidence from Jewish and Hellenistic literature suggest that it denotes purpose or goal in our passage. See also Barrett, *Epistle*, 197; Cranfield, *Romans 9-16*, 515; Dunn, *Romans 9-16*, 589; Badenas, *Christ*, 78-80, 115-116.

[118] The phrase εἰς δικαιοσύνην can be taken either with Χριστός ('Christ ends the law *and brings* δικαιοσύνη for everyone who believes') or νόμος ('Christ is the τέλος of *the-law-as-a-way-of-δικαιοσύνη* for everyone who believes'). The former seems to make more sense, because Christ is the subject of the whole clause.

[119] Here δικαιοσύνη can be understood as some sort of gift given to a believer. This parallels Paul's expressions in the second half of 5:17, οἱ λαμβάνοντες as the recipients of the abundance of grace and the gift of δικαιοσύνη *will reign* in ζωῇ through Jesus, whereas in the first half ὁ θάνατος *reigned* through Adam. This seems to support Cranfield's argument that δικαιοσύνη is a status. But does the expression ἡ δωρεὰ τῆς δικαιοσύνης really give legitimacy to a perspective that regards the term as an object, a package received and retained, as if it was one's own property? Dunn (*Romans 1-8*, 282) argues not. For Dunn, δικαιοσύνη is both 'the status of one acceptable to God' (p 281) and something that is always God's in a relational sense, i.e. δικαιοσύνη is 'a gift given

18:5: Μωϋσῆς γὰρ γράφει τὴν δικαιοσύνην τὴν ἐκ νόμου ὅτι ὁ ποιήσας αὐτὰ ἄνθρωπος ζήσεται ἐν αὐτοῖς. That brings us to the third argument from 10:5-13.

The argument, as discussed above, goes: Paul understands the citation of Lev 18:5 in 10:5 as advocating justification by works as against justification by faith (cf. 10:6 with Deut 9:4; 30:12). This argument is based on contrasting 10:5 with 10:6-8. But there are syntactical and theological grounds to understand what Paul says in verses 6-8 as a continuation of what he says in verse 5.[120] Also, in verses 5-8 Paul seems to be appropriating the Levitical and Deuteronomic passages and, in so doing, intending a christological meaning for the citations. That is to say, Paul took the word of the divine commandment for the Deuteronomist as Christ and Moses' declaration in Lev 18:5 in terms of something that was said about Christ. That means that in 10:5, ὁ ποιήσας ἄνθρωπος (cf. Phil 2:7-10) is a reference to Christ. K. Barth, Cranfield and M. Barth hold this christological reading.[121] Not surprisingly, some dismiss this reading. The reason being that the Levitical passage is understood to confirm the widely held Jewish view about complying with the code of commandments in the Mosaic law (Lutheran) or conforming to the works of the law as a way of life or the way of living appropriate to the covenant (New Perspective).[122] Neither argument, however, takes into account the fact that Paul uses ὁ ποιήσας αὐτὰ ἄνθρωπος ζήσεται ἐν αὐτοῖς (v 5) to support or prove his claim that τέλος γὰρ νόμου Χριστὸς εἰς δικαιοσύνην παντὶ τῷ πιστεύοντι

---

not by passing the gift from God's hands but by drawing the receiver into his arms' (p 282).

[120] For different reasons: first, if the γάρ in verse 5 is taken as introducing a logical connection between verses 4 and 5, verse 5 should be seen as a scriptural proof of Paul's statement in verse 4 and a further elaboration of Paul's train of thought in verses 2-4. If valid, second, the δέ in verse 6 is a connective particle, which, in this context, should not necessarily denote 'but' or, as Dunn (*Romans 9-16*, 602) would have it, 'whereas'. Third, that both passages contain the idea that obedience to God's commandment leads to life prevents us from assuming that Paul is pitting scripture against scripture. On the whole, the syntactical basis for a contrast between Lev 18:5 and Deut 30:11-14 (cf. vv 15-16) is slim, to say the least. See Cranfield, *Romans 9-16*, 521-522; Badenas, *Christ*, 122-130.

[121] Barth, *Commentary*, 127; Cranfield, *Romans 9-16*, 521-522; M. Barth, *The People of God*, 39-41. For further discussion, see Badenas, *Christ*, 120-121.

[122] Dunn (*Romans 9-16*, 601-602; cf. *Theology*, 373), for example, argues that such a construal of 10:5 'completely misses the point', because 'it would make Jesus an exemplar of nationalist righteousness'. Paul, according to Dunn, seems to retain the covenantal nomistic sense of Lev 18:5. That is, the Levitical passage confirms the widely held Jewish view that keeping the statutes and ordinances of the law was the way of living appropriate to the covenant. So, for Dunn, while Paul retains the covenantal nomistic interpretation of Lev 18:5 in 10:5, he gives Hab 2:4b in Rom 1:17b a meaning that stands against or redefines covenantal nomism. Would Paul have applied different interpretative principles to the Habakkuk and Levitical passages? Possible, but unlikely.

(v 4). The result of this usage is that ὁ ποιήσας ἄνθρωπος and Χριστός are paralleled.

The question then should be: why does Paul present Christ as the τέλος of the law? Cranfield argues that he presents him as such because he believed that Christ, through his obedience to God, brought the order of relations characterised by the law in order to earn a righteous status before God which human beings can have through faith in him.[123] But this view (perhaps unwittingly) assumes that Christ was not righteous before his obedient death, which is contrary to Paul's own view (cf. Rom 5:6 with 5:19). We would argue that Paul presents Christ as the τέλος of the law because he believed that God's eschatological saving act through Christ brought to an end a system characterised by an exclusivistic and particularistic interpretation of the law and, consequently, made righteousness possible for *all* those who accept the gospel. This obviously is reminiscent of Rom 1:16. As the power of God is for salvation for everyone who believes in Rom 1:16, Christ is the τέλος of the law for righteousness for everyone who believes [in God or Christ] in 10:4 (cf. 10:9: εἰς σωτηρίαν = εἰς δικαιοσύνην). In both passages, πᾶς ὁ πιστεύων characterises the essence of Paul's gospel, namely the universality of the work of Christ (the power of God) that enables Jews and Gentiles to share in righteousness.[124] In short, Rom 10:4 and 10:5 underline, probably mainly, what Christ was able to accomplish for Jews and Gentiles rather than what a Jew or Gentile could or could not do. This brings us to vv 6-8.

How can the personified ἡ ἐκ πίστεως δικαιοσύνη be understood christologically? The personification is based on the Deuteronomist's idea about the word of the divine commandment, which is near the mouth and heart of the children of Israel and for which they do not need to go up to heaven or cross the sea. What the divine word says in Deuteronomy, ἡ ἐκ πίστεως δικαιοσύνη says for Paul. The phrase ἡ δὲ ἐκ πίστεως δικαιοσύνη could mean 'righteousness by [human] faith' or 'righteousness through [God's] faithfulness'.[125] Either argument, particularly the former, may fit into the

---

[123] Cranfield, *Romans 9-16*, 521-522.

[124] This seems to cohere (albeit loosely) with Rom 1:17, where Paul uses ὁ δίκαιος ἐκ πίστεως ζήσεται as a proof text for his claim that the righteousness of God is being revealed ἐκ πίστεως εἰς πίστιν. As will be discussed later, the living (the resurrection life) of the 'righteous one' (who is faithful or obedient to God) in Rom 1:17b seems to prove not only that God's formerly hidden salvific power became a reality in the Christ event but also that that same power continues to be revealed to the believing Jew and Gentile alike. See Strobel (*Untersuchungen*, 189-191), who reads Rom 10:1-13 in the light of not only Rom 1:16-17 but also Hab 2:3-4.

[125] Dunn (*Romans 9-16*, 602), for example, argues that ἐκ πίστεως in 10:6, in keeping with 'the dual thread of thought which Paul draws from his text (1:17a)', refers primarily

context, but neither explains the relationship between the Deuteronomist's word of the divine commandment and the personified ἡ δὲ ἐκ πίστεως δικαιοσύνη. In our view, τὸ ῥῆμα τῆς πίστεως in verse 8 probably explains the meaning of the personified ἡ ἐκ πίστεως δικαιοσύνη better. This point is not noticed by any commentator on Romans, but it seems to us to be reasonable, because the phrase τὸ ῥῆμα τῆς πίστεως (the word that is πίστις) in this verse is described as διὰ ῥήματος Χριστοῦ (the word that is Christ) that brings about πίστις in verse 17. The personified phrase as a whole could stand for Christ, for he is the sole content of the gospel events as well as the embodiment of πίστις. But Paul does not divorce who Christ is from what he does. So although one cannot be sure if ἐκ πίστεως in verse 6 stands for ἐκ πίστεως [Χριστοῦ], the christological elements in the context suggest that the πίστις in the personified ἡ ἐκ πίστεως δικαιοσύνη could refer to Christ's faithful act, through which a new order of relations that is universal and inclusive is established (10:9-10, 12).

The main problem with this reading is that it does not seem to cohere with the reading of δικαιοσύνην τὴν ἐκ πίστεως in 9:30, because ἐκ πίστεως in 9:30-32 as a whole probably stands for faith in Christ. However, if ἐκ πίστεως in 10:6 is understood in the light of the overwhelming christological elements in 10:4-10, righteousness on the basis of Christ's becoming the τέλος of the law in 10:5 can be understood as righteousness *through Christ's faithfulness* in 10:6. Then the meaning of ἐκ πίστεως in 9:30-32 can complement the meaning of the same phrase in 10:6 and *vice versa*. But this new suggestion would make only little sense unless and until the meaning of ἐκ πίστεως in relation to the πίστις Χριστοῦ construction is considered and what we mean by 'faith in Christ' and 'faithfulness of Christ' is explained exegetically. To that we now turn.

4.4. Ἐκ Πίστεως and Πίστις Χριστοῦ

We start this section by discussing briefly the πίστις Χριστοῦ debate from its genesis through to its present state. That will lay a foundation for our subsequent considerations, the first of which will be to do with linguistic issues relating to πίστις Χριστοῦ. After briefly examining the significance of the absence of the definite article in the construction, we will critically analyse Matlock's lexical-semantic approach where he argues against rendering πίστις Χριστοῦ as the 'faithfulness of Christ'. We will contend, however, that such a rendering is linguistically and exegetically viable. We will attempt to show that through treating Gal 2:16 (and context) and Rom 3:22 (and context) separately. Then as the Abraham argument in Romans 4

---

to 'man's response to divine grace (9:32)', but quite likely also to 'God's faithfulness as that which establishes the covenant' rather than 'Israel's covenant loyalty'.

has been used against interpreting πίστις Χριστοῦ as Christ's faithfulness, we will analyse that argument in the final sub-section.

4.4.1. Existing Interpretations of Πίστις Χριστοῦ

Given its central importance in Paul and Christian religion, the πίστις Χριστοῦ construction has been perennial but divisive. It is unlikely that the same sort of interpretative division occurred in Pauline churches in the 50s or early 60s. Scholarly opinions differ as to whether it was interpreted as objective or subjective genitive by some Church Fathers,[126] but from the Reformation period through to the nineteenth century the objective genitive was the universally accepted reading of the construction.[127] Then came Haussleiter towards the end of the nineteenth century, who first introduced the subjective genitive reading of the phrase,[128] leading to the πίστις Χριστοῦ controversy. Sanday and Headlam[129] and Hatch[130] argued against Haussleiter. Some, however, accepted his view. Deissmann, for instance, spoke of the phrase in terms of the mystical genitive where πίστις Χριστοῦ = πίστις ἐν Χριστῷ, hence the phrase expresses one's union with Christ rather than denoting Christ as an object of religious belief.[131] With slight divergence from Deissmann, Schmitz understood the genitive in πίστις Χριστοῦ as a 'characterising genitive' (*charakterisierenden Genitiv*) and rendered the phrase 'Christ-faith' (*Christus-Glaube*).[132] But it was Kittel who substantially advanced the subjective genitive interpreta-

---

[126] Harrisville ('ΠΙΣΤΙΣ ΧΡΙΣΤΟΥ: Witness of the Fathers', *NovT* XXXVI [1994] 233-241) argues that the early Church Fathers use πίστις αὐτοῦ with a subjective sense, but their use of πίστις Χριστοῦ is ambiguous. Harrisville nevertheless insists that the objective rendering must be applied to the Fathers' use of πίστις Χριστοῦ, because there is clear evidence that both Greek and Latin writers understand the phrase in an objective sense. Wallis (*Faith*, 181ff), on the other hand, has argued that the subjective interpretation played a significant role in the first three centuries of the Christian era.

[127] It was Luther's reading of the phrase διὰ πίστεως ᾽Ιησοῦ Χριστοῦ in Rom 3:22 as an objective genitive ('through faith in Jesus Christ') that was echoed by many. *Luther's Works* 25:31; Luther, *Lectures*, 19, 109. For some historical and interpretative backgrounds, see, for example, Käsemann, *Commentary*, 94; Wilckens, *Brief I*, 188; Cranfield, *Romans 1-8*, 203; Dunn, *Romans 1-8*, 166; *Theology*, 128ff; Fitzmyer, *Romans*, 345-346; Ulrichs, *Christusglaube*, 13-18.

[128] Haussleiter, 'Glaube', 109-145, 205-230; 'Was versteht Paulus unter christlichem Glauben?': *Greifswalder Studien für H Cremer*, 1895.

[129] Sanday and Headlam, *Epistle*, 83-84.

[130] Hatch, *Pauline Idea of Faith*.

[131] Deissmann, *Paul: A Study in Social and Religious History*, 161-165. See also Hays, *Faith*, 144; R. Longenecker, *Galatians*, 87.

[132] Schmitz, *Die Christusgemeinschaft des Paulus im Lichte seines Genitivgebrauche*. The phrase 'Christ faith' is adopted by Engberg-Pederson in his recent work *Paul and the Stoics*, 179ff.

tion in Germany,[133] followed by Hebert and T. F. Torrance in Britain in the 1950s.[134] Hebert and Torrance's arguments, in which they saw an equivalence of meaning between Paul's πίστις and the Hebrew אמונה so that both meant 'faithfulness' rather than 'believing', received vigorous criticisms from Moule,[135] Murray,[136] and Barr,[137] who advocated the opposite.

What is interesting, and perhaps confusing, about the debate is that it not only draws together scholars who belong to opposing interpretative streams, it also divides those who belong to the same interpretative stream. For instance, Hays, who is one of the most recent notable advocates of the subjective genitive interpretation, is in agreement with Dunn, who has been one of the most notable advocates of the objective genitive interpretation, with regard to the prominence of God's covenant faithfulness in Romans 1-3 in general and 1:17a in particular.[138] Furthermore, by way of taking further Sanders' 'covenantal nomism' in Pauline discussions, Dunn has stressed that the law served as an identity- and boundary-marker for ethnic Israel.[139] B. Longenecker, who seems to attempt to advance Dunn's view through what he calls 'ethnocentric covenantalism', disagrees with Dunn on his interpretation of πίστις Χριστοῦ.[140] B. Longenecker more or less accepts Martyn's 'apocalyptic' framework, but Martyn's framework regards any interpretative claims for πίστις Χριστοῦ that are based on covenant faithfulness as alien to Paul's thinking. For Martyn, Paul contrasts the observance of the law with πίστις 'Ιησοῦ Χριστοῦ and, in so doing, sets himself against 'the Teachers' who interpreted Jesus as confirming rather than contradicting the law.[141] In the midst of such confusing interpretative overlaps and differences, the advocates of the subjective genitive interpretation emphasise what Jesus did, i.e. his demonstration and exemplification of πίστις ('faithfulness' or 'fidelity') to the God of Israel within his own life (christological), while the advocates of the objective

---

[133] Kittel, 'Πίστις 'Ιησοῦ Χριστοῦ bei Paulus', *TSK* 79 (1906) 419-436.

[134] Hebert, '"Faithfulness" and "Faith"', *Theology* 58 (1955) 373-379; Torrance, 'One Aspect of the Biblical Conception of Faith', *ExpT* 68 (1956-57) 111-114.

[135] Moule, 'The Biblical Conception of "Faith"', *ExpT* 68 (1956-57), 157, 222.

[136] Murray, *Epistle*, 32, 110-112, 363-374 (Appendix B).

[137] Barr, *Semantics*, 161-205.

[138] Hays, 'ΠΙΣΤΙΣ', 35-60; and *Faith*, 150f; Dunn, 'Once', 61-81; *Theology*, 371-385.

[139] Dunn, 'Works of the Law and the Curse of the Law (Gal 3:10-14)', *NTS* 31 (1985) 523-542; 'The New Perspective on Paul (E. P. Sanders, *Paul and Palestinian Judaism*; Gal 2:16)', *Bulletin of the John Rylands University Library of Manchester* 65:2 (1983) 95-122; *Theology*, 128ff.

[140] B. Longenecker, *Triumph*, esp. 89-103. See also his 'ΠΙΣΤΙΣ in Romans 3:25: Neglected Evidence for the "Faithfulness of Christ"?', *NTS* 39 (1993) 478-480.

[141] Martyn, 'A Law Observant Mission to Gentiles: The Background of Galatians', *SJT* 38:3 (1985) 307-324; *Issues*, esp. 141-175.

genitive interpretation emphasise what human beings can do in their 'faith in Jesus' in acknowledgement of what Jesus did (anthropological).[142] In the following sections, we wish to examine both readings and see which one would enable us to determine a meaning that is exegetically and contextually appropriate for ἐκ πίστεως in Rom 1:17.

4.4.2. Some Linguistic Issues

The question as to whether or not the genitive in πίστις Χριστοῦ is objective or subjective depends on linguistic as much as exegetical and contextual considerations. In that respect, Barr's semantic approach in his *The Semantics of Biblical Language* proved particularly helpful, but due to his focus on the OT use of the אמן word-group and its translation in the LXX, his treatment of the Pauline πίστις texts remained tantalising and unsatisfactory.[143] That was partly remedied in the 1980s by Hultgren (who favoured the objective genitive interpretation) and Williams (who favoured the subjective genitive interpretation), whose syntactical and grammatical arguments gave the debate a new impetus.[144] Their debate centred partly on the absence of the definite article in the construction, to which brief attention should be paid here.

It has been argued that the genitive in the phrase πίστεως 'Ιησοῦ Χριστοῦ is subjective, because there are examples in Romans and elsewhere in Paul where πίστις is followed by the genitive of a personal pronoun or the genitive of a substantive denoting a person. So, for example, the genitives in ἡ πίστις ὑμῶν (1:8; cf. 1 Thess 1:8), τὴν πίστιν τοῦ θεοῦ (3:3), τὸν ἐκ πίστεως 'Ιησοῦ (3:26) and τῷ ἐκ πίστεως 'Αβραάμ (4:16) are subjective.[145] However, this can be rejected on the basis that πίστις 'Ιησοῦ Χριστοῦ is used without the definite article. Indeed, it has been said that ἡ πίστις ἡμῶν (rather than πίστις ἡμῶν), for example, is subjective because it is arthrous and that Paul's failure to employ ἡ πίστις τοῦ Χριστοῦ in the same way as he uses this construction and the genitival substantives mentioned above meant that Paul in πίστις Χριστοῦ had not been talking about Christ's own faith/faithfulness.[146] Admittedly, Paul does not use an arthrous noun with the genitive of a substantive denoting a person as often

---

[142] See also Dunn, 'In Quest of Paul's Theology: Retrospect and Prospect', in Johnson and Hay, *Pauline*, 95-115, 100-101; B. Longenecker, *Triumph*, 95f.

[143] See Barr, *Semantics*, 161ff.

[144] Hultgren, 'The *Pistis Christou* Formulation in Paul', *NovT* 22 (1980) 248-263; Williams, 'Again *Pistis Christou*', *CBQ* 49 (1987), 431-447.

[145] Howard, 'Notes and Observations on the "Faith of Christ"', *HTR* 60 (1967) 459-465; '"The Faith of Christ"', *ET* 85 (1974) 212-215; 'Romans 3:21-31 and the Inclusion of the Gentiles', *HTR* 63 (1970) 223-233; see also Torrance, 'Aspect', 111-114.

[146] Hultgren, '*Pistis*', 248-263; Dunn, *Theology*, 381.

as he uses the anarthrous noun with genitive relations. But it is often the case in the NT that a noun with a genitive pronoun is arthrous[147] and Paul's use of ἡ πίστις ἡμῶν (cf. 2 Cor 9:2), for example, is consistent with that. In addition to this, insisting on taking Paul's failure to use ἡ πίστις τοῦ Χριστοῦ as an argument against the reading of the genitive ᾽Ιησοῦ Χριστοῦ as subjective would lead to the unlikely conclusion that the use of an arthrous substantive with another arthrous genitival substantive (such as τὴν πίστιν τοῦ θεοῦ) should be the only form where the subjective genitive interpretation can be appropriate. That conclusion would consequently lead to the absurd view that Paul's δικαιοσύνη θεοῦ is different from his ἡ δικαιοσύνη τοῦ θεοῦ (cf. 1:16; 3:5, 20 with 3:7; 10:3).[148] In short, Paul's failure to use πίστεως ᾽Ιησοῦ Χριστοῦ with the definite article does not rule out taking the genitive ᾽Ιησοῦ Χριστοῦ as subjective.

However, Matlock, in his article titled 'Detheologizing the ΠΙΣΤΙΣ ΧΡΙΣΤΟΥ Debate', has added his voice to the objective genitive interpretation of the phrase through a lexical consideration of the πιστ- terms.[149] Matlock does not pay attention to the debate between Hultgren and Williams, but his inattention may be justified on the basis that his purpose is lexical-semantic rather than grammatical. Matlock sets out to remedy the lack of interest among Pauline scholarship to attempt to explain the πίστις Χριστοῦ formulation from the perspective of lexical-semantics and aims to 'critique and improve argumentation over πίστις Χριστοῦ' in a way that is beneficial for proponents of both the objective genitive and subjective genitive interpretations.[150] So a critical engagement with his arguments is in order.

Matlock distinguishes meanings of πίστις based on the premise that the term has polysemous senses. For him, an attempt to find an underlying meaning which broadly applies to all uses of πίστις and translate the term, for example, as 'faithfulness' to the exclusion of other meanings such as 'faith' betrays failure to pay attention to the sort of ambiguity that exists in the way the term is employed. It also means that the polysemous nature of the term is ignored.[151] To support this point, Matlock follows Louw-Nida's six lexemes of πίστις/πιστεύω categorised according to their semantic sub-

---

[147] E.g. Matt 9:2, 22; Mk 2:5; 10:52; Lk 5:20; 8:25; 17:19; Rom 4:5; 1 Cor 2:5; 15:17; 2 Cor 10:15; 1 Thess 1:8; 3:2; Eph 3:17; Col 1:4.

[148] So Williams ('Again', 431-447).

[149] Matlock ('Detheologizing the ΠΙΣΤΙΣ ΧΡΙΣΤΟΥ Debate: Cautionary Remarks from a Lexical Semantic Perspective', *NovT* 42 [2000] 1-23, 20) says that '[t]he subjective genitive reading cannot be judged to have made much progress since Barr's linguistic critique'. Matlock does not refer to Hultgren's and Williams' articles at all.

[150] Matlock, 'Detheologizing', 3.

[151] For Matlock ('Detheologizing', 6), '"[p]olysemy" should be considered a normal and indispensable feature of language, and not an anomaly to be avoided if possible'.

domains. He first distinguishes lexemes 'a' (Acts 17:31) and 'f' (1 Tim 5:12), which, according to Louw-Nida, cite probably the only NT instances (in the former πίστις means 'proof' and in the latter 'promise, pledge to be faithful'), and then lexeme 'c' where πίστις means 'trustworthiness', 'faithfulness', 'dependability'. The remaining three senses are judged to have semantic closeness. In fact, πίστις^d ('to believe in, to be a believer or Christian') and its semantic derivative πίστις^e ('to be a believer, Christian faith') could have been placed with πίστις^b ('to believe in, to have confidence in, to have faith in, to trust, faith, trust').[152]

By taking Louw-Nida's definitions of πίστις^c (e.g. Rom 3:3), where the meaning of the term is to do with a personal characteristic or quality ('trustworthiness', 'dependability', 'faithfulness'), as an example, Matlock attempts to explain the πίστις Χριστοῦ formulation in Gal 2:16 from the perspective of the subjective genitive reading. Louw-Nida's definition should lead one to argue that justification is achieved by the quality that Jesus possesses or displays, but the subjective genitive interpreters take a more active sense of 'faithfulness' and get πίστις to mean 'Jesus' faithful death'. This, for Matlock, shows a reliance on the semantic features of the English gloss of 'faithfulness' – 'faithfulness-unto-death'. This sense may be found in Paul, but depending on glosses rather than real definitions does not make both 'for clarity and for accountability'.[153] It is understanding πίστις as 'faith, trust' that makes both for clarity and accountability and is decisive for reading πίστις Χριστοῦ as objective genitive. The strongest cases for this are found in Rom 4:3 and 4:9, where the verb in the quotation from Gen 15:6 in the former is replaced with the noun in the latter, and in Gal 2:16, 3:22 and Rom 3:22, where the verbal form sits side-by-side with the πίστις Χριστοῦ formulation.[154] Although the use of πίστις with the objective genitive was 'relatively rare' before the NT, that changed when the use of πίστις as 'faith' in 'stereotypical association with certain objects' increased. It is in this process that the 'early Christian idiom' 'faith in Christ' and 'works of the law' was born.[155] In Matlock's view, it is in service of this polemical contrast that the instrumental prepositions ἐκ and διά along with πίστεως are employed in Galatians (and Romans) and Hab 2:4 cited (in Gal 3:11 [and Rom 1:17]).[156] The answer to the question as to why Paul's form of expression is so bound to this contrast is to be found in the question of circumcision that became a pressing

---

[152] Matlock, 'Detheologizing', 10.
[153] Matlock, 'Detheologizing', 11-12.
[154] Matlock, 'Detheologizing', 13, 15-16, 18. See also Dunn, *Romans 1-8*, 166.
[155] Matlock, 'Detheologizing', 19-20.
[156] Matlock, 'Detheologizing', 21.

need of the moment for Paul and his readers/hearers.[157] This leads Matlock
to appeal to Pauline scholarship to stop straining 'to find every theological
initiative condensed into droplets of Pauline grammar'.[158]

It is true that proposed grammatical solutions thus far, for all their merits, have not streamlined the intricacies of the issues involved in the πίστις
Χριστοῦ debate. Failure to combine those solutions with a consideration of
internal evidence plus contextual analysis also means there is still more
smoke than fire in the debate.[159] Indeed, the debate has at times been
obscured by legitimate but generalised theological concerns that are sometimes misplaced.[160] But it is, perhaps, naïve to regard lexical-semantics as
something that permits a theologically neutral construal of the πίστις language, because no lexicographer can deal with the language in question
and make a judgement that is purely linguistic and devoid of theology.[161]
Matlock's analysis, however, shows us how important it is to sufficiently
emphasise the polysemous senses of πίστις. Indeed, one must recognise
that πίστις, like most Greek word forms, has a number of different lexemes
with meanings belonging to different semantic sub-domains before making
any decision about the contextual and syntactical suitability of the sense
the term carries. While Matlock takes the sense 'faith, trust' over against
'faithfulness' as his lexical choice to explain the πίστις Χριστοῦ construction, he probably rightly sees 'faithfulness' as valid a sense as any other
senses in understanding Paul's use of πίστις.[162] Moreover, Matlock is right
in pointing out that the subjective genitive readers have not always been
clear about the relation of the sense of πίστις as 'faithfulness' and Jesus'
death in the πίστις Χριστοῦ construction.

---

[157] For Matlock ('Detheologizing', 22), since 'works of the law' is what humans do
(e.g. circumcision), the fact that it is used in antithetical relation to πίστις Χριστοῦ
means that the latter refers to human action as well ('…with faith aplenty but foreskins
resolutely intact').

[158] Matlock, 'Detheologizing', 23.

[159] See also Hooker, 'ΠΙΣΤΙΣ ΧΡΙΣΤΟΥ', *NTS* 35 (1989) 321-342, 321; B. Longenecker, 'ΠΙΣΤΙΣ', 479.

[160] In our view, soteriological concerns, for example, are misplaced, particularly in
the case of Romans where almost all of the σῳζῶ and σωτηρία language is used futuristi-
cally. While it cannot be denied that Paul sometimes equates δικαιοσύνη and σωτηρία in
Romans, it may be wrong to think of 'justification' as the same thing as eschatological
salvation.

[161] See also Hays' comments in the introduction to the second edition of his *The Faith
of Jesus Christ*, xliv-xlvii.

[162] As Campbell (*The Quest*, 185-186) points out, the meaning 'faithfulness' can be
found in numerous passages in Paul: Rom 1:5, 8, 12; 16:26; 2 Cor 5:7; 1 Thess 1:3, 8;
3:2, 6; 5:8; arguably Gal 5:5, 6, 22; Phil 1:25, 27; Phile 5, 6 (cp. Eph 1:15; 6:16, 23; Col
1:4, 23; 2:5, 7, etc.).

Matlock goes further and argues that the subjective genitive reading is incompatible with the meaning of the antithetical ἔργα νόμου and πίστις Χριστοῦ in Gal 2:16. He also argues that the stylistic shift from noun-with-genitive to verb-with-preposition and then to noun-with-genitive in Rom 3:22, 26 (as in Gal 2:16) appear to form a strong argument in favour of taking 'faith in Christ' as an appropriate rendering of πίστις Χριστοῦ. As indicated above, it is the lexical-semantic argument that forms a basis for this: πίστις Χριστοῦ belongs in lexeme[b] ('to believe in', 'to have faith in') rather than lexeme[c] ('trustworthiness', 'faithfulness'). If, on these grounds, one accepts Matlock's argument that interpreting πίστις Χριστοῦ as the faithfulness of Christ is not linguistically and exegetically viable, then one cannot interpret ἐκ πίστεως in Rom 1:17 christologically either. But in the following two sub-sections (4.4.3 and 4.4.4) we will test Matlock's contentions and other alternatives and, in so doing, attempt to defend the christological interpretation of πίστις Χριστοῦ through providing fresh contextually- and exegetically-based arguments. Sub-section 4.4.3 will focus on Gal 2:16 and context while sub-section 4.4.4 will be based on Rom 3:22 and context.

4.4.3. Galatians 2:16 and Context

If the πίστις Χριστοῦ formulations are understood to belong in lexeme[b] ('to believe in', 'to have faith in') rather than lexeme[c] ('trustworthiness', 'faithfulness'), the argument that had not Paul had what humans do in his mind when he used πίστις Χριστοῦ he would not have contrasted it with ἔργα νόμου can be sustained.[163] As far as Galatians is concerned, the main contextual argument in favour of this view is that Paul and his first Galatian audience were presented with the pressing need of the moment, which, as Matlock also says (though without elaborating on it), was mainly to do with the agitators' insistence on observing works of the law, circumcision in particular. In response to this, Paul declares that δικαιωθῶμεν ἐκ πίστεως Χριστοῦ. That is, Paul presents faith/believing in Christ as an alternative but proper means of justification.

But Matlock, like other proponents of this traditional perspective, has not asked whether πίστις Χιρστοῦ as 'Christ's faithfulness-to-death' can sit together with the meaning of εἰς Χριστὸν 'Ιησοῦν ἐπιστεύσαμεν in Gal 2:16. Neither have the advocates of the subjective genitive interpretation of πίστις Χριστοῦ. But this is an important question and we wish to explore it. Before that, however, it is methodologically necessary to consider the

---

[163] Matlock, 'Detheologizing', 12. This antithesis is strengthened by ἡμεῖς εἰς Χριστὸν 'Ιησοῦ ἐπιστεύσαμεν, which, as Dunn (*Theology*, 381) would also argue, is intended to mean that those who 'believed in Jesus' 'demonstrated and established the principle of *pistis Christou* as rendering works of the law unnecessary'.

contextual factors behind Paul's statements in Gal 2:16. Our focal question here is: is the apparent contrast between πίστις Χριστοῦ and ἔργα νόμου based on Paul's concern that his Jewish-Christian critics mistakenly held 'works of the law' as a means of justification? We attempt to answer this question through a brief examination of two arguments. The first argument will be based on the so-called New Perspective, where works of the law are understood with an ethnocentric role whereby they are misguidedly used as exclusive national identity markers. The second argument will be based on the recent defences of the Old Perspective, where it has been said that Paul's Jewish-Christian critics, pursuant with the perspective of Judaism, held the view that obedience to Torah was the basis for justification or salvation.

1) Contextual Factors in Relation to Works of the Law:

1.1) Works of the Law and their Ethnocentric Role. Here, we summarise briefly the argument that Paul uses the term 'works of the law' in reaction against the ethnocentric role that works of the law were afforded by his Jewish-Christian critics. The apostle, probably based on his own first-hand experience in Antioch and the report he probably received about his Jewish-Christian critics' engagement in compelling Gentile Christians to be circumcised (Gal 5:10-12; 6:12), seems to see the danger of making Jewish nomistic practices part of the ingredients of Christian life and iden- tity (Gal 2:11-14). He responds by asserting that the reason why he, Peter and others 'believed in Christ Jesus' was because they knew humanity as a whole (πᾶσα σάρξ) would not be justified ἐξ ἔργων νόμου but ἐκ/διὰ πίστεως Χριστοῦ (cf. Rom 3:20-22). Part of this assertion echoes Ps 142:2 (LXX), where, after crying to the Lord to hear his supplications in his faithfulness and righteousness in verse 1, the psalmist pleads with the Lord not to enter into judgement with him but to save him on the basis of his חסד (vv 8, 12 [ἔλεος σοῦ]), because 'no one living is righteous before you'. For the psalmist, as no human being is righteous before the Lord, the sal- vation and standing before the divine presence of any Israelite depends on the justice, goodness, compassion, mercy and love of the Lord rather than her good deeds or moral-ethical perfections. Such an idea was also com- mon in other circles of Second Temple Judaism (cf., for example, *1 En* 81:3, 5; 1QS 11:9-15; 1QHᵃ 12:29-37; 15:26-31; 17:14). This, of course, is based on the Jewish theological axiom that God's covenant with Israel pre- ceded any good works that Israelites might perform as the way of showing gratitude to the Lord for his entirely free love and their legitimacy as the covenant people (Deut 9:6; 10:12-15; Isa 63:8-10).

Such a theological axiom, coupled with the story of Abraham, seems to have provided Paul with a framework that became central in his thinking (cf. Gal 2:16 with Rom 3:20). Paul, like many other Jews in the Second Temple period, knows that his standing as a righteous person and member of the elect is not dependent on his observance of religious requirements, but only on God's goodness and mercy. It is Christ (rather than the law) who mediates that divine mercy for Jews and Gentiles. Those Gentiles, who have received this mercy by participating in Christ through faith, have also shared in the righteousness occasioned by Christ (Gal 2:16, 21) or received the blessing of Abraham (Gal 3:14), the promise of the Spirit (Gal 3:14) and the 'hope of righteousness' (Gal 5:5). What should be required of them, therefore, is neither circumcision nor uncircumcision but living their faith through and within the framework of ἀγάπη (Gal 5:6). Why did Paul contrast ἔργα νόμου with πίστις Χριστοῦ in Gal 2:16? From our discussions above, it seems unlikely that the reason for such a contrast was because his critics preached works of the law, circumcision in particular, as the basis of justification. It probably was because they attached the ethnocentric role to works of the law whereby *compliance with the practice of circumcision in particular was seen as something that established the legitimacy of Gentile Christians as God's people and true descendants of Abraham.* This, in Paul's view, would undermine what God did in and through Christ to deliver Jews and Gentiles from the bondage of Law, Sin and Flesh into the freedom of the Spirit (Gal 2:11-14; 3:14, 21-22; 5:1-6, 16-25; 6:12-15).

1.2) Works of the Law: A Means of Justification? As discussed in the first chapter of this book, scholars such as Westerholm, Kim, Gathercole and Silva have criticised arguments such as the one discussed above and provided fresh defences of the traditional perspective on justification. Westerholm, for example, argues that what Paul rejects (i.e. 'righteousness of the law') in Galatians has a scriptural basis rather than being confined to ethnocentrism or legalism. Before his conversion, Paul was of the view that one needed to observe the law in order to enjoy the life and blessings it promises. After his conversion, however, he comes to believe that human beings are neither able nor willing to obey this divine law (Ps 142:2 [LXX]; Gal 2:15-16). That belief leads him to the doctrine of justification by faith as opposed to justification by works.[164] According to Westerholm, Paul's Jewish-Christian critics in Galatia did not present the Jewish law as 'an alternative to faith in Jesus Christ but as the framework within which such faith was to be lived'.[165] Paul saw this as advocating the stance that God's favour was to be found in the confines of the Jewish law and, there-

---

[164] Westerholm, *Perspectives Old and New on Paul: The "Lutheran" Paul and His Critics*, 1ff.

[165] Westerholm, *Perspectives*, 369.

fore, as essentially similar to that of non-Christian Jews.[166] Westerholm
specifies the Jewish law here as the 'Sinaitic law'. From a Jewish perspective, what distinguishes Jews as 'righteous' is their observance of this law.
From Paul's perspective, however, those who are under the law (Jews) and
those who are not (Gentiles) are 'sinners', as confirmed by the universal
statement in Ps 142:2 (LXX). So both Jews and Gentiles are *only* declared
righteous by *faith in Jesus Christ*. There is, therefore, no need for Gentile
believers to be circumcised or adopt distinctively Jewish practices,[167] although Paul does not go so far as to fault the Sinaitic law or declare Jewish
practices as invalid.[168] So what is Paul's problem with Judaism in Galatia?
Westerholm argues that Paul's problem is not that Judaism limits God's
covenant blessings to those who observe the boundary markers, as argued
by Dunn, but rather that it fosters 'the belief that people can be declared
righteous on the basis of their faithfulness to the Sinaitic law'.[169] And
Paul's Jewish-Christian critics have more or less adopted such a position.
When Paul argues against them, his 'point is not that people are not required to do what is right or that the law is wrong in telling them to do so,
but that only faith in Jesus Christ provides a solution for humanity's cap-
tivity to sin'.[170]

Westerholm's argument can be summarised as follows. 1) Non-Christian Jews exclusively focus on faithfulness to the law as a means of justification. 2) Paul's Jewish-Christian critics hold both faith in Christ and obedience to the law together and argue that the former should be lived within
the framework of the latter. 3) Paul exclusively focuses on faith in Christ
as the means of justification.

Westerholm has made a substantial case in defence of the traditional
perspective. But there are at least three things that should be said in response to his argument. First, while Westerholm is probably right to say
that Paul's Jewish-Christian critics did not insist that works of the law
should be seen as an alternative to 'faith', he takes for granted that πίστις
Χριστοῦ means 'faith in Christ'. As is well known, the construction can
also be rendered as 'faithfulness of Christ'. The latter rendering might
even help us explain the question as to whether Paul's critics saw works of
the law, circumcision in particular, as a means of justification. We shall
come back to that below.

---

[166] Westerholm, *Perspectives*, 369.

[167] Westerholm, *Perspectives*, 370-374, 380.

[168] Westerholm, *Perspectives*, 380.

[169] Westerholm, *Perspectives*, 380.

[170] Westerholm, *Perspectives*, 381.

Second, Westerholm correctly observes that circumcision was the chief cause of controversy in Galatia,[171] but he does not emphasise sufficiently that it was the imposition of the practice of circumcision on Gentile Christians that troubled Paul.[172] Paul does not say that he sees no point in Jewish Christians continuing to observe Jewish religious practices.[173] But he vehemently opposes any attempt to compel 'the Gentiles to live like Jews' (Gal 2:14; Gal 6:12). This suggests that he holds works of the law as an appropriate (but not compulsory) practice for Jewish Christians, while emphasising 'faith in Christ' (as to whether or not this is the meaning of πίστις Χριστοῦ will be discussed below) for both Jewish Christians and Gentile Christians.

Third, Westerholm refers to Ps 142:2 (LXX) as the scriptural basis for Paul's idea of justification by faith. Certainly, Paul cites or alludes to this psalm in Gal 2:16, 3:11 and Rom 3:20 where he discusses the concept of justification, but Westerholm's argument that Paul developed this concept in view of Jewish belief that people would be declared righteous through their fulfilment of the commandments of the law is to be questioned at least for two reasons.

A) Judaism or the Torah is not about a collection of demands through which human beings acquire righteousness, rather it is to be explained and understood within the framework of God's loving initiative to choose Israel to be 'a people holy to the Lord' and 'a people for his own possession' (Deut 7:6).[174] Of course, with this initiative comes a demand to observe God's commandments. But such demand is to be met by all Jews as a way of sustaining their relationship with God rather than as a means of being declared righteous (Deut 7:9, 11). Israel is righteous by virtue of being chosen to be the 'son' of the righteous God,[175] but that does not exclude individual and collective failures to maintain that righteousness (e.g. Deut 9:4-7; Ezra 9:6-15). The psalmist in Ps 142 is deeply aware of that, as he asserts: 'no one living is righteous before you' (v 2).

As indicated above, Paul concurs with the psalmist. Paul's Jewish-Christian critics would probably agree with the psalmist's assertion as well. But Paul differs from both the psalmist and his critics. The psalmist

---

[171] Westerholm, *Perspectives*, 366.

[172] In Gal 6:12, ὑμᾶς could refer to the Galatian Christians as a whole. But since Jewish Christians do not need to be compelled to be circumcised, it should be understood as a reference to the Christian community among which Paul's critics were active in attempting to compel Gentile Christians to accept circumcision as a compulsory practice.

[173] See also Westerholm, *Perspectives*, 380-381.

[174] Westerholm (*Perspectives*, 381) too concedes this point. But he explains away by saying that the issue of election is not mentioned in Galatians.

[175] Compare, for example, Ex 4:22; Deut 14:1-2; 32:4-5, 8-9 with 2 Sam 7:14; Ps 2:7; 89:3, 14; Isa 11:1-5; 53:11; Jer 23:5.

would say that Jews should continue to at once depend on God's mercy for the forgiveness of their sins and observe the commandments of the law as a way of maintaining their righteousness. To this, Paul's Jewish-Christian critics would add Christ as the one through whom God's mercy was mediated while demanding observance of works of the law from both Jews and Gentiles who are in Christ. Differently from both, Paul would argue that since God's mercy is now mediated for Jews and Gentiles through the death of Christ so that those who are in Christ are righteous (Gal 3:11-14; cf. Deut 27:26; 28:58; 30:10), there is no need for Gentile Christians in particular to do works or to be circumcised. In Gal 5:4, Paul even goes so far as to say that those Galatians who are compelled by his Jewish-Christian critics' perspective and attempt 'to be *counted as righteous* in the sphere of the law' (ἐν νόμῳ δικαιοῦσθε)[176] 'are cut off from Christ' (κατηργήθητε ἀπὸ Χριστοῦ).[177] This seems an overreaction or exaggerated threat, but it originates from Paul's conviction that those who are in Christ have also received the 'hope of righteousness' (5:5-6).[178] In short, Paul uses Ps 142:2 in order to make his point that *the righteousness of those who are in Christ remains intact* and, therefore, Galatian Christians do not need to be circumcised in order to maintain their righteousness.

B) Westerholm's perspective from Ps 142 is based on his argumentative framework that within Judaism Jews are righteous because they have done

---

[176] The prepositional phrase ἐν νόμῳ can be taken as locative ('by law') or instrumental ('in the sphere of the law'). Longenecker (*Galatians*, 228) seems to prefer the former, while Burton (*Galatians*, 276) and Dunn (*Epistle*, 267) prefer the latter. Both are acceptable, but the latter is more probable because of its presumed contrast with ἐν Χριστῷ in 5:6.

[177] It is important to note here that commentators have differing views on the sort of assumption that is being criticised in Gal 5:4. Dunn (*Epistle*, 267-269) argues that Paul is criticising the view that justification in the final judgement is a consequence of *membership* of the chosen people. For Longenecker (*Galatians*, 228), Paul is warning against an assurance that the Galatian Christians had been given by Paul's critics that 'in accepting supervision for their lives from the prescriptions of the Mosaic law they were not forsaking Christ or renouncing grace, but were completing their commitment to both'. Slightly differently, Martyn (*Galatians*, 471) argues that some Galatians have come to think that salvation is dependent on enacting 'allegiance to Christ' within observance of the law. Paul is telling them that that is a wrong thinking. Martyn accepts that a dual attachment to Christ and observance of the law is acceptable to Paul, but he rejects attaching law-observance 'some degree of salvific potency'. Martyn is probably right in saying this, but it should be stressed that Paul would only accept such a dual attachment as far as Jewish Christians are concerned (Gal 1:22; 2:1ff).

[178] Paul's 'hope of righteousness' in Gal 5:5 probably refers to the kind of final vindication [of righteousness] that he talks about in Rom 2:12. Now, it is not doing works that guarantees ultimate vindication, nor circumcision or uncircumcision, but participation in Christ.

what they ought.[179] This view suggests, probably wrongly, that even the original acquisition of righteousness or life by Israel was based on doing what is right (cf. Deut 7:6-8 with Ezek 16:6-8). Furthermore, Westerholm's argument does not seem to take sufficient account of the kind of critical self-assessment and consciousness of sin that existed among those Second Temple Jews who regarded themselves as righteous (as against those who were unrighteous). Some even allude to Ps 142:2. For example, the writer of 1QH[a] in 15:28 admits: 'Who will be righteous before you when he is judged? No one!'.[180] The writer of 1QS in 11:9 says: 'I belong to evil humankind, to the assembly of unfaithful flesh'. Upon his return from his heavenly tour, Enoch was instructed to tell his children that 'no flesh is righteous before the Lord, for he created them' (*1 En* 81:5). These admissions, to be sure, could be taken as originating from a sense of failure to fulfil God's commandments. That may well be the case, but the goal of our authors' attempt to fulfil God's commandments could not have been justification or being transferred from the state of ungodliness to godliness. Despite their self-critical attitude and consciousness of sin, all three, like our psalmist (Ps 141:7 [LXX]), would believe that they were in the company of the righteous. They would accept that they should observe God's commandments as a way of sustaining their relationship with God and, therefore, their status as righteous people. None of them, however, would accept that they should do so *in order to be declared righteous*. In alluding to Ps 142:2, the producers of 1QH[a], 1QS and the Astronomical Book of Enoch probably reflect the paradoxical but scriptural idea that the salvation and destiny of Israel depend on God's unfailing patience, compassion and mercy, not on her own righteousness (Deut 9:4-7; Ps 142:1-2, 8, 12).[181]

In relation to our concern in this section, Westerholm may agree with the view that Paul's critics would have accepted that God's mercy, through which God established his covenant with Israel, was now mediated for Jews and Gentiles in and through Christ and that Jews and Gentiles must acknowledge that. But by arguing that Judaism had the idea that one is declared righteous through works of the law and Paul's critics' position was not essentially different from this, he portrays Paul's Jewish-Christian

---

[179] Westerholm, *Perspectives*, 286-291.

[180] My translation of 15:28: ומי יצדק לפניכה בהשפטו ואין. García Martínez and Tigchelaar's translation reads: 'Who is just before you when he goes to court? No ...'

[181] For example, the author of 1QH[a] declares that 'you pu[ri]fy [the sons of your truth] from their offences by the greatness of your goodness, and by the abundance of your com[pas]sion, to make them stand in your presence, for ever and ever' (15:30-31). Enoch, after reading the heavenly book that contains accounts of human deeds and so on, praised the Lord 'because of his patience' (*1 En* 81:3). And the author of 1QS confidently claims that if he stumbles 'the mercies of God' shall always be his salvation and that God will atone for all his sins in 'his plentiful goodness' (11:12, 14).

critics as those who engaged in compelling Gentile Christians in Galatia to be circumcised in order to be justified.[182] His argument, in this regard, is unconvincing.

But Silva refers to *Sir* 3:30 ('As water extinguishes a blazing fire, so almsgiving [צדקה] atones for sin') and argues that the idea that one should work for or contribute to 'one's own salvation' through good works existed within Jewish communities known to Paul.[183] Whether Silva's 'one's own salvation' is the same thing as one's acquisition of a righteous status is not clear. But if he is equating atonement for sin in *Sirach* with acquisition of righteousness, there are two things that can be said against his view. First, as indicated above and as Elliott has rightly argued, some Jewish groups in the Second Temple period expressly placed clear boundaries between their *righteous* community and those whom they saw as unrighteous (i.e. the majority of Israel).[184] As discussed earlier, Gathercole has also extensively argued that a substantial number of Jewish apocryphal and pseudepigraphal writings present obedience to Torah as the basis for eschatological vindication or salvation of *the righteous*. Ben Sira is instructing the righteous, whose acquisition of righteousness did not depend on almsgiving but primarily on God's election of Israel and his covenant with her. Furthermore, the covenant given to the chosen people of God also included provisions of atonement through which sins could be forgiven.

Second, Ben Sira's expression that 'almsgiving atones for sin' (that is, supposing that 'almsgiving' is an appropriate rendering for צדקה in *Sir* 3:30[185]) cannot be understood in terms of almsgiving serving as a means of earning righteousness in the sense of an ungodly person becoming godly. As *Sir* 35:1-3 shows, giving alms is part and parcel of heeding the divine commandments, which includes 'forsaking unrighteousness ', which is also

---

[182] As Sanders (*PPJ*, 427) admits, some individual Jews may have been guilty of distorting Jewish ideas in Paul's time. Although we cannot be sure about the accurate reporting of it, Luke in Acts 15 tells us that some were teaching that salvation was not possible without circumcision or keeping the law of Moses (vv 1, 5). But this sort of idea cannot be noticed in Galatians unless one understands Gal 5:4 along this line, which, in our view, is a misreading. In Gal 6:12, Paul accuses his critics for attempting to compel Galatian Christians to be circumcised in order to spare themselves from persecution, not because they believed that salvation was through circumcision. We need more evidence to suggest that Paul's Jewish-Christian critics regarded obedience to the law as the basis of becoming a child of God.

[183] Silva, 'Faith', 246.

[184] Elliott, *The Survivors of Israel: A Reconsideration of the Theology of Pre-Christian Judaism*, 185-186.

[185] While צדקה can be rendered 'almsgiving' in the light of 4:1ff, in the light of 3:26-29 it can mean 'righteousness' (of the wise man) as opposed to 'sin' or 'evil' of the sinner or 'stubborn mind'. But 3:30 seems to introduce what is said in 4:1ff, so 'almsgiving' probably is the correct rendering for צדקה in it.

paralleled with 'atonement' (v 3). In these verses and in *Sir* 35 as a whole, it is the righteous person who is urged to observe God's commandments. However, being righteous or godly neither exempts one from observing God's commandments nor makes one complacent. Of course, critical self-assessment or consciousness of sin coupled with complete confidence in God's mercy is not as elaborate in *Sirach* as it is in 1QS 11, for example,[186] but that it is not completely absent seems incontrovertible. Indeed, it is the consciousness of sin that seems to lead Ben Sira to urge his readers to heed God's commandments. Gathercole understands this heeding as a means of 'this-worldly' and 'individualistic' reward.[187] The promise of earthly blessing certainly follows obedience in *Sirach*, but, as *Sir* 35:1-3 shows, heeding divine commandments is a way of maintaining the status of righteousness rather than becoming righteous. For Ben Sira, it seems, to maintain righteousness is the same thing as choosing life rather than death (15:16; cf. Deut 30:15f). But Ben Sira also believes that God in his mercy (not on the basis of Israel's obedience to the law) will redeem his people Israel at the appointed time (36:1-17). In brief, in *Sirach* election and covenant do not prevent one from choosing a way of unrighteousness or death, so sustaining righteousness or life through observing divine statutes is encouraged.[188]

To conclude our consideration of issues involved in the contextual background of Gal 2:16, Silva's argument that *Sir* 3:30 supports the idea that one works for one's own salvation probably wrongly implies that those Jews who considered themselves as righteous believed that their acquisition of righteousness or life was occasioned by their fulfilment of the commandments of the Torah. This is not to deny that the righteous saw the necessity of observance of the commandments of the Torah, which would also have been advocated by Paul's Jewish-Christian critics. Paul does not seem to object to Jewish compliance with this so long as it is carried out

---

[186] The writer of 1QS confesses: 'I belong to evil humankind, to the assembly of unfaithful flesh; my failings, my iniquities, my sins ... belong to those ... who walk in darkness' (11:9-10). Then he goes on to say: 'if I stumble the mercies of God shall be my salvation always; and if I fall in the sin of the flesh, in the justice of God (בצדקת אל), which endures eternally, shall my judgement be ... he will judge me in the justice of his truth, and in his plentiful goodness always atone for all my sins; in his justice (בצדקתו) he will cleanse me ...' (11:12, 14). The translation is from García Martínez and Tigchelaar. Here בצדקתו can be rendered 'through his righteousness'.

[187] Gathercole, *Boasting*, 40.

[188] While life is this-worldly in *Sirach*, it is otherworldly in 2 Maccabees (7:22, 23, 29, 37), *Psalms of Solomon* (3:11-12) and *1 Enoch*. But in both strands of thinking, as in the general thinking of the OT, the life of the righteous is divinely given and is maintained through obeying divine commandments. See also Dunn, *Theology*, 152-153; Winninge, *Sinners*, 74-75.

within the framework of the death of Christ and its implications. But he rejects any demand that Gentile Christians too observe works of the law including circumcision. The reason for this rejection could not have been because his critics saw circumcision as the basis of justification.[189]

In the light of all the above, it seems overconfident to say that Paul's contrast between πίστις Χριστοῦ and ἔργα νόμου in Gal 2:16 is framed against his critics' mistaken view that works of the law is a means of justification (= acquisition of righteousness or life). The main reason is that Paul's critics would probably have held the view that God's purpose in giving the law to Israel was so that Jews might obey its commandments not as a means of justification but rather as a way of demonstrating that they are sharers of the national righteousness based on election, that they are true descendants of Abraham and that their living is consistent with God's values. The proponents of the New Perspective are probably right in espousing this sort of argument, but by basing such a view on the premise that justification by faith [in Christ] is the solution to the problem of the weakness of the flesh (cf. Gal 2:16 with Rom 3:20 and 8:3), they appear to have oversimplified the issue. For one thing, πίστις Χριστοῦ in Gal 2:16 could have a subjective genitive meaning that is equivalent to Christ's obedient death on the cross. This brings us to our earlier question as to whether πίστις Χριστοῦ as 'Christ's faithfulness-to-death' can sit together with the meaning of εἰς Χριστὸν Ἰησοῦν ἐπιστεύσαμεν in Gal 2:16.

2) Πίστις Χριστοῦ: Christ's Faithfulness-to-Death?

In Gal 2:16, Paul declares that πίστις Χριστοῦ is the means through which justification is achieved. In the context of Gal 2:16, to be justified in or through Christ is part and parcel of receiving the Spirit (3:2), becoming the children of Abraham (3:7), and receiving the blessings of Abraham (3:14) and the promise of the Spirit (3:14, 22). Moreover, for Paul, justification is inextricably linked with being freed from the sphere of Flesh and the power of Sin and coming into the sphere of the Spirit and under the redemptive power of God (3:22; 4:4-7; 5:16-25; cf. Rom 8:3-4).[190] Thus, to

---

[189] As can be noticed in Gal 6:12, Paul's critics wanted to compel Gentile Christians to be circumcised in the hope that they would 'make a good showing in the flesh or outwardly' (εὐπροσωπῆσαι ἐν σαρκί) and, in so doing, spare themselves from persecution. See also R. Longenecker's comments on Gal 6:12 (*Galatians*, 290-291). As Longenecker rightly points out, σάρξ in 6:12-13 is used in the physical sense (cf. 2:20; 4:13, 14, 23, 29) rather than in the apocalyptic and/or ethical sense as in 5:16, 17, 19, 24; 6:8.

[190] In the Hellenistic background, 'flesh' and 'spirit' are counterposed spheres of damnation and salvation. But in Galatians, σάρξ and πνεῦμα are presented as two opposing cosmic spheres within which power and authority with opposing mindset, outlook, values, desires, aspirations, purposes and goals are exercised is confirmed by Rom 8:5f; Gal 5:17 (see also Martyn, *Issues*, 120f, 253; Hays, *Faith*, xl); the Rule of Community

say that *those who believe in Christ Jesus* are justified ἐκ πίστεως Χριστοῦ (2:16) is the same thing as saying that *those who believe* [in Christ] are given the promise ἐκ πίστεως ᾽Ιησοῦ Χριστοῦ (3:22).

So can πίστις Χριστοῦ mean 'Christ's faithfulness-to-death'? As the construction in Gal 2:16 stands, the answer is 'no', because Christ's death is not indicated in the passage. However, when we understand what Paul means by justification or the reception of the promise [of the Spirit] ἐκ/διὰ πίστεως Χριστοῦ in the light of his idea of justification ἐν Χριστῷ (2:17) and the reception of the blessings of Abraham ἐν Χριστῷ ᾽Ιησοῦ (3:14), the answer can be 'yes'. The equation of justification ἐκ/διὰ πίστεως Χριστοῦ with justification ἐν Χριστῷ may be explained as follows. The Christ through whom Paul and other believers are justified or have received the blessings of Abraham is *the Son of God who loved them and gave himself for them* (2:20). Christ not only gave himself for Paul and other believing Jews and Gentiles, he also now lives in them. On this basis, Paul uses such linguistic image of identification as being crucified with Christ (2:19-20). As he later declares in 6:14, Paul boasts in the cross of Christ and, probably implicitly, in the crucified redeemer Christ, which is what Christ always is for Paul.[191] In short, Paul is of the view that he and the Galatian Christians owed their justification and their newly acquired life primarily to Christ's self-giving and sacrificial act. He speaks of that as justification ἐν Χριστῷ. It is then reasonable to read δικαιοῦται...διὰ πίστεως᾽Ιησοῦ Χριστοῦ and δικαιωθῶμεν ἐκ πίστεως Χριστοῦ in 2:16 in terms of justification through Christ's faithfulness-to-death.

There are two arguments against this conclusion. First, as Matlock contends, that Paul did not contrast ἐκ πίστεως Χριστοῦ with ἐξ ἔργα Χριστοῦ shows that he did not intend a christological meaning for the former. Second, πίστις Χριστοῦ shares the same meaning as εἰς Χριστὸν ᾽Ιησοῦν ἐπιστεύσαμεν. We deal with both arguments in turn. In support of the first argument, it can be said that Paul did not intend a separate meaning for the noun (with its genitive relation Χριστοῦ) here from that which he intended for the verb.[192] It can also be said that Paul uses πίστις without a personal pronoun in Gal 3:2-9 probably because he wants to set the term against 'works'. In 3:2-4 in particular, he emphasises, through a rhetorical question, that the Galatians did not receive the Spirit ἐξ ἔργων νόμου but rather ἐξ ἀκοῆς πίστεως. Furthermore, in the light of the reference to Abraham's

---

(1QS 4:15-17, 19f, 25) and *1 Enoch* (15:4; 106:17). See also Schweizer, 'πνεῦμα, πνευματικός', *TDNT VI*, 389-451; 'σάρξ', *TDNT VII*, 98-151.

[191] Here δι᾽ οὗ can be taken as 'through whom' or 'through which'. Either way, it makes no difference in Paul's thinking. See also Longenecker, *Galatians*, 294-295.

[192] So Matlock ('Detheologizing', 15-16), who argues that the verb πιστεύω here contributes (as it also does in Rom 4) to the selection of the sense 'faith, trust' for the noun.

trust in God (3:6), οἱ ἐκ πίστεως in 3:7 could mean those who are of faith (i.e. the children of Abraham)[193] as opposed to those who are of works of the law.[194] Πίστις in both οἱ ἐκ πίστεως and ἐξ ἀκοῆς πίστεως can be taken as having the same sense as the verb.[195] In short, justification, for Paul, is dependent on human faith (cf. 3:8 with 3:24), whose alternative must be human works.

Gal 3:8 clearly states that God is the one who justifies the Gentiles ἐκ πίστεως. This statement seems to correspond to Paul's earlier assertion regarding the Galatian Christians' reception of the Spirit 'through the hearing of faith' rather than 'through works of the law' (3:2-4). 'Faith' here and in 3:7, for example, can be argued to mean believing. There is thus a strong case for the traditional argument here. But at least three arguments can be put forward in favour the christological argument as well. First, ἐκ πίστεως in 3:8 should not necessarily be limited to human faith, because ἐκ πίστεως δικαιοῖ in this verse is identical to ἐκ πίστεως δικαιωθῶμεν in 3:24, which probably is a short for δικαιωθῶμεν ἐκ πίστεως Χριστοῦ in 2:16. As discussed in sub-section 4.1, Paul sometimes uses ἐκ πίστεως as an abbreviated form of ἐκ πίστεως Χριστοῦ. If that is also the case in Gal 3:8, Paul can be understood as talking about God's act of justifying the Gentiles 'through the faithfulness-[of-Christ-to-death]'. Second, that Paul says that the Galatian Christians did not receive the Spirit through works of the law does not necessarily suggest that his critics attempted to compel Gentile Christians to be circumcised in order to be justified or gain righteous status. Our discussion of the contextual background earlier cast serious doubt on that view. It also made us hesitant about readily claiming that Paul's scriptural assertion in Gal 2:16 that 'no human being will be justified through works of the law' suggests that ἔργα νόμου is always a direct contrast to ἐκ πίστεως. That seems to be the case in Gal 3:8 as well, as πίστις here should not necessarily carry the same meaning as πιστεύω, because ἐκ πίστεως appears to be an abbreviation of ἐκ πίστεως Χριστοῦ, which, one could argue, should be taken as subjective genitive. Third, if Gal 3:8 is understood in terms of God's act of justifying the Gentiles through human faith, such an argument could be seen to be akin to the view that the mental disposition of having faith must replace the old Jewish idea of observing the law and living by it as a precondition for justification.[196] It would, of course, be wrong to deny that Paul saw faith as

---

[193] Or as Burton (*Galatians*, 155) says: 'those who have believed and whose standing and character are determined by that faith'.

[194] See Silva ('Faith', 224-226) who refers to οἱ ἐξ ἔργων νόμου as 'Judaizers', Christian Jews who insisted that Gentiles be circumcised, as opposed to 'the good guys'.

[195] Matlock, 'Detheologizing', 8; Silva, 'Faith', 232.

[196] In order to sustain this argument, one needs to understand πίστις in relation to the

one's cognitive response in acknowledgement of God's saving act in Christ. But as Taylor argues, the reading that makes justification dependent on human faith-response appears to assign 'to man too much of a function and to Christ too little', because it seems to substitute 'the mental act of having faith for the bodily one of being circumcised', leaving Jesus 'in the passive rôle of being the object of our justifying faith'.[197]

Our adjudication above shows that the traditional approach, where πίστις Χριστοῦ is understood as an antithetical human action to ἔργα νόμου, can only be cogent if πίστις Χριστοῦ is interpreted as 'faith in Christ'. But as shown above and will be shown below, there are good reasons to interpret it as the 'faithfulness of Christ' and, therefore, as Christ's action. If this was what Paul had in mind when he penned Gal 2:16, it would have enabled him to successfully argue against his critics who probably held the view that Gentiles' acceptance of the message of the gospel should be followed by their performance of Jewish nomistic practices as legitimating factors and markers of their new identity as God's people and true descendants of Abraham. More specifically, Paul's critics engaged in compelling Gentile Christians to be circumcised. This, in Paul's view, goes against the decision taken by the Jerusalem leadership that in Gentile mission the compliance of Gentile converts with the practice of circumcision and certain Jewish dietary rules should be out of the equation.[198] Furthermore, insisting on Gentile circumcision will not only

---

genitive Χριστοῦ as a cognitive-religious exercise in response to some divine act or claim, or in order to win some divine favour or reward (believing-acceptance or believing-expectation). But as Hays ('Πίστις', 55) argues, Paul does not say that we are 'justified' or 'saved' by 'our own cognitive disposition'.

[197] Taylor, 'The Function of πίστις Χριστοῦ in Galatians', *JBL* 85 [1966] 58-76, 75.

[198] If the critics had anything to do with the Antiochene crisis, Paul's recounting of the crisis before Gal 2:16 must inform our decision as to the reason for Paul's contrast. The Jerusalem 'pillars' had agreed that Barnabas and Paul should preach the gospel among the uncircumcised or Gentiles while Peter should go to the circumcised or Jews (2:7-9). Partly on this basis, it seems, Paul in Antioch challenged Peter, Barnabas and all the other Jewish Christians for not acting consistently with τὴν ἀλήθειαν τοῦ εὐαγγελίου when they compelled Gentiles to live like Jews (2:11-14). In 2:11-14, 'living like Jews' (as opposed to 'living like Gentiles') does not seem to include circumcision, as Paul's focus is on the impropriety of compelling Gentiles to share in table fellowship only when meals are prepared in accordance with Jewish dietary laws – according to Gal 6:12, Gentile Christians were also being 'compelled' (note the use of ἀναγκάζεις in both 2:14 and 6:12) to be circumcised. If the account in Acts 10 is deemed to offer interpretative guidance, Luke tells us that Peter was compelled to accept that dietary laws should no longer prevent him from spreading the message of Christ among the Gentiles. Paul, therefore, found Peter's agreement with those who were compelling Gentile Christians to observe Jewish dietary laws not only hypocritical but also contrary to the 'truth of the gospel'. In Acts 15 too, Peter was the one who asked: 'Now therefore why do you make trial of God by putting a yoke upon the neck of the disciples which neither our fathers nor we have

seriously undermine Gentile mission due to the physical pain it involves, it is also inconsistent with the 'truth of the gospel' (Gal 2:14). The 'truth', according to Gal 2:16, is that God justified Jews and Gentiles through πίστις Χριστοῦ. On this basis, Paul emphatically declares that since works of the law never played any part in Christian justification, it should not be made to play any part in Christian living either. Paul does not say that it is wrong for Jewish Christians to do works or be circumcised. He rather emphasises that what matters is neither circumcision nor uncircumcision but the 'new creation' brought about through the cross of Christ (Gal 6:14-15). If πίστις Χριστοῦ denotes Christ's act of obedient-faithfulness expressed in his death, ἔργα νόμου should not be understood as its direct contrast in spite of the antithetical parallelism that there is between the two phrases.

However, πίστις Χριστοῦ and ἔργα νόμου can refer to what humans do if πίστις Χριστοῦ has the same meaning as εἰς Χριστὸν Ἰησοῦν ἐπιστεύσαμεν. This, as indicated above, is the second argument against taking πίστις Χριστοῦ as 'Christ's faithfulness-to-death'. That πίστις Χριστοῦ and εἰς Χριστὸν Ἰησοῦν ἐπιστεύσαμεν have the same meaning is supported by the fact that πιστεύω is never used of Christ's own faith/faithfulness, but always with reference to human faith in God or Christ.[199] This argument cannot be dismissed on the basis that Paul's use of εἰς Χριστὸν Ἰησοῦν ἐπιστεύσαμεν (2:16) and later τοῖς πιστεύουσιν (3:22) is an outcome of his indulgence in tautology.[200] Nor is it sufficient to say that since Gal 2:16 is the only place in Paul's Seven Letter Corpus where 'believing in Christ' is explicitly mentioned, it is not methodologically plausible to use it to interpret all uses of πίστις Χριστοῦ. However, πίστις Χριστοῦ can be rendered as the faithfulness of Christ on the grounds that Paul often uses πίστις as 'faithfulness' (e.g. Rom 1:5, 8, 12; 16:26; 2 Cor 5:7; 1 Thess 1:3, 8; 3:2, 6; 5:8) and the use in Gal 2:16 could well be the same.[201] Also, while most uses of πίστις carry the same mean-

---

been able to bear?' (v10). He agreed with James' decision that Gentiles should only abstain from idolatry, sexual immorality, eating meat from strangled animals and blood (v 20). Whether Peter knew the food served in Antioch had meat from strangled animals or blood, we don't know. In any case, the reason for Paul's contrast between ἔργα νόμου and πίστις Χριστοῦ is some Jewish-Christians' attempt to compel Gentile Christians to live like Jews.

[199] So Silva ('Faith', 232-233).

[200] See also Matlock, 'Detheologizing', 14 and n. 44.

[201] Silva does not accept this, but he accepts that πίστις Χριστοῦ can be interpreted as the 'faithfulness of Christ'. He ('Faith', 227) says: 'Such a view [i.e. understanding the phrase in its traditional sense of "faith in Christ"] does not deny for a moment that the expression could, in principle, be taken as a subjective genitive, or even that Paul himself, in certain context (but none that has survived, as far as I can tell), may have used the phrase with reference to Jesus' own faith or faithful obedience.'

ing as πιστεύω in Gal 3:2-9, we noticed above that the same should not necessarily be the case in 3:8. We can also say that πίστις and πιστεύω in Gal 2:16 need not necessarily share the same meaning.[202] This does not settle the issue, however. For anthropological and christological interpreters can continue to emphasise their respective arguments in a polarised manner. In our view, such polarisation is not necessary. We propose a *via media* that maintains 'Christ's faithfulness-to-death' as the (explanatory) meaning of the substantival construction and 'faith in Christ' as the meaning of the verbal construction. We provide three explanatory reasons for doing so.

First, the synonymity between the revelation of πίστις and Christ in Gal 3:23 (cf. 1:12, 16) seems to lead Paul to say that God justified the Gentiles through πίστις (Gal 3:8). As discussed earlier, the revealed πίστις is virtually indistinguishable from the revealed Christ, so to be justified through πίστις is to be in a position to receive or share in the blessings of Abraham ἐν Χριστῷ 'Ἰησοῦ, which is another way of saying that the promise of the Spirit is received διὰ τῆς πίστεως (cf. 3:14 with 3:23-24). Accepting the revealed πίστις can thus be understood as having πίστις (or believing) in Christ whereby πίστις is an acknowledgement of Christ as the agent and means of God's act of justification. Our faith is a trusting-recognition of what God did in and through Christ who was faithful even unto death.[203]

---

[202] Silva's ('Faith', 232) recent argument that Paul's purpose in using the verbal construction in Gal 2:16 is to 'disambiguate' the genitival construction for the reader is not helpful. Had Paul's aim been disambiguating the genitival construction, he should have done the same elsewhere. But the way he uses the verb in Rom 3:22 and Gal 3:22 introduces more ambiguity, because in both places the verb is used without an object. Silva does not admit 'believing in Christ' is a singular reference in Paul's Seven Letter Corpus. But he argues that the verb 'πιστεύω is indisputably used of our faith in God or Christ [in Gal 2:16, 3:6 and 3:22]' and, in so doing, gives the impression that all these three Galatian passages refer to 'faith in God or Christ'. But we cannot decide as to whether the verbal uses in Gal 3:22 and Rom 3:22 refer to 'faith in Christ'. The meaning of the verb in these verses is ambiguous. Something that is itself ambiguous can hardly disambiguate the meaning of πίστις Χριστοῦ in both passages.

[203] It must be emphasised again that our argument here is based on the view that ἵνα ἐκ πίστεως δικαιωθῶμεν in 3:24 has the same meaning as ἵνα δικαιωθῶμεν ἐκ πίστεως Χριστοῦ in 2:16. If one follows the traditional perspective where the period of the Law and the period of the faith are regarded as two antithetical mytho-historical periods, then the phrase stands for the faith by which we are justified as opposed to the Torah that represents the negative backdrop (3:10, 22; 4:1-10). This faith is faith in Christ Jesus, as 2:16 shows. Such a view is held, for example, by Betz (*Galatians*, 115-119, 175-178). For him (*Galatians*, 117), πίστις 'Ἰησοῦ Χριστοῦ is 'an abbreviation' for 'faith of (= in) Christ Jesus', i.e. 'believing' that Christ is Jesus is 'the channel which mediates "justification" before the throne of God, instead of "doing" the works of the Torah'. For a slightly different perspective, see Dunn, *Epistle*, 200, see also 196-201.

Second, since the relationship between ἡμεῖς εἰς Χριστὸν Ἰησοῦν ἐπιστεύσαμεν and δικαιωθῶμεν ἐκ πίστεως Χριστοῦ in Gal 2:16 is clearly furnished by ἵνα (which could serve as a conjunction of purpose, result or even as a marker of a direct statement), Paul should be understood as saying here that 'we believed in Christ Jesus, so that we may be justified through the faithfulness of Christ'. This understanding separates human action from Christ's action. The basis of our justification is Christ's death.[204] Our faith in Christ is *our acknowledgement* of what God did in and through Christ. It is also *our participation* in Christ (Gal 2:20; 5:5; 6:14).

Third, an act of faith in Christ is something that characterises the manner in which Jewish and Gentile Christians live in Christ. This can be noticed in Gal 2:20, where ἐν πίστει ζῶ τῇ τοῦ υἱοῦ τοῦ θεοῦ, which should be read as objective genitive. Paul's declaration here seems to somehow parallel ἡμεῖς εἰς Χριστὸν Ἰησοῦν ἐπιστεύσαμεν in Gal 2:16. In the former, πίστις with a genitive relation τοῦ υἱοῦ τοῦ θεοῦ is associated with a Christian's present way of life as a justified person; while in the latter πιστεύω with a prepositional relation (εἰς Χριστὸν Ἰησοῦν) is associated with the means through which God justified a person. Paul relates God's act of justifying to one's believing or having faith not in order to say that God's act is contingent on one's believing-acceptance but in order to say that one's continued trusting-recognition of the revealed πίστις results in apprehending and living in accordance with the effect of God's salvific act in and through the crucified redeemer Christ.

In conclusion, while recognising that the contrast between πίστις and ἔργα exists in Galatians, the phrase ἔργα νόμου probably is not intended to be a direct contrast to πίστις Χριστοῦ. The former stands for human action, whereas the latter probably stands for Christ's action. The former refers to Jewish religious practices, whereas the latter refers to Christ's death through which God's grace is mediated for Jews and Gentiles. So why does Paul contrast ἔργα νόμου with πίστις Χριστοῦ? He contrasts them probably because some Jewish-Christian teachers have engaged in compelling Gentile Christians to observe Jewish religious practices. Paul's argument, in so doing, is that since God did not justify anyone through works of the law but through Christ's faithfulness-to-death, the legitimacy of Gentile Christians as God's people and Abraham's descendants must depend exclusively on what God did through Christ, which, of course, they should acknowledge. 'Faith/believing in Christ' denotes acknowledging Christ as someone through whose obedient death God brought about the

---

[204] Campbell (*The Quest*, 227-230) parallels Abraham's trust in God with Christ's trust in God. But this does not enable us to explain what our faith or trust in Christ means.

new creation. The phrase also represents the concepts of participating in Christ and living in him. So ἡμεῖς εἰς Χριστὸν Ἰησοῦν ἐπιστεύσαμεν and δικαιωθῶμεν ἐκ πίστεως Χριστοῦ in Gal 2:16 can respectively be maintained as anthropological and christological declarations. In a word, both are complementary expressions with differing meanings.

4.4.4. Romans 3:22 and Context

In this sub-section, as in the foregoing one, we explore whether interpreting πίστις Χριστοῦ as Christ's faithfulness-to-death is linguistically and exegetically viable. As noted above, Matlock concludes that the rendering 'faithfulness of Christ' as 'faithfulness-of-Christ-to-death' depends on the English gloss of 'faithfulness' rather than a real linguistic definition of πίστις, where πίστιςᶜ is defined as (1) 'the state of being someone on whom complete confidence can be placed' and (2) as a personal characteristic or quality, hence 'faithfulness, trustworthiness, dependability'.[205] The main textual example for this definition, as pointed out above, is πίστις θεοῦ in Rom 3:3. The latter definition clearly applies to this passage, but it does not seem to apply to πίστις Χριστοῦ, because neither of the definitions fits into the meaning where 'faithfulness of Christ' is understood as 'faithfulness-of-Christ-to-death'. This argument fatally undermines reading ἐκ πίστεως in Rom 1:17 christologically. We start with the question whether πίστις in Rom 3:22, 26 can be rendered as 'faithfulness' and discuss arguments that might support taking πίστις Χριστοῦ as Christ's faithfulness-to-death.

As indicated earlier, we agree with Matlock that it is lexically possible to translate the term in Rom 3:3 and 3:22, 26 as 'faith'. But when πίστις is used with the genitive, the sense 'faithfulness' becomes as suitable as the sense 'faith'. So, for example, ἡ πίστις ὑμῶν and διὰ τῆς ... πίστεως ὑμῶν in Rom 1:9 and 1:12 respectively can be understood as the *faithfulness* of the Roman Christians – an epexegetical reading of εἰς ὑπακοὴν πίστεως ('for obedient-faithfulness') in 1:5 further strengthens this.[206] Similarly, one could argue, πίστις with the genitive Χριστοῦ can be understood as 'faithfulness', because it would be nonsensical to talk about Christ (the Son of God) exercising faith in God.[207] Here, the sense 'faithfulness' clearly is necessitated by theological considerations. But is it also the lexical sense that is selected by the context?

---

[205] Matlock, 'Detheologizing', 11.
[206] See also Campbell, *The Quest*, 186-187.
[207] See also Moo, *Epistle*, 225; Fitzmyer, *Romans*, 345.

It has been argued that Paul's use of the πίστις Χριστοῦ construction in Rom 3:22, 26 between similar genitival constructions in 3:3 (τὴν πίστιν τοῦ θεοῦ) and 4:12, 16 (τῆς πίστεως ᾿Αβραάμ, τῷ ἐκ πίστεως ᾿Αβραάμ) shows that he may have meant that the genitives in the former should be taken as subjective. In other words, Paul uses the subjective genitive in 3:3 and 4:12, 16 to talk about the 'faithfulness of God' and the 'faithfulness of Abraham' respectively, making it unlikely that he would talk about 'faith in Jesus Christ' in 3:22, 26.[208] The parallel between τῷ ἐκ πίστεως ᾿Αβραάμ in 4:16 and τὸν ἐκ πίστεως ᾿Ιησοῦ in 3:26 seems to reinforce this view.[209] One could, of course, argue, as Matlock does, that for Paul to do such a thing may not be surprising, because the genitive relation of even an identically constructed phrase suddenly changes, for example, in Acts 9:31.[210] Sudden change in terms of genitive relations, indeed, takes place in this passage. Also, Paul may well have intended different meanings for the genitive constructions in 3:3 and 3:22. But an example such as that from Acts 9:31 cannot be found in Paul's Seven Letter Corpus. We can find phrases such as ζῆλον θεοῦ in Rom 10:2 and τῇ πίστει τοῦ εὐαγγελίου in Phil 1:27. These are clear evidence that a noun-with-genitive cannot always be subjective genitive. It is the context that should decide the relevant senses of both phrases. Elsewhere in the NT too, the meaning of a given phrase (e.g. πίστις θεοῦ) is not necessarily dependent on the way the phrase is used.[211] This provides us with the principle that a grammatical decision must be made on the basis of how a given form functions within its context. But even when we apply this principle to the πίστις of 3:3 (πίστις θεοῦ) and that of 3:22 (πίστις Χριστοῦ), a semantic shift between the two passages is not necessitated, because πίστις in both passages can still mean 'faithfulness'. This is consistent with the Hebrew

---

[208] So Kittel ('Πίστις', 424), Howard ('"Faith"', HTR 60, 460), Stowers (Rereading, 201-202), Hays ('ΠΙΣΤΙΣ', 47) and Campbell (Rhetoric, 66-67).

[209] It is interesting that τῷ ἐκ πίστεως ᾿Αβραάμ in 4:16 parallels τὸν ἐκ πίστεως ᾿Ιησοῦ in 3:26. In the latter passage, MSS D L Ψ 33 614 945 et al have the accusative ᾿Ιησοῦν, which results in reading 3:26c in terms of God justifying Jesus ἐκ πίστεως. That these manuscripts' change from the genitive to the accusative indicates that some Christian copyists in later periods (from the 7th century CE onwards) would even go so far as to say that Jesus was 'justified' by [his] πίστις (thus, 3:26c reading: 'so that [God] himself might be righteous and the one who justifies Jesus through [his] faithfulness'). From a text-critical standpoint, these manuscripts are not authoritative, because the earliest and most reliable manuscripts have the genitive ᾿Ιησοῦ. Incidentally, among modern scholars, Hanson (Studies, 51), without referring to the textual apparatus in Rom 3:26 but in relation to an explication of Rom 1:17b, argues that Jesus as the Messiah was vindicated or justified by God.

[210] Matlock, 'Detheologizing', 16.

[211] Cf. Mk 11:22; Acts 3:16a; 2 Thess 2:13; Jas 2:1; Rev 14:22. See also Dunn, Theology, 380; Matlock, 'Detheologizing', 17; Silva, 'Faith', 231.

אֱמוּנָה, which is to do with a conduct that is in accordance with אָמַת ('stability', 'reliability', 'permanence', 'faithfulness') and therefore includes 'sincerity', 'faithfulness', etc. So if it is valid to render πίστις Χριστοῦ as 'faithfulness of Christ', is it also legitimate to explain what 'faithfulness of Christ' actually means by offering the 'death of Christ' as an explanatory notion? Nowhere in his Seven Letter Corpus does Paul clearly equate πίστις with Jesus' death, but we provide four arguments in favour of the legitimacy of using the faithfulness-of-Christ-to-death as an explanatory notion for the faithfulness of Christ.

1) Since πίστις can be understood in terms of Jesus' action that emanates from a quality he possesses, πίστις Χριστοῦ can also behave like the proposed explanatory meaning. Matlock's (witting or unwitting) choice of the meaning 'trustworthiness' for lexeme^c (as he attempts to understand Louw-Nida's treatment of the πίστις/πιστεύω lexemes) explains πίστις in Rom 3:3 as God's personal characteristic or quality, but it does not actually explain his action embedded in the sense 'faithfulness'.[212] Of course, the *quality* of being faithful and an *event* which demonstrates that quality are different, but they are inextricably linked and one is not known without the other. The context of Rom 3:3 shows that when Paul talks about the faithfulness of God, he is talking mainly about his commitment to his covenant expressed through his salvific activities. If the meaning of πίστις in Rom 3:3 does not include God's action, one wonders how ἡ ἀπιστία αὐτῶν, which is contrasted with ἡ πίστις τοῦ θεοῦ in the passage, would be construed other than as the unfaithfulness of the Jews expressed in their actions with regard to matters relating to their relationship with God. In short, πίστις θεοῦ encompasses God's action. Along this line, it is legitimate to construe πίστις Χριστοῦ as Christ's faithful or obedient action, i.e. his death on the cross.

2) Paul appears to understand πίστις as obedience, which is quite evident in Rom 1:5 and 16:26 where ὑπακοὴν πίστεως can be understood epexegetically. This can be applied to the issue in question via Rom 5:19, where Jesus is presented as 'the obedient one' through whom many are constituted as righteous and where there is no reference to any human action in the form of faith or believing.[213] Although there is no reference to πίστις in this passage, Jesus' obedience points to nothing other than his death on the cross, which not only is *the* ultimate expression of his faithfulness to God but also the means through which the state of Adamic humanity that is characterised by unfaithfulness or disobedience is reversed.[214] Paul does not obviously refer to Jesus as ὁ δίκαιος in 5:19,[215]

---

[212] Matlock, 'Detheologizing', 11-12.
[213] See also Hooker, 'ΠΙΣΤΙΣ', 337.
[214] Hooker ('ΠΙΣΤΙΣ', 324) may be right in saying: '*A priori*, we may expect the Sec-

but his statement in Rom 5:19 further reflects the Servant tradition in Isa 53:11 (δικαιῶσαι δίκαιον εὖ δουλεύοντα πολλοῖς). The Servant's death is not equated with his faithfulness but his actions in the song as a whole (Isa 52:13-53:11) clearly represent his obedience to YHWH. This seems to influence Jewish traditions such as *4 Maccabees*, in which the deaths of Eleazar (6:28-29[216]) and the Seven Brothers (and their Mother) (17:21-22[217]) are good examples. The Mother of the Seven Brothers is referred to as ἡ δικαία τοῖς τέκνοις (18:7) and her seven children are also described as δίκαιοι, whose obedience to their Mother, their loyalty to the law and their faithfulness to God led them to martyrdom (15:10; 16:22; cf. 15:24; 17:22). In their faithful action, the martyrs not only became instrumental for the purification of their nation and punishment of the tyrant (17:17-22), but also they imitated Δανιὴλ ὁ δίκαιος, his three friends (16:21; cf. 18:15) and the patriarchs whose actions set a framework that one who dies for God lives to God (16:21-25; cf. *2 Macc* 7:23).[218] All this seems to support the view that Jesus' obedience-to-death probably is the same thing as his faithfulness-to-death.

3) Taking ὃν προέθετο with διὰ τῆς πίστεως and ἱλαστήριον with ἐν τῷ αἵματι αὐτοῦ in 3:25, we can render ὃν προέθετο (relative pronoun + aorist middle) with the sense of 'whom [God] set forth publicly'[219] and

---

ond Adam to be obedient, to give glory to God, and to be faithful. Moreover, what the Christian becomes depends on what Christ is; if the Christian is a son of God, it is only because Christ is Son of God (Rom 8; Gal 4); if righteous, this is dependent on Christ's righteousness (2 Cor 5:21).'

[215] It is also to be noted that Paul does not refer to Jesus as πιστός, which he does in relation to God (1 Cor 1:9; 10:13; 2 Cor 1:18; 1 Thess 5:24 [?]) and some individuals including himself (1 Cor 4:17; 7:25; Gal 3:9). But given Paul's association of πίστις with Jesus on numerous occasions, there is no question that he viewed Jesus as the Faithful *par excellence*. This is consistent with what we can find in some other NT writings, such as Hebrews where Jesus is presented as the 'pioneer and perfecter' of the πίστις (12:2; cf. 11:1-39) and the Apocalypse where he is described as ὁ μάρτυς ὁ πιστός (Rev 1:5; 3:15).

[216] It reads: 'Be merciful to your people, and let our punishment suffice for them. Make my blood their purification, and take my life in exchange for theirs.' (NRSV)

[217] It reads: 'the tyrant was punished, and the homeland purified – they having become, as it were, a ransom (ἀντίψυχον [lit. 'given for life']) for the sin of our nation. And through the blood of those devout ones and their death as an atoning sacrifice (τοῦ ἱλαστηρίου θανάτου αὐτῶν [Codex A]), divine Providence preserved Israel that previously had been mistreated.' (NRSV)

[218] Like the Servant, who will be glorified and lifted high beyond his suffering (52:13; 53:12), the martyrs will be honoured before the divine throne (17:17, 20).

[219] προέθετο (aorist middle) has been interpreted with three general senses. First, 'set forth publicly' or 'displayed' (Sanday and Headlam, *Epistle*, 87; Murray, *Epistle*, 117; Käsemann, *Commentary*, 91, 97 ['publicly set forth']; Stuhlmacher, *Letter*, 57-58 ['publicly appointed']. Second, 'purposed', 'designed': the two other uses of προτίθημι in the NT (1:13; Eph 1:9) and the two uses of the cognate noun πρόθεσις in Romans (8:28;

understand the cryptic phrase διὰ τῆς πίστεως as an abbreviation of διὰ πίστεως᾽Ιησοῦ Χριστοῦ (v 22), much as ἐκ πίστεως ᾽Ιησοῦ Χριστοῦ (e.g. Rom 3:26; Gal 2:16) can be taken as an extension of ἐκ πίστεως (e.g. Rom 1:17; Gal 3:24). This enables us to take διὰ τῆς πίστεως with ὅν προέθετο and as subjective genitive. We can then render 3:25a: 'whom God set forth publicly through *his* faithfulness as a *hilasterion* by means of his blood'.[220] According to such syntactical and translational choice, the faithfulness [of Jesus] is instrumental. Even if one accepts the view that the cryptic phrase διὰ τῆς πίστεως modifies ἱλαστήριον in 3:25, which some do,[221] it is unlikely that Paul thought that any human action played an instrumental role in the process of God setting Jesus as ἱλαστήριον, the ἔνδειξις ('evidence', 'demonstration') of the righteousness of God (3:24-25).[222]

9:11; cf. Matt 12:4; Mark 2:26; Luke 6:4; Acts 11:23; 27:13; Eph 1:11; 3:11; 2 Tim 1:9; 3:10; Heb 9:2) have the sense 'purpose' (Cranfield, *Romans*, 201; Campbell, *Rhetoric*, 134; NEB: 'God designed him'). Third, 'offered as sacrifice' (Barrett, *Epistle*, 77; GNB: 'God offered him'; Ziesler, *Letter*, 112). Although respectable cases can be made in favour of the second and third arguments, the first argument is stronger, given the terms πεφανέρωται, εἰς ἔνδειξιν, πρὸς τὴν ἔνδειξιν in the context.

[220] See also B. Longenecker, 'ΠΙΣΤΙΣ', 478-480. So what is the ultimate object of God setting forth Jesus as ἱλαστήριον, in Paul's view in 3:26? Fitzmyer (*Romans*, 353): so that God might show that 'he is upright' and 'justifies the one [who] puts faith in Jesus'. Cranfield (*Romans 1-8*, 213): 'in order that he might *be* righteous and that he might justify the person who believes in Jesus'. But in our view, God's ultimate object in this operation is that he might be 'righteous' and seen to be 'righteous' by justifying one through the faithfulness of Jesus. As Hays ('ΠΙΣΤΙΣ', 47) suggests, the justified person can be understood as 'the one who shares the faith of Jesus' (τὸν ἐκ πίστεως ᾽Ιησοῦ).

[221] In this reading, διὰ τῆς πίστεως indicates an expression of the mode in which a person shares in the expiation of sin or 'the means by which individuals appropriate the benefits of the sacrifice' (Moo, *Epistle*, 236). Some understand Jesus in this passage as the concrete manifestation of God's righteousness. Human beings appropriate to themselves the effects of that manifested divine righteousness through faith in him. Indeed, the divine righteousness is comprehended only by those who have the eyes of faith. See Fitzmyer, *Romans*, 345, 350; Hultgren, *Paul's Gospel and Mission*, 38-39, 82f.

[222] Paul uses ἔνδειξις twice in Rom 3:25-26, and twice in 2 Cor 8:24 and Phil 1:28. In 2 Corinthians and Philippians, the term is employed in relation to a certain action that serves as evidence or a sign (an act of love and an adversarial attitude respectively). But in Rom 3:25-26 it is used in relation to Jesus. This is how the syntax can be explained: εἰς ἔνδειξιν in 3:25 is taken in connection with ὅν προέθετο ὁ θεὸς ἱλαστήριον. The subject of the relative pronoun ὅν is Christ Jesus (see v 24). Thus the one who is set forth as *hilasterion* is the ἔνδειξις of God's righteousness. Such a view is almost unique in the NT, although in Acts 2:22 Jesus of Nazareth is exhibited by God to the Jews with deeds of power and, as the subsequent verses show, to exercise power (vv 25, 30, 33-36; cf. Ps 110:1). The evidence from Acts may be regarded as subsidiary, but it nevertheless supports an understanding of ἔνδειξις in relation to Jesus, who reveals or displays God's righteousness.

As argued in chapter 3 of this book, the term 'righteousness of God' does not seem to stand for human propensity consistent with God's moral standards or some abstract object given as a gift or a package received and retained so as to become one's own property. Paul could not have understood the righteousness of God in Romans (1:17; 3:5, 21-26; 10:3) apart from Christ, because only Christ can be the embodiment of God's own righteousness (cf. Rom 1:16-17 with 1 Cor 1:30; 2 Cor 5:21). This is consistent with Paul's portrayal of Christ as God's power (1 Cor 1:24), as someone who is set *with power* to exercise authority as the Son of God in his resurrection life (Rom 1:4) and as the co-sharer of divine identity and role (Rom 8:34; cf. Ps 110:1). [223] Rom 8:34, along with Rom 6:6-8, further blurs the distinction between the crucified Christ and the risen or exalted Christ. In Rom 3:25 too, it appears, Paul subsumes the crucifixion and exaltation categories under the notion that is behind the image of the ἱλαστήριον that is set forth in order to become the ἔνδειξις of the righteousness of God.[224] In short, Christ's πίστις in Rom 3:25 is inextricably linked with his death through which God verified the reality of his righteousness not only to Israel but also to the world as a whole (that in turn demonstrated God's faithfulness to the world).

Paul's ἔνδειξις in 3:25 probably expresses the same idea as πεφανέρωται in 3:21.[225] Paul does not use πεφανέρωται in 3:22. The absence of the verb does not affect the objective genitive reading, but without the verb the subjective genitive readers cannot claim that the righteousness of God has been revealed through Christ's faithfulness.[226] But the omission of

---

[223] That is to say, Paul does not view Christ as the counsel and God as the judge. Hengel (*Studies in Early Christology*, 136 and n. 41, 139), probably rightly, argues that the counsel does not stand at the right hand of the judge but at the right side of the accused, facing the judge (cf. Ps 109:6, 31; Zech 3:1).

[224] The syllogism goes: A (Jesus) is B (ἱλαστήριον); B displays C (δικαιοσύνη θεοῦ); therefore A is (the embodiment of) C. It is important to note here that Paul departs from the Pentateuchal cultic tradition in Lev 16:2f, where ἱλαστήριον is the lid on the ark of the covenant, which is sprinkled with the animal blood of the sin-offering on the Yom Kippur. He also departs from *4 Macc* 17:22, where ἱλαστήριον appears to refer to the martyrological death that at once purifies the nation of Israel and triggers judgement against the enemy of God and his people. As far as *4 Macc* 17:22 is concerned, following either the longer reading of Codex ℵ (καὶ διὰ τοῦ αἵματος τῶν εὐσεβῶν ἐκείνων καὶ τοῦ ἱλαστηρίου τοῦ θανάτου αὐτῶν ἡ θεία πρόνοια τὸν Ἰσραηλ προκακωθέντα διέσωσεν) or the shorter reading of Codex A (it does not have τοῦ before θανάτου) does not seem to make any difference to this conclusion. Note that NRSV translates the passage as follows: 'And through the blood of those devout ones and their death as an atoning sacrifice, divine Providence preserved Israel that previously had been mistreated'.

[225] See also Blackman, 'Romans 3:26b', 203-204; Campbell, *Rhetoric*, 157-159.

[226] Some subjective genitive interpreters have often pointed out that when the noun-with-genitive (διὰ πίστεως Ἰησοῦ Χριστοῦ) in Rom 3:22 is understood as an objective

πεφανέρωται in 3:22 does not mean that it is not assumed at all. For this sort of ellipsis is not unusual in Romans. In Rom 5:3, for example, Paul says ἡ θλῖψις ὑπομονὴν κατεργάζεται, but in verse 4 he says ἡ δὲ ὑπομονὴ δοκιμήν, ἡ δὲ δοκιμὴ ἐλπίδα. Although κατεργάζεται is omitted in the latter, Paul's declaration there cannot be understood without supplying the verb. Similarly, πεφανέρωται is to be supplied in 3:22. We can, therefore, take the assumed πεφανέρωται with διὰ πίστεως Ἰησοῦ Χριστοῦ (as we took ἀποκαλύπτεται with ἐκ πίστεως in Rom 1:17) and understand Paul as saying that the righteousness of God has been revealed 'through the faithfulness of Jesus Christ to all who believe [in Christ]'.[227] So while verse 21 describes the source by which the righteousness of God was witnessed (namely the law and the prophets), verse 22 could be taken as describing the means through which that divine righteousness has been revealed to those who believe. The means in question is the faithfulness-of-Christ-to-death.

In the light of Rom 3:25, it is Christ himself who is set forth as the evidence of God's righteousness that has been revealed. It thus follows that it is Christ himself who is revealed to the hearers of the gospel and reveals God. Rom 1:2-4 shows that the gospel of God, for which Paul was separated, is about the crucified and risen Christ who is now set with power as Son of God, Lord and Christ (cf. 8:33-34; 10:9-10, 16). This gospel, promised in the prophetic writings περὶ τοῦ υἱοῦ [θεοῦ] (Rom 1:2-3), enables Jews and Gentiles to gain the knowledge and understanding of Christ.[228] Rom 15:21 neatly encapsulates this: 'those who have never been told about him (περὶ αὐτοῦ) shall *see* (ὄψονται), and those who have never heard shall *understand* (συνήσουσιν)'.[229] Thus, in Rom 3:21-22 Paul seems

---

genitive ('through faith in Jesus Christ'), the resulting reading positions εἰς πάντας τοὺς πιστεύοντας ('to all who believe') tautologously and meaninglessly. But since δικαιοσύνη θεοῦ can be qualified by διὰ πίστεως Ἰησοῦ Χριστοῦ, the objective genitive reading can work perfectly well. It can be put: what is revealed to all those who believe [in Christ or God] is righteousness that is by faith in Jesus Christ.

[227] See also Keck, "'Jesus'", 456.

[228] Cranfield, *Romans 9-16*, 765; Fitzmyer, *Romans*, 716; Stuhlmacher, *Letter*, 238.

[229] Paul can, therefore, claim that his gospel is not of human origin but received δι' ἀποκαλύψεως Ἰησοῦ Χριστοῦ (Gal 1:11-12). The content of this apocalypse is not explained but, as Stuhlmacher suggests, it may have to do with Paul's encounter with Christ, as expressed in Gal 1:13-17, which, to an extent, parallels Rom 1:2-4. Stuhlmacher ('Gospel', 154) writes: 'Its essential content was the appearance of Jesus as 'Son of God'. On the basis of Rom 1:3; 1 Cor 9:1; and Phil 2:9ff. one must understand that expression as follows: In his Damascus vision Paul saw Christ exalted to the right hand of God (in accordance with Ps 110:1) and installed as Son of God in the position of "Lord". This vision turned the persecutor of the Church and champion of the law into an apostle and the preacher of the gospel among the Gentiles. Hence the revelation of Christ before the walls of Damascus effected in Paul's life a turning away from his Pharisaic

to want to show that when Jews and Gentiles believingly accept the gospel
events represented in πίστις Χριστοῦ (Christ's faithful death), they come
to comprehend that the righteousness of God is no longer a hidden reality.[230] We now come to our fourth and final argument.

4) If Paul understood Christ's death in terms of his faithfulness, such an
understanding would not be peculiar to him in the first century Christian
world. For two reasons: first, as discussed in the second chapter of this
book, the writer of Hebrews presents Jesus as the pioneer and perfector of
πίστις in 12:1-2. The writer does that by way of comparing his faithful-
ness-unto-the-cross with the faithfulness of Abel and other biblical heroes
and heroines. He also does that by way of showing that Jesus is the prime
and superior model of faithfulness and singular means of attaining the
promise (cf. 10:36 with 11:39). Second, at the beginning of his Apocalypse, John describes Jesus as ὁ μάρτυς ὁ πιστός, ὁ πρωτότοκος τῶν
νεκρῶν καὶ ὁ ἄρχων τῶν βασιλέων τῆς γῆς (Rev 1:5). Almost a similar
expression can be observed in 3:15, where Jesus is called ὁ μάρτυς ὁ
πιστὸς καὶ ἀληθινός ἡ ἀρχὴ τῆς κτίσεως τοῦ θεοῦ. For John, Jesus the
martyr is Jesus the faithful. Like the author of Hebrews, John sees the
faithfulness of Jesus as the same thing as his faithfulness-to-death.

In conclusion, our discussions above showed two things. First, a lexical
definition of πίστις[c] (according to Louw-Nida) should not be limited to a
personal quality or characteristic, because such senses as 'faithfulness' and
'dependability' in the lexeme obviously reflect actions that characterise the
referent of πίστις, which, in the case of Rom 3:3 and 3:22, 26 are God and
Christ respectively. Second, there is sufficient evidence that supports understanding Christ's faithfulness in terms of Christ's faithful death. If

---

zeal for the law and a turning to the Christ who revealed himself.' See also Kim (*Origin*,
59-60) who advocates a similar perspective.

[230] Such a view holds justification and Christ together in the sense that the means of
justification is what Christ did for us. The objective genitive reading, however, separates
justification from Christ because justification is dependent on what humans do, although
the latter is necessary. Matlock ('Detheologizing', 22) doubts that Paul sees that emphasis on 'justification by faith in Christ' separates Christ from justification. Lohse (*Der
Brief*, 131) also argues that πίστις Ἰησοῦ Χριστοῦ in Rom 3:22 is 'der Glaube εἰς
Χριστόν'. But Wallis (*Faith*, 75), probably rightly, complains that the objective genitive
reading of πίστις Χριστοῦ not only makes 'human faith' something that occasions the
revelation of God's salvific power, it also tends to deny the significance of the initial
revelation of this power. We should add here that what was believed to be hidden in the
Second Temple period for Paul and any thinking Second Temple Jew would have been
the righteousness of God as something that represents and expresses God's activity and
the presence of his salvific power in the world. If this is valid, to suggest that faith in
Christ is instrumental for such a revelation is tantamount to saying that God's saving
initiative and activity is contingent on human act of faith, which appears to be unPauline,
to say the least.

valid, this could be said in relation to the purpose of our study: as Rom 1:17 anticipates and is developed in 3:21-26 and ἐκ πίστεως in the former probably is an abbreviation of διὰ πίστεως Χριστοῦ or ἐκ πίστεως Χριστοῦ in the latter, Paul in both Rom 1:17 and 3:22 is probably talking about the revelation of the righteousness of God *through Christ's faithfulness* that was expressed in his death on the cross.[231]

4.4.5. The Abraham Argument in Romans 4

One of the main arguments against a christological interpretation of ἐκ πίστεως in Rom 1:17 and the subjective genitive interpretation of πίστις Χριστοῦ in Rom 3:21-26 is derived from Romans 4. In this section, we will first consider the arguments for and against creating a correlation between Christ's πίστις and Abraham's πίστις. We will then ask if an understanding of πίστις Χριστοῦ in 3:21-26 (an extension of ἐκ πίστεως in Rom 1:17) as the faithful death of Christ might not help us explain Paul's argument in Romans 4.

Against correlating Abraham's πίστις with Christ's, it is said that since Abraham is presented as a model for Christians having πίστις and becoming righteous and that Abraham's faith serves as a witness to 'faith in Christ' (πίστις Χριστοῦ) in Rom 3:21-26, pointing to the faithfulness of Christ as a means of justification is unwarranted.[232] That πίστις Χριστοῦ is not employed in Rom 4 and that Paul does not parallel Christ with Abraham but rather regards him as the seed of Abraham (Rom 4:13f; Gal 3:16) support this. Abraham's faith, therefore, is to be taken as 'a typological

---

[231] The statement that the faithful death of Jesus is the means through which the righteousness of God, proclaimed in the gospel, has been revealed to all who believe can mean three things. 1) It can mean that Jesus' death occasioned revelation in the sense that one epistemologically perceives upon the proclamation of the gospel what has already been revealed through Jesus' faithful death. 2) The statement can also mean that as Paul proclaims his gospel to his hearers the resulting perception or knowledge enables them to understand that the whole point of Jesus' death and resurrection was so that God's eschatological saving power (δικαιοσύνη θεοῦ) may become a reality in the world and, consequently, God may be seen as righteous in his judgement and salvation. 3) The statement can further mean that Paul declares that God's saving activity/power has been revealed through the faithful death of Jesus because he (Paul) has a concept of the death of Jesus as an ongoing event (Rom 6:3-6; cf. Gal 2:19; 6:14). All these meanings can complement one another and strengthen the idea that the faithful death of Jesus is instrumental for the revelation of δικαιοσύνη θεοῦ to those who believe.

[232] But see Watson who, in his earlier work (*Paul, Judaism and the Gentiles*, 135-142), argues that Paul in Rom 4 is attacking two views held in Judaism: that Abraham is the original recipient of God's covenant promises and a model of obedience. This, in other words, means that it would be natural for Paul to attack the perspectives that Abraham is *the* exemplar of πίστις for Christians and that their commitment to following in his footsteps must be symbolised by circumcision.

forbear of Christian faith' that is christologically grounded in the sense of not identifying Abrahamic faith as faith in Christ but the 'resurrection-content' of Abraham's faith being witness to Paul's understanding of faith in Romans 3 in particular.[233] Furthermore, the parallel between οἱ πιστεύοντες and Abraham in Rom 4:24 should most naturally be taken as suggesting that the correlation is exclusively between Abraham and Christians. Although the faith of the former is said to be directed not towards Jesus but towards the God who raised Jesus, the Abraham-Christian correlation can still be valid on the basis that, as Abraham trusted in a life-giving God, so Christians trust in a God who raised Jesus from the dead. Paul's midrashic interpretation, in this case, aims to transpose the idea that existed within Judaism about Abraham's faith being the type of all who believe in God (e.g. *Gen Rab* 40:8: 'All that is recorded of Abraham is repeated in the history of his children') to his Christian thinking. In short, since Paul seems to establish a correlation between Abraham's faith and Christian faith in Rom 4, Abraham's faith is to be understood as a typological precursor of Christian faith.

This argument is held by the majority of Pauline scholars, but there are some who would argue against stressing too much the view that Abraham is the definitive *exemplum* of the mode by which one becomes a Christian.[234] They give at least three reasons. First, understanding Abraham as the definitive *exemplum* of being a Christian could potentially undermine the Pauline notion that Abraham's fatherhood is as equally significant to the uncircumcision or those who have his kind of πίστις in his pre-circumcision life as it is to the circumcision or those who are faithful to the law (4:12-16; cf. 3:1-2). Paul continued to believe, albeit paradoxically, that Abraham was the father of Jews (Christian and non-Christian) and Gentiles (Christian). To make a parallelism between the righteousness that was reckoned to Abraham on the basis of his 'faith' and the 'justification' that is 'absolutely' dependent on 'faith' for believers can lead to a definition of Judaism and Christianity strictly in terms of Abraham. This can result in the potential elimination of the law for the Jews and the proclamation of the gospel for the Gentiles.[235]

---

[233] Gathercole, 'Faith', 163-165.

[234] See, for example, Stowers, 'ΕΚ ΠΙΣΤΕΩΣ', 672-673; Campbell, 'Presuppositions', 718; Hays, 'Reconsideration', 97-98.

[235] Campbell ('Presuppositions', 718) puts his argument as follows: if one takes Abraham as the definitive example of the pious person, one must also define Judaism (especially through the OT) and Christianity 'in terms of him, and of him alone. Not only is the law eliminated for Jews then, but the proclamation of the gospel and the coming of Christ are, for precisely the same reasons, eliminated for Christians – this is of course the automatic corollary of taking a pre-Christian as a definitive paradigm of Christianity'.

Second, the view in question seems to underemphasise the work of Christ and overemphasise the role of human faith when it comes to the question as to how one becomes a Christian. One could even allege that such a view originates from the Law-Grace antithesis that perhaps wrongly attributes the effectiveness of God's saving grace to one's cognitive decision upon hearing the gospel message or one's intellectual assent to a set of doctrinal propositions. This assent or decision is tantamount to a meritorious act without which justification is not possible. What leads to justification or salvation is not a cognitive decision, but as Campbell, for example, would argue a *trust* like that which is described in 4:17 and which no one, apart from Christ, can have.[236]

Third, Hays argues that Paul's adaptation of the Abraham story in Romans 4 suggests that Abraham's faith is to be understood primarily as a scriptural precedent about the faithfulness of a single figure chosen by God through whom God's blessing is brought to many. For Hays, Abraham is someone whose faithfulness typologically foreshadows or prefigures Christ's faithfulness.[237] That Paul somehow saw 'the faithfulness of Abraham' in a similar light to 'the faithfulness of Jesus' shows that (cf. 4:16 with 3:26).[238] Also, the locus of Paul's interpretation of Gen 15:6 in verse

---

[236] Campbell ('Presuppositions', 718) asks rhetorical questions on the basis of 4:17: 'Who apart from Christ can claim to have trust like this? (Put slightly differently: If this is what we must do to be saved, then who will be?)'. Campbell seems to understand 'trust' not merely as one's confidence in or reliance on God, but also as one's firmness in fidelity to God on the basis of his reliability. He recognises that πίστις and πιστεύω are used interchangeably in Romans 4 (cf. v 3 with vv 5 and 9) and 10:1-11, where they carry the sense of 'faith', 'believe' or 'trust'. But he argues that when Paul speaks of basal Christian beliefs such as Christ's resurrection and Christian resurrection, he speaks not only of believing something to be true but also of trusting God who raised Jesus from the dead. See also his *Quest*, 183-188.

[237] Hays ('Reconsideration', 97-98) expounds this as follows: 'Abraham's faith/obedience ... ought to be understood not primarily as a paradigm for the faith of Christian believers but first of all as a prefiguration of the faith of Jesus Christ (cf. Rom. 3:22), whose faith/obedience now has vicarious soteriological consequences for those who know him as Lord. Broadly speaking, then, the relevance of Paul's appeal to the story of Abraham would lie in the fact that he finds there a precedent within Scripture for the idea that the faithfulness of a single divinely-chosen protagonist can bring God's blessing upon 'many' whose destiny is figured forth in that protagonist's action. In this respect, Abraham serves for Paul not just as an exemplar of Christian believing but also as a typological foreshadowing of Christ, the 'one man' (Rom 5:19) through whose obedience 'the many were constituted as righteous'. See also his 'ΠΙΣΤΙΣ', 47-48; Campbell, 'Presuppositions', 718.

[238] Such an understanding does not necessarily preclude the patriarch being an exemplar of a Christian. So Hays ('Reconsideration', 95) says, Paul could be understood as saying either '[b]ecause we participate in the blessing pronounced upon him we mirror his faith' or 'because our faith parallels his, we may be said to be his seed'.

17 coupled with the theological importance of Jesus' death and resurrection in verse 24 seems to suggest a corollary between the πίστις of the figure of Abraham and that of Christ. In both verses, God's action is unsolicited. In 4:25, Christian justification (δικαίωσις) too is entirely dependent on God's unsolicited initiative through Christ.[239]

From what we have seen so far, there are two competing views. 1) Abraham's πίστις should be understood to serve as a witness to 'faith in Christ'. 2) Abraham's πίστις is to be construed as a typological precursor of Christ's faithfulness. The former case is easier to argue than the latter, but we would argue that establishing a correlation between Christian faith and Abraham's faith or Abraham's faithfulness and Christ's faithfulness is not Paul's primary concern in Rom 4. Paul's concern in Rom 4 as a whole, it seems, is to *substantiate his argument in 3:30* where he says that the one God justifies the circumcision ἐκ πίστεως and the uncircumcision διὰ τῆς πίστεως. This leads him to the question as to whether the law is abolished or confirmed διὰ τῆς πίστεως (3:31). By way of arguing that the latter is the case, Paul says that Abraham himself was not 'justified' ἐξ ἔργων and, therefore, he had nothing to boast about before God (4:2). Paul uses Gen 15:6 as his evidence here (v 3), which he explains further in the following verses. In doing all this, in our view, *Paul's chief concern is to show why Gentile Christians should be regarded as legitimate members of the new community of Abraham's descendants without circumcision.*

Some argue that circumcision was seemingly a non-issue in Rome because either Gentile Christians adopted it in keeping with existing synagogue principles laid down for Gentile proselytes, or Jewish Christians judged it unnecessary to impose it on the former.[240] But since Abraham as an *exemplum* of πίστις was an existing Judeo-Christian theologoumenon in the Second Temple period (e.g. *Sir* 44:19-21; 1 Macc 2:50-52; Heb 11:8-19 and Js 2:20-24), circumcision would probably have featured in the debates and discussions in Rome over the ways in which the new Christian movement could be related to the Jewish socio-religious milieu and thought-world. Some in Rome would also have presented Abraham as a classic model whose circumcision symbolised his covenant with God and argued that Gentile Christians must also show that they are part of the covenant through circumcision. Paul's view that real circumcision was a matter of the heart rather than the flesh of the foreskin (Rom 2:29) would not be palatable to these people. Such a claim emanates from his conviction that both Jews and Gentiles are God's people and Abraham's descendants on the basis of God's salvific act through Christ. In addition to this, to speak against Gentile circumcision in particular is evangelistically ex-

---

[239] See also Hays, 'ΠΙΣΤΙΣ', 48; Campbell, 'Presuppositions', 718.

[240] For this theory and related issues, see Wedderburn, *Reasons*, 60-61.

pedient, because if circumcision is ruled out for Gentile converts the excruciating physical pain it involved would not hinder other Gentiles from showing enthusiasm for the gospel.

Those people in Rome who were critical of Paul's position would, in the main, have been Jewish Christians.[241] How would they have come to know about Paul's stance on Jewish nomistic practices *vis-à-vis* Gentile Christians? We can suppose that they were aware of Paul's position in the Jerusalem conference (Acts 15) and his confrontation with Peter and others in Antioch (Gal 2) and had gone to Rome ahead of the arrival of the letter of Romans and its sender.[242] Furthermore, as Aquila, Prisca and Epaenetus, who were influenced by Paul's perspective, had returned to Rome (Rom 16:3-5),[243] it is likely that they would have challenged any

---

[241] We have some evidence within the letter to support the existence of such people. 1) 2:1-16 shows that Paul may have been reflecting real circumstances amongst his readers by using a Jewish conversation partner who knows and teaches the law and who can be comparable to the ones accused of temple robbery that probably took place in 19 CE (cf. Josephus: *Ant* 18:81-84). 2) We cannot be certain about the referents of τινες in 3:8, but it is reasonable to assume that the term refers to certain individuals who were critical of Paul's teaching. 3) 7:1 suggests that Paul had some knowledge of the sort of people his readers were made up of. His parenthetical expression γινώσκουσιν γὰρ νόμον λαλῶ in particular appears to describe some Christians who were well-versed in the teachings of the law. 4) In 13:1-7, Paul could be reflecting on the ways in which certain individuals – who perhaps had close links both to the synagogues and the house-churches, were in charge of the temple tax, and may have been socially prominent – handled issues in relation to tax payment and the recognition of the authority of government officials. 5) 14:1-15:13 clearly shows that Paul knew about differences of opinion amongst his readers in Rome over Jewish dietary and calendrical regulations. 6) If chapter 16 is addressed to the readership in Rome, which, we think it is (see the note below), vv 17-18 indicate that Paul urges his readers to reject those who cause 'dissensions' or 'doubts', because they serve their own appetites (or bellies) rather than the Lord Christ.

[242] Ambrosiaster supposes that Paul's critics, who are implied in 3:8 and 16:17-18, as they are throughout the letter, *are already in Rome*. It is worth noting parts of his comments on 3:8 and 16:17-18. 3:8: '...The matter was raised by opponents ... Paul calls this blasphemy and rejects it as a bad interpretation of God's teaching. Faith is not meant to encourage people to sin by preaching that God will ultimately be vindicated. Rather, it gives sinners a remedy so that having recovered their health they may live under the law of God and not sin again' (*CSEL* 81:103, 105). 16:17-18: 'They were forcing believers to become Jews and thereby making the benefits of God worthless. ... They compiled long genealogies and used them to support their teaching by which they were deceiving the hearts of the simple' (*CSEL* 81:489). The latter appears to betray the influence of 1 Timothy or some known tradition same as that reflected in the epistle. See also Campbell ('Gospel', 321-331), who argues that Paul's critics may have already been in Rome. For a brief analysis of Campbell's thesis, see Miller, *The Obedience of Faith, the Eschatological People of God, and the Purpose of Romans*, 11-12. Miller criticises Campbell for failing to show how his thesis fits into 12:1-15:13.

[243] Some have argued that Rom 16 is addressed to the church in Ephesus, but this theory is generally rejected. For further discussion, see Wedderburn, *Reasons*, 11-21.

ethnocentric role that circumcision was afforded. That, consequently, would have made circumcision as controversial as calendrical and dietary issues (Rom14:1-15:13).[244]

So how does Paul in Rom 4 argue against his critics who may have insisted that Gentile Christians must be circumcised in order to symbolise their legitimacy as members of the people of God and therefore heirs to the promise given to Abraham? Through two things: first, Abraham's believing-acceptance of the divine word of promise was reckoned to him as righteousness before his circumcision. He argues this case in 4:1-12 and drives his point home in verse 12 by saying that Abraham's fatherhood is not limited to those who are from the circumcision (ἐκ περιτομῆς), but it also extends to those ἐν ἀκροβυστίᾳ who walk in the footsteps of the πίστις of Abraham. Second, in verses 13-22 Paul argues that Abraham's continued trust and faithfulness *until* and *after* his circumcision is not presented as a precondition for receiving the promised heir, because that was dependent on *God's ability to bring life out of the dead or non-existent*.[245] In verse 16 again, he divides Abraham's seed into two camps: those who are ἐκ τοῦ νόμου and those who are ἐκ πίστεως 'Αβραάμ. By using the μόνον here, he makes the point that the promise is guaranteed not only to the Jews but also to those Gentiles who have the kind of πίστις that Abraham had before and after his circumcision (cf. 3:30). But Paul's argument in verses 13-22 in the main reflects Gen 17, where circumcision, as *the* key symbolising factor of the covenant between God and Abraham, preceded the fulfilment of God's promise (i.e. the birth of Isaac). So we can safely assume that Paul's critics in Rome would have pointed out that before the promise materialised for Abraham, circumcision took place as the sign of

---

[244] On the weak-strong argument, see Reasoner, *The Strong and the Weak: Rom 14:1-15:13 in Context*, 5-20. Who were the weak? Different answers can be offered: a literary construct based on the Corinthian situation (1 Cor 8), a group of Jewish Christians, Gentile Christians, Jewish and Gentile Christians, or practising Jews outside the house-churches. The 'weak' could stand for a mixed audience if before the arrival of the gospel in Rome and Claudian expulsion there were some Gentiles who had already been attached to synagogues. These people could see the necessity of combining the observance of Jewish elements with following Christ after their acceptance of the gospel. So Wedderburn (*Reasons*, 60). Dunn (*Romans 1-8*, xlix) also argues that even before the imperial banishment in the late 40s there may have been some God-fearing or God-worshipping Gentiles.

[245] Paul seems to take the sequence of events in Abraham's life literally and seriously: at over the age of 75 Abraham was promised an heir and he believed the Lord with regard to that promise (Gen 15:1-16; cf. 12:1-4); at the age of 85 he was given Hagar as another wife (16:3); at the age of 86 Ishmael was born (16:15-16); at the age of 99 Abraham and his male family members were circumcised (17:24-25); and at the age of 100 Sarah gave birth to Isaac, who was circumcised when he was eight days old (21:1-5).

the covenant between Abraham and God (Gen 17:9-14, 23-27). Those who become the people of God in accordance with this covenant must then be circumcised, because, as Watson rightly says, the foreskin is 'the signifier of that which is outside the covenant'.[246] The person whose foreskin is not destroyed will be destroyed himself on the grounds of breaking the covenant. According to Gen 17, the rite of circumcision is presented in such a way that 'the flesh of the foreskin' is something that 'must be surrendered as a vicarious sacrifice for the well-being of the rest of the body'.[247] Circumcision is not an ordinary rite and, in Paul's view, it remains significant for the Jews (Rom 3:1-2). Then, how can the Gentile Christians get away without fulfilling this rite?

Probably for two things: first, neither Abraham's standing before God as a righteous person nor his reception of the promise that was to ensure his universal fatherhood depended on the destruction of the flesh of the foreskin but on God's unsolicited initiative based on grace and his divine power to fulfil the promise (4:16-17). God's initiative accompanied with a word of promise elicited Abraham's believing-response and his continuing trust or faithfulness for 24 years. Even more crucially, second, Christ's death (rather than circumcision) is the means through which God establishes Jewish as well as Gentile Christians as members of his new community. Subsequent to arguing his case by using Abraham's narrative in Gen 17 in the run up to the birth of Isaac in an extremely selective and compressed manner, Paul goes back to Gen 15:6 in Rom 4:22. The reason for going back to Gen 15:6, we would argue, is because of the analogy he is about to draw in verse 24 between Abraham's faith in God who brings life *ex nihilo* and Christians' faith in God who raised Jesus from the dead.[248] In verse 25, Paul stresses that the transgression of Christians has been dealt with by Jesus' death and their justification has been achieved through his resurrection.[249] Their change of identity from being sinful pagans to being

---

[246] Watson, *Paul*, 213.

[247] Watson, *Paul*, 213.

[248] See also Barrett, *Romans*, 99; Gathercole, 'Faith', 162-163; Watson, *Paul*, 217.

[249] The christological formula in 4:25 (ὃς παρεδόθη διὰ τὰ παραπτώματα ἡμῶν καὶ ἠγέρθη διὰ τὴν δικαίωσιν ἡμῶν) is likely to be a confessional fragment based on Isa 53:11 (יַצְדִּיק צַדִּיק עַבְדִּי לָרַבִּים, δικαιῶσαι δίκαιον εὖ δουλεύοντα πολλοῖς). The Servant tradition provides Paul with a framework as he attempts to express the significance of Jesus' action for 'our' δικαίωσις. The way in which we understand the role of the Deutero-Isaianic Servant figure is important for understanding Jesus' role. Scholars hold diverse but interrelated views. Hooker (*Jesus and the Servant: The Influence of the Servant Concept of Deutero-Isaiah in the New Testament*, 48ff) understands it in terms of the accomplishment of Israel's mission as 'a light to the nations' through her suffering; Orlinsky ('The So-Called "Servant of the Lord" and "Suffering Servant" in Second Isaiah', in Orlinsky *et al*, *Studies on the Second Part of the Book of Isaiah*, 53ff) in terms of an unpopular mission of 'the prophet' that benefited the people; and Williams (*Jesus'*

justified people is based on God's act through Christ. For it is the death of
Christ, rather than circumcision, that achieves and signifies the state of
being the people of God and becoming descendants of Abraham.

The term παρεδόθη in verse 25 underscores the idea of Christ being
given over to death by God.[250] A few verses later, Paul says that Christ
died ὑπὲρ ἀσεβῶν while we were still weak (5:6) and Christ died ὑπὲρ
ἡμῶν while we were still sinners (5:8b). If Christ's death is instrumental
for our present justification, Christ's resurrection life is instrumental for
our eschatological salvation (5:9-10). God gave Christ over to death to deal
with that which signified Jews and Gentiles as those who were outside the
covenant and under the wrath of God (i.e. sin) and he raised Christ from
the dead to deal with that which would prevent them from acquiring the
resurrection life (i.e. death). So the faith of the Roman Christians is an expression of their believing-acceptance and acknowledgement of that divine
action. Abraham's faith too was his acknowledgement of God's word of
promise and God's ability to fulfil his promise of universal fatherhood
through his offspring.[251]

In conclusion, Paul in Rom 4 is not mainly concerned with a correlation
between Abraham's believing-acceptance of the divine word of promise
and people's believing-acceptance of the gospel message. His main concern is to answer the question as to why Gentile Christians should be considered as legitimate children of Abraham without circumcision, so the issue lies in the significance of circumcision for Gentile Christians *vis-à-vis*

Death as Saving Event: The Background and Origin of a Concept, 102ff) in terms of a
vicarious expiatory suffering of a righteous figure for the sins of his fellows.

[250] Indeed, in the light of Rom 8:32 ([ὁ θεὸς] ... ὑπὲρ ἡμῶν πάντων παρέδωκεν
αὐτόν), the act of giving over in the verb παραδίδωμι can be attributed to God – the conjunction between παρεδόθη and τὰ παραπτώματα ἡμῶν again invokes καὶ διὰ τὰς
ἁμαρτίας αὐτῶν παρεδόθη in Isa 53:6 (cf. v 12). Elsewhere in the NT, particularly the
Gospels, παραδίδωμι is used with reference to Judas delivering Jesus to the representa-
tives of the chief priests, Sanhedrin to Pilate, and Pilate to the soldiers (Matt 27:2, 3; Mk
14:44; 15:1, 10; Luke 23:25; 24:7, 20). See also Cranfield, *Romans 1-8*, 251;
Stuhlmacher, *Letter*, 75; Hays, 'Reconsideration', 93.

[251] Watson (*Paul*, 218), probably rightly, says: 'Abraham's faith, then, is nothing
other than his acknowledgment of a divine address in which God commits himself un-
conditionally to future action on his behalf, with the intention that he should henceforth
live in the light of that assured future'. Along this line, πίστις in Rom 5:1 can be taken as
instrumental not so much for God's act of justifying those believing Jews and Gentiles as
for believers' initial and on-going knowledge of God's act through Christ. Dunn (*Romans
1-8*, 246) too argues that πίστις here denotes a person's initial act of conversion or commitment which is not to be separated from 'the *continued* act of believing'. Stuhlmacher
(*Letter*, 77) also argues that πίστις is to be understood as '*fides ex auditu*, that is, faith
that grows out of the obedient hearing of the message in which Jesus is proclaimed as the
savior and Lord of the world'.

God's saving action through Christ. Paul's argument seems to us to be that Gentile Chrisitians do not need to be circumcised, because their legitimacy as members of God's chosen people (the descendants of Abraham) has been ensured not through the destruction of the flesh of the foreskin, but rather through the death of Christ (the ultimate expression of his faithfulness to God) and the life-giving ability of God.

6. Conclusions

In this chapter, we set out to answer the question as to whether ἐκ πίστεως in Rom 1:17 refers to human faith or Christ's faithfulness. From our discussion of the textual issues, we noticed that this question could not be answered in a straightforward manner. The reason for this is that Paul does not follow the Hebrew reading and add αὐτοῦ after ἐκ πίστεως; nor does he add the pronoun μου after ὁ δίκαιος or ἐκ πίστεως, as in the minority or majority LXX variations respectively. In fact, the absence of the pronoun opens up the possibility of interpreting ἐκ πίστεως not only anthropologically and/or christologically, but also theocentrically/covenantally. We ruled out the latter reading on the grounds of exegetical implausibility and procedural incoherence and focussed our discussion on the former two interpretative options.

On the basis of the priority of the date of Galatians over that of Romans, we started our attempt to answer the question with an exegesis of Gal 3:11. Although this passage does not enable us to determine whether ἐκ πίστεως is used anthropologically or christologically, it provides a good case for arguing that ἐκ πίστεως expresses what humans do and therefore stands for human faith as against human deeds. But this does not settle the issue for at least three reasons. First, the traditional understanding of ἔργα νόμου and ἐκ πίστεως is based on a probably mistaken view that the two phrases are *always* used in direct contrast to one another and that ἔργα νόμου, which stand for Jewish nomistic practices including circumcision, were held by Judaism and Paul's Jewish-Christian critics as a means through which Jews are declared righteous. We will come back to this below. Second, as ἐκ πίστεως most probably is a short form for ἐκ/διὰ πίστεως Ἰησοῦ Χριστοῦ, any decision regarding the prepositional phrase in the Galatians citation must depend on the interpretation we accept for the πίστις Χριστοῦ construction. Third, Paul, in Gal 3:24, hypostatises πίστις and seems to depict it as something that represents Christ. So, one's understanding of the referent of ἐκ πίστεως must include wider considerations of the πίστις debate in Romans and Galatians.

The issue is not made any easier in Rom 1:17. The facts that Paul uses the δικαιοσύνη θεοῦ language in relation to ἐκ πίστεως, that there is no contextual signal that implicitly or explicitly suggests a faith-works antithesis in the Romans citation and that Paul uses the cryptic double preposition ἐκ πίστεως εἰς πίστιν in the first half of Rom 1:17 make the whole issue far more complex than in Gal 3:11. But one thing our discussion showed was that the syntax of Rom 1:17a suggests that ἐκ πίστεως probably is the means through which the righteousness of God as God's eschatological saving power and presence has been revealed and εἰς πίστιν stands for the 'faith'/'trust' that divine righteousness achieves for the Jew and Greek (Rom 1:16). We could not, however, decide whether the subject of ἐκ πίστεως is Christ or a human person. As Paul seems to depict ἐκ πίστεως in Rom 1:17 as an abbreviation of διὰ πίστεως 'Ιησοῦ Χριστοῦ (Rom 3:22) and ἐκ πίστεως 'Ιησοῦ (3:26), our decision must take into account the meaning of the πίστις Χριστοῦ construction.

But before that, we considered the use of ἐκ πίστεως in Rom 9:30-10:13. Our discussion showed basically two things. First, ἐκ πίστεως in 9:30-32 is used to express human faith/believing in Christ. The error of the referents of 'Israel' (probably non-Christian Jews) is to focus on works to the exclusion of this faith/believing. This error has its origin in their ignorance that the righteousness of God as God's saving power has been made known in and through Christ. Second, the πίστις in the personified ἡ ἐκ πίστεως δικαιοσύνη in 10:6 could be understood to refer to Christ's faithful act. This reading does not seem to cohere with the reading of δικαιοσύνην τὴν ἐκ πίστεως in 9:30, where ἐκ πίστεως probably stands for faith in Christ. And yet, given the overwhelming christological elements in 10:4-10, the anthropological meaning of ἐκ πίστεως in 9:30-32 could be understood as complementary to the christological meaning of the same phrase in 10:6 and *vise versa*. But any decision here should be consistent with the meaning of ἐκ πίστεως in relation to πίστις Χριστοῦ.

When we considered the πίστις Χριστοῦ debate, our chief concern was not to resolve the existing disagreements over the grammatical question as to whether the phrase is objective or subjective genitive (although we paid some attention to that), but to determine whether an anthropological ('faith in Christ') or christological ('faithfulness of Christ', i.e. 'Christ's faithfulness-to-death') interpretation suits Paul's use of πίστις Χριστοῦ particularly in Gal 2:16 and 3:22. We could then decide on the suitability of either of the readings to ἐκ πίστεως in Rom 1:17 (and Gal 3:11).

The exegetical and linguistic viability of the christological meaning of πίστις Χριστοῦ has been questioned mainly on the grounds that πίστις and πιστεύω share a common meaning ('faith', 'trust') and that Paul sets ἐκ πίστεως Χριστοῦ against ἔργα νόμου in Galatians and Romans. This, ac-

cording to anthropological interpreters, is reinforced by the parallel between πίστις Χριστοῦ and ἡμεῖς εἰς Χριστὸν ᾽Ιησοῦν ἐπιστεύσαμεν in Gal
2:16. Thus the substantive πίστις, even when it is used with a genitive relation, should be understood as having the same sense as the verb. The
central argument is that πίστις Χριστοῦ in Gal 2:16 and Rom 3:22 means
'faith in Christ'. On this basis, it is argued that Paul contrasts faith in
Christ with works of the law in order to present the former as the correct
means of justification. This argument is based on the hypothesis that Paul's
Jewish-Christian critics regarded observing works of the law as a means
through which people are declared righteous (So Westerholm).

Our investigation showed that there are places in Romans and Galatians
where πίστις and πιστεύω indeed share a common meaning, 'have faith,
believe' (e.g. Rom 4:5, 9; Gal 3:6, 7). But there are also instances where
πίστις could mean 'faithfulness' (e.g. Rom 1:5, 8, 12; 16:26; 2 Cor 5:7; 1
Thess 1:3, 8; 3:2, 6; 5:8). So while Paul has the idea of 'faith in Christ', for
example, in Gal 2:16 (ἡμεῖς εἰς Χριστὸν ᾽Ιησοῦν ἐπιστεύσαμεν) and Rom
9:30-32, and possibly in Gal 3:22 (τοῖς πιστεύουσιν) and Rom 3:22 (εἰς
πάντας τοὺς πιστεύοντας), πίστις Χριστοῦ in such passages as Gal 2:16
and Rom 3:22 should be understood along the same line as πίστις θεοῦ in
Rom 3:3 (cf. 3:26; 4:16). That is, as πίστις θεοῦ means 'faithfulness of
God', so also πίστις Χριστοῦ probably means 'faithfulness of Christ'. But
no knowledge about God's quality of being faithful would be possible
without an event which demonstrates that quality. Similarly, we cannot
know about Christ's quality of being faithful without his death on the
cross, which is the demonstration of his ultimate faithfulness to God.
'Faithfulness of Christ' is Christ's obedient death (Rom 3:25; 5:19; cf. 1:5;
16:26). To be sure, Paul does not clearly equate πίστις with Jesus' death
anywhere in his Seven Letter Corpus, but for him the Christ through whom
people are justified or have received the blessings of Abraham (Gal 2:17;
3:14; Rom 3:24) is the Son of God who loved them and gave himself for
them (Gal 2:20; Rom 4:25; 5:6). So it is proper to deduce that justification
through the faithfulness of Christ means the same thing as justification
through Christ's faithfulness-to-death. On this basis, we adopted a *via
media* approach for reading Gal 2:16, where πίστις Χριστοῦ is read with a
christological meaning and the obvious ἡμεῖς εἰς Χριστὸν ᾽Ιησοῦν
ἐπιστεύσαμεν with an anthropological meaning. This enables us to say that
human faith in Christ is an acknowledgement of God's justifying or saving
act through or on the basis of the faithfulness of Christ.

If this reading is valid, the hypothesis that Paul's Jewish-Christian critics presented works of the law, circumcision in particular, as a means of
justification for Gentile Christians is doubtful, because πίστις Χριστοῦ
cannot be understood as any person's act of faith that is contrasted with her

works. To be sure, Paul in some places sets πίστις against ἔργα. But πίστις Χριστοῦ and ἔργα νόμου in Gal 2:16 (cf. also Rom 3:20 with 3:22), for example, should not be understood as identical contrasts because πίστις Χριστοῦ probably denotes Christ's faithful death, but also because there is no convincing evidence in Judaism that doing works of the law was seen as the basis on which God declared Jews righteous. It should be admitted here that, as Gathercole has shown, in some Jewish writings ultimate vindication is linked to obedience to God's commandments. But this vindication is different from original acquisition of righteous status on the basis of election through God's grace. Indeed, what is ultimately vindicated is one's obedience to divine commandments. Obedience is a way of maintaining righteousness and choosing to remain in the sphere of life rather than a means of acquiring righteousness. We saw that Jews in the Second Temple period continued to regard themselves as righteous and to have confidence in God's goodness, patience and mercy for their salvation. But they coupled that confidence with intense recognition of their failures and sinfulness. This is precisely what we notice in the context of Ps 142:2 (LXX), which some Second Temple Jews cite or allude to (e.g. 1QH^a 15:28; 1QS 11:9; *1 En* 81:5). Paul, who also cites or alludes to this psalm (Gal 2:16; 3:11; Rom 3:20), and (probably) his critics diverged from the psalmist and these Jews in that they believed that God's mercy shown to Israel was now mediated for Jews and Gentiles in and through Christ. But Paul and his critics differed on how Jewish religious practices, circumcision in particular, should be applied to those who are *in Christ*. Paul's critics insisted that Gentile Christians should practice circumcision in order to establish their legitimacy as the righteous children of Abraham. For Paul, on the other hand, imposing circumcision on Gentile Christians would undermine the significance of Christ's death (his faithfulness), in and through which God's mercy is now mediated for Jews and Gentiles, and be a hindrance for Gentile mission.

What all this means in relation to our central question is that if πίστις Χριστοῦ in Rom 3:21-26 is interpreted in terms of Christ's relation to God, ἐκ πίστεως in Rom 1:17 should be understood likewise. The problem, however, is twofold. First, the anthropological reading of πίστις Χριστοῦ remains as valid as the christological reading. This renders the christological meaning of ἐκ πίστεως less than safe. Second, there is a lack of decisive evidence in favour of the messianic reading of ὁ δίκαιος in the Habakkuk citation in Rom 1:17. That makes defending the thesis that ἐκ πίστεως means the faithfulness of [the Righteous One] harder. But nevertheless, our exegeses of Rom 1:17 and key related texts from Galatians and Romans showed that the christological meaning of ἐκ πίστεως is possible.

Summary and Final Conclusions

As we come to the end of our study, we should now remind ourselves that the central task we set out to undertake was a critical evaluation of existing interpretations of Rom 1:17. We aimed to achieve this through a detailed study of the passage in question (and its immediate context) and exegetical analyses of relevant texts from the OT, Second Temple Judaism and the NT (Pauline and some non-Pauline texts). We recognised that those existing interpretations could be categorised as anthropological (how one is justified by faith [Old Perspective]), covenantal (who is maintained within God's covenant relationship [New Perspective]) and christological (what the messiah achieves for the believer). But we thought it sensible to limit ourselves to the anthropological and christological interpretative categories, chiefly because the anthropological interpretation represents a perspective which has been consistently prevalent since Luther. Indeed, since the Reformation Rom 1:17 has been seen as a passage that introduces and provides a framework for the doctrine of justification by faith. It would thus be the integrity of such a perspective that the christological construal of Rom 1:17 could potentially undermine if it (the christological reading) were shown to have internal coherence and argumentative cogency.

In the first chapter, we analysed these two categories after briefly discussing Luther's reading of Rom 1:17. We then summarised the interpretations that modern scholarship has afforded concerning the term δικαιοσύνη θεοῦ ('righteousness of God'). Luther's rejection of the hitherto universal meaning of the righteousness of God as God's retributive justice and interpretation of the phrase in terms of a righteousness that comes from God as a gift became foundational for later interpretations. It is true that in modern scholarship the meaning of the righteousness of God is not limited to a 'gift' sense, as it is also interpreted, for example, with covenantal and power senses (see below). But it is this gift sense that is often adopted in the anthropological reading of Rom 1:17. Along the same line, Luther's understanding of πίστις ('faith') as a divine gift by which a sinner is declared righteous before God's tribunal is adopted in this reading. So for the anthropological reader, the righteousness of God in Rom 1:17 is understood as a righteousness that is given to a person (ὁ δίκαιος) and received by faith (ἐκ πίστεως). The revelation in the gospel, therefore, is the revelation of this new idea of *righteousness by faith* rather than *righteousness by observing the law or works of the law*. Distinguishing this reading from a christological reading is not difficult. For according to the latter, as Hanson, Hays, Campbell and Wallis have argued, ὁ δίκαιος in the Habakkuk citation is Christ rather than the Christian, and ἐκ πίστεως in both halves of Rom 1:17 is the faithfulness of Christ rather than human faith.

Plausible cases have been made in favour of these readings, but both readings have problems. Anthropological interpreters continue to take for granted the traditional perspective that Rom 1:17, as the thesis of Romans, provides a framework for the doctrine of justification by faith. What is revealed, in their view, is that righteousness which is acquired by faith upon the proclamation of the gospel. This reading, however, is problematic because it equates the righteousness of God with a righteous status bestowed upon the justified ungodly in the divine court. Interpreting the righteousness of God as a righteous status is incompatible with an understanding of the revelation of the righteousness of God as an event that can be understood to have taken place in the Christ event. This is not to suggest that anthropological readers understand God's act of endowing righteousness to the believer in abstraction from the cross. But by virtue of reducing the righteousness of God to a righteous status, and revelation to one's epistemological understanding, they limit their explanation to the efficacy of God's act on the cross for an individual who accepts the message of Paul's gospel. Such an explanation seems to leave no room for a universalistic perspective of the revelation of the righteousness of God; a revelation that first took place in the gospel events and continues to take place in Paul's proclamation. If the revelation of the righteousness of God took place in the gospel events, how should ἐκ πίστεως be understood? It cannot be understood as human faith, because God's act of revealing his righteousness in the gospel obviously cannot depend on what a person does. Reading the prepositional phrase with a sense of God's faithfulness is possible but not plausible. The alternative is construing ἐκ πίστεως as Christ's faithfulness and ὁ δίκαιος as Christ.

This reading is also problematic, because christological interpreters have not provided us with any evidence from Second Temple Judaism where the 'righteous one' in Hab 2:4 is understood as a messiah. The absence of such evidence demands comprehensive attention to the Jewish background that could provide us with interpretative guidance. But the analysis of the christological readers relating to the use of the epithet within Judaism has been very scanty – in Campbell's studies, such an attempt is almost non-existent. Furthermore, none of the christological readers has done a comprehensive exegetical study of Hab 2:3-4 in its interpretative traditions. They have complained that the traditional reading of

Rom 1:17 wrongly rendered ἐκ πίστεως as human faith and viewed this human faith as the means through which the righteousness of God is revealed. But they have not adequately explained what the revelation of the righteousness of God means in such a way that the meaning would be suitable to the interpretation they accepted for ἐκ πίστεως. As a result, they have failed to provide us with a coherent interpretation of Rom 1:16-17. In the course of remedying these interpretative shortcomings and adjudicating between what we believe are the problems in the two competing readings, our central question was whether the christological reading would be cogent enough to undermine the traditional view that Rom 1:17 introduces or provides a framework for the idea of justification by faith.

As mentioned above, reading ὁ δίκαιος as a reference to the messiah, rather than the generic believer, is one of the key elements that characterise the christological interpretation, so in the second chapter of the book we engaged in a comprehensive investigation into the background evidence with specific attention to the interpretations of Hab 2:3-4 in the LXX, Qumran Commentary, the Nahal Hever text and the letter of Hebrews. Our exegesis of the LXX text showed us the extent of the discrepancies between the Masoretic and Septuagintal readings. It also enabled us to determine that the eschatological coming of YHWH in the Masoretic text of Hab 2:3 is probably interpreted in terms of the messianic coming by the Septuagintal translator. This seems to be shown by the renderings καὶ ἀνατελεῖ εἰς πέρας (2:3a) and ἐρχόμενος ἥξει (2:3b), and the personalised expression ὑπόμεινον αὐτόν (2:3b). But such messianic interpretation cannot be noticed immediately in Hab 2:4. The issue is further complicated by the fact that the minority reading of LXX MSS has μου after ὁ δίκαιος while the pronoun comes after ἐκ πίστεως in the majority reading. Whichever reading one chooses to accept as contextually suitable, it seems exegetically valid to understand the 'righteous one' as a generic individual. However, 'my righteous one' can be construed to be messianic as well. Syntax allows us to read the epithets [ὁ] ἐρχόμενος and ὁ δίκαιός μου as referring to the same figure. The epithet 'my righteous one' appears to have the same meaning as the messianic 'my son' (Ps 2:7) or 'my righteous servant' (Isa 53:11; cf. Ps 89:3, 20). This may be reinforced by the phraseological parallelism between Deutero-Isaiah's reference to the Servant as the one in whom YHWH's soul is delighted (Isa 42:1) and Habakkuk's reference to 'my righteous one' as someone in whom YHWH's soul will be delighted. In short, Hab 2:3-4 as a whole in the Greek text can be read messianically.

The same cannot be said in relation to either the *Pesher* Habakkuk or the Nahal Hever text. Although the conflict between the Teacher of Righteousness and the Wicked Priest in the *Pesher* seems to be influenced or informed by the conflict between 'the righteous one' and 'the wicked one' in Habakkuk, the sort of messianic elements that can be noticed in the LXX are not evident in the *Pesher* Habakkuk. This is not to deny that the community could have viewed the Teacher of Righteousness as a messianic figure, as this seems to be suggested by the portrayal of the Teacher as a divinely appointed ideal figure through whom divine mysteries are disclosed and the eschatological deliverance of his devotees is ensured. However, since the MT's 'righteous one' is used with reference to the community rather than the Teacher, it would be wrong to claim that 1QpHab interprets Hab 2:3-4 with a messianic reference. Slightly differently from the pesherist, the producer or reviser of the Nahal Hever text uses the 'righteous one' generically. But significantly differently from the pesherist and indeed from the LXX translator, he translates the MT's באמונתו as ἐν αὐτῷ, thereby making the 'righteous one' the subject of πίστις. But the fragments as a whole appear to show that the producer of the Nahal Hever text was not that concerned with a messianic understanding of Hab 2:3-4.

When we come to Hebrews 10:37-38, however, the issue is less clear-cut. On the one hand, Heb 10:37 is straightforwardly christological by virtue of the fact that ἐρχόμενος is titularised and applied to Jesus, while Heb 10:38 can be read anthropologically. But on the other, it can be argued that the whole citation of Hab 2:3-4, along with the conflated phrase from Isa 26:20 in Heb 10:37 should be read christologically. From the point of view of the former argument, it seems clear that in Heb 10:37 the author interprets Hab 2:3b in terms of the coming of Christ. Differently from this, Heb 10:38 can be understood to be used to address concerns about the real possibility of some Jewish-Christians drifting away from their faith, hence ὁ δίκαιός μου being an individual believer. This is the view that the commentaries on Hebrews unanimously hold. However, there are grounds to read ὁ δίκαιός μου as a messianic figure. The inversion of Hab 2:4a and 2:4b could be understood as deliberate attempt to parallel ὁ ἐρχόμενος with ὁ δίκαιός μου whereby both are construed messianically. This can be supported by two things. First, the term ἐρχόμενος can be understood as ὁ δίκαιός [μου] in the LXX. And secondly, 'my righteous one' seems to have a similar sense to the messianic 'my son' in Heb 1:5 (cf. Ps 2:7) and be informed or influenced by Deutero-Isaiah's 'my righteous servant' in 53:11 (cf. Ps 89:3, 20). So Heb 10:37-38 may be read as saying that the Messiah who acquired eschatological life through his faithfulness ('my righteous one') is the one who will come ('the coming one') to save the faithful. In the wider context, Jesus the Messiah is not only presented as the pioneer and perfecter of faith/faithfulness (12:1-2) but also as the superior model of faith/faithfulness and means of attaining the promise of salvation (cf. 10:36 with 11:39).

From our detailed discussion of the question as to whether the LXX translators, the Qumran pesherist, the producer of the Nahal Hever text and the author of Hebrews interpreted Hab 2:3-4 messianically, we saw that while it is possible that some LXX textual traditions read Hab 2:3-4 messianically, the evidence is fairly scant, and there is little evidence elsewhere of such reading. Indeed, the evidence from Qumran and Nahal Hever support the generic reading of the text. Our exegesis of the citation of Hab 2:3-4 in Heb 10:37-38 showed that both generic and christological interpretations are possible. This, cumulatively, must be seen as strengthening the traditional reading of Rom 1:17 and Gal 3:11 over against christological readings, and we need more positive evidence in the co-texts of those passages and in relevant Jewish texts in order to justify a christological reading.

In chapter 3 we dealt with Paul's expressions in Rom 1:17a. But as Rom 1:16 is closely linked with Rom 1:17, we thought it methodologically essential to deal with Rom 1:16-17a. Our question was whether and to what extent Paul's expressions in Rom 1:16-1:17a can be understood christologically. Christological interpreters of Rom 1:17 have not asked this question and, consequently, failed to offer a coherent reading of the passage. Our answer to this question was that although direct references to Christ or obvious christological clues are absent in Rom 1:16-17a, the power of God can be interpreted as being a linguistic image or co-referential term for Christ and the righteousness of God as standing for God's salvific power and presence in and through Christ. Traditionally, of course, the power of God is understood as the gospel that brings about salvation or the righteousness of God as that righteousness which is reckoned to or bestowed on the unbeliever, i.e. on those who were hitherto unbelievers.

We did not deny the plausibility of this understanding. But we attempted to offer an alternative and perhaps better understanding. When Rom 1:16b and 1:17a are taken as independent statements probably intended to justify and affirm Paul's claim that he is not ashamed of the gospel, both halves can be interpreted in juxtaposition and the power of God and the righteousness of God can be understood as the contents of the gospel. In the light of Pss 98 and 143 (LXX: Pss 97 and 142), which appear to have informed Paul's declaration in Rom 1:17 and 3:21-22, and some Second Temple Jewish writings (e.g. *1 En* 71:14; 99:10; 101:3; 1QM 4:6; 1QS 11:12), we interpret the righteousness of God as God's saving power. If this is valid, the righteousness of God will have the same sense as the power of God. Such a reading enables us to understand the righteousness of God christologically. In the context of Rom 1:17, Christ is presented as someone who is set as the Son of God *with power* beyond resurrection (1:4) and the gospel Paul preaches is a gospel concerning the Son of God

(1:3) or of the Son of God (1:9), who, for him, always remains the crucified but exalted redeemer (6:1-11; 8:34). Even more so, Christ is depicted
as the power of God and the righteousness of/from God in 1 and 2 Corinthians (1 Cor 1:24, 30; 2 Cor 5:21).

Rom 1:17a (in relation to 1:16) is traditionally understood as Paul's
declaration that the gospel is the means through which *righteousness from
or by faith* is revealed to the ungodly person, leading her to believe and be
endowed with a righteous status in the divine court. We argued that the
revelation Paul talks about in Rom 1:17a should not be limited to the
revelation that took place within his mission. As Rom 3:21-26, in which
Rom 1:17 is expanded, shows, the revelation in Rom 1:17a also refers to
the gospel events. In this case, we can hardly talk about a status that was
revealed in the gospel events. We did not deny that Paul regarded 'righteousness' as a gift in some places. Our point was that there probably is a
distinction between the *righteousness of God* and *righteousness*. For Paul,
it seems, the righteousness of God, like the wisdom of God and the power
of God, is a linguistic term that expresses God's identity and action embodied in Christ and revealed in the cross. As one's acquisition of a righteous (Christ-like) status depends on one's identification with or participation in Christ (2 Cor 5:21), the righteousness of God should be understood
as the divine power that occasions righteousness.

The question then is: if Paul's *claim* in Rom 1:17a is concerned with the
revelation of God's saving power that was the subject matter of Paul's proclaimed gospel, what meaning should the cited *proof* in Rom 1:17b (Hab
2:4b) be offered? As both anthropological and christological interpretations depend on the meanings of ὁ δίκαιος and ἐκ πίστεως in the citation,
in chapter 4 of the book we focused on the question as to whether ὁ
δίκαιος in the citation is a reference to the generic individual or a messiah.
One problem in the process of answering this question is Paul's disinterest
in employing the δίκαιος language with reference to Christ. Indeed, the
only passage where he could be understood as *implicitly* referring to Christ
as the 'righteous one' is Rom 5:19. This, coupled with the absence in
Second Temple Jewish writings of a citation of Hab 2:4 with a messianic
meaning, can engender, probably understandably, a tendency to conclude
that the conventional construal of the adjective in Rom 1:17b as the generic believer should be regarded as final. But our discussion in chapter 4
showed that such a conclusion fails to appreciate the interpretative guidance internal and external evidence can provide. There is ample evidence
that the adjective is used with reference to a messianic figure in Second
Temple Judaism. We saw that the epithet 'Righteous One' (a variant of
Son of Man, Chosen One, Messiah) in the Parables of *1 Enoch* in particular
is a reference to an eschatological or messianic figure. To develop this

idea, the author depends on the Danielic Son of Man and Deutero-Isaianic Servant traditions, and the messianic traditions of Proto-Isaiah and Jeremiah. Most of these traditions are shared by other Jewish and Christian writers, many of whom do not explicitly refer to a messianic or eschatological figure as the 'righteous one' but refer to him as 'righteous king', 'righteous messiah' or someone whose life is characterised by righteousness and faithfulness. Furthermore, there are non-Pauline NT uses of δίκαιος that can be regarded as indirectly messianic. Matt 10:41 is one example (cf. 11:2-3). In 1 Pet 3:18 and 1 Jn 2:1, δίκαιος is employed primarily as an attribute of Jesus, but it also refers *indirectly* to Jesus as *the suffering messiah*. In Acts 3:14, 7:52 and 22:14, however, [ὁ] δίκαιος is a direct reference to Jesus as messiah.

All this evidence may not prove that Paul used ὁ δίκαιος in the Habakkuk citation as a reference to Christ, but they show us that such an understanding would not have been completely strange in the first century world. Indeed, as a sharer of scriptural and interpretative traditions, Paul could well have understood ὁ δίκαιος as a christological designation via Isa 53:11, a passage that appears to have influenced Paul's and early Christians' understanding of the role of Christ and the significance of the gospel events. But the epithet could have been used as a reference to the generic individual believer as well. Our adjudication of existing arguments for and against a messianic reading of the adjective in the citation and analyses of Rom 1:17 and 1:18-3:20 in the light of parallel contextual elements from Second Temple Jewish writings, for example, showed that both generic and christological interpretations of ὁ δίκαιος in Rom 1:17 are plausible. So the probability of either of the interpretations must depend on how ἐκ πίστεως in relation to the πίστις Χριστοῦ construction in Galatians and Romans is interpreted. We dealt with this issue in chapter 5.

Our central question in this chapter was whether ἐκ πίστεως in Rom 1:17 is human faith or Christ's faithfulness. Paul's failure to or choice not to follow both the MT (he omits αὐτοῦ after ἐκ πίστεως) and LXX (he omits μου after ὁ δίκαιος [minority texts] or ἐκ πίστεως [majority texts]) readings in both Gal 3:11 and Rom 1:17 means that this issue cannot be settled on the basis of textual considerations alone. As far as Rom 1:17 is concerned, it is probably the case that ἐκ πίστεως in 1:17a is informed by the Habakkuk citation in 1:17b. So, procedurally, how the latter is interpreted should determine the reading of the first half. But the fact that Paul diverges from both the MT and LXX opens up the possibility of interpreting the phrase not only as human faith and/or Christ's faithfulness but also as God's covenant faithfulness. We argued that the latter reading was exegetically implausible and procedurally incoherent. Focussing on the former two interpretative options, we first studied Gal 3:11. Our exegetical study showed that there is a good case for arguing that ἐκ πίστεως in the citation expresses what humans do and therefore stands for human faith as against human deeds. The premise for this argument is that Paul contrasts ἔργα with πίστις against his critics' teaching that people are declared righteous on the basis of works. But as will be discussed below, this premise is questioned. Also, in the context of Gal 3 ἐκ πίστεως should not always be understood as a human action. The phrase ἐκ πίστεως most probably is a short form for ἐκ/διὰ πίστεως Ἰησοῦ Χριστοῦ, which can be interpreted as human faith or Christ's faithfulness. Paul's hypostatisation of πίστις in Gal 3:24 as Christ and other christological elements in the context of Galatians 3 seem to suggest that Paul understood πίστις as something that represents Christ. These and other reasons led us to the view that any decision regarding the referent of ἐκ πίστεως in Gal 3:11 must include wider considerations of the πίστις debate in Romans and Galatians.

Paul cites Hab 2:4b in exactly the same way in Rom 1:17 as he does in Gal 3:11. But Rom 1:17 as a whole differs from Gal 3:11 in that in the former Paul uses the double preposition ἐκ πίστεως εἰς πίστιν. The phrase ἐκ πίστεως in Rom 1:17a seems to be informed by the same phrase from Hab 2:4b, which is cited in Rom 1:17b. According to the syntax of Rom 1:17a, ἐκ πίστεως appears to be used as a reference to the process that causes the revelation of the righteousness of God, while εἰς πίστιν is used purposively as a reference to the process that is caused by the revelation of the righteousness of God. That is to say, if ἐκ πίστεως is X and εἰς πίστιν Y, for example, the righteousness of God is revealed through X and the same divine righteousness can be understood to cause Y. The question then is: do both X and Y stand for human faith? Traditionally, the answer has been 'yes'. Certainly, Y stands for human faith. In the light of Rom 1:16, the divine righteousness that causes Y is probably the same thing as the power of God that achieves salvation for those who believe. As the power of God is the content of Paul's gospel, it is an understanding of the reality of that power that leads Jews and Gentiles to believe in the gospel message and identify with Christ. So the causation of both faith (εἰς πίστιν) and salvation (εἰς σωτηρίαν) can be attributed to God's power. But can the same be said about ἐκ πίστεως? If the phrase is understood as the means by which one acquires a righteous status, the answer would again be 'yes'. But if it is understood as the means through which the righteousness of God is revealed, the answer should be 'no', because, as argued earlier, the righteousness of God is not a righteous status and the revelation Paul talks about in Rom 1:17 is a past as well as a present event. But as in Gal 3:11, our attempt to answer the question as to whether ἐκ πίστεως is anthropological or christological must necessarily take into account issues relating to the πίστις Χριστοῦ construction, because ἐκ πίστεως in Rom 1:17

seems to be an abbreviation of διὰ πίστεως 'Ιησοῦ Χριστοῦ and ἐκ πίστεως 'Ιησοῦ in 3:22, 26.

But before that we examined the arguments surrounding ἐκ πίστεως in Rom 9:30-10:13. We outlined three arguments in favour of the anthropological reading. First, ἐκ πίστεως in 9:30-33 stands for the faith of those who put their trust in the rock (Isa 28:16, cited in 9:33). The referents of 'Israel' (probably non-Christian Jews) erred, because they focussed on works to the exclusion of faith in Christ, i.e. an acknowledgement of God's saving action in and through Christ. Second, in 10:3-4 Christ is the τέλος of the law as a way of righteousness or salvation for everyone who believes [in him]. Third, in 10:5-13 Paul cites Deut 30:12 and argues that what a person needs to do to be saved is confess with her mouth that Jesus is Lord and believe in her heart that God raised him from the dead. We accept the viability of these arguments.

However, we note several things. First, the believing in verses 9 and 10 is directly linked with God who raised Jesus from the dead. So believing in Christ is an acknowledgement of what God did through Christ's death and resurrection. Second, the origin of the error of the referents of 'Israel' is their ignorance of God's righteousness, i.e. God's saving power revealed in and through Christ (10:3-4; cf. 1:17; 3:21-26; 2 Cor 5:21). Third, Christ brought the order of relations characterised by the law and its works in order to make righteousness possible for *all*, so doing works to the exclusion of πίστις that is associated with Christ does not enable one to share in that universal righteousness created and characterised by Christ (10:4-5). Fourth, it is possible to read the πίστις in the personified ἡ ἐκ πίστεως δικαιοσύνη in 10:6 as Christ's faithfulness. From this, while 9:30-10:13 on the whole strongly supports the anthropological interpretation of ἐκ πίστεως, there are indications that the text does not exclude a christological interpretation of the phrase. We suggested, on this basis, that the meaning of ἐκ πίστεως as 'faith [in Christ]' in 9:30-32 and the meaning of the same phrase as 'faithfulness [of Christ]' in 10:6 could complement each other. In other words, one's faith [in Christ] is an acknowledgement of God's saving action through Christ's death (which is a demonstration of his ultimate faithfulness to God). But this reading can only be maintained when it fits into the meaning of Paul's πίστις Χριστοῦ. That brings us to the question as to how the πίστις Χριστοῦ construction can contribute to our interpretation of ἐκ πίστεως in Rom 1:17.

We cannot be absolutely certain as to why Paul failed to add 'Ιησοῦ Χριστοῦ after ἐκ πίστεως in our passage and in many instances in Galatians and Romans. The best that can be said is that Paul's failure to add the genitive in Rom 1:17 and elsewhere probably is habitual rather than deliberate, because he sometimes uses ἐκ/διὰ πίστεως where he could have said ἐκ/διὰ πίστεως Ἰησοῦ Χριστοῦ (cf., for example, Rom 3:22 with 3:25 and Gal 2:16 with 3:24). So as ἐκ/διὰ πίστεως Ἰησοῦ Χριστοῦ itself is most probably informed by ἐκ πίστεως from Hab 2:4, it is legitimate to understand ἐκ πίστεως in Rom 1:17a, for example, as an abbreviated form of the longer ἐκ/διὰ πίστεως Ἰησοῦ Χριστοῦ. What πίστις Χριστοῦ means continues to polarise Pauline scholarship, however. Some of those who argue for the anthropological meaning (faith in Christ) of the construction leave little or no room for the christological meaning (Christ's faithfulness) and *vice versa*. In this study, we attempted to adopt a *via media* approach.

It cannot be denied that πίστις sometimes shares a common sense with πιστεύω ('have faith' or 'believe'). Even some uses of ἐκ πίστεως, which most probably are informed by the same phrase in Hab 2:4, have an anthropological meaning, in which case Campbell's insistence that all uses of ἐκ πίστεως in Romans and Galatians are christological is overconfident. However, it cannot be denied that πίστις sometimes has the sense 'faithfulness' as well. So which of the two senses would be suitable to πίστις in places where the πίστις Χριστοῦ construction is employed (e.g. Gal 2:16, 3:22 and Rom 3:22, 26) should be determined by a combination of things: the context in which Paul uses the construction, the meaning we afford concerning 'faith in Christ' and 'faithfulness of Christ', and so on. In our view, 'faith in Christ' means a believing-acceptance of the gospel message as an (continuing) acknowledgement of God's salvific initiative and act through Christ. Conversely, the 'faithfulness of Christ' probably means Christ's fidelity to God and his mission even unto death (Rom 3:21-26; 6:6-11; 8:34; cf. Isa 53:11; Heb 12:1-2; Rev 1:5; 3:15; *2 Macc* 7:23; *4 Macc* 17:21-22). Our exegeses showed that both construals could be accommodated in Gal 2:16, 3:22 and Rom 3:22 in particular. Paul unambiguously says 'we believed in Christ Jesus' (ἡμεῖς εἰς Χριστὸν Ἰησοῦν ἐπιστεύσαμεν) in Gal 2:16. He places the verb side-by-side with πίστις Χριστοῦ in this passage, as he does in Gal 3:22 and Rom 3:22. But in Gal 3:22 (τοῖς πιστεύουσιν) and Rom 3:22 (εἰς πάντας τοὺς πιστεύοντας) an object is not used with the verb, so Christ or God or the gospel can be supplied in both. Whatever the case, in all three passages the verbal construction probably means a human acknowledgement of God's initiative and action through Christ and πίστις Χριστοῦ the faithfulness of Christ-to-death. This interpretation enables us to understand human action in distinction from Christ's action, for the former is obviously dependent on the latter. To be sure, there are instances where Paul contrasts ἔργα as a way of life characterised by observing Jewish religious practices and πίστις as a way of life characterised by faith [in Christ], i.e. one's continuous acknowledgement of what God did in and through Christ (e.g. Rom 9:30-33; cf. Gal 2:16 with 2:20). But πίστις Χριστοῦ and ἔργα νόμου should not be construed as antithetical human actions, because the former probably denotes Christ's faithfulness-to-death. There is also another contextual reason why this should not be done.

As indicated above, the argument that πίστις Χριστοῦ and ἔργα νόμου are antithetical human actions is based on the traditional view that Paul contrasts ἔργα with πίστις against his critics' teaching that people are declared righteous on the basis of works. We examined the recent defences of this perspective over against the perspective that was first proposed by Sanders and then developed and defended by Dunn and others. Our conclusion is that while there is evidence in Second Temple Judaism that obedience to God's commandments is linked to eschatological vindication, there is no convincing evidence to suggest that obedience is the basis of acquiring righteousness. Indeed, we saw that obedience, pursuant with the prevalent Jewish theological axiom, is a way of maintaining the righteous status which Israel received by virtue of election and covenant on the basis of God's free love and mercy. Eschatological vindication is thus the vindication of those who have maintained their righteous status and, therefore, their divinely given life by obediently observing divine commandments.

Paul's Jewish-Christian critics diverged from this by believing that God's free love and mercy were now mediated by Christ. But they also insisted that Gentile Christians, like Jewish Christians, should observe works of the law, circumcision in particular, in order to establish their legitimacy as the righteous people of God and true descendants of Abraham. Paul opposed this on both theological and practical grounds. Theologically, God's salvific act, which is the subject matter of his gospel, was first performed and disclosed in the cross of Christ. Since the death of Christ, an expression of his faithfulness to God, not only mediates God's mercy but also establishes those who are in Christ as legitimate people of God and true descendants of Abraham, removing the flesh of the foreskin is meaningless. Practically, while to say that circumcision has no theological meaning does not mean that Jewish Christians should not perform it, insisting that Gentile Christians too should perform it would become a hindrance to the Gentile mission. For Paul, it is unnecessary and even wrong to focus on works of the law in general while knowing, as the psalmist in Ps 142:2 [LXX] (cf. Rom 3:20; Gal 2:16; 3:11) declares, that no human being will be justified through works of the law. Justification is achieved through God's gracious act in and through Christ. Paul expresses this notion using statements such as 'we are justified through the faithfulness of Jesus Christ' (Gal 2:16), 'the promise *is given* through the faithfulness of Jesus Christ to those who believe' (Gal 3:22), and 'the righteousness of God has been revealed through the faithfulness of Jesus Christ to all who believe'

(Rom 3:21-22). Paul's declarations in Rom 1:17 can be understood as part and parcel of these expressions.

To conclude, the results in this book, in the main, show that the validity of the conventional view that Rom 1:17 introduces and provides a framework for the doctrine of justification by faith does not seem to be fundamentally threatened by the christological view. Indeed, the idea that Rom 1:17 is about the gospel revealing righteousness that is from or by faith – where the righteousness of God denotes righteous status divinely endowed on a believer, ἐκ πίστεως means human faith [in Christ] and ὁ δίκαιος refers to the justified believer – remains plausible. This interpretation should not be taken for granted, however, because our exegeses of the passage and internal and external evidence cumulatively showed that the passage could also be understood to be concerned with introducing and providing a framework for the idea of *God's act of salvation through Christ's faithfulness-to-death* (πίστις Χριστοῦ), the knowledge of which triggers the human act of faith-response.

That would mean that the revelation of the righteousness of God in the passage denotes God's salvific appearance in and through Christ, with ἐκ πίστεως meaning Christ's faithfulness-to-death and ὁ δίκαιος refering to Christ. Admittedly, pre-Pauline and Pauline evidence in favour of reading ὁ δίκαιος in the Habakkuk citation as Christ seems to be insufficient and the christological meaning of ἐκ πίστεως is heavily dependent on the disputed subjective genitive interpretation of πίστις Χριστοῦ. However, that this reading is internally coherent and has some degree of argumentative cogency cannot be denied.

So, accepting that Rom 1:17 is a passage in which Paul set forth his programmatic statement for the letter as a whole, and accepting that his thoughts and concerns in the letter were shaped by his understanding of what Christ achieved for the salvation and life of Jews and Gentiles, we judge that the christological reading should be afforded more weight within Pauline scholarship than has been the case thus far.

Bibliography

Primary Literature

Aland, K., et al. (eds), *The Greek New Testament* (4th edn), Stuttgart: Deutsche Bibelgesellschaft, 1993.

Aristotle, *The Nicomachean Ethics* (new and rev. edn, trans. H. Rackham), London: Heinemann, 1934.

Black, M., *The Book of Enoch (1 Enoch)*, Leiden: Brill, 1985.

Black, M (ed.), *Apocalypsis Henochi Graece,* Leiden: Brill, 1970.

Brenton, L. C. L., *The Septuagint with Apocrypha: Greek and English* (17th edn), Grand Rapids: Zondervan, 1990.

Charles, R. H., *The Apocrypha and Pseudepigrapha of the Old Testament in English: With Introductions and Critical and Explanatory Notes to the Several Books Edited in Conjunction with Many Scholars*, 2 vols, Oxford: Clarendon Press, 1913.

–, *The Book of Enoch: With an Introduction by W. O. E. Oesterley*, London: SPCK, 1917.

Charlesworth, J., *The Old Testament Pseudepigrapha: Apocalyptic Literature and Testaments*, vol. 1, London: Darton, Longman & Todd, 1983.

–, *The Old Testament Pseudepigrapha: Expansions of the 'Old Testament' and Legends; Wisdom and Philosophical Literature; Prayers, Psalms and Odes; Fragments of Judeo-Hellenistic Works*, vol. 2, London: Darton, Longman & Todd, 1983.

Cicero, Marcus Tullius, *Pro Flacco* (ed., with introduction and notes, T. B. L. Webster), Oxford: Clarendon Press, 1931.

De Bruyn, T., *Pelagius's Commentary on St Paul's Epistle to the Romans: Translated with Introduction and Notes*, Oxford: Clarendon Press, 1993.

Denis, Albert-Marie, *Fragmenta Pseudepigraphorum Quae Supersunt Graeca,* Leiden: Brill, 1970.

Eissfeldt, O. et al., *Biblia Hebraica Stuttgartensia*, Stuttgart: Württembergische Bibelanstalt, 1969.

Feldman, L., and Reinhold, M., *Jewish Life and Thought Among Greeks and Romans: Primary Readings*, Edinburgh: T & T Clark, 1996.

García Martínez, F., *The Dead Sea Scrolls Translated: The Qumran Scrolls in English*, Leiden: Brill, 1994.

García Martínez, F., and Tigchelaar, E. J. C., *The Dead Sea Scrolls Study Edition*, 2 vols, Leiden: Brill, 1997–1998.

Josephus, Flavius, *Works* (trans. and ed. H. S. J. Thackeray, R. Marcus, A. Wikgren and L. H. Feldman), 9 vols, London: Heinemann, 1926–1969.

Knibb, M. A., *The Ethiopic Book of Enoch, Volumes I and II*, Oxford: Clarendon Press, 1978.

Luther, Martin, *Works* (ed. J. Pelikan and H. T. Lehman), Philadelphia: Fortress, 1958–1967.

Nestle, E. and Aland, K., *Novum Testamentum Graece* (27th edn), Stuttgart: Deutsche Bibelgesellschaft, 1993.

Philo of Alexandria, *Works* (ed. F. H. Colson, G. H. Whitaker, J. W. Earp and R. Marcus), 12 vols, London: Heinemann, 1929–1941.

Plato, *The Republic* (rev. edn, trans. P. Shorey), Cambridge, Massachusetts: Harvard University Press, 1937.

Sparks, H. F. D. (ed.), *The Apocryphal Old Testament*, Oxford: Clarendon Press, 1984.

Suetonius, *The Lives of the Caesars I* (trans. J. C. Rolfe), London: Heinemann, 1913.

Tov, E., 'The Greek Minor Prophets Scroll from Nahal Hever (8HevXIIgr): The "Seiyal" Collection' (with the collaboration of R. A. Kraft and a contribution of P. J. Parsons), in *Discoveries in the Judean Desert VIII*, Oxford: Clarendon Press, 1990.

Uhlig, S., *Das äthiopische Henochbuch, Jüdische Schriften aus hellenistisch-römischer Zeit, herausgegeben von Werner Georg Kümmel*, Gütersloh: Gütersloher Verlag, 1984.

Vermes, G., *The Complete Dead Sea Scrolls in English*, London: Allen Lane, 1997.

General Reference Works

Abbot-Smith, G., *A Manual Greek Lexicon of the New Testament* (3rd edn), Edinburgh: T & T Clark, 1937.

Bauer, W., Arndt, W. F., Gingrich, F. W. and Danker, F. W., *A Greek–English Lexicon of the New Testament and Other Early Christian Literature* (6th edn), Chicago: University of Chicago Press, 1979.

Blass, F. and Debrunner, A., *A Greek Grammar of the New Testament and Other Early Christian Literature* (trans. and rev. R. W. Funk), Chicago: University of Chicago Press, 1961.

Denis, Albert-Marie, *Concordance grecque des pseudépigraphes d'Ancien Testament*, Louvain-la-Neuve, Université Catholique de Louvain, Institut Orientaliste, 1987.

Dillmann, C. F. A., *Lexicon Linguae Aethiopicae*, Lipsiae: T. O. Weigel, 1865.

Holladay, W. L., *A Concise Hebrew and Aramaic Lexicon of the Old Testament*, Leiden: Brill, 1971.

Liddell, H. G. and Scott, R., *Greek–English Lexicon* (abridged form), Oxford: Clarendon Press, 1989.

Louw, J. P. and Nida, E. A., *Greek–English Lexicon of the New Testament Based on Semantic Domains*, New York: United Bible Societies, 1990.

Metzger, B. M., *A Concordance to the Apocrypha/Deuterocanonical Books of the Revised Standard Version, Derived from the Bible Data Bank of the Centre Informatique et Bible (Abbey of Maredsous)*, London: Collins, 1983.

–, *A Textual Commentary on the Greek New Testament* (2nd edn), Stuttgart: Deutsche Bibelgesellschaft, 1994.

Rienecker, F. and Rogers, C. L., *Linguistic Key to the Greek New Testament*, Grand Rapids: Zondervan, 1980.

Wigram, G. V., *The Englishman's Greek Concordance of the New Testament* (reprinted from the 9th edn originally published by Samuel Bagster & Sons, London, 1903, with Strong's numbering), Peabody: Hendrickson, 1996.

Zerwick, M. and Grosvenor, M., *A Grammatical Analysis of the Greek New Testament II: Epistles – Apocalypse*, Rome: Biblical Institute Press, 1979.

Secondary Literature

Achtemeier, E. R., 'Righteousness in the Old Testament', *IDB IV*, 80–85.

Achtemeier, P. J., 'Righteousness in the New Testament', *IDB IV*, 91–96.

–, 'Unsearcheable Judgements and Inscrutable Ways: Reflections on the Discussion of Romans', in E. Johnson and D. Hay (eds), *Pauline Theology IV: Looking Back, Pressing On* (SBL Symposium Series), Atlanta: Scholars Press, 1997, 3-21.

Adams, E., *Constructing the World: A Study in Paul's Cosmological Language*, Edinburgh: T& T Clark, 1999.

Adler, W., 'Introduction', in J. VanderKam and W. Adler (eds), *The Jewish Apocalyptic Heritage in the Early Christianity*, Minneapolis: Fortress, 1996, 1-31.

Allegro, J. M., 'Further Messianic References in Qumran Literature', *JBL* 75 (1956) 174–176.

Allen, L. C., 'The Old Testament Background of (ΠΡΟ)᾽OPIZEIN in the New Testament', *NTS* 17 (1970–71) 104–108.

Andersen, F. I., *Habakkuk: A New Translation with Introduction and Commentary*, New York: Doubleday, 2001.

Atkinson, K., 'On the Herodian Origin of Militant Davidic Messianism at Qumran: New Light from *Psalms of Solomon* 17', *JBL* 118 (1999) 435–460.

Attridge, H. W., *The Epistle to the Hebrews*, Philadelphia: Fortress, 1989.

Balentine, S. E., *The Hidden God: The Hiding of the Face of God in the Old Testament*, Oxford: Oxford University Press, 1983.

Barclay, J., *Jews in the Mediterranean Diaspora: From Alexander to Trajan (323 BCE–117 CE)*, Edinburgh: T & T Clark, 1996.

Barker, M., 'The High Priest and the Worship of Jesus', in C. C. Newman et al. (eds), *The Jewish Roots of Christological Monotheism* (JSJS), Leiden: Brill, 1999, 93–111.

Barr, J., *The Semantics of Biblical Language*, Oxford: Oxford University Press, 1961.

Barrett, C. K., *From First Adam to Last*, London: A. & C. Black, 1962.

–, 'I am Not Ashamed of the Gospel', in M. Barth et al., *Foi et salut selon S. Paul* (épître aux Romains 1,16), Rome: Biblical Institute Press, 1970, 19-50.

–, *A Commentary on the Second Epistle to the Corinthians*, London: BNTC, 1973.

–, *The Epistle to the Romans* (BNTC, 2nd edn), London: A. & C. Black, 1991.

Barth, K., *The Epistle to the Romans*, London: Oxford University Press, 1933.

–, *Christ and Adam: Man and Humanity in Romans 5* (trans. T. A. Smail), London: Oliver & Boyd, 1956.

–, *A Shorter Commentary on Romans*, London: SCM, 1959.

Barth, M., *The People of God* (JSNTS 5), Sheffield: JSOT, 1983.

Bassler, J. M., *Divine Impartiality: Paul and a Theological Axiom*, Chico: Scholars Press, 1981.

Bauckham, R., *God Crucified: Monotheism and Christology in the New Testament*, Carlisle: Paternoster, 1998.

–, 'The Throne of God and the Worship of Jesus', in C. C. Newman et al. (eds), *The Jewish Roots of Christological Monotheism* (JSJS), Leiden: Brill, 1999, 43–69.

Baumbach, G., 'The Sadducees in Josephus', in L. Feldman et al. (eds), *Josephus, the Bible, and History*, Leiden: Brill, 1988, 173–195.

Baumgarten, J., 'The Pharisaic–Sadducean Controversies about Purity, and the Qumran Texts', *JJS* (1980) 157–170.

–, 'Scripture and Law in 4Q265', in M. Stone et al. (eds), *Biblical Perspectives: Early Use and Interpretation of the Bible in the Light of the Dead Sea Scrolls* (Proceedings of the First International Symposium of the Orion Center for the Study of the Dead Sea Scrolls and Associated Literature, 12–14 May 1996), Leiden: Brill, 1998, 25–33.

Beker, J. C., *Paul's Apocalyptic Gospel: The Coming Triumph of God*, Philadelphia: Fortress, 1982.

–, *Paul the Apostle: The Triumph of God in Life and Thought*, Philadelphia: Fortress, 1984.

–, 'Recasting Pauline Theology', in J. M. Bassler (ed.), *Pauline Theology 1: Thessalonians, Philippians, Galatians, Philemon*, Minneapolis: Fortress, 1991, 15–24.

Benjamins, H. S., 'Paradisiacal Life: The Story of Paradise in the Early Church', in G. Luttikhuizen (ed.), *Paradise Interpreted: Representations of Biblical Paradise in Judaism and Christianity*, Leiden: Brill, 1999, 153–167.

Bernstein, M. S., 'Pesher Habakkuk', in L. Schiffman and J. VanderKam (eds), *Encyclopedia of the Dead Sea Scrolls I*, Oxford: Oxford University Press, 2000, 647–650.

Best, E., 'The Revelation to Evangelize the Gentiles', *JTS* (1984) 1-30.

Betz, H. D., *Galatians: A Commentary on Paul's Letter to the Churches in Galatia* (Hermeneia series), Philadelphia: Fortress, 1979.

Black, M., *Romans*, London: Marshall, Morgan & Scott, 1973.

Blackman, C., 'Romans 3:26b: A Question of Translation', *JBL* 87 (1968) 203–204.

Blumenfeld, B., *The Political Paul: Justice, Democracy and Kingship in a Hellenistic Framework* (JSNT 200), Sheffield: Sheffield Academic Press, 2001.

Boccaccini, G., *Beyond the Essene Hypothesis: The Parting of the Ways between Qumran and Enochic Judaism*, Grand Rapids: Eerdmans, 1998.

Bockmuehl, M., 'Das Verb φανερόω im Neuen Testament', *BZ* 32 (1988) 87-99.

–, *Revelation and Mystery in Ancient Judaism and Pauline Christianity* (WUNT 2/36), Tübingen: Mohr Siebeck, 1990.

–, *Jewish Law in Gentile Churches: Halakhah and the Beginning of Christian Public Ethics*, Edinburgh: T & T Clark, 2000.

Boring, M. E., 'The Language of Universal Salvation in Paul', *JBL* 105 (1986) 269–292.

Bornkamm, G., *Paul* (trans. D. M. G. Stalker), New York: Harper & Row, 1971.

Brownlee, W. H., *The Midrash Pesher of Habakkuk*, Missoula: Scholars Press, 1979.

Bruce, F. F., *The Epistle to the Galatians: A Commentary on the Greek Text* (NIGTC), Grand Rapids: Eerdmans, 1982.

–, 'The Romans Debate – Continued', in K. P. Donfried (ed.), *The Romans Debate* (rev. and expanded edn), Edinburgh: T & T Clark, 1991, 175–194.

–, 'Paul in Acts and Letters', in G. F. Hawthorne et al. (eds), *Dictionary of Paul and His Letters*, Leicester: IVP, 1993, 679–692.

Bruce, G. A., *Apocalyptic Eschatology and Reality: An Investigation of Cosmic Transformation*, Unpublished PhD Dissertation, University of South Africa, 1987.

Buchanan, G. W., *To the Hebrews*, New York: Doubleday, 1972.

Büchsel, F. and Procksch O., 'λύω, ἀναλύω, ἀνάλυσις, ἐπιλύω, ἐπίλυσις, καταλύω, κατάλυμα, ἀπατάλυτος, λύτρον, ἀντίλυτρον, λυτρόω, λύτρωσις, λυτρωτής, ἀπολύτρωσις', in G. Kittel (ed.), *TDNT IV* (trans. G. W. Bromiley), Grand Rapids: Eerdmans, 1967, 328–356.

Bultmann, R., *Theology of the New Testament*, London: SCM, 1956.

–, 'Adam and Christ according to Romans 5', in W. Klassen and G. F. Snyder (eds), *Current Issues in New Testament Interpretation: Essays in Honor of Otto A. Piper*, London: SCM, 1962, 143–165.

–, 'ΔΙΚΑΙΟΣΥΝΗ ΘΕΟΥ', *JBL* 83 (1964) 12–16.

Byrne, B., *Romans* (SP), Collegeville, Minn.: Glazier, Liturgical Press, 1996.

–, 'Interpreting Romans Theologically in a Post – "New Perspective" Perspective', *HTR* (2001) 227-241.

Caird, G. B., *The Language and Imagery of the Bible*, London: Duckworth, 1980.

Calvin, J., *The Epistles of Paul the Apostle to the Romans and to the Thessalonians* (trans. R. Mackenzie), T & T Clark: Edinburgh, 1961.

Campbell, D. A., *The Rhetoric of Righteousness in Romans 3.21–26* (JSNTS 65), Sheffield: JSOT, 1992.

–, 'The Meaning of Πίστις and Νόμος in Paul: A Linguistic and Structural Perspective', *JBL* 111 (1992) 91–103.

–, 'Determining the Gospel through Rhetorical Analysis in Paul's Letter to the Roman Christians', in L. A. Jervis and P. Richardson (eds), *Gospel in Paul: Studies on Corinthians, Galatians and Romans for Richard N. Longenecker*, Sheffield: Sheffield Academic Press, 1994, 315–336.

–, 'Rom 1:17 – A *Crux Interpretum* for the Πίστις Χριστοῦ Debate', *JBL* 113 (1994) 265–285.

–, 'False Presuppositions in the Πίστις Χριστοῦ Debate: A Response to Brian Dodd', *JBL* 116 (1997) 713–719.

–, 'Natural Theology in Paul? Reading Romans 1:19–20', *IJST* 1:3 (1999) 231–252.

–, *The Quest for Paul's Gospel: A Suggested Strategy*, London: Continuum, 2005.

Campbell, W. S., 'Why Did Paul Write Romans?', *ExpT* (1974) 264–269.

–, 'Romans III as a Key to the Structure and Thought of the Letter', *NovT* (1981) 22–40.

Carson, D. A. *et al* (eds), *Justification and Variegated Nomism: The Complexities of Second Temple Judaism* (WUNT 2/140), Tübingen: Mohr Siebeck, 2001.

–, *Justification and Variegated Nomism: The Paradoxes of Paul* (WUNT 2/181), Tübingen: Mohr Siebeck, 2004.

Casey, M., *Son of Man: The Interpretation and Influence of Daniel 7*, London: SPCK, 1979.

Cavallin, H. C. C., '"The Righteous Shall Live by Faith": A Decisive Argument for the Traditional Interpretation', *ST* 32 (1978) 33-43.

Charles, R. H., *A Critical History of the Doctrine of a Future Life in Israel, in Judaism and in Christianity*, London: A & C Black (2nd edn), 1913.

Charlesworth, J., *The Old Testament Pseudepigrapha and the New Testament*, Harrisburg: Trinity Press International, 1985.

Cheon, S., 'Three Characters in the Wisdom of Solomon', *JSP* 12 (2001) 105-113.

Collins, J. J., 'The Heavenly Representative: The Son of Man in Enoch', in J. J. Collins and G. Nickelsburg, *Ideal Figures in Ancient Judaism: Profiles and Paradigms*, Chico: Scholars Press, 1980.

–, 'The Son of Man in First-century Judaism', *NTS* 38 (1992) 448–466.

–, *Daniel* (Hermeneia series), Minneapolis: Fortress, 1993.

–, 'Messiahs in Context: Method in the Study of Messianism in the Dead Sea Scrolls', in M. Wise et al., *Methods of Investigation of the Dead Sea Scrolls and the Khirbet Qumran Site*, New York: New York Academy of Sciences, 1994, 213–227.

–, *The Scepter and the Star: The Messiahs of the Dead Sea Scrolls and Other Ancient Literature*, London: Doubleday, 1995.

–, *Apocalypticism in the Dead Sea Scrolls*, London: Routledge, 1997.

–, *The Apocalyptic Imagination: An Introduction to Jewish Apocalyptic Literature* (2nd edn), Grand Rapids: Eerdmans, 1998.

Collins, Y., *Cosmology and Eschatology in Jewish and Christian Apocalypticism*, Leiden: Brill, 1996.

Conzelmann, H., *An Outline of the Theology of the New Testament*, London: SCM, 1969.

Cotterell, P. and Turner, M., *Linguistics and Biblical Interpretation*, London: SPCK, 1989.

Cowley, R., *Ethiopian Biblical Interpretation: A Study in Exegetical Tradition and Hermeneutics* (University of Cambridge Oriental Publications 38), Cambridge, 1988.

Cranfield, C. E. B., *Romans* (ICC), 2 vols, Edinburgh: T & T Clark, 1975.

–, *On Romans and Other New Testament Essays*, Edinburgh: T & T Clark, 1998.

Cremer, H., *Die paulinische Rechtfertigungslehre im Zusammenhang ihrer geschichtlichen Voraussetzungen* (2nd edn), Gütersloh: Bertelsmann, 1900.

Cullmann, O., *Christ and Time: The Primitive Christian Conception of Time and History* (trans. F. V. Filson), London: SCM, 1962 (2nd edn) (German edn. 1946; 3rd German edn. 1962).

–, *The Christology of the New Testament*, London: SCM, 1963.

–, *Salvation in History* (trans. S. G. Sowers et al.), London: SCM, 1967 (German edn. 1965).

Dabourne, W., *Purpose and Cause in Pauline Exegesis in Romans 1–4*, Cambridge: Cambridge University Press, 1999.

Dahl, N. A., *Studies in Paul: Theology for the Early Christian Mission*, Minneapolis: Augsburg Publishing House, 1977.

–, 'Rom 3:9: Text and Meaning', in M. D. Hooker et al. (eds), *Paul and Paulinism, Essays in Honour of C. K. Barrett*, London: SPCK, 1982, 184–204.

Dangl, F., 'Habakkuk in Recent Research', *Currents in Research: Biblical Studies* (CR: BS), vol 9, 2001, 131-168.

Davies, G. N., *Faith and Obedience in Romans, A Study in Romans 1–4* (JSNTS 39), Sheffield: JSOT, 1990.

Davies, W. D., *Paul and Rabbinic Judaism: Some Rabbinic Elements in Pauline Theology* (4th edn), London: SPCK, 1980.

–, 'The Teacher of Righteousness and the "End of Days"', *Mémorial Jean Carmignac, RevQ* (1988) 313–317.

Davies, W. D and Allison, D. C., *The Gospel According to Matthew*, vol. II, Edinburgh: T & T Clark, 1991.

De Boer, M., *The Defeat of Death: Apocalyptic Eschatology in 1 Corinthians 15 and Romans 5* (JSNTS 22), Sheffield: JSOT, 1988.

–, 'Paul and Apocalyptic Eschatology', in J. Collins (ed.), *The Encyclopedia of Apocalypticism*, vol. I, New York: Continuum, 2000, 345-383.

Deidun, T., 'James Dunn and John Ziesler on Romans in New Perspective', *HeyJ* (1992) 79-84.

Deissmann, G. A., *Light from the Ancient East* (2nd edn; trans. L. R. M. Strachan), London: Hodder & Stoughton, 1910.

–, *St Paul: A Study in Social and Religious History* (trans. L. Strachan), London: Hodder & Stoughton, 1912.

Descamps, A., *Les justes et la justice dans les évangiles et le christianisme primitif hormis la doctrine proprement paulinienne*, Louvain: Publications Universitaires des Louvain, 1950.

Dodd, B., 'Romans 1:17 – A *Crux Interpretum* for the Πίστις Χριστοῦ Debate?', *JBL* 114 (1995) 470–473.

Dodd, C. H., *The Apostolic Preaching and Its Developments*, London: Hodder & Stoughton, 1936 (reset 1944).

–, *The Meaning of Paul for Today* (2nd edn), London: Fontana, 1956.

–, *The Epistle of Paul to the Romans* (rev. edn), London: Collins, 1959.

Donfried, K. P., 'False Presuppositions in the Study of Romans', *CBQ* 36 (1974) 332–355.

–, *The Romans Debate* (rev. and expanded edn), Edinburgh: T & T Clark, 1991.

–, 'A Short Note on Romans 16', in K. P. Donfried (ed.), *The Romans Debate* (rev. and expanded edn), Edinburgh: T & T Clark, 1991, 44–52.

Dunn, J. D. G., *Unity and Diversity in the New Testament: An Enquiry into the Character of Earliest Christianity*, London: SCM, 1977.

–, 'The New Perspective on Paul (E. P. Sanders, *Paul and Palestinian Judaism*; Gal 2:16)', *Bulletin of the John Rylands University Library of Manchester* 65:2 (1983), 95–122.

–, 'Works of the Law and the Curse of the Law (Gal 3:10–14)', *NTS* 31 (1985) 523–542.

–, *Romans* (WBC 38), 2 vols, Dallas, Texas: Word Books, 1988.

–, *Christology in the Making: An Inquiry into the Origins of the Doctrine of the Incarnation* (2nd edn), London: SCM, 1989.

–, *The Epistle to the Galatians*, London: A & C Black, 1993.

–, 'Once More, ΠΙΣΤΙΣ ΧΡΙΣΤΟΥ', in E. Johnson and D. Hay (eds), *Pauline Theology IV: Looking Back, Pressing On* (SBL Symposium Series), Atlanta: Scholars Press, 1997, 61–81.

–, 'In Quest of Paul's Theology: Retrospect and Prospect', in E. Johnson and D. Hay (eds), *Pauline Theology IV: Looking Back, Pressing On* (SBL Symposium Series), Atlanta: Scholars Press, 1997, 95-115.

–, 'Paul and Justification by Faith', in R. Longenecker (ed.), *The Road From Damascus: The Impact of Paul's Conversion on His Life, Thought and Ministry*, Grand Rapids: Eerdmans, 1997, 85–101.

–, *The Theology of Paul the Apostle*, Edinburgh: T & T Clark, 1998.

Eichrodt, W., *Theology of the Old Testament*, London: SCM, 1961.

Ellingworth, P., *The Epistle to the Hebrews*, Grand Rapids, Michigan: Eerdmans, 1993.

Elliott, N., *The Rhetoric of Romans: Argumentative Constraint and Strategy and Paul's Debate with Judaism*, Sheffield: Sheffield Academic Press, 1990.

–, 'The Anti-Imperial Message of the Cross', in R. Horsley (ed.), *Paul and Empire: Religion and Power in Roman Imperial Society*, Harrisburg: Trinity Press International, 1997, 167–183.

Elliott, J., *1 Peter: A New Translation and Commentary*, New York: Doubleday, 2000.

Elliott, M., *The Survivors of Israel: A Reconsideration of the Theology of Pre-Christian Judaism*, Grand Rapids: Eerdmans, 2000.

Emerton, J. A., 'The Textual and Linguistic Problems of Habakkuk II.4–5', *JTS* 28 (1977) 1–18.

Engberg-Pedersen, T., *Paul and the Stoics*, Edinburgh: T & T Clark, 2000.

Fitzmyer, J., *Paul and His Theology: A Brief Sketch* (2nd edn), Englewood Cliffs: Prentice Hall, 1989.

–, *Romans: A New Translation with Introduction and Commentary* (The Anchor Bible), London: Doubleday, 1992.

–, *According to Paul: Studies in the Theology of the Apostle*, New York: Paulist Press, 1992.

–, 'Habakkuk 2:3-4 and the New Testament', in J. Fitzmyer, *To Advance the Gospel: New Testament Studies* (2nd edn), Grand Rapids, Michigan: Eerdmans, 1998, 236-246.

–, 'Paul and the Dead Sea Scrolls', in P. Flint and J. VanderKam (eds), *The Dead Sea Scrolls After Fifty Years II*, Leiden: Brill, 1999, 599–621.

Fletcher-Louis, C., *Luke-Acts: Angels, Christology and Soteriology* (WUNT 2/94), Tübingen: Mohr Siebeck, 1997.

Fohrer, G., *Introduction to the Old Testament* (trans. D. Green), London: SPCK, 1970.

Frankfurter, D., 'The Legacy of Jewish Apocalypses in Early Christianity: Regional Trajectories', in J. VanderKam and W. Adler (eds), *The Jewish Apocalyptic Heritage in the Early Christianity*, Minneapolis: Fortress, 1996, 129–200.

Gamble, H., *The Textual History of the Letter to the Romans*, Grand Rapids: Eerdmans, 1977.

García Martínez, F., 'Qumran Origins and Early History: A Groningen Hypothesis', *Folia Orientalia* 25 (1988) 113–136.

–, *Qumran and Apocalyptic: Studies on the Aramaic Texts from Qumran*, Leiden: Brill, 1992.
–, 'Man and Woman: Halakah Based upon Eden in the Dead Sea Scrolls', in G. Luttikhuizen (ed.), *Paradise Interpreted: Representations of Biblical Paradise in Judaism and Christianity*, Leiden: Brill, 1999, 95–115.
García Martínez, F., and Trebolle Barrera, J.C., *The People of the Dead Sea Scrolls: Their Writings, Beliefs and Practices*, Leiden: Brill, 1993.
Garlington, G., *Faith, Obedience and Perseverance: Aspects of Paul's Letter to the Romans* (WUNT 2/79), Tübingen: Mohr Siebeck, 1994.
Garnsey, P. and Whittaker, C. (eds), *Imperialism in the Ancient World: The Cambridge University Research Seminar in Ancient History*, Cambridge: Cambridge University Press, 1978.
Gaston, L., *Paul and the Torah*, Vancouver: University of British Columbia Press, 1987.
Gathercole, S., *Where is Boasting?: Early Jewish Soteriology and Paul's Response in Romans 1-5*, Grand Rapids, Michigan: Eerdmans, 2002.
–, 'Justified by Faith, Justified by his Blood: The Evidence of Romans 3:21-4:5', in D. A. Carson *et al* (eds), *Justification and Variegated Nomism: The Paradoxes of Paul* (WUNT 2/181), Tübingen: Mohr Siebeck, 2004, 147-184.
George, T., 'Modernizing Luther, Domesticating Paul: Another Perspective', in D. A. Carson *et al* (eds), *Justification and Variegated Nomism: The Paradoxes of Paul* (WUNT 2/181), Tübingen: Mohr Siebeck, 2004, 437-463.
Georgi, D., *Theocracy in Paul's Praxis and Theology* (trans. D. E. Green), Minneapolis: Fortress, 1991.
–, 'God Turned Upside Down', in R. Horsley (ed.), *Paul and Empire: Religion and Power in Roman Imperial Society*, Harrisburg: Trinity Press International, 1997, 148–157.
Gherghita, R., *The Role of the Septuagint in Hebrews* (WUNT 2/160), Tübingen: Mohr Siebeck, 2003.
Glatt-Gilad, D. A., 'Reflections on the Structure and Significance of the *'ᵃmānāh* (Neh 10, 29–40)', *ZAW* 112 (2000) 386–395.
Gordon, R., *Studies in the Targum to the Twelve Prophets, From Nahum to Malachi*, Leiden: Brill, 1994.
–, *Hebrews*, Sheffield: Sheffield Academic Press, 2000.
Goulder, M., 'Hebrews and the Ebionites', *NTS* 49 (2003) 393-406.
Gräbe, P. J., *The Power of God in Paul's Letters* (WUNT 2/123), Tübingen: Mohr Siebeck, 2000.
Greenspoon, L. J., 'The Dead Sea Scrolls and the Greek Bible', in P. Flint and J. VanderKam (eds), *The Dead Sea Scrolls After Fifty Years I*, Leiden: Brill, 1998, 101–127.
Gundry, R. H., *Matthew: A Commentary on His Literary and Theological Art*, Grand Rapids: Eerdmans, 1982.
Haacker, K., *Der Brief des Paulus an die Römer,* ThHK 6, Leipzig: Evangelische Verlagsanstalt, 1999.
Haak, R., *Habakkuk* (Supplements to Vetus Testamentum series, 44), Leiden: Brill, 1992.
Hagner, D., *Matthew 1-13*, Dallas, Texas: Word Books, 1993.
Hamm, D., 'Faith in the Epistle to the Hebrews: the Jesus Factor', *CBQ* 52 (1990) 270-291.
Hansen, G., 'A Paradigm of the Apocalypse: the Gospel in the Light of the Epistolary Analysis', in L. A. Jervis and P. Richardson (eds), *Gospel in Paul: Studies on Corinthians, Galatians and Romans for Richard N. Longenecker*, Sheffield: Sheffield Academic Press, 1994, 194–209.
Hanson, A., *Studies in Paul's Technique and Theology*, London: SPCK, 1974.
Harrington, D., *The Gospel of Matthew*, Collegeville, Minnesota: Liturgical Press, 1991.

Harris, M, J., *The Second Epistle to the Corinthians: A Commentary on the Greek Text*, Grand Rapids, Michigan: Eerdmans, 2005.

Harrison, P. N., *Paulines and Pastorals*, London: Villiers, 1964.

Harrisville, R. A., 'ΠΙΣΤΙΣ ΧΡΙΣΤΟΥ: Witness of the Fathers', *NovT* 36 (1994) 233–241.

Hatch, W. H. P., *The Pauline Idea of Faith in Relation to Jewish and Hellenistic Religion*, Cambridge: Harvard University Press, 1917.

Haussleiter, J., 'Der Glaube Jesu Christi und der christliche Glaube', *NKZ* 2 (1891) 109–145; 205–230.

–, 'Was versteht Paulus unter christlichem Glauben?': *Greifswalder Studien für H. Cremer*, 1895.

Hay, D., '*Pistis* as "Ground for Faith" in Hellenized Judaism and Paul', *JBL* 108 (1989) 461–476.

Hays, R. B., 'Psalm 143 and the Logic of Romans 3', *JBL* 99 (1980) 109–115.

–, '"Have We Found Abraham to be Our Forefather According to the Flesh"? A Reconsideration of Rom. 4:1', *NovT* (1985) 76–98.

–, '"The Righteous One" as Eschatological Deliverer', in J. Marcus and M. L. Soards (eds), *Apocalyptic and the New Testament: Essays in Honor of J. Louis Martyn* (JSNTS 24), Sheffield: JSOT, 1989, 191–215.

–, *Echoes of Scripture in the Letters of Paul*, New Haven: Yale University Press, 1989.

–, 'Πίστις and Pauline Christology', in E. Johnson and D. Hay (eds), *Pauline Theology IV: Looking Back, Pressing On* (SBL Symposium Series), Atlanta: Scholars Press, 1997, 35–60.

–, *The Faith of Jesus Christ: An Investigation of the Narrative Structure of Galatians 3:1–4:11* (SBL Dissertation Series 56, 2nd edn), Grand Rapids: Eerdmans, 2002.

Hebert, A. G., '"Faithfulness" and "Faith"', *Theology* 58 (1955) 373–379.

Hengel, M., *Judaism and Hellenism: Studies in their Encounter in Palestine during the Early Hellenistic Period*, vol. 1 (and vol. 2, *Notes and Bibliography*), London: SCM, 1974.

–, *Studies in Early Christology*, Edinburgh: T & T Clark, 1995.

Hiebert, T., *God of My Victory: the Ancient Hymn in Hab 3*, Atlanta: Scholars Press, 1986.

Holladay, J. R., 'Plausible Circumstances for the Prophecy of Habakkuk', *JBL* 120 (2001) 123–130.

Hooker, M., *Jesus and the Servant: The Influence of the Servant Concept of Deutero-Isaiah in the New Testament*, London: SPCK, 1959.

–, 'Adam in Romans 1', *NTS* 6 (1959/60) 297–306.

–, 'A Further Note on Romans 1', *NTS* 13 (1966/67) 181–183.

–, *The Son of Man in Mark: A Study of the Background of the Term 'Son of Man' and Its Use in St. Mark's Gospel*, London: SPCK, 1967.

–, 'ΠΙΣΤΙΣ ΧΡΙΣΤΟΥ', *NTS* 35 (1989) 321–342.

Horsley, R. (ed.), *Paul and Politics: Ekklesia, Israel, Imperium, Interpretation: Essays in Honor of Krister Stendahl*, Harrisburg: Trinity Press International, 2000.

Howard, G., 'Notes and Observations on the "Faith of Christ"', *HTR* 60 (1967) 459–465.

–, 'Romans 3:21–31 and the Inclusion of the Gentiles', *HTR* 63 (1970) 223–233.

–, '"The Faith of Christ"', *ExpT* 85 (1974) 212–215.

Hultgren, A. J., 'The *Pistis Christou* Formulation in Paul', *NovT* 22 (1980) 248–263.

–, *Paul's Gospel and Mission*, Philadelphia: Fortress, 1985.

Hurtado, L., 'The Doxology at the End of Romans', in E. J. Epp and G. D. Fee (eds), *New Testament Textual Criticism: Its Significance for Exegesis. Essays in Honor of Bruce M. Metzger*, Oxford: Clarendon Press, 1981, 185-199.

–, *One God, One Lord: Early Christian Devotion and Ancient Jewish Monotheism*, Edinburgh: T & T Clark, 1998.

–, 'Jesus' Divine Sonship in Paul's Epistle to the Romans', in S. Soderlund and N. T. Wright (eds), *Romans and the People of God: Essays in Honor of Gordon D. Fee on the Occasion of His 65ᵗʰ Birthday*, Grand Rapids: Eerdmans, 1999, 217-233.

Isaac, E., '1 (Ethiopic Apocalypse of) Enoch', in J. Charlesworth, *The Old Testament Pseudepigrapha I: Apocalyptic Literature and Testaments*, New York: Doubleday, 1983.

Janzen, J. G., 'Hab 2:2–4 in the Light of Recent Philological Advances', *HTR* 73 (1980) 53–78.

–, 'Eschatological Symbol and Existence in Habakkuk', *CBQ* 44 (1982) 394–414.

Jepsen, A., 'אמן', in G. J. Botterweck and H. Ringgren (eds), *TDOT I*, Grand Rapids: Eerdmans, 1974, 292–323.

Jeremias, J., 'πολλοί', in G. Kittel (ed.), *TDNT VI* (trans. G. W. Bromiley), Grand Rapids: Eerdmans, 1968, 536–545.

Jervis, L. A., *The Purpose of Romans: A Comparative Letter Structure Investigation*, Sheffield: JSOT, 1991.

Jewett, R., 'Ecumenical Theology for the Sake of Mission: Romans 1:1–17 + 15:14–16:24', in D. Hay and E. Johnson (eds), *Pauline Theology III: Romans* (SBL Symposium Series), Minneapolis: Fortress, 1995, 89–108.

Johnson, D., 'The Paralysis of Torah in Habakkuk I 4', *VT* 35 (1985) 257–266.

Käsemann, E., *New Testament Questions of Today* (trans. W. J. Montague), London: SCM, 1969.

–, *Perspectives on Paul* (trans. M. Kohl), London: SCM, 1974.

–, *Commentary on Romans* (trans. and ed. W. Bromiley), London: SCM, 1980.

Keck, L., '"Jesus" in Romans', *JBL* (1989) 443–460.

–, 'What Makes Romans Tick?', in D. Hay and E. Johnson (eds), *Pauline Theology III: Romans* (SBL Symposium Series), Minneapolis: Fortress, 1995, 3–29.

Kertelge, K., *'Rechtfertigung' bei Paulus: Studien zur Struktur und zum Bedeutungsgehalt des paulinischen Rechtfertigungsbegriffs*, NTA (NS) 3, Münster, 1967.

–, *Paul's Epistle to the Romans*, New York: Herder & Herder, 1972.

Kim, S., *The Origin of Paul's Gospel, Grand Rapids*: Eerdmans, 1982.

–, *Paul and the New Perspective: Second Thoughts on the Origins of Paul's Gospel*, Cambridge: Eerdmans, 2001.

Kittel, G., 'Πίστις' Ιησοῦ Χριστοῦ bei Paulus', *TSK* 79 (1906) 419–436.

Knibb, M. A., 'The Date of the Parables: A Critical Review', *NTS* 25 (1979) 345–359.

–, *The Qumran Community* (Cambridge Commentaries on Writings of the Jewish & Christian World: 200 BC to AD 100), Cambridge: Cambridge University Press, 1987.

–, 'The Teacher of Righteousness – A Messianic Title?', in W. D. Davies et al. (eds), *A Tribute to Geza Vermes, Essays on Jewish and Christian Literature and History*, Sheffield: JSOT, 1990, 50–65.

–, 'Messianism in the Pseudepigrapha in the Light of the Scrolls', in *DSD* 2 (1995) 165–184.

–, 'Eschatology and Messianism in the Dead Sea Scrolls', in P. Flint and J. VanderKam (eds), *The Dead Sea Scrolls After Fifty Years II*, Leiden: Brill, 1999, 379–402.

–, *Translating the Bible, The Ethiopic Version of the Old Testament* (The Schweich Lectures of the British Academy), Oxford: Oxford University Press, 1999.

Koch, Dietrich-Alex, 'Der Text von Hab 2:4b in der Septuaginta und im Neuen Testament', *ZNW* (1985) 68-85.

Kreitzer, L., *Jesus and God in Paul's Eschatology*, Sheffield: JSOT, 1987.

Kruse, G. C., *Paul, the Law and Justification*, Peabody, Massachusetts: Hendrickson, 1997.

Kümmel, W. G., '*Paresis* and *Endeixis*: A Contribution to the Understanding of the Pauline Doctrine of Justification', *JTC* 3 (1967) 1–13.

–, 'Die Botschaft des Römerbriefs' (Review of Käsemann's *An die Römer*, 1973), *ThLZ* 99 (1974) 481–488.

Kvanvig, H., *Roots of Apocalyptic: The Mesopotamian Background of the Enoch Figure and of the Son of Man*, Zürich: Neukirchener Verlag, 1988.

Lane, A. N. S., *Justification by Faith in Catholic – Protestant Dialogue: An Evangelical Assessment*, Edinburgh: T & T Clark, 2002.

Lane, W. L., *Hebrews* (WBC 47b), Dallas, Texas: Word Books, 1991

Lee, B., *A Developing Messianic Understanding of Hab 2:3–5 in the New Testament in the Context of Early Jewish Writings*, Unpublished PhD Dissertation, Southern Baptist Theological Seminary, 1998.

Leenhardt, F. J., *The Epistle to the Romans* (trans. Harold Knight), London: Lutterworth, 1961.

Légasse, S., 'Paul's Pre-Christian Career According to Acts', in R. Bauckham (ed.), *The Book of Acts in its First-century Setting: Palestinian Setting* (vol. 4), Carlisle: Paternoster, 1995, 365–390.

Levine, L. I., *Judaism and Hellenism in Antiquity: Conflict or Confluence*, Seattle: University of Washington, 1998.

Levinskaya, I., *The Book of Acts in Its First-century Setting: Diaspora Setting*, Grand Rapids: Eerdmans, 1996.

Levison, J. R., *Portraits of Adam in early Judaism: from Sirach to 2 Baruch*, Sheffield: JSOT, 1988.

Lietzmann, H., *Einführung in die Textgeschichte der Paulusbriefe: in die Römer* (HNT 8, 5th edn), Tübingen: Mohr Siebeck, 1971.

Lim, T., *Holy Scriptures in the Qumran Commentaries and Pauline Letters*, Oxford: Oxford University Press, 1997.

Lindsay, D. R., *Josephus and Faith, Πίστις and Πιστεύειν as Faith Terminology in the Writings of Flavius Josephus and in the New Testament*, Leiden: Brill, 1993.

Lohse, E., *Der Brief an die Römer*, KEK 4, Göttingen: Vandenhoeck & Ruprecht, 2003.

Longenecker, B., *Eschatology and the Covenant: A Comparison of 4 Ezra and Romans 1–11* (JSNTS), Sheffield: JSOT, 1991.

–, 'ΠΙΣΤΙΣ in Romans 3:25: Neglected Evidence for the 'Faithfulness of Christ'?', *NTS* 39 (1993) 478–480.

–, 'Contours of Covenant Theology in Post-Conversion Paul', in R. Longenecker (ed.), *The Road From Damascus: The Impact of Paul's Conversion on His Life, Thought and Ministry*, Grand Rapids: Eerdmans, 1997, 125-146.

–, *The Triumph of Abraham's God: The Transformation of the Identity in Galatians*, Edinburgh: T & T Clark, 1998.

Longenecker, R., *Paul, Apostle of Liberty*, New York: Harper & Row, 1964.

–, *The Christology of Early Jewish Christianity*, London: SCM, 1970.

–, *Biblical Exegesis in the Apostolic Period*, Grand Rapids: Eerdmans, 1975.

–, *Galatians* (WBC), Dallas: Word, 1990.

–, 'A Realised Hope, a New Commitment, a Developed Proclamation: Paul and Jesus', in R. Longenecker (ed.), *The Road From Damascus: The Impact of Paul's Conversion on His Life, Thought and Ministry*, Grand Rapids: Eerdmans, 1997, 18–42.

Luther, M., *Lectures on Romans* (trans. and ed. W. Pauck), London, 1961.

Malchow, B. V., 'A Manual for Future Monarchs', *CBQ* 47 (1985) 238–245.

Manson, T. W., 'The Argument from Prophecy', *JTS* 46 (1945) 129–136.

Marshall, I. H., 'Romans 16:25–27 – An Apt Conclusion', in S. Soderlund and N. T. Wright (eds), *Romans and the People of God: Essays in Honor of Gordon D. Fee on the Occasion of His 65th Birthday*, Grand Rapids: Eerdmans, 1999, 170–184.

Martin, L. L., *The Righteousness of God in Romans: A Study in Paul's Use of Jewish Tradition*, Unpublished PhD Dissertation, Marquette University, 1991.

Martyn, J. L., 'Apocalyptic Antinomies in Paul's Letter to the Galatians', *NTS* 31 (1985) 410–424.

–, 'A Law Observant Mission to Gentiles: The Background of Galatians', *SJT* 38 (1985) 307–324.

–, *Theological Issues in the Letters of Paul*, Edinburgh: T & T Clark, 1997.

–, *Galatians*, Edinburgh: T & T Clark, 1998.

Mason, R., *Zephaniah, Habakkuk, Joel*, Sheffield: JSOT, 1994.

Mason, S., *Flavius Josephus on the Pharisees: A Composition-Critical Study* (SPB 39), Leiden: Brill, 1991.

–, '"For I am not ashamed of the gospel" (Rom 1:16): The Gospel and the First Readers of Romans', in L. A. Jervis and P. Richardson (eds), *Gospel in Paul: Studies on Corinthians, Galatians and Romans for Richard N. Longenecker*, Sheffield: Sheffield Academic Press, 1994, 254–287.

–, 'Chief Priests, Sadducees, Pharisees and Sanhedrin in Acts', in R. Bauckham (ed.), *The Book of Acts in its First-century Setting: Palestinian Setting* (vol. iv), Carlisle: Paternoster, 1995, 115–177.

Matlock, R. B., *Unveiling the Apocalyptic Paul: Paul's Interpreters and the Rhetoric of Criticism* (JSNTS 127), Sheffield: Sheffield Academic Press, 1996.

–, 'Detheologizing the ΠΙΣΤΙΣ ΧΡΙΣΤΟΥ Debate: Cautionary Remarks from a Lexical Semantic Perspective', *NovT* 42 (2000) 1–23.

McGrath, A., *Iustitia Dei: A History of Christian Doctrine of Justification I* (Beginnings to 1500), 23–36; *II* (From 1500 to the present day), Cambridge: Cambridge University Press, 1986.

Michaels, J. R., *1 Peter* (WBC 49), Waco, Texas: Word Books, 1988.

Michel, O., *Der Brief an die Römer*, KEK 4, Göttingen: Vandenhoeck & Ruprecht, 1978.

Milik, J. T., –, *Ten Years of Discovery in the Wilderness of Judea* (trans. J. Strugnell), London: SCM, 1959.

–, *The Books of Enoch, Aramaic Fragments of Qumran Cave 4*, Oxford: Clarendon Press, 1976.

Millar, F., *The Emperor in the Roman World (31 BC–AD 337)* (2nd edn), London: Duckworth, 1992.

Miller, J. C., *The Obedience of Faith, the Eschatological People of God, and the Purpose of Romans*, Atlanta, Georgia: Society of Biblical Literature, 2000.

Minear, P. S., *The Obedience of Faith*, London: SCM, 1971.

Moffatt, J., *Hebrews: International Critical Commentary*, Edinburgh: T & T Clark, 1924.

Moo, D. J., *The Epistle to the Romans* (NICNT), Grand Rapids: Eerdmans, 1996.

Moody, R. M., 'The Habakkuk Quotation in Romans 1:17', *ExpT* (1981) 205–208.

Morris, L., *The Epistle to the Romans*, Leicester: IVP, 1988.

–, 'Faith', in G. F. Hawthorne et al. (eds), *Dictionary of Paul and His Letters*, Leicester: IVP, 1993, 285–291.

Motyer, A., *The Prophecy of Isaiah*, Leicester: IVP, 1993.

Moule, C. F. D., 'The Biblical Conception of "Faith"', *ExpT* 68 (1956–57) 157, 222.

–, *The Origin of Christology*, Cambridge: Cambridge University Press, 1977.

–, *JTS* 32 (1981), 498–502 (untitled review of Käsemann's *Commentary on Romans*).

Moxnes, H., 'Honour and Righteousness in Romans', *JSNT* 32 (1988) 61–77.

Moyise, S., 'Intertextuality and the Study of the Old Testament in the New Testament', in S. Moyise, *The Old Testament in the New Testament: Essays in Honour J. L. North*, Sheffield: Sheffield Academic Press, 2000.

Müller, C., *Gottes Gerechtigkeit und Gottes Volk: Eine Untersuchung zu Römer 9–11*, FRLANT 86, Göttingen, 1964.

Murphy-O'Connor, J., 'The Essenes and their History', *RB* 81 (1971) 215–244.

–, 'The Damascus Document Revisited', *RB* 92 (1985) 239–244.

–, *Paul: A Critical Life*, Oxford: Clarendon Press, 1996.

Murray, J., *The Epistle to the Romans: The English Text with Introduction, Exposition and Notes* (2 vols), Grand Rapids: Eerdmans, 1959.

Neusner, J., *Judaism and Its Social Metaphors: Israel in the History of Jewish Thought*, Cambridge: Cambridge University Press, 1989.

Nickelsburg, G., *Resurrection, Immortality and Eternal Life in Intertestamental Judaism*, Cambridge, Massachusetts: Harvard University Press, 1972.

–, *Jewish Literature Between the Bible and Mishnah: A Historical and Literary Introduction*, London: SCM, 1981.

–, 'Salvation Without and With a Messiah: Developing Beliefs in Writings Ascribed to Enoch', in J. Neusner et al. (eds), *Judaisms and their Messiahs at the Turn of the Christian Era*, Cambridge: Cambridge University Press, 1987, 49–68.

–, 'The Nature and Function of Revelation in 1 Enoch, Jubilees and Some Qumranic Documents', in E. Chason and M. Stone (eds), *Pseudepigraphic Perspectives: The Apocrypha and Pseudepigrapha in Light of the Dead Sea Scrolls,* Leiden: Brill, 1999, 91–120.

Nickelsburg, G. and Stone, M., *Faith and Piety in Early Judaism: Texts and Documents*, Philadelphia: Fortress, 1983.

Nielsen, E., 'The Righteous and the Wicked in Habaqquq', *ST* 6 (1953) 54–78.

Noort, E., 'Gan-Eden in the Hebrew Bible', in G. Luttikhuizen (ed.), *Paradise Interpreted: Representations of Biblical Paradise in Judaism and Christianity*, Leiden: Brill, 1999, 21–36.

Nygren, A., *Commentary on Romans* (trans. C. C. Rasmussen), London: SCM, 1955.

O'Neill, J. C., *Paul's Letter to the Romans*, London: Penguin, 1975.

Oepke, A., 'εἰς', in G. Kittel (ed.), *TDNT II*, Grand Rapids: Eerdmans, 1964, 420–434.

Olson, D. C., 'Enoch and the Son of Man in the Epilogue of the Parables', *JSP* 18 (1998) 27–38.

Orlinsky, H. M., 'The So-Called "Servant of the Lord" and "Suffering Servant" in Second Isaiah', in H. M. Orlinsky et al. (eds), *Studies on the Second Part of the Book of Isaiah*, Leiden: Brill, 1967.

Orlov, A., 'The Origin of the Name "Metatron" and the Text of 2 (Slavonic Apocalypse of) Enoch', *JSP* 21 (2000) 19–26.

Otto, E., 'Die Stellung der Wehe-Worte in der Verkündigung des Propheten Habakuk', *ZAW* 89 (1977) 73–107.

Owen, H. P., 'The Scope of Natural Revelation in Romans 1 and Acts 17', *NTS* (1959) 133–143.

Palmer, M. W., 'How Do We Know a Phrase is a Phrase? A Plea for Procedural Clarity in the Application of Linguistics to Biblical Greek', in S. Porter and D. Carson [eds], *Biblical Greek and Linguistics: Open Questions in Current Linguistic Research* (JSNTS 80), Sheffield: Sheffield Academic Press, 1993, 152-186.

Pardee, D., '*YPH* "Witness" in Hebrew and Ugaritic', *VT* 28 (1978) 204–213.

Parker, T. H. L., *Commentaries on the Epistle to the Romans, 1532–1542*, Edinburgh: T & T Clark, 1986.

Porter, S., *Verbal Aspect in the Greek of the New Testament, with Reference to Tense and Mood*, New York: Peter Lang, 1989.

–, *Idioms of the Greek New Testament* (2nd edn), Sheffield: JSOT, 1994.

–, 'The Use of the Old Testament: A Brief Comment on Method and Terminology', in C. A. Evans and J. A. Sanders (eds), *Early Christian Interpretation of the Scriptures of Israel*, Sheffield: Sheffield Academic Press, 1997, 79-96.

Quarles, L. C., 'From Faith to Faith: A Fresh Examination of the Prepositional Series in Romans 1:17', *NovT* 45 (2003) 1-21, 18.

Räisänen, H., *Paul and the Law*, Philadelphia: Fortress, 1982.

·–, *Beyond New Testament Theology: A Story and A Programme* (2nd edn), London: SCM, 2000.

Ramaroson, L., 'La justification par la foi *du* Christ Jésus', *ScEspr* 39 (1987) 81–92.

Reasoner, M., *The Strong and the Weak: Rom 14:1-15:13 in Context* (JSNTS 103), Cambridge: Cambridge University Press, 1999.

Reumann, J., *'Righteousness' in the New Testament: 'Justification' in the United States Lutheran-Roman Catholic Dialogue, With Responses by Joseph A. Fitzmyer and Jerome D. Quinn*, Philadelphia: Fortress, 1982.

–, 'Righteousness (*Greco-Roman World*)', in D. N. Freedman (editor-in-chief), *ABD V*, London: Doubleday, 1992, 742–745.

Ridderbos, H., *Paul: An Outline of His Theology* (trans. J. R. deWitt), Grand Rapids: Eerdmans, 1975.

Ringgren, H., 'חיה', *TDOT IV*, G. J. Botterweck and H. Ringgren (eds), Grand Rapids: Eerdmans, 1980, 324–344.

–, *Israelite Religion* (trans. D. Green), Lanham: University Press of America, 1988.

Roberts, J. J. M., *Nahum, Habakkuk, and Zephaniah* (OTL series), Louisville: Westminster/John Knox, 1991.

Robinson, J., *Wrestling with Romans*, London: SCM, 1979.

Rowland, C. C., *The Open Heaven: A Study in Apocalyptic in Judaism and Early Christianity*, London: SPCK, 1982.

–, *Christian Origins: An Account of the Setting and Character of the Most Important Sect of Judaism*, London: SPCK, 1985.

Sacchi, P., *Jewish Apocalyptic and its History* (trans. W.J. Short) (JSPS 20), Sheffield: Sheffield Academic Press, 1990.

Sanday, W. and Headlam, A. C., *The Epistle to the Romans: A Critical and Exegetical Commentary* (5th edn), Edinburgh: T & T Clark, 1914.

Sanders, E. P., *Paul and Palestinian Judaism, A Comparison of Patterns of Religion*, London: SCM, 1977.

–, *Paul, the Law, and the Jewish People*, Philadelphia: Fortress, 1983.

–, *Paul* (Past Masters series), Oxford: Oxford University Press, 1991.

–, *Judaism: Practice and Belief, 63 BCE – 66 CE*, London: SCM, 1992.

Schiffman, L. H., *Reclaiming the Dead Sea Scrolls: The History of Judaism, the Background of Christianity, the Lost Library of Qumran*, Philadelphia: JPS, 1994.

–, 'The Qumran Scrolls and Rabbinic Judaism', in P. Flint and J. VanderKam (eds), *The Dead Sea Scrolls After Fifty Years II*, Leiden: Brill, 1999, 552–571.

Schlatter, A., *Romans: The Righteousness of God* (trans. S. S. Schatzmann), Hendrickson: Peabody, 1995.

Schlier, H., *Der Römerbrief*, Herder: Freiburg, 1977.

Schmid, H. H., 'Creation, Righteousness, and Salvation' in B. W. Anderson (ed.), *Creation in the Old Testament*, London: SPCK, 1984, 102–117.

Schmidt, H. W., *Der Brief des Paulus an die Römer* (2nd edn), Berlin: Evangelische Verlagsanstalt, 1966.

Schmidt, K. L., 'ὁρίζω, ἀφορίζω, ἀποδιορίζω, προορίζω', in G. Kittel (ed.), *TDNT V*, (trans. G. W. Bromiley), Grand Rapids: Eerdmans, 1967.

Schmitz, O., *Die Christusgemeinschaft des Paulus im Lichte seines Genetivgebrauchs* (NTF 1/2), Gütersloh: Bertelsmann, 1924.

Schnackenburg, R., *The Johannine Epistles* (trans. Reginald and Ilsa Fuller), Kent, Great Britain: Burnes and Ooates, 1996.

Schreiber, S., 'Henoch als Menschensohn. Zur problematischen Schlussidentifikation in den Bilderreden des äthiopischen Henochbuches (äthHen 71, 14)', *ZNW* 91 (2000) 1–17.

Schreiner, S., 'Erwägungen zum Text von Hab 2.4–5', *ZAW* 86 (1974) 538–542.

Schreiner, T., *Romans* (Baker Exegetical Commentary on the New Testament), Grand Rapids: Baker Books, 1998.

Schrenk, G., 'δίκη, δίκαιος, δικαιοσύνη, δικαιόω, δικαίωμα, δικαίωσις, δικαιοκρισία', in G. Kittel (ed.), *TDNT II* (trans. G. W. Bromiley), Grand Rapids: Eerdmans, 1964, 174–225.

Schweitzer, A., *Paul and His Interpreters: A Critical History* (trans. W. Montgomery), London: A & C Black, 1912.

–, *My Life and Thought: An Autobiography* (trans. C.T. Campion), London: Allen & Unwin, 1933.

–, *The Mysticism of Paul the Apostle* (trans. W. Montgomery), London: A & C Black, 1953.

–, *The Teaching of Reverence for Life* (trans. R. H. Fuller), London: SPCK, 1970.

Schweizer, E., 'The Son of Man Again', *NTS* 10 (1963/64) 256–261.

–, 'πνεῦμα, πνευματικός', in G. Kittel (ed.), *TDNT VI*, (trans. G. W. Bromiley), Grand Rapids: Eerdmans, 1968, 332–445.

–, 'σάρξ, σαρκικός, σάρκινος', in G. Kittel (ed.), *TDNT VII*, (trans. G. W. Bromiley), Grand Rapids: Eerdmans, 1971, 98–151.

Scroggs, R., *The Last Adam. A Study in Pauline Anthropology*, Philadelphia: Fortress, 1966.

–, 'Paul as Rhetorician: Two Homilies in Romans 1–11', in R. Hamerton-Kelly and R. Scroggs (eds), *Jews, Greeks, and Christians: Religious Cultures in Late Antiquity: Essays in Honor of William David Davies*, Leiden: Brill, 1976, 271–298.

Scullion, J. J., 'Righteousness (OT)', in Freedman, D. N. (editor-in-chief), *ABD V*, London: Doubleday, 1992, 725–736.

Seifrid, M. A., *Justification by Faith: The Origin and Development of a Central Pauline Theme* (NovTS 68), Leiden: Brill, 1992.

–, *Christ, Our Righteousness: Paul's Theology of Justification*, Downers Grove: Apollos, 2000.

–, 'Unrighteous by Faith: Apostolic Proclamation in Romans 1:18-3:20', in D. A. Carson *et al* (eds), *Justification and Varigated Nomism: The Paradoxes of Paul* (WUNT 2/181), Tübingen: Mohr Siebeck, 2004, 105-145.

Seitz, O. J. F., 'Two Spirits in Man: An Essay in Biblical Exegesis', *NTS* 6 (1959/60) 82–95.

Sherwin-White, N., *Roman Society and Law in the New Testament: The Sarum Lectures 1960–1961*, Oxford: Clarendon Press, 1963.

Siegfried, H., *A History of Israel in Old Testament Times* (2nd edn), Philadelphia: Fortress, 1981.

Silva, M., 'Faith versus Works of the Law in Galatians', in D. A. Carson *et al* (eds), *Justification and Variegated Nomism: The Paradoxes of Paul* (WUNT 2/181), Tübingen: Mohr Siebeck, 2004, 217-248.

Sjöberg, E., *Der Menschensohn im äthiopischen Henochbuch*, Lund, 1946.

Smalley, S. S., *1, 2, 3 John* (WBC 51), Waco, Texas: Word Books, 1984.

Smith, J. Z., 'Prayer of Joseph', in J. Charlesworth (ed.), *The Old Testament Pseudepigrapha: Expansions of the 'Old Testament' and Legends; Wisdom and Philosophical Literature; Prayers, Psalms and Odes; Fragments of Judeo-Hellenistic Works*, vol. 2, London: Darton, Longman & Todd, 1983, 699–700.

–, 'On the History of ΑΠΟΚΑΛΥΠΤΩ and ΑΠΟΚΑΛΥΨΙΣ', in D. Hellholm (ed.), *Apocalypticism in the Mediterranean World and the Near East*, Tübingen: Mohr Siebeck, 1983, 9-20.

Snodgrass, K., 'The Gospel in Romans: A Theology of Revelation', in L. A. Jervis et al. (eds), *Gospel in Paul, Studies on Corinthians, Galatians and Romans for Richard Longenecker*, Sheffield: Sheffield Academic Press, 1994, 288–314.

Sollamo, R., 'The Koine Background for the Repetition and Non-Repetition of the Possessive Pronoun in Co-ordinate Items', in D. Fraenkel and J. W. Wevers (eds), *Studien zur Septuaginta: Robert Hanhart zu Ehren*, Göttingen: Vanderhoeck & Ruprecht, 1990, 52-63.

–, 'Repetition of Possessive Pronouns in the Greek Psalter: The Use and Non-Use of Possessive Pronouns in Renderings of Hebrew Coordinate Items with Possessive Pronouns', in V. Hiebert, C. E. Cox & P. J. Gendry (eds), *The Old Greek Psalter: Studies in Honour of Albert Pietersma*, Sheffield: Sheffield Academic Press, 44-53.

Stanley, C. D., *Paul and the Language of Scripture: Citation Technique in the Pauline Epistles and Contemporary Literature* (JSNTS 74), Cambridge: Cambridge University Press, 1992.

–, 'The Social Environment of "Free" Biblical Quotations in the New Testament', C. A. Evans and J. A. Sanders (eds), *Early Christian Interpretation of the Scriptures of Israel: Investigations and Proposals*, Sheffield: Sheffield Academic Press, 1997, 19-27.

–, '"Pearls before Swine": Did Paul's Audience Understand His Biblical Quotations?', *NovT* 41 (1999) 124-144.

Stendahl, K., 'The Apostle Paul and the Introspective Conscience of the West', *HTR* 56 (1963), 199–215.

–, *Paul among Jews and Gentiles, and Other Essays*, London: SCM, 1976.

Stone, M. E. and Greenfield, J. C., 'The Enochic Pentateuch and the Date of the Similitudes', *HTR* 70 (1977) 51–65.

Stowers, S., 'ΕΚ ΠΙΣΤΕΩΣ and ΔΙΑ ΤΗΣ ΠΙΣΤΕΩΣ in Romans 3:30', *JBL* 108 (1989) 665–674.

–, *A Rereading of Romans: Justice, Jews, and Gentiles*, New Haven: Yale University Press, 1994.

Strecker, G., *The Johannine Letters* (trans. Linda Maloney), Minneapolis: Fortress, 1996.

Strobel, A., *Untersuchungen zum eschatologischen Verzögerungsproblem: Auf Grund der spätjüdisch-urchristlichen Geschichte von Habakuk 2,2ff*, Leiden: Brill, 1961.

Stuhlmacher, P., *Gerechtigkeit Gottes bei Paulus*, FRLANT 87, Göttingen, 1965.

–, *Reconciliation, Law, and Righteousness: Essays in Biblical Theology* (trans. E. R. Kalin), Philadelphia: Fortress, 1986.

–, 'The Pauline Gospel', in P. Stuhlmacher (ed.), *The Gospel and the Gospels*, Grand Rapids: Eerdmans, 1991, 149-172.

–, *Paul's Letter to the Romans: A Commentary* (trans. S. C. Hafemann), Louisville: Westminster/John Knox Press, 1994.

–, 'Eschatology and Hope in Paul', *EQ* 72 (2000) 315–333.

Sturm, R. E., *An Exegetical Study of the Apostle Paul's Use of the Word Apocalypto/Apokalypsis: The Gospel as God's Apokalypse*, Unpublished PhD Dissertation, New York: Union Theological Seminary, 1985.

–, 'Defining the Word "Apocalyptic": A Problem in Biblical Criticism', in J. Marcus and M. L. Soards (eds), *Apocalyptic and the New Testament: Essays in Honor of J. Louis Martyn* (JSNTS 24), Sheffield: JSOT, 1989, 17–48.

Sweeney, M. A., 'Structure, Genre, and Intent in the Book of Habakkuk', *VT* 41 (1991) 63–83.

Swete, H. B., *An Introduction to the Old Testament in Greek* (rev. R. R. Ottley and H. Thackeray), Cambridge: Cambridge University Press, 1900

Taylor, G. M., 'The Function of πίστις Χριστοῦ in Galatians', *JBL* 85 (1966) 58–76.

Taylor, J., 'Why were the Disciples First Called "Christians" at Antioch? (Acts 11:26)', *RB* 101:1 (1994) 75–94.

–, 'From Faith to Faith: Romans 1.17 in the Light of Greek Idiom', *NTS* (2004) 337-348.

Theisohn, J., *Der auserwählte Richter: Untersuchungen zum traditionsgeschichtlichen Ort der Menschensohngestalt der Bilderreden des Äthiopischen Henoch* (SUNT 12), Göttingen, 1975.

Thomas, H. O., *John Wesley's and Rudolf Bultmann's Understanding of Justification by Faith, Compared and Contrasted*, Unpublished PhD Dissertation, Bristol University, 1990.

Thrall, M. E., *A Critical and Exegetical Commentary on the Second Epistle to the Corinthians*, Edinburgh: T&T Clark, 1994.

Tigchelaar, E. J. C., 'Eden and Paradise: The Garden Motif in Some Early Jewish Texts (1 Enoch and Other Texts Found at Qumran)', in G. P. Luttikhuizen (ed.), *Paradise Interpreted, Representation of Biblical Paradise in Judaism and Christianity*, Leiden: Brill, 1999, 37–62.

Torrance, T. F., 'One Aspect of the Biblical Conception of Faith', *ExpT* 68 (1956–57) 111–114, 221-222.

Tov, E., *Textual Criticism of the Hebrew Bible*, Minneapolis: Fortress, 1992.

–, 'Groups of Biblical Texts Found at Qumran', in D. Dimant & L. Schiffman, *Time to Prepare the Way in the Wilderness: Papers on the Qumran Scrolls by Fellows of the Institute for Advanced Studies of the Hebrew University, Jerusalem*, Leiden: Brill, 1995, 85-102.

–, *The Text-Critical Use of the Septuagint in Biblical Research* (2nd edn), Jerusalem: Simor, 1997

–, 'The Significance of the Texts from the Judean Desert for the History of the Text of the Hebrew Bible: A New Synthesis', in F. H. Cryer and T. L. Thompson (eds), *Qumran Between the Old and New Testaments*, 277-309, Sheffield: Sheffield Academic Press, 1998.

–, *The Greek and Hebrew Bible: Collected Essays on the Septuagint*, Leiden: Brill, 1999.

–, 'The Biblical Texts from the Judean Desert', in E. Herbert and E. Tov, *The Bible as Book: the Hebrew Bible and the Judean Desert Discoveries*, London: The British Library, 2002, 139-166.

–, *Scribal Practices and Approaches Reflected in the Texts from the Judean Desert*, Leiden: Brill, 2004.

Ullendorff, E., 'An Aramaic "Vorlage" of the Ethiopic Text of Enoch?', *Atti del Convegno Internazionale di Studi Etiopici*, Rome, 1960, 259–268.

–, *Ethiopia and the Bible: The Schweich Lectures*, Oxford: Oxford University Press, 1968.

Ulrich, E., 'The Dead Sea Scrolls and the Biblical Text', in P. Flint and J. VanderKam (eds), *The Dead Sea Scrolls After Fifty Years II*, Leiden: Brill, 1998, 79-100.

Ulrichs, K. F., *Christusglaube: Studien zum Syntagma πίστις Χριστοῦ und zum paulinischen Verständnis von Glaube und Rechtfertigung* (WUNT 2/227), Tübingen: Mohr Siebeck, 2007.

Van Ruiten, J. T. A. G. M., 'Eden and the Temple: The Rewriting of Genesis 2:4–3:24 in the Book of Jubilees', in G. P. Luttikhuizen (ed.), *Paradise Interpreted, Representation of Biblical Paradise in Judaism and Christianity*, Leiden: Brill, 1999, 63–81.

VanderKam, J. C., *Enoch and the Growth of an Apocalyptic Tradition*, Washington, DC: Catholic Biblical Association of America, 1984.

–, 'Righteous One, Messiah, Chosen One, and Son of Man', in J. Charlesworth (ed.), *The Messiah: Developments in Earliest Judaism and Christianity*, Minneapolis: Fortress, 1992, 169–191.

–, '1 Enoch, Enochic Motifs, and Enoch in Early Christian Literature', in J. VanderKam and W. Adler (eds), *The Jewish Apocalyptic Heritage in the Early Christianity*, Minneapolis: Fortress, 1996, 33–101.

–, *Calendars in the Dead Sea Scrolls: Measuring Time*, London: Routledge, 1998.

–, 'Identity and History of the Community', in P. Flint and J. VanderKam (eds), *The Dead Sea Scrolls After Fifty Years II*, Leiden: Brill, 1999, 487–533.

–, *From Revelation to Canon: Studies in the Hebrew Bible and Second Temple Literature*, Leiden: Brill, 2000.

Vermes, G., *The Dead Sea Scrolls: Qumran in Perspective* (rev. edn), London: SCM, 1994.

Von Rad, G., *Old Testament Theology*, 2 vols, New York: Harper & Row, 1965.

Walker Jr, W. O., 'Romans 1.18-2.29: A Non-Pauline Interpolation?', *NTS* 45 (1999) 533–552.

Wallace, D. B., *Greek Grammar Beyond the Basics: An Exegetical Syntax of the New Testament with Scripture, Subject and Greek Word Indexes*, Grand Rapids: Zondervan, 1996.

Wallis, I. G., *The Faith of Jesus Christ in Early Christian Traditions*, Cambridge: Cambridge University Press, 1995.

Watson, F., *Paul, Judaism and the Gentiles*, Cambridge: Cambridge University Press, 1986.

–, *Paul and the Hermeneutics of Faith*, London: T & T Clark International, 2004.

Watts, R. E., '"For I Am Not Ashamed of the Gospel": Romans 1:16–17 and Habakkuk 2:4', in S. K. Soderlund and N. T. Wright (eds), *Romans and the People of God: Essays in Honor of Gordon D. Fee on the Occasion of His 65th Birthday*, Grand Rapids: Eerdmans, 1999, 3–25.

Way, D., *The Lordship of Christ: Ernst Käsemann's Interpretations of Paul's Theology*, Oxford: Clarendon Press, 1991.

Wedderburn, A. J., 'Adam in Paul's Letter to the Romans', in E. A. Livingstone (ed.), *Studia Biblica* 3: *Papers on Paul and Other New Testament Writers*, Sheffield: JSOT, 1980, 413–430.

–, *The Reasons for Romans*, Edinburgh: T & T Clark, 1988.

–, 'The Purpose and Occasion of Romans Again', in K. P. Donfried (ed.), *The Romans Debate* (rev. and expanded edn), Edinburgh: T & T Clark, 1991, 195–202.

Werman, C., 'Qumran and the Book of Noah', in E. Chason and M. Stone (eds), *Pseudepigraphic Perspectives: The Apocrypha and Pseudepigrapha in Light of the Dead Sea Scrolls*, Leiden: Brill, 1999, 171–182.

Westerholm, S., 'The "New Perspective" at Twenty Five', in D. A. Carson *et al* (eds), *Justification and Variegated Nomism: The Paradoxes of Paul* (WUNT 2/181), Tübingen: Mohr Siebeck, 2004, 1-38.

–, *Perspectives Old and New on Paul: The "Lutheran" Paul and His Critics*, Grand Rapids, Michigan: Eerdmans, 2004.

Whitsett, C. G., 'Son of God, Seed of David: Paul's Messianic Exegesis in Romans 1:3–4', *JBL* (2000) 661–681.

Wiefel, W., 'Jewish Community in Ancient Rome and the Origins of Roman Christianity', in K. P. Donfried (ed.), *The Romans Debate* (rev. and expanded edn), Edinburgh: T & T Clark, 1991, 85–101.

Wilckens, U., *Der Brief an die Römer I*, Zürich: Benziger, 1978.

Williams, S. K., *Jesus' Death as Saving Event: The Background and Origin of a Concept*, Missoula: Scholars Press, 1975.

–, 'The "Righteousness of God" in Romans', *JBL* 99 (1980) 241–290.

–, 'Again *Pistis Christou*', *CBQ* 49 (1987) 431–447.

Winninge, M., *Sinners and the Righteous: A Comparative Study of the Psalms of Solomon and Paul's Letters*, Stockholm: Almqvist & Wiksell International, 1995.

Wise, M. O., '4QFlorilegium and the Temple of Adam', *RevQ* 15 (1991) 103–132.

Woude, A. S., 'Wicked Priest or Wicked Priests: Reflections on the Identification of the Wicked Priest in the Habakkuk Commentary', *JJS* 33 (1982) 349–359.

Wright, N. T., *The Messiah and the People of God: A Study in Pauline Theology with Particular Reference to the Argument of the Epistle to the Romans*, Unpublished DPhil Dissertation, Oxford University, 1980.

–, 'A New Tübingen School?: Ernst Käsemann and His Commentary on Romans', *Themelios* 7:3 (1982) 6–16.

–, *The Climax of the Covenant, Christ and the Law in Pauline Theology*, Edinburgh: T & T Clark, 1991.

–, *The New Testament and the People of God*, London: SPCK, 1992.

–, 'On Becoming the Righteousness of God: 2 Corinthians 5:21', in D. Hay and E. Johnson, *Pauline Theology II: 1 and 2 Corinthians*, Minneapolis: Fortress, 1993, 200-208.

–, 'Romans and the Theology of Paul', in D. Hay and E. Johnson, *Pauline Theology III: Romans* (SBL Symposium Series), Minneapolis: Fortress, 1995, 30–67.

–, *Jesus and the Victory of God*, London: SPCK, 1996.

–, *What Saint Paul Really Said: Was Paul of Tarsus the Real Founder of Christianity?*, Oxford: Lion, 1997.

–, 'New Exodus, New Inheritance: The Narrative Structure of Romans 3–8', in S. Soderlund and N. T. Wright (eds), *Romans and the People of God: Essays in Honor of Gordon D. Fee on the Occasion of His 65th Birthday*, Grand Rapids: Eerdmans, 1999, 26–35.

–, 'The Letter to the Romans: Introduction, Commentary and Reflections', in *The New Interpreters Bible*, Nashville, Tenn.: Abingdon, 2002, 395-770.

Yefru, W., 'An Inquiry into the Ethiopic Book of Henok: The European and Ethiopian Views', in W. Yefru (ed.), *Henok* (1994) 57-72.

Ziesler, J. A., *The Meaning of Righteousness in Paul: A Linguistic and Theological Enquiry*, Cambridge: Cambridge University Press, 1972.

–, *Pauline Christianity* (rev. edn), Oxford: Oxford University Press, 1983.

–, *Paul's Letter to the Romans*, London: SCM, 1989.

Zimmerli, W., *Ezekiel*, vol. 2 (trans. J. D. Martin), Philadelphia: Fortress, 1983.

Index of References

Old Testament

Apocrypha

Pseudepigrapha

New Testament

Ancient Writings

Index of Authors

Index of Subjects

Wissenschaftliche Untersuchungen zum Neuen Testament
Alphabetical Index of the First and Second Series

Bock, Darrell L.: Blasphemy and Exaltation in Judaism and the Final Examination of Jesus. 1998. *Vol. II/106.*

Bockmuehl, Markus N.A.: Revelation and Mystery in Ancient Judaism and Pauline Christianity. 1990. *Vol. II/36.*

Bøe, Sverre: Gog and Magog. 2001. *Vol. II/135.*

Böhlig, Alexander: Gnosis und Synkretismus. Vol. 1 1989. *Vol. 47* – Vol. 2 1989. *Vol. 48.*

Böhm, Martina: Samarien und die Samaritai bei Lukas. 1999. *Vol. II/111.*

Böttrich, Christfried: Weltweisheit – Menschheitsethik – Urkult. 1992. *Vol. II/50.*

– / *Herzer, Jens* (Ed.): Josephus und das Neue Testament. 2007. *Vol. 209.*

Bolyki, János: Jesu Tischgemeinschaften. 1997. *Vol. II/96.*

Bosman, Philip: Conscience in Philo and Paul. 2003. *Vol. II/166.*

Bovon, François: Studies in Early Christianity. 2003. *Vol. 161.*

Brändl, Martin: Der Agon bei Paulus. 2006. *Vol. II/222.*

Breytenbach, Cilliers: see *Frey, Jörg.*

Brocke, Christoph vom: Thessaloniki – Stadt des Kassander und Gemeinde des Paulus. 2001. *Vol. II/125.*

Brunson, Andrew: Psalm 118 in the Gospel of John. 2003. *Vol. II/158.*

Büchli, Jörg: Der Poimandres – ein paganisiertes Evangelium. 1987. *Vol. II/27.*

Bühner, Jan A.: Der Gesandte und sein Weg im 4. Evangelium. 1977. *Vol. II/2.*

Burchard, Christoph: Untersuchungen zu Joseph und Aseneth. 1965. *Vol. 8.*

– Studien zur Theologie, Sprache und Umwelt des Neuen Testaments. Ed. by D. Sänger. 1998. *Vol. 107.*

Burnett, Richard: Karl Barth's Theological Exegesis. 2001. *Vol. II/145.*

Byron, John: Slavery Metaphors in Early Judaism and Pauline Christianity. 2003. *Vol. II/162.*

Byrskog, Samuel: Story as History – History as Story. 2000. *Vol. 123.*

Cancik, Hubert (Ed.): Markus-Philologie. 1984. *Vol. 33.*

Capes, David B.: Old Testament Yaweh Texts in Paul's Christology. 1992. *Vol. II/47.*

Caragounis, Chrys C.: The Development of Greek and the New Testament. 2004. *Vol. 167.*

– The Son of Man. 1986. *Vol. 38.*

– see *Fridrichsen, Anton.*

Carleton Paget, James: The Epistle of Barnabas. 1994. *Vol. II/64.*

Carson, D.A., O'Brien, Peter T. and *Mark Seifrid* (Ed.): Justification and Variegated Nomism.
Vol. 1: The Complexities of Second Temple Judaism. 2001. *Vol. II/140.*
Vol. 2: The Paradoxes of Paul. 2004. *Vol. II/181.*

Chae, Young Sam: Jesus as the Eschatological Davidic Shepherd. 2006. *Vol. II/216.*

Chester, Andrew: Messiah and Exaltation. 2007. *Vol. 207.*

Chibici-Revneanu, Nicole: Die Herrlichkeit des Verherrlichten. 2007. *Vol. II/231.*

Ciampa, Roy E.: The Presence and Function of Scripture in Galatians 1 and 2. 1998. *Vol. II/102.*

Classen, Carl Joachim: Rhetorical Criticsm of the New Testament. 2000. *Vol. 128.*

Colpe, Carsten: Iranier – Aramäer – Hebräer – Hellenen. 2003. *Vol. 154.*

Crump, David: Jesus the Intercessor. 1992. *Vol. II/49.*

Dahl, Nils Alstrup: Studies in Ephesians. 2000. *Vol. 131.*

Daise, Michael A.: Feasts in John. 2007. *Vol. 229.*

Deines, Roland: Die Gerechtigkeit der Tora im Reich des Messias. 2004. *Vol. 177.*

– Jüdische Steingefäße und pharisäische Frömmigkeit. 1993. *Vol. II/52.*

– Die Pharisäer. 1997. *Vol. 101.*

Deines, Roland and *Karl-Wilhelm Niebuhr* (Ed.): Philo und das Neue Testament. 2004. *Vol. 172.*

Dennis, John A.: Jesus' Death and the Gathering of True Israel. 2006. *Vol. 217.*

Dettwiler, Andreas and *Jean Zumstein* (Ed.): Kreuzestheologie im Neuen Testament. 2002. *Vol. 151.*

Dickson, John P.: Mission-Commitment in Ancient Judaism and in the Pauline Communities. 2003. *Vol. II/159.*

Dietzfelbinger, Christian: Der Abschied des Kommenden. 1997. *Vol. 95.*

Dimitrov, Ivan Z., James D.G. Dunn, Ulrich Luz and *Karl-Wilhelm Niebuhr* (Ed.): Das Alte Testament als christliche Bibel in orthodoxer und westlicher Sicht. 2004. *Vol. 174.*

Dobbeler, Axel von: Glaube als Teilhabe. 1987. *Vol. II/22.*

Dryden, J. de Waal: Theology and Ethics in 1 Peter. 2006. *Vol. II/209.*

Du Toit, David S.: Theios Anthropos. 1997. *Vol. II/91.*

Dübbers, Michael: Christologie und Existenz im Kolosserbrief. 2005. *Vol. II/191.*

Dunn, James D.G.: The New Perspective on Paul. 2005. *Vol. 185.*

Dunn , James D.G. (Ed.): Jews and Christians. 1992. *Vol. 66.*

– Paul and the Mosaic Law. 1996. *Vol. 89.*

– see *Dimitrov, Ivan Z.*

–, *Hans Klein, Ulrich Luz* and *Vasile Mihoc* (Ed.)*:* Auslegung der Bibel in orthodoxer und westlicher Perspektive. 2000. *Vol. 130.*

Ebel, Eva: Die Attraktivität früher christlicher Gemeinden. 2004. *Vol. II/178.*

Ebertz, Michael N.: Das Charisma des Gekreuzigten. 1987. *Vol. 45.*

Eckstein, Hans-Joachim: Der Begriff Syneidesis bei Paulus. 1983. *Vol. II/10.*

– Verheißung und Gesetz. 1996. *Vol. 86.*

Ego, Beate: Im Himmel wie auf Erden. 1989. *Vol. II/34.*

Ego, Beate, Armin Lange and *Peter Pilhofer* (Ed.): Gemeinde ohne Tempel – Community without Temple. 1999. *Vol. 118.*

– and *Helmut Merkel* (Ed.): Religiöses Lernen in der biblischen, frühjüdischen und frühchristlichen Überlieferung. 2005. *Vol. 180.*

Eisen, Ute E.: see *Paulsen, Henning.*

Elledge, C.D.: Life after Death in Early Judaism. 2006. *Vol. II/208.*

Ellis, E. Earle: Prophecy and Hermeneutic in Early Christianity. 1978. *Vol. 18.*

– The Old Testament in Early Christianity. 1991. *Vol. 54.*

Endo, Masanobu: Creation and Christology. 2002. *Vol. 149.*

Ennulat, Andreas: Die 'Minor Agreements'. 1994. *Vol. II/62.*

Ensor, Peter W.: Jesus and His 'Works'. 1996. *Vol. II/85.*

Eskola, Timo: Messiah and the Throne. 2001. *Vol. II/142.*

– Theodicy and Predestination in Pauline Soteriology. 1998. *Vol. II/100.*

Fatehi, Mehrdad: The Spirit's Relation to the Risen Lord in Paul. 2000. *Vol. II/128.*

Feldmeier, Reinhard: Die Krisis des Gottessohnes. 1987. *Vol. II/21.*

– Die Christen als Fremde. 1992. *Vol. 64.*

Feldmeier, Reinhard and *Ulrich Heckel* (Ed.): Die Heiden. 1994. *Vol. 70.*

Fletcher-Louis, Crispin H.T.: Luke-Acts: Angels, Christology and Soteriology. 1997. *Vol. II/94.*

Förster, Niclas: Marcus Magus. 1999. *Vol. 114.*

Forbes, Christopher Brian: Prophecy and Inspired Speech in Early Christianity and its Hellenistic Environment. 1995. *Vol. II/75.*

Fornberg, Tord: see *Fridrichsen, Anton.*

Fossum, Jarl E.: The Name of God and the Angel of the Lord. 1985. *Vol. 36.*

Foster, Paul: Community, Law and Mission in Matthew's Gospel. *Vol. II/177.*

Fotopoulos, John: Food Offered to Idols in Roman Corinth. 2003. *Vol. II/151.*

Frenschkowski, Marco: Offenbarung und Epiphanie. Vol. 1 1995. *Vol. II/79* – Vol. 2 1997. *Vol. II/80.*

Frey, Jörg: Eugen Drewermann und die biblische Exegese. 1995. *Vol. II/71.*

– Die johanneische Eschatologie. Vol. I. 1997. *Vol. 96.* – Vol. II. 1998. *Vol. 110.* – Vol. III. 2000. *Vol. 117.*

Frey, Jörg and *Cilliers Breytenbach* (Ed.): Aufgabe und Durchführung einer Theologie des Neuen Testaments. 2007. *Vol. 205.*

– and *Udo Schnelle (Ed.):* Kontexte des Johannesevangeliums. 2004. *Vol. 175.*

– and *Jens Schröter* (Ed.): Deutungen des Todes Jesu im Neuen Testament. 2005. *Vol. 181.*

–, *Jan G. van der Watt,* and *Ruben Zimmermann* (Ed.): Imagery in the Gospel of John. 2006. *Vol. 200.*

Freyne, Sean: Galilee and Gospel. 2000. *Vol. 125.*

Fridrichsen, Anton: Exegetical Writings. Edited by C.C. Caragounis and T. Fornberg. 1994. *Vol. 76.*

Gäbel, Georg: Die Kulttheologie des Hebräerbriefes. 2006. *Vol. II/212.*

Gäckle, Volker: Die Starken und die Schwachen in Korinth und in Rom. 2005. *Vol. 200.*

Garlington, Don B.: 'The Obedience of Faith'. 1991. *Vol. II/38.*

– Faith, Obedience, and Perseverance. 1994. *Vol. 79.*

Garnet, Paul: Salvation and Atonement in the Qumran Scrolls. 1977. *Vol. II/3.*

Gemünden, Petra von (Ed.): see *Weissenrieder, Annette.*

Gese, Michael: Das Vermächtnis des Apostels. 1997. *Vol. II/99.*

Gheorghita, Radu: The Role of the Septuagint in Hebrews. 2003. *Vol. II/160.*

Gordley, Matthew E.: The Colossian Hymn in Context. 2007. *Vol. II/228.*

Gräbe, Petrus J.: The Power of God in Paul's Letters. 2000. *Vol. II/123.*

Gräßer, Erich: Der Alte Bund im Neuen. 1985. *Vol. 35.*

– Forschungen zur Apostelgeschichte. 2001. *Vol. 137.*

Grappe, Christian (Ed.): Le Repas de Dieu / Das Mahl Gottes. 2004. *Vol. 169.*

Green, Joel B.: The Death of Jesus. 1988. *Vol. II/33.*

Gregg, Brian Han: The Historical Jesus and the Final Judgment Sayings in Q. 2005. *Vol. II/207.*

Gregory, Andrew: The Reception of Luke and Acts in the Period before Irenaeus. 2003. *Vol. II/169.*

Grindheim, Sigurd: The Crux of Election. 2005. *Vol. II/202.*

Gundry, Robert H.: The Old is Better. 2005. *Vol. 178.*

Gundry Volf, Judith M.: Paul and Perseverance. 1990. *Vol. II/37.*

Häußer, Detlef: Christusbekenntnis und Jesusüberlieferung bei Paulus. 2006. *Vol. 210.*

Hafemann, Scott J.: Suffering and the Spirit. 1986. *Vol. II/19.*

– Paul, Moses, and the History of Israel. 1995. *Vol. 81.*

Hahn, Ferdinand: Studien zum Neuen Testament.
Vol. I: Grundsatzfragen, Jesusforschung, Evangelien. 2006. *Vol. 191.*
Vol. II: Bekenntnisbildung und Theologie in urchristlicher Zeit. 2006. *Vol. 192.*

Hahn, Johannes (Ed.): Zerstörungen des Jerusalemer Tempels. 2002. *Vol. 147.*

Hamid-Khani, Saeed: Relevation and Concealment of Christ. 2000. *Vol. II/120.*

Hannah, Darrel D.: Michael and Christ. 1999. *Vol. II/109.*

Harrison; James R.: Paul's Language of Grace in Its Graeco-Roman Context. 2003. *Vol. II/172.*

Hartman, Lars: Text-Centered New Testament Studies. Ed. von D. Hellholm. 1997. *Vol. 102.*

Hartog, Paul: Polycarp and the New Testament. 2001. *Vol. II/134.*

Heckel, Theo K.: Der Innere Mensch. 1993. *Vol. II/53.*

– Vom Evangelium des Markus zum viergestaltigen Evangelium. 1999. *Vol. 120.*

Heckel, Ulrich: Kraft in Schwachheit. 1993. *Vol. II/56.*

– Der Segen im Neuen Testament. 2002. *Vol. 150.*

– see *Feldmeier, Reinhard.*

– see *Hengel, Martin.*

Heiligenthal, Roman: Werke als Zeichen. 1983. *Vol. II/9.*

Heliso, Desta: Pistis and the Righteous One. 2007. *Vol. II/235.*

Hellholm, D.: see *Hartman, Lars.*

Hemer, Colin J.: The Book of Acts in the Setting of Hellenistic History. 1989. *Vol. 49.*

Hengel, Martin: Judentum und Hellenismus. 1969, ³1988. *Vol. 10.*

– Die johanneische Frage. 1993. *Vol. 67.*

– Judaica et Hellenistica. Kleine Schriften I. 1996. *Vol. 90.*

– Judaica, Hellenistica et Christiana. Kleine Schriften II. 1999. *Vol. 109.*

– Paulus und Jakobus. Kleine Schriften III. 2002. *Vol. 141.*

– Studien zur Christologie. Kleine Schriften IV. 2006. *Vol. 201.*

– and *Anna Maria Schwemer:* Paulus zwischen Damaskus und Antiochien. 1998. *Vol. 108.*

– Der messianische Anspruch Jesu und die Anfänge der Christologie. 2001. *Vol. 138.*

Hengel, Martin and *Ulrich Heckel* (Ed.): Paulus und das antike Judentum. 1991. *Vol. 58.*

– and *Hermut Löhr* (Ed.): Schriftauslegung im antiken Judentum und im Urchristentum. 1994. *Vol. 73.*

– and *Anna Maria Schwemer* (Ed.): Königsherrschaft Gottes und himmlischer Kult. 1991. *Vol. 55.*

– Die Septuaginta. 1994. *Vol. 72.*

–, *Siegfried Mittmann* and *Anna Maria Schwemer* (Ed.): La Cité de Dieu / Die Stadt Gottes. 2000. *Vol. 129.*

Hentschel, Anni: Diakonia im Neuen Testament. 2007. *Vol. 226.*

Hernández Jr., Juan: Scribal Habits and Theological Influence in the Apocalypse. 2006. *Vol. II/218.*

Herrenbrück, Fritz: Jesus und die Zöllner. 1990. *Vol. II/41.*

Herzer, Jens: Paulus oder Petrus? 1998. *Vol. 103.*

– see *Böttrich, Christfried.*

Hill, Charles E.: From the Lost Teaching of Polycarp. 2005. *Vol. 186.*

Hoegen-Rohls, Christina: Der nachösterliche Johannes. 1996. *Vol. II/84.*

Hoffmann, Matthias Reinhard: The Destroyer and the Lamb. 2005. *Vol. II/203.*

Hofius, Otfried: Katapausis. 1970. *Vol. 11.*

– Der Vorhang vor dem Thron Gottes. 1972. *Vol. 14.*

– Der Christushymnus Philipper 2,6–11. 1976, ²1991. *Vol. 17.*

– Paulusstudien. 1989, ²1994. *Vol. 51.*

– Neutestamentliche Studien. 2000. *Vol. 132.*

– Paulusstudien II. 2002. *Vol. 143.*

– and *Hans-Christian Kammler:* Johannesstudien. 1996. *Vol. 88.*

Holtz, Traugott: Geschichte und Theologie des Urchristentums. 1991. *Vol. 57.*

Hommel, Hildebrecht: Sebasmata.
Vol. 1 1983. *Vol. 31.*
Vol. 2 1984. *Vol. 32.*

Horbury, William: Herodian Judaism and New Testament Study. 2006. *Vol. 193.*

Horst, Pieter W. van der: Jews and Christians in Their Graeco-Roman Context. 2006. *Vol. 196.*

Hvalvik, Reidar: The Struggle for Scripture and Covenant. 1996. *Vol. II/82.*

Jauhiainen, Marko: The Use of Zechariah in Revelation. 2005. *Vol. II/199.*

Jensen, Morten H.: Herod Antipas in Galilee. 2006. *Vol. II/215.*

Johns, Loren L.: The Lamb Christology of the Apocalypse of John. 2003. *Vol. II/167.*

Jossa, Giorgio: Jews or Christians? 2006. *Vol. 202.*

Joubert, Stephan: Paul as Benefactor. 2000. *Vol. II/124.*

Jungbauer, Harry: „Ehre Vater und Mutter". 2002. *Vol. II/146.*

Kähler, Christoph: Jesu Gleichnisse als Poesie und Therapie. 1995. *Vol. 78.*

Kamlah, Ehrhard: Die Form der katalogischen Paränese im Neuen Testament. 1964. *Vol. 7.*

Kammler, Hans-Christian: Christologie und Eschatologie. 2000. *Vol. 126.*

– Kreuz und Weisheit. 2003. *Vol. 159.*

– see *Hofius, Otfried.*

Kelhoffer, James A.: The Diet of John the Baptist. 2005. *Vol. 176.*

– Miracle and Mission. 1999. *Vol. II/112.*

Kelley, Nicole: Knowledge and Religious Authority in the Pseudo-Clementines. 2006. *Vol. II/213.*

Kieffer, René and *Jan Bergman (Ed.):* La Main de Dieu / Die Hand Gottes. 1997. *Vol. 94.*

Kierspel, Lars: The Jews and the World in the Fourth Gospel. 2006. *Vol. 220.*

Kim, Seyoon: The Origin of Paul's Gospel. 1981, ²1984. *Vol. II/4.*

– Paul and the New Perspective. 2002. *Vol. 140.*

– "The 'Son of Man'" as the Son of God. 1983. *Vol. 30.*

Klauck, Hans-Josef: Religion und Gesellschaft im frühen Christentum. 2003. *Vol. 152.*

Klein, Hans: see *Dunn, James D.G.*

Kleinknecht, Karl Th.: Der leidende Gerechtfertigte. 1984, ²1988. *Vol. II/13.*

Klinghardt, Matthias: Gesetz und Volk Gottes. 1988. *Vol. II/32.*

Kloppenborg, John S.: The Tenants in the Vineyard. 2006. *Vol. 195.*

Koch, Michael: Drachenkampf und Sonnenfrau. 2004. *Vol. II/184.*

Koch, Stefan: Rechtliche Regelung von Konflikten im frühen Christentum. 2004. *Vol. II/174.*

Köhler, Wolf-Dietrich: Rezeption des Matthäusevangeliums in der Zeit vor Irenäus. 1987. *Vol. II/24.*

Köhn, Andreas: Der Neutestamentler Ernst Lohmeyer. 2004. *Vol. II/180.*

Konradt, Matthias: Israel, Kirche und die Völker im Matthäusevangelium. 2007. *Vol. 215.*

Kooten, George H. van: Cosmic Christology in Paul and the Pauline School. 2003. *Vol. II/171.*

Korn, Manfred: Die Geschichte Jesu in veränderter Zeit. 1993. *Vol. II/51.*

Koskenniemi, Erkki: Apollonios von Tyana in der neutestamentlichen Exegese. 1994. *Vol. II/61.*

– The Old Testament Miracle-Workers in Early Judaism. 2005. *Vol. II/206.*

Kraus, Thomas J.: Sprache, Stil und historischer Ort des zweiten Petrusbriefes. 2001. *Vol. II/136.*

Kraus, Wolfgang: Das Volk Gottes. 1996. *Vol. 85.*

Kraus, Wolfgang and *Karl-Wilhelm Niebuhr* (Ed.): Frühjudentum und Neues Testament im Horizont Biblischer Theologie. 2003. *Vol. 162.*

– see *Walter, Nikolaus.*

Kreplin, Matthias: Das Selbstverständnis Jesu. 2001. *Vol. II/141.*

Kuhn, Karl G.: Achtzehngebet und Vaterunser und der Reim. 1950. *Vol. 1.*

Kvalbein, Hans: see *Ådna, Jostein.*

Kwon, Yon-Gyong: Eschatology in Galatians. 2004. *Vol. II/183.*

Laansma, Jon: I Will Give You Rest. 1997. *Vol. II/98.*

Labahn, Michael: Offenbarung in Zeichen und Wort. 2000. *Vol. II/117.*

Lambers-Petry, Doris: see *Tomson, Peter J.*

Lange, Armin: see *Ego, Beate.*

Lampe, Peter: Die stadtrömischen Christen in den ersten beiden Jahrhunderten. 1987, ²1989. *Vol. II/18.*

Landmesser, Christof: Wahrheit als Grundbegriff neutestamentlicher Wissenschaft. 1999. *Vol. 113.*

– Jüngerberufung und Zuwendung zu Gott. 2000. *Vol. 133.*

Lau, Andrew: Manifest in Flesh. 1996. *Vol. II/86.*

Lawrence, Louise: An Ethnography of the Gospel of Matthew. 2003. *Vol. II/165.*

Lee, Aquila H.I.: From Messiah to Preexistent Son. 2005. *Vol. II/192.*

Lee, Pilchan: The New Jerusalem in the Book of Relevation. 2000. *Vol. II/129.*

Lichtenberger, Hermann: Das Ich Adams und das Ich der Menschheit. 2004. *Vol. 164.*

– see *Avemarie, Friedrich.*
Lierman, John: The New Testament Moses. 2004. *Vol. II/173.*
– (Ed.): Challenging Perspectives on the Gospel of John. 2006. *Vol. II/219.*
Lieu, Samuel N.C.: Manichaeism in the Later Roman Empire and Medieval China. ²1992. *Vol. 63.*
Lindgård, Fredrik: Paul's Line of Thought in 2 Corinthians 4:16–5:10. 2004. *Vol. II/189.*
Loader, William R.G.: Jesus' Attitude Towards the Law. 1997. *Vol. II/97.*
Löhr, Gebhard: Verherrlichung Gottes durch Philosophie. 1997. *Vol. 97.*
Löhr, Hermut: Studien zum frühchristlichen und frühjüdischen Gebet. 2003. *Vol. 160.*
– see *Hengel, Martin.*
Löhr, Winrich Alfried: Basilides und seine Schule. 1995. *Vol. 83.*
Luomanen, Petri: Entering the Kingdom of Heaven. 1998. *Vol. II/101.*
Luz, Ulrich: see *Dunn, James D.G.*
Mackay, Ian D.: John's Raltionship with Mark. 2004. *Vol. II/182.*
Mackie, Scott D.: Eschatology and Exhortation in the Epistle to the Hebrews. 2006. *Vol. II/223.*
Maier, Gerhard: Mensch und freier Wille. 1971. *Vol. 12.*
– Die Johannesoffenbarung und die Kirche. 1981. *Vol. 25.*
Markschies, Christoph: Valentinus Gnosticus? 1992. *Vol. 65.*
Marshall, Peter: Enmity in Corinth: Social Conventions in Paul's Relations with the Corinthians. 1987. *Vol. II/23.*
Martin, Dale B.: see *Zangenberg, Jürgen.*
Mayer, Annemarie: Sprache der Einheit im Epheserbrief und in der Ökumene. 2002. *Vol. II/150.*
Mayordomo, Moisés: Argumentiert Paulus logisch? 2005. *Vol. 188.*
McDonough, Sean M.: YHWH at Patmos: Rev. 1:4 in its Hellenistic and Early Jewish Setting. 1999. *Vol. II/107.*
McDowell, Markus: Prayers of Jewish Women. 2006. *Vol. II/211.*
McGlynn, Moyna: Divine Judgement and Divine Benevolence in the Book of Wisdom. 2001. *Vol. II/139.*
Meade, David G.: Pseudonymity and Canon. 1986. *Vol. 39.*
Meadors, Edward P.: Jesus the Messianic Herald of Salvation. 1995. *Vol. II/72.*
Meißner, Stefan: Die Heimholung des Ketzers. 1996. *Vol. II/87.*
Mell, Ulrich: Die „anderen" Winzer. 1994. *Vol. 77.*

– see *Sänger, Dieter.*
Mengel, Berthold: Studien zum Philipperbrief. 1982. *Vol. II/8.*
Merkel, Helmut: Die Widersprüche zwischen den Evangelien. 1971. *Vol. 13.*
– see *Ego, Beate.*
Merklein, Helmut: Studien zu Jesus und Paulus. Vol. 1 1987. *Vol. 43.* – Vol. 2 1998. *Vol. 105.*
Metzdorf, Christina: Die Tempelaktion Jesu. 2003. *Vol. II/168.*
Metzler, Karin: Der griechische Begriff des Verzeihens. 1991. *Vol. II/44.*
Metzner, Rainer: Die Rezeption des Matthäusevangeliums im 1. Petrusbrief. 1995. *Vol. II/74.*
– Das Verständnis der Sünde im Johannesevangelium. 2000. *Vol. 122.*
Mihoc, Vasile: see *Dunn, James D.G..*
Mineshige, Kiyoshi: Besitzverzicht und Almosen bei Lukas. 2003. *Vol. II/163.*
Mittmann, Siegfried: see *Hengel, Martin.*
Mittmann-Richert, Ulrike: Magnifikat und Benediktus. 1996. *Vol. II/90.*
Miura, Yuzuru: David in Luke-Acts. 2007. *Vol. II/232.*
Mournet, Terence C.: Oral Tradition and Literary Dependency. 2005. *Vol. II/195.*
Mußner, Franz: Jesus von Nazareth im Umfeld Israels und der Urkirche. Ed. von M. Theobald. 1998. *Vol. 111.*
Mutschler, Bernhard: Das Corpus Johanneum bei Irenäus von Lyon. 2005. *Vol. 189.*
Niebuhr, Karl-Wilhelm: Gesetz und Paränese. 1987. *Vol. II/28.*
– Heidenapostel aus Israel. 1992. *Vol. 62.*
– see *Deines, Roland*
– see *Dimitrov, Ivan Z.*
– see *Kraus, Wolfgang*
Nielsen, Anders E.: "Until it is Fullfilled". 2000. *Vol. II/126.*
Nissen, Andreas: Gott und der Nächste im antiken Judentum. 1974. *Vol. 15.*
Noack, Christian: Gottesbewußtsein. 2000. *Vol. II/116.*
Noormann, Rolf: Irenäus als Paulusinterpret. 1994. *Vol. II/66.*
Novakovic, Lidija: Messiah, the Healer of the Sick. 2003. *Vol. II/170.*
Obermann, Andreas: Die christologische Erfüllung der Schrift im Johannesevangelium. 1996. *Vol. II/83.*
Öhler, Markus: Barnabas. 2003. *Vol. 156.*
– see *Becker, Michael.*
Okure, Teresa: The Johannine Approach to Mission. 1988. *Vol. II/31.*
Onuki, Takashi: Heil und Erlösung. 2004. *Vol. 165.*

Oropeza, B. J.: Paul and Apostasy. 2000. *Vol. II/115.*

Ostmeyer, Karl-Heinrich: Kommunikation mit Gott und Christus. 2006. *Vol. 197.*

– Taufe und Typos. 2000. *Vol. II/118.*

Paulsen, Henning: Studien zur Literatur und Geschichte des frühen Christentums. Ed. von Ute E. Eisen. 1997. *Vol. 99.*

Pao, David W.: Acts and the Isaianic New Exodus. 2000. *Vol. II/130.*

Park, Eung Chun: The Mission Discourse in Matthew's Interpretation. 1995. *Vol. II/81.*

Park, Joseph S.: Conceptions of Afterlife in Jewish Insriptions. 2000. *Vol. II/121.*

Pate, C. Marvin: The Reverse of the Curse. 2000. *Vol. II/114.*

Pearce, Sarah J.K.: The Land of the Body. 2007. *Vol. 208.*

Peres, Imre: Griechische Grabinschriften und neutestamentliche Eschatologie. 2003. *Vol. 157.*

Philip, Finny: The Origins of Pauline Pneumatology. 2005. *Vol. II/194.*

Philonenko, Marc (Ed.): Le Trône de Dieu. 1993. *Vol. 69.*

Pilhofer, Peter: Presbyteron Kreitton. 1990. *Vol. II/39.*

– Philippi. Vol. 1 1995. *Vol. 87.* – Vol. 2 2000. *Vol. 119.*

– Die frühen Christen und ihre Welt. 2002. *Vol. 145.*

– see *Becker, Eve-Marie.*

– see *Ego, Beate.*

Pitre, Brant: Jesus, the Tribulation, and the End of the Exile. 2005. *Vol. II/204.*

Plümacher, Eckhard: Geschichte und Geschichten. 2004. *Vol. 170.*

Pöhlmann, Wolfgang: Der Verlorene Sohn und das Haus. 1993. *Vol. 68.*

Pokorný, Petr and *Josef B. Souček:* Bibelauslegung als Theologie. 1997. *Vol. 100.*

– and *Jan Roskovec* (Ed.): Philosophical Hermeneutics and Biblical Exegesis. 2002. *Vol. 153.*

Popkes, Enno Edzard: Die Theologie der Liebe Gottes in den johanneischen Schriften. 2005. *Vol. II/197.*

Porter, Stanley E.: The Paul of Acts. 1999. *Vol. 115.*

Prieur, Alexander: Die Verkündigung der Gottesherrschaft. 1996. *Vol. II/89.*

Probst, Hermann: Paulus und der Brief. 1991. *Vol. II/45.*

Räisänen, Heikki: Paul and the Law. 1983, [2]1987. *Vol. 29.*

Rehkopf, Friedrich: Die lukanische Sonderquelle. 1959. *Vol. 5.*

Rein, Matthias: Die Heilung des Blindgeborenen (Joh 9). 1995. *Vol. II/73.*

Reinmuth, Eckart: Pseudo-Philo und Lukas. 1994. *Vol. 74.*

Reiser, Marius: Syntax und Stil des Markusevangeliums. 1984. *Vol. II/11.*

Rhodes, James N.: The Epistle of Barnabas and the Deuteronomic Tradition. 2004. *Vol. II/188.*

Richards, E. Randolph: The Secretary in the Letters of Paul. 1991. *Vol. II/42.*

Riesner, Rainer: Jesus als Lehrer. 1981, [3]1988. *Vol. II/7.*

– Die Frühzeit des Apostels Paulus. 1994. *Vol. 71.*

Rissi, Mathias: Die Theologie des Hebräerbriefs. 1987. *Vol. 41.*

Roskovec, Jan: see *Pokorný, Petr.*

Röhser, Günter: Metaphorik und Personifikation der Sünde. 1987. *Vol. II/25.*

Rose, Christian: Theologie als Erzählung im Markusevangelium. 2007. *Vol. II/236.*

– Die Wolke der Zeugen. 1994. *Vol. II/60.*

Rothschild, Clare K.: Baptist Traditions and Q. 2005. *Vol. 190.*

– Luke Acts and the Rhetoric of History. 2004. *Vol. II/175.*

Rüegger, Hans-Ulrich: Verstehen, was Markus erzählt. 2002. *Vol. II/155.*

Rüger, Hans Peter: Die Weisheitsschrift aus der Kairoer Geniza. 1991. *Vol. 53.*

Sänger, Dieter: Antikes Judentum und die Mysterien. 1980. *Vol. II/5.*

– Die Verkündigung des Gekreuzigten und Israel. 1994. *Vol. 75.*

– see *Burchard, Christoph*

– and *Ulrich Mell* (Hrsg.): Paulus und Johannes. 2006. *Vol. 198.*

Salier, Willis Hedley: The Rhetorical Impact of the Semeia in the Gospel of John. 2004. *Vol. II/186.*

Salzmann, Jorg Christian: Lehren und Ermahnen. 1994. *Vol. II/59.*

Sandnes, Karl Olav: Paul – One of the Prophets? 1991. *Vol. II/43.*

Sato, Migaku: Q und Prophetie. 1988. *Vol. II/29.*

Schäfer, Ruth: Paulus bis zum Apostelkonzil. 2004. *Vol. II/179.*

Schaper, Joachim: Eschatology in the Greek Psalter. 1995. *Vol. II/76.*

Schimanowski, Gottfried: Die himmlische Liturgie in der Apokalypse des Johannes. 2002. *Vol. II/154.*

– Weisheit und Messias. 1985. *Vol. II/17.*

Schlichting, Günter: Ein jüdisches Leben Jesu. 1982. *Vol. 24.*

Schließer, Benjamin: Abraham's Faith in Romans 4. 2007. *Vol. II/224.*

Schnabel, Eckhard J.: Law and Wisdom from Ben Sira to Paul. 1985. *Vol. II/16.*
Schnelle, Udo: see *Frey, Jörg.*
Schröter, Jens: Von Jesus zum Neuen Testament. 2007. *Vol. 204.*
– see *Frey, Jörg.*
Schutter, William L.: Hermeneutic and Composition in I Peter. 1989. *Vol. II/30.*
Schwartz, Daniel R.: Studies in the Jewish Background of Christianity. 1992. *Vol. 60.*
Schwemer, Anna Maria: see *Hengel, Martin*
Scott, Ian W.: Implicit Epistemology in the Letters of Paul. 2005. *Vol. II/205.*
Scott, James M.: Adoption as Sons of God. 1992. *Vol. II/48.*
– Paul and the Nations. 1995. *Vol. 84.*
Shum, Shiu-Lun: Paul's Use of Isaiah in Romans. 2002. *Vol. II/156.*
Siegert, Folker: Drei hellenistisch-jüdische Predigten. Teil I 1980. *Vol. 20* – Teil II 1992. *Vol. 61.*
– Nag-Hammadi-Register. 1982. *Vol. 26.*
– Argumentation bei Paulus. 1985. *Vol. 34.*
– Philon von Alexandrien. 1988. *Vol. 46.*
Simon, Marcel: Le christianisme antique et son contexte religieux I/II. 1981. *Vol. 23.*
Snodgrass, Klyne: The Parable of the Wicked Tenants. 1983. *Vol. 27.*
Smit, Peter-Ben: Food and Fellowship in the Kingdom. 2007. *Vol. II/234.*
Söding, Thomas: Das Wort vom Kreuz. 1997. *Vol. 93.*
– see *Thüsing, Wilhelm.*
Sommer, Urs: Die Passionsgeschichte des Markusevangeliums. 1993. *Vol. II/58.*
Sorensen, Eric: Possession and Exorcism in the New Testament and Early Christianity. 2002. *Vol. II/157.*
Souček, Josef B.: see *Pokorný, Petr.*
Spangenberg, Volker: Herrlichkeit des Neuen Bundes. 1993. *Vol. II/55.*
Spanje, T.E. van: Inconsistency in Paul? 1999. *Vol. II/110.*
Speyer, Wolfgang: Frühes Christentum im antiken Strahlungsfeld. Vol. I: 1989. *Vol. 50.*
– Vol. II: 1999. *Vol. 116.*
– Vol. III: 2007. *Vol. 213.*
Stadelmann, Helge: Ben Sira als Schriftgelehrter. 1980. *Vol. II/6.*
Stenschke, Christoph W.: Luke's Portrait of Gentiles Prior to Their Coming to Faith. *Vol. II/108.*
Sterck-Degueldre, Jean-Pierre: Eine Frau namens Lydia. 2004. *Vol. II/176.*
Stettler, Christian: Der Kolosserhymnus. 2000. *Vol. II/131.*
Stettler, Hanna: Die Christologie der Pastoralbriefe. 1998. *Vol. II/105.*

Stökl Ben Ezra, Daniel: The Impact of Yom Kippur on Early Christianity. 2003. *Vol. 163.*
Strobel, August: Die Stunde der Wahrheit. 1980. *Vol. 21.*
Stroumsa, Guy G.: Barbarian Philosophy. 1999. *Vol. 112.*
Stuckenbruck, Loren T.: Angel Veneration and Christology. 1995. *Vol. II/70.*
– , *Stephen C. Barton* and *Benjamin G. Wold* (Ed.): Memory in the Bible and Antiquity. 2007. *Vol. 212.*
Stuhlmacher, Peter (Ed.): Das Evangelium und die Evangelien. 1983. *Vol. 28.*
– Biblische Theologie und Evangelium. 2002. *Vol. 146.*
Sung, Chong-Hyon: Vergebung der Sünden. 1993. *Vol. II/57.*
Tajra, Harry W.: The Trial of St. Paul. 1989. *Vol. II/35.*
– The Martyrdom of St.Paul. 1994. *Vol. II/67.*
Theißen, Gerd: Studien zur Soziologie des Urchristentums. 1979, ³1989. *Vol. 19.*
Theobald, Michael: Studien zum Römerbrief. 2001. *Vol. 136.*
Theobald, Michael: see *Mußner, Franz.*
Thornton, Claus-Jürgen: Der Zeuge des Zeugen. 1991. *Vol. 56.*
Thüsing, Wilhelm: Studien zur neutestamentlichen Theologie. Ed. von Thomas Söding. 1995. *Vol. 82.*
Thurén, Lauri: Derhethorizing Paul. 2000. *Vol. 124.*
Thyen, Hartwig: Studien zum Corpus Iohanneum. 2007. *Vol. 214.*
Tibbs, Clint: Religious Experience of the Pneuma. 2007. *Vol. II/230.*
Tolmie, D. Francois: Persuading the Galatians. 2005. *Vol. II/190.*
Tomson, Peter J. and *Doris Lambers-Petry* (Ed.): The Image of the Judaeo-Christians in Ancient Jewish and Christian Literature. 2003. *Vol. 158.*
Trebilco, Paul: The Early Christians in Ephesus from Paul to Ignatius. 2004. *Vol. 166.*
Treloar, Geoffrey R.: Lightfoot the Historian. 1998. *Vol. II/103.*
Tsuji, Manabu: Glaube zwischen Vollkommenheit und Verweltlichung. 1997. *Vol. II/93.*
Twelftree, Graham H.: Jesus the Exorcist. 1993. *Vol. II/54.*
Ulrichs, Karl Friedrich: Christusglaube. 2007. *Vol. II/227.*
Urban, Christina: Das Menschenbild nach dem Johannesevangelium. 2001. *Vol. II/137.*
Visotzky, Burton L.: Fathers of the World. 1995. *Vol. 80.*
Vollenweider, Samuel: Horizonte neutestamentlicher Christologie. 2002. *Vol. 144.*

Vos, Johan S.: Die Kunst der Argumentation bei Paulus. 2002. *Vol. 149.*

Wagener, Ulrike: Die Ordnung des „Hauses Gottes". 1994. *Vol. II/65.*

Wahlen, Clinton: Jesus and the Impurity of Spirits in the Synoptic Gospels. 2004. *Vol. II/185.*

Walker, Donald D.: Paul's Offer of Leniency (2 Cor 10:1). 2002. *Vol. II/152.*

Walter, Nikolaus: Praeparatio Evangelica. Ed. von Wolfgang Kraus und Florian Wilk. 1997. *Vol. 98.*

Wander, Bernd: Gottesfürchtige und Sympathisanten. 1998. *Vol. 104.*

Waters, Guy: The End of Deuteronomy in the Epistles of Paul. 2006. *Vol. 221.*

Watt, Jan G. van der: see *Frey, Jörg*

Watts, Rikki: Isaiah's New Exodus and Mark. 1997. *Vol. II/88.*

Wedderburn, A.J.M.: Baptism and Resurrection. 1987. *Vol. 44.*

Wegner, Uwe: Der Hauptmann von Kafarnaum. 1985. *Vol. II/14.*

Weissenrieder, Annette: Images of Illness in the Gospel of Luke. 2003. Vol. II/164.

–, *Friederike Wendt* and *Petra von Gemünden* (Ed.): Picturing the New Testament. 2005. *Vol. II/193.*

Welck, Christian: Erzählte ‚Zeichen'. 1994. *Vol. II/69.*

Wendt, Friederike (Ed.): see *Weissenrieder, Annette.*

Wiarda, Timothy: Peter in the Gospels. 2000. *Vol. II/127.*

Wifstrand, Albert: Epochs and Styles. 2005. *Vol. 179.*

Wilk, Florian: see *Walter, Nikolaus.*

Williams, Catrin H.: I am He. 2000. *Vol. II/113.*

Wilson, Todd A.: The Curse of the Law and the Crisis in Galatia. 2007. *Vol. II/225.*

Wilson, Walter T.: Love without Pretense. 1991. *Vol. II/46.*

Wischmeyer, Oda: Von Ben Sira zu Paulus. 2004. *Vol. 173.*

Wisdom, Jeffrey: Blessing for the Nations and the Curse of the Law. 2001. *Vol. II/133.*

Wold, Benjamin G.: Women, Men, and Angels. 2005. *Vol. II/2001.*

– see *Stuckenbruck, Loren T.*

Wright, Archie T.: The Origin of Evil Spirits. 2005. *Vol. II/198.*

Wucherpfennig, Ansgar: Heracleon Philologus. 2002. *Vol. 142.*

Yeung, Maureen: Faith in Jesus and Paul. 2002. *Vol. II/147.*

Zangenberg, Jürgen, Harold W. Attridge and *Dale B. Martin* (Ed.): Religion, Ethnicity and Identity in Ancient Galilee. 2007. *Vol. 210.*

Zimmermann, Alfred E.: Die urchristlichen Lehrer. 1984, ²1988. *Vol. II/12.*

Zimmermann, Johannes: Messianische Texte aus Qumran. 1998. *Vol. II/104.*

Zimmermann, Ruben: Christologie der Bilder im Johannesevangelium. 2004. *Vol. 171.*

– Geschlechtermetaphorik und Gottesverhältnis. 2001. *Vol. II/122.*

– see *Frey, Jörg*

Zumstein, Jean: see *Dettwiler, Andreas*

Zwiep, Arie W.: Judas and the Choice of Matthias. 2004. *Vol. II/187.*

*For a complete catalogue please write to the publisher
Mohr Siebeck • P.O. Box 2030 • D–72010 Tübingen/Germany
Up-to-date information on the internet at www.mohr.de*